KOREA AND ITS FUTURES

ALSO BY ROY RICHARD GRINKER

Houses in the Rainforest: Ethnicity and Inequality among Farmers and Foragers in Central Africa

Perspectives on Africa: A Reader in Culture, History, and Representation (Co-edited and introduced with Christopher B. Steiner)

KOREA AND ITS FUTURES

UNIFICATION AND THE UNFINISHED WAR

Roy Richard Grinker

St. Martin's Press
New York, NY

ISBN 0-312-21091-4 (cloth)
ISBN 0-312-22472-9 (paper)

Library of Congress Cataloging-in-Publication Data

Grinker, Roy Richard, 1961-
    Korea and its futures : Unification and the unfinished war / Roy
    Richard Grinker.
        p.   cm.
    Includes bibliographical references and index.
    ISBN 0-312-21091-4 (cloth) ISBN 0-312-22472-9 (paper)
    1. Korean reunification question (1945-   )   I. Title.
    DS917.444.G75 1998   97-49577
                                                           CIP

Design by Acme Art, Inc.
First paperback edition: January 2000

10 9 8 7 6 5 4 3 2 1

For Chin Mook Chung and Hak Soon Lee
and for
Sue, Carol, Joyce, and Cathy

CONTENTS

PREFACE

This book is about two interdependent symbols of Korean identity: national division and national unification.[1] It is about how they have become hegemonic components of south Korean conceptions of the nation, and how their hegemony stands as an obstacle to reconciliation. At its most basic level this study outlines the ways in which north Korea and the concept of unification *(t'ongil)* appear in various south Korean discourses: the national media, school textbooks, exhibitions, scholarly and creative writing, and everyday discussion in Seoul. In these different settings, unification is defined in terms of homogeneity and recovery, terms that I suggest undermine movements toward unification. More specifically, I argue that current south Korean discourses on unification and division reinforce popular and political resistances to reconciliation and south-north dialogue. The received view is that national division disrupted Korean cultural and national identity and homogeneity and that unification will recover them. I show instead that unification, as it is often conceived in projections and fantasies of the future, is a contemporary threat to south Korean identity and that much of the resistance to unification in south Korea stems from the tension between two worlds: the unified nation as an idealized past and future, and the divided nation as the world in which nearly every south Korean has been born and raised.

This book is also about the absence of discourses of unification in other contexts, especially the many times and places in which north Korea and north Koreans are invisible to the people of south Korea. Most south Koreans admit to knowing almost nothing about the north Korean people and their everyday lives; some say they have difficulty envisioning what they look like. These discursive gaps, I argue, are expressive of the ambivalences and uncertainties surrounding Koreans' visions of themselves and their past, present, and future. The paucity of information on the north Korean people alongside the abundance of information (much of which could be termed propaganda) on the evils of the north Korean state means that south Koreans can easily detest communism without specifying how they feel about the north Korean people.

As for unification, I have found it curious, though not totally surprising, that an idea so central to Korean identity has, for most of the last fifty years, eluded extensive critical scholarly examination, public debate, or disagreement, and that politicians say little if anything about unification during political speeches and election bids beyond politically correct admonitions. Indeed, it is fair to say that Korean scholars have not had a great deal of academic freedom regarding the subject of north Korea or unification. Although public discussion of unification increased during Roh Tae Woo's Sixth Republic (1988-1991), during this time it also became a nearly traitorous act to assert that one did not want unification. And despite the south Korean government's attacks upon students and other radicals as "sentimentalists" whose passions threatened national security, the majority of political and social elites in south Korea have not focused intensively on developing their own unification schemes and policies. Moreover, planning for postunification Korea is even harder to find. Although political scientists and government policymakers have long analyzed different "official" schemes and strategies, such as gradual versus quick unification, or unification through a confederation or commonwealth, little is known about how south Korean citizens think and feel about unification.

The absences are striking not only because Korean unification is important to Koreans, but also because it is central to international peace. Political leaders throughout the world have come to assume that the Korean War, the buildup of nuclear weapons on the Korean peninsula, and regional instability in northeast Asia will end only when south and north Korea become one. Most south Koreans assume that the true and real Korea is a unified Korea, whereas the current condition of division and separate alignments with (or perhaps dependence on) the superpowers is a false and temporarily aberrant Korea. Despite concerns about the financial, social, and political ramifications of unification, in both north and south Korea unification is often framed as a sacred and universally desired goal. It is therefore extraordinarily difficult for people to say in general conversation what some of my interviewees considered a confession: that while unification must remain Korea's "paramount goal," they do not want to see unification during their lifetimes. In other words, to speak about unification is to speak about something so sensitive, and so central to the way that Koreans envision themselves and their relation to the rest of the world, that it is nearly unspeakable.

In private and in discussions with friends, colleagues, classmates, and family many people surely try to imagine what unification would look like; the image is formed by the little knowledge south Koreans have about north Korea and by the various hypothetical scenarios of unification that appear in the media and in official discourses. On the one hand, north Korea and a unified Korea are therefore blank slates open to fantasy and projection. On the other hand, the political sensitivity of unification limits the kinds of imaginative constructions that might be generated. I am referring here to the socially and politically structured prohibitions on expressions of sympathy with the north, ambivalence about unification, or the wish for a sustained division.[2] Many scholars, politicians, and ordinary citizens are consequently unwilling to discuss north Korea and north Koreans in any depth or detail.

This is not to say that there is an absence of discourse on unification and north Korea. Far from it: this book is about the ways in which people talk about these topics. But there is an absence of certain kinds of discourses, namely, detailed and critical debates on the concept of unification itself. Since the late 1980s, a number of texts have been published in south Korea on the subject of unification, an extraordinary number of conferences on unification have been held in south Korea and abroad, access to information about the north has improved, and political liberalization and greater access to literature in China and Russia have offered new information for unification studies. A recent compendium of information on north Korea and unification lists several dozen researchers and private, governmental, and educational institutions engaged in unification-related work (P'yŏnghwa Munje Yŏnguso 1997). These include government think tanks specializing in finding diplomatic and military solutions to division, and nongovernmental and church-affiliated organizations that try to facilitate family reunions and food aid transfers across the border. Even the south Korean government's ministry of unification has begun distributing articles, written by academics, on the subject of unification and cultural difference (Cho, H. J. 1997; Chung J. K. 1997). Yet this recent abundance does not mean that discussions about unification have been diverse, wide-ranging, or dynamic. Instead, south Korean academic approaches to unification have been dominated by affirmations of its necessity, with few efforts to critically assess the idea of unification and its ancillary concepts, such as homogeneity and nationalism, or the processes through which unification has come to be considered a necessity. There is a need for cultural analyses, studies that draw attention to the specific vehicles—language and other forms of representation—through which the concept of unification is constructed.

In sum, I want to stress two points about the ways in which south Koreans have been preoccupied with unification. First, unification has received considerable attention from policy analysts and political scientists, but they have treated the subject in quite stereotypical and predictable ways. This book takes as its starting point the proposition that formulaic treatments of unification in a bureaucratic frame are insufficient either to reveal the deeply imbricated meanings of unification for south Koreans or to achieve a perspective on unification that will facilitate reconciliation between south and north Korea. Second, there is a good deal of unification discourse in south Korea that lies beyond the policy world. Its registers are less academic than popular; it appears in the realms of language and literature, public exhibitions, forms of dissidence, jokes, and the media.

One might explain some of the barriers to scholarly work on unification in terms of political realities, for example, the lack of dialogue between the south and north about anything, let alone unification. In my view, however, the most compelling explanation for the absences I have noted is not among those cited above—the lack of information, free speech, or academic freedom—for these constitute the myriad ways in which unification has taken its hegemonic hold. They are the effects, as it were, the cultural glosses and rationalizations that mask the power of the symbol of unification to constrain competing discourses. Rather, the most compelling answer may be found in the process through which unification became a sacred goal, that is, the process through which unification became a singular object separated from critical discussion. The failure to see division and unification for what they are—constructed symbols—has produced an impasse in the peace process. Because Koreans idealize unification as the end of suffering, a site of social and economic homogeneity, they cannot begin to take the practical and, one might say, uncomfortable or "muddy" steps necessary to unify the nation. Indeed, in the first chapter I argue that there is much evidence that Koreans want to maintain the dream of unification even more than they want to achieve an actual unification.

One reason for the difficulty in discussing unification *(t'ongil)* is that it is linked to a series of other taken-for-granted concepts, one of the most important of which is "homogeneity" *(tongjilsŏng)*, since unification is often glossed as the "recovery of homogeneity" *(tongjilsŏng hoebok)*.[3] The association between unification and homogeneity hinders progress on unification, because north and south Korea are not homogeneous; in fact, one could argue, though not without inciting intense disagreement, that Koreans have never been homogeneous and never will be. Politicians boast that south Koreans are themselves homogeneous, and yet there are long-standing regional tensions even within south Korea. Koreans do not have a concept of difference that evokes the sense of a melting pot, and the word used to explain cultural and political difference *(ijil)* has a negative connotation. Because there is little interest in or acknowledgment of diversity, one of the most important questions about Korea's future is nearly impossible to ask: How are south and north Koreans different? Moreover, unification and homogeneity are so inextricably linked that it seems no one has yet figured out a way to talk about north-south differences without appearing to somehow justify the status quo of division or being accused of offering justification for those who might want to keep Korea divided.

The ostensibly simple statement "All Koreans want unification" can be fruitfully transformed here into another difficult question: "Why do Koreans want something that they call unification?" Perhaps, given the often coercive nature of Korea's political system and the degree to which unification discourses are hegemonic, it takes a foreigner to ask this bold and even unseemly question. Exploring unification as a constructed symbol might suggest that unification is somehow a choice, if not an illusion, rather than an ineluctable goal. The now popular definitions of cultures as "invented traditions" or nations as "imagined communities" suffer from this problem of misinterpretation as well; they have often been taken to mean that traditions and communities are somehow illegitimate or invalid. Yet to refer to something as constructed, invented, or imagined is not to deny its reality, only to suggest that its reality is not a natural given, that the reality is conceived or "thought" and is actually created by human actors. Resistance to subjecting a phenomenon to this sort of analytical (one might also say "deconstructive") treatment is expressive of the power of that phenomenon to secure itself; indeed, many south Koreans I know are afraid to talk about the complexities and ambivalences of Korean unification for fear that it will result in "too many ideas," and thus somehow harm the unification process. The phrase "democracy but not too much democracy" is sometimes employed in Korea for the same reason: people fear that a multiplicity of voices will inhibit decisive action.

Despite the fact that south Koreans clearly recognize how afraid the north Koreans are of "unification by absorption" *(hŭpsu t'ongil)* into the south, south Korea has not given any signals to the north that unification might preserve some of the distinctiveness the north has developed during division. For many south Koreans, "unification" is a euphemism for conquest, the annihilation of north Korea and the total assimilation of north Koreans into south Korea. From this perspective, unification as assimilation will not only end division and heterogeneity, but it also will complete south Korea's latent victory in Korea's unfinished war.

Thus, a central goal of this study is to begin to uncover the process of the symbolic construction of unification as an unexamined desire, and, as one consequence, to open up an avenue for exploring alternative Korean realities such as diversity or heterogeneity; that is, for exploring the future(s) in plural rather than singular terms. In the pages that follow, I will not only outline the discourses through which south Koreans symbolically pattern their identity in opposition to images of north Korea, but I also will argue that these discourses point to the need for south Koreans to engage in more practical discussions on unification that move beyond the myth of homogeneity and the view that difference is "otherness." Difference, according to this argument, could be seen as a foundation for new communities that bring together Koreans' separate and yet shared experiences of division in a way that strengthens the nation. Thus, the unification of all Koreans into a single nation may require popular and political views and domestic policies oriented more toward a national organization of difference than a divided organization of imagined similarity.

In the literature of political science and international affairs, one can easily find many books and articles that posit various scenarios for both the processes and consequences of unification. There are so many

newspaper and magazine articles that directly or indirectly deal with
unification that one could never read them all. Yet they tend to be
founded on the premise that unification is the "endgame," to use a
foreign-policy term. Much less attention has been paid to unification as
a point of origin or as a multidimensional process that has no boundary
or endpoint. Although early in his administration south Korea's President Kim Young Sam ordered several government agencies to analyze
the social aspects of the inevitable unification, they have not cooperated
with one another, and their results are unavailable for either government
or public discussion. Moreover, despite the presence of well over seven
hundred defectors from north Korea living in the south, who are the
only available model for assessing potential social and economic problems in a unified Korea, virtually nothing has been published about the
defectors' adjustment to south Korean life. Although the recent food
crisis in north Korea has increased somewhat the visibility of north
Korean people in the media, most images of the north are never aired,
and radio and television broadcasts from the north are jammed, because
most media from the north, including magazines and newspapers, are
classified by the government of south Korea and unavailable to the
public.[4]

If the north Korean state does collapse in the next few years, as
many predict, the two Koreas may find themselves on the brink of
unification. At the very least, most observers of Korea expect that north
Korea will not survive for long without radical changes, and that north
Korea will increasingly be a burden on south Korean politics and
economics (Oberdorfer 1997). South Koreans risk repeating two mistakes made by the former west Germany prior to German unification:
failing to discuss practical and specific dimensions of unification until
after it occurs, and ignoring the extent to which half a century of
division can produce significant social and cultural differences between
the two sides of a nation. The failure of Germans to discuss their
differences prior to unification led the author Peter Schneider to say in
a New York Times editorial that "the wall created the illusion that only
the wall separated East and West Germans." Most south Koreans will
agree that north Koreans can one day help make Korea a greater world
power. However, the chances for success are much smaller, and the
chances of social and economic disaster much greater, if the south does
not begin to talk about the north Korean people, unmask the mythology

of Korean homogeneity, and offer a plural society in which north and south Koreans can one day live.

A Note on Language

I have transliterated the Korean words and names that appear in this text according to the McCune-Reischauer system for romanizing Korean. Exceptions include those well-known words or names whose conventional spellings do not conform to the system (for example, Kim Il Sung, Synghman Rhee, Seoul) and the names of authors who prefer a particular romanization (for example, Paik Nak Chung instead of Paek Nak-ch'ŏng; Lee Bann instead of Yi Ban). I have transliterated the names of Korean authors who have published in English according to the spellings that appear in their English-language publications. Korean names are ordered according to standard Korean practice—surname first—with the exception of anglicized Korean names such as John Lie. The names of interviewees are pseudonyms, and some elements of interview narrative, such as residence and workplace names, have been changed to protect interviewee identities.

ACKNOWLEDGMENTS

I owe an enormous debt of gratitude to the numerous people and institutions that supported my work. My first thanks must go to Dr. Chin Mook Chung, Hak Soon Lee, and Kim Eun Yŏn, who first introduced me to Korea. Indeed, it was through many long discussions with Dr. Chung about Korean history and politics that I first became interested in Korean studies. The extended Chung family has supported my interests and made my work both possible and enjoyable.

All of the anthropologists with whom I have worked in Seoul have given me a remarkable amount of encouragement to conduct research and write on Korean culture; Professors Chun Kyung Soo, Cho Hae Joang, and Han Kyung Koo, in particular, have been extraordinarily generous with their time and attention. I am grateful for their insights, criticism, and advice.

In the United States, Professors Nancy Abelmann and Michael Robinson read several versions of my chapters; Sheila Miyoshi Jager, Park Chan-bong and Scott Snyder read the entire manuscript. Each of these generous colleagues consistently offered criticisms that have made this a much better book than it would have otherwise been. Kim Choong Soon provided much-needed intellectual and personal support as I was embarking on my study. Mr. Han Sŏng-ryŏng and Mr. Ch'oi Tong-u of the Democratic People's Republic of North Korea Permanent Mission to the United Nations were very helpful in providing me with some literature from north Korea. All of the staff at the Korea section of the Library of Congress, especially Mrs. Ahn In-kyŏng, and David Parker of the Korea Information Center of the Embassy of the Republic of Korea in Washington, D.C., gave much of their time to locate documents relating to my research. The artist Lee Bann was generous with his time and inspirational in his art. Young-Key Kim-Renaud deserves special thanks because she has been one of my closest colleagues on Korean matters.

The George Washington University, especially Jonathan Higman, the Department of Anthropology, and the Gaston Sigur Center for East Asian Affairs under its former director, Young C. Kim, provided me with hospitable environments in which to work. Through my association with the Atlantic Council of the United States, and with the guidance of its executive vice-president, Dr. Alfred Wilhelm, I was introduced to foreign policy concerns, especially in East Asia, and given access to a wide community of thinkers interested in north-south Korean relations.

My research was supported by generous grants from the Social Science Research Council/American Council of Learned Societies Postdoctoral Fellowship in Korean studies, the George Washington University, and the United States Institute of Peace. I am especially grateful to Mimi Kim of the SSRC, Linda Salamon of George Washington University, and Scott Snyder of the USIP. I also thank Young C. Kim of George Washington University's Gaston Sigur Center for East Asian Studies for providing my airfare to Korea on more than one occasion.

Others who have provided me with assistance at various stages of my research include Lee Hong Koo of the south Korean government, Kil Jeong-woo of *Joong Ang Ilbo*, Hong Eun-taek of *Tonga Ilbo*, Yu Dong-hee of the Munhwa Broadcasting Company, and Philo Kim of the National Institute for Unification Research; Kim Bong Sik, Ch'oi Song Hee, Kim Sang-joon, Shim Soo-in, Hwang Yu-jin, Shin Jee Young, and Kim Soo-jin; Kim Yoon-yul of the United Nations Development Program, Sonia Ryang of Australia National University, Han Sang-bok, Lee Kwang-kyu, and Paik Nak Chung of Seoul National University, and Ch'oi Dae-yŏng of the Prime Minister's Office, Republic of Korea; Yang Ch'ang Seok of the Korean Embassy; Robert Sutter of the Congressional Research Service; Laura Nelson; Dr. Yim Hyŏng-bin of the Ch'u-gye School Foundation and Choong-Ang Girl's High School; Dr. Oe Su-ch'ŏl, Yun Taeng-nim; Philip Yun of the United States Department of State, Karen Sutter and Theoni Xintaris of the Atlantic Council of the United States, and Richard Smock of the United States Institute of Peace; Paul Brodwin, Terry O'Nell, Gautam Ghosh, Alf Hiltebeitel, and Joel Kuipers. In addition, an author could not find a more professional and efficient editorial and production team than Karen Wolny and Wendy Kraus of St. Martin's. I am particularly indebted to Shim Soo-in for her outstanding research assistance. I want to extend an extra amount of gratitude to Han Kyung Koo and Han Seung Mee for their friendship and openness, and for telling me things I needed but may not have wanted to hear about the sensitivity and significance of the work I was doing. Many thanks to Zafer Senocak for permission to reprint his poem "Doppelman"; to David R. McCann for use of his translation of Kim So-wŏl's poem "Azaleas"; and to Cho Hae Joang for use of a poem that appeared in her book *T'alsikminji side chisikinŭi kŭl ilgiwa sam ilgi 1: paro yŏgi kyosilaesŏ* [Reading texts and rereading everyday lives in the post-colonial era 1: From the classroom].

Of course, I take all responsibility for errors and sins of omission.

I also wish to thank my parents, Roy and Florence Grinker, and a close friend, Lee Dong-ik. Dong-ik has engaged me in endless and helpful debates that deeply influenced my understanding of Korea. Finally, I extend my warmest thanks and love to my family—Joyce, Isabel, and Olivia. They have enriched my life and work immeasurably, and so this book also belongs to them.

Roy Richard Grinker
Washington, D.C.

ONE

INTRODUCTION: UNIFICATION AND THE DISRUPTION OF IDENTITY IN SOUTH KOREA

> Mourning is regularly the reaction to the loss of a loved person, or to the loss of some abstraction which has taken the place of one, such as fatherland, liberty, an ideal, and so on.
>
> —Sigmund Freud,
> "Mourning and Melancholia"

FROM AUGUST 13 TO 20, 1996, thousands of students and police clashed at Yonsei University and other university campuses throughout Seoul, as they had many times before. The students protested for the unification of Korea and for the removal of the 37,000 U.S. troops from south Korea. Supported by numerous helicopters, 10,000 riot police stormed the university, arrested more than 5,000 students, and shuttled hundreds of wounded and weary police and students to hospitals for treatment. One policeman died a few days after being struck by a rock. President Kim Young Sam personally labeled the students "north Korean sympathizers," "guerrillas," "communists," and "supporters of the enemy" and ordered the Ministry of Education to revamp school curricula so that young people would henceforth develop "correct" ideologies and philosophies.

This protest, as substantial as it may appear, stands as one of many that came before and many that will surely follow, to be met with the standard response, "The students protested, *again*." Students have long been active and successful in promoting democratization for south Korea in the face of extraordinary government opposition. And until recently there was considerable popular support for student and academic activists, who were characterized throughout much of Korea's contemporary history as moral compasses and as a check against extreme governmental powers. Yet on the desire for Korean unification, there is little disagreement between students, the government, and academics. No south Korean administration has ever wavered from the position that unification is Korea's universal and "paramount goal," and one would be hard pressed to find any Korean who would admit that he or she did not want Korea to unify. Some Korean churches hold unbroken twenty-four-hour-a-day circle prayers for unification, and surveys of preteens consistently show that south Korean schoolchildren heed their textbooks' admonitions that every Korean must work toward overcoming national division and regaining the political and cultural homogeneity of the peninsula. If the students, the government, and everyone else are so committed to unification, then what are the students protesting against? What motivates these young people to exert their will and risk their lives and families' reputations by protesting?

Another question involves the motivations of those who oppose the protestors. The students who participated in the August 1996 riots at Yonsei were violent—student organizations provided protestors with firebombs and steel pipes—but the south Korean government also uses violent means to suppress peaceful pro-unification demonstrations and has promised that in the future they will not hesitate to use firearms on college campuses. In fact, violence on the part of the students has been minimal compared to that of the government. Indeed, nearly every study of the history of Korean student protests documents that the most common form of student protest in the 1980s and 1990s was nonconfrontational demonstration (Jang J. O. 1994: 128-129).

Government officials generally view student protests in the 1990s as anachronistic and pro-north, as evidenced by President Kim Young Sam's recent statement that "their group activities are no longer a pure student movement," by which he implies that the students have been influenced directly by north Koreans (*Korea Herald*, August 22, 1996, on-line edition). He banned peaceful demonstrations too, on the grounds that the students have no legitimate reason to protest now that he, a civilian and a former dissident, is president of the country. Some citizens complain that the protests need to be suppressed for the sake of everyday business and traffic flow. Others argue that if the government permits peaceful demonstrations, the students will escalate to violent demonstrations.

I once asked a taxi driver, "What if the students had a peaceful march and the police stayed away?" He replied, "Then they'd have demonstrations every day and never go to school." The government, in other words, has to set limits on students, who are irresponsible children engaged in an adolescent struggle. Student protests, like other forms of conflict in south Korea, including national division, tend to be framed in such familial or Confucian terms. In turn, the students, it appears, are marching for the right to protest as much as they are protesting for specific issues. Of course, none of these answers seems adequate to explain the intense anger and force with which the students are so often confronted, or the ban on peaceful demonstrations. If the government is so explicitly pro-unification and pro-democracy, what is the government reacting against?

The answers to these admittedly naive questions about student-government conflict are complex, yet they are so politically sensitive that people are tempted to give them simple and conclusive answers: on the one side, that the students are naive pawns of the north ("they say they want unification, but in Kim Il Sung's vision"), and, on the other side, that politicians are elites who want to preserve their hegemony ("they do not want unification, but rather the status quo"). Both sides make the same basic claim that the other is responsible for delaying unification. Many students link the government with the political forces—such as wealthy elites, the superpowers (especially the American military), and conservatives—that they believe caused and continue division. The government, on the other hand, associates the students with the north Koreans.

Despite the certainty with which the desire for unification is so often affirmed, discourses on unification in south Korea involve many layers of narrative and counternarrative, contests over the terms of debate, and ambivalence about Korea's future. One of the purposes of this book is to explore the history and foundations of contemporary division and unification discourses, not only because they help us understand the meanings of particular events such as student protests, but also because analyzing the discourses themselves can contribute to a wider comprehension of some of the more troubling and important issues in south and north Korea today.

Analysis of the ways in which unification and division become represented in south Korea can also help us discern how these concepts have often eluded public or scholarly debates on their symbolic meanings and vicissitudes. If the opposition between students and the government sounds like a simple equation it is because their opposition to each other and the opposition of their discourses have, like the discourses on unification and division, become routinized since the 1960s. Government pronouncements on students, student slogans, and even the events during which they clash have become fairly predictable—unfortunately so, since the events typically result in extensive injuries to both police and students. Unification and division, too, have lost an affective presence; they are uneventful terms, part and parcel of everyday life, and so it is not surprising that they are seldom subject to extensive critical examination.

I have two central goals in this book: first, to describe the complicated role of north Korea in defining south Korean identity; second, to show how the symbolic and imaginative incorporation of north Korea into south Korean identity is made possible by a well-patterned south Korean discourse about relationships of similarity and difference between the north and the south.

My analysis also involves a neutral and sometimes explicitly positive discussion of Korean identity in terms of heterogeneity and difference, a discussion that is clearly antithetical to some conventional nationalist discourses.[1] Indeed, the term *ijil*, used to refer to heterogeneity (usually between south and north), is almost always preceded by the verb "overcoming." How culturally different or incompatible are north and south Koreans? Are northerners and southerners comparable units? Is it possible to construct a unified Korea that is not defined by the master narrative of homogeneity and which provides a place for diversity? Is there anything in the north to be preserved after unification? These questions are difficult to ponder. South Koreans have often found it extraordinarily hard to challenge conventional nationalist historiography, to see the Korean "people," or *minjok,* as a modern construction, despite there being much evidence that prior to the nineteenth century Koreans had little sense of an abstract Korean nation-state (Eckert, 1991: 226-227).

Although I explicitly address the problem of confronting heterogeneity, it is important to stress that I do not provide an answer to the question of how north and south Koreans are different. The question appears to offer an interesting avenue for exploring the significance of "north" and "south" to national identity, but the question also attributes to these abstractions of north and south a false stability or essence. A scholarly study of southern representations of the differences between south and north cannot involve an attempt to determine what those differences "really are," but only what those differences are as articulated in the representations found in the south. This is sometimes a difficult logic for me to explain to friends and acquaintances in both Korea and the United States; indeed, on a number of occasions they have suggested that once I understand what south Koreans think about the north I should go to the north and see if the south Koreans are right or wrong. Although I have been trying, unsuccessfully, to obtain a visa to travel to north Korea, I have never intended to do a comparative study. This is not only because far too little is known about north Korea and north Koreans to say much about north Korean culture and society and what north Korean people think about south Korea, but more fundamentally because comparative studies always suffer from the methodological problem of determining the categories and criteria for comparison. What would it mean to say that millions of people in one territory are similar to or different from millions of people in another? Which criteria would one use? For example, even if one could demonstrate through a massive collection of linguistic data that the languages used in the north and south are quite different, how could we argue that they are more or less different than the Korean language as it is spoken by people in Kyŏngsang-do and Chŏlla-do in the south, or between rich and poor in the south, or between men and women, children and adults?

I should also point out a violation against convention: when referring to relations between the north and south I do not write the terms "north" and "south" in the order that either south Koreans or north Koreans usually place them. Southerners speak about south-north relations as *nambuk* (*nam-*, "south"; *buk-*, "north"), rarely placing the word "north" before the word "south"; northerners do exactly the opposite by consistently writing *puknam* (note that *puk* and *buk* are the same words; when it is the initial consonant, /b/ is romanized as /p/). The importance of the order is humorously illustrated in a short story by the author Chói Il-nam (1989) in which a north Korean instinctively responds to a south Korean's suggestion to drink *somaek,* a distilled liquor *(soju)* with a beer *(maekju)* chaser, by calling it *maekso.* At times in this text I refer to "north-south" relations and at other times to "south-north" because I believe that, while the order is politically important in the two Koreas, the order bears little relation to the arguments I am making, and to use one order instead of the other might suggest that I was "taking sides." However, as the reader will already have noticed, I do not capitalize "south" and "north." Use of the lower case is consistent with the widely held Korean view that there is one Korea, for now divided into a north and a south, and that north and south Korea do not constitute distinct nations. This is not a specifically southern or northern literary convention.

REPRESENTATION

I have already noted that this is a study of representations. By "representation" I mean the ways in which people individually and collectively depict something or someone verbally, visually, or through other expressive techniques, such as music. These depictions, even those believed to be "realistic," also have to be understood as *interpretations.* From this perspective, science, poetry, and religion are all forms of representation, each form being a subjective lens of interpretation, whether for the person who makes the representation or for those who perceive it. Subjectivity implies that representations have to be analyzed in terms of the strategies through which something becomes represented, for example, when events are represented through narrative, observations represented through science, or personal experiences represented through long-standing emotions. As we will see in chapter 7, for example, students, scholars, and the government often argue over whether the reality of north Korea is that it consists of a people or a state, and the form of representation follows that opposition: many students and scholars argue that unification must be represented in terms of sentiment (for the north Korean people), whereas the government argues that it must be represented in terms of scientific, nonsentimental understanding (of the north Korean state). The value of a study of representation is that it takes analytic distinctions such as the one posited between the people and the state and subjects them to the same analytical methods used to look at other social phenomena.

Representations are symbolic because the representation "speaks," as it were, in a way that the phenomenon represented cannot. They are also multivocal, because the meanings of a representation can be wide-ranging, with some meanings salient in some contexts but not others, depending on its social uses. The American flag means one thing when it is at half-mast, another when it is carried into an Olympic stadium, another when it is hoisted upon an enemy's land, and quite another when used as a patch on torn blue jeans. The power of representations also varies with the power of the agents who construct them. These aspects of representation tell us that it may be quite misleading to think about representations as existing inside people's heads as part of a cognitive structure; rather, the meanings unfold, and are conveyed, through specific practices, be they speeches, rituals, or other social performances.

Yet representations are real in the sense that even when they are not tangible objects they can have real effects. In the study of African history and cultures, for example, the concept of representation has long taken center stage (Grinker and Steiner 1997d). Mudimbe (1988, 1994) has forcefully shown how Africa has been represented in Western scholarship, since the time of the ancient Greeks, through the lens of European fantasies and constructs. Images of Africans and other non-Western peoples as savage, cannibalistic, and culturally impoverished have often been used by Western writers to "establish opposites and 'others' whose actuality is always subject to the continuous interpretation and reinterpretation of their differences from 'us'" (Said 1995: 3). For this reason, representations of an "Other" generally tell us far less about those who are being represented than they do about the preoccupations and prejudices of those engaged in the act of representing. But representations, such as the artistic images of Africans constructed by Europeans, also directly shaped the ways in which empires racially divided the world, and they were used to justify colonialism and other violations of human rights. Representations are thus political as well as aesthetic.

Turning to south Korea, we know that the south is filled with a variety of different kinds of representations of north Korea and that

many of these representations are based on extraordinarily little knowledge about the north. For instance, south Korean newspapers and
magazines frequently contain speculative articles about Kim Jong Il's
numerous health problems, and yet we know that to truly suffer from all
of the illnesses that have been ascribed to him, he would have to be either
superhuman or dead. These representations can be evaluated in part on
the basis of evidence presented in their support, but they can also be
evaluated for what they tell us about south Korea's demonization of the
north, and the degree to which south Koreans establish their own
identity as the opposite of the north. The extent to which the north and
south define each other in their opposition is an important feature of
division and unification discourses.

The process of "othering" in south Korea is hard to miss. Many south
Koreans regularly represent north Koreans quite negatively as people who,
after years of indoctrination, have no freedom of thought and behavior;
they are represented as uncivilized, inhabiting a time before progress and
enlightenment, heathen, backward, and blinded by the cult of Kim Il
Sung. At other times, north Koreans appear more positively, as primordial
Koreans before the fall of the south into the evils of modernity; they
preserve traditions that the south Koreans have forgotten; they are less
"Western" and more "pure." Although the two sets of representations may
seem at odds at first glance, a closer look reveals that they are both ways of
framing north Korea as the south's opposite. Part of this process of
othering, therefore, is that north Korea becomes a strong component and
defining characteristic of south Koreans' representations of themselves—
representations made by the detour of the north.

THE ARGUMENT

I shall argue that the continued conflict between north and south, and
the prospects for future peace on the Korean peninsula, must be
comprehended within the broader social and cultural context in which
Koreans come to believe in the necessity and inevitability of unification.
I suggest that a fundamental obstacle to peace on the Korean peninsula
(where the two Koreas remain, technically, in a state of war) is that south
Korea has become a nation in which nearly all aspects of economic,
political, and cultural identity are defined in opposition to north Korea,

and that, despite being a sacred goal, unification is paradoxically a threat to south Korean identity.

Korean identity is largely defined by division. In fact, almost every Korean living today was born and raised in a divided Korea and no Korean living today can remember a Korean state that is both sovereign and undivided. Instead of arguing the conventional line that it is difference and division that have disrupted Korean identity, I want to explore the possibility that the prospect of unification, too, as it is often imagined, idealized, and fantasized in projections into the future, is a disruption to contemporary Korean identity. Similarly, rather than focus on how unification will overcome heterogeneity, I want to explore whether Koreans ought to overcome the myth of homogeneity that stifles relations between south and north and prevents either side from recognizing that a unified Korea must also be a somewhat diverse Korea. When I refer to "identity" I mean the master narrative of homogeneity that is destabilized by the growing but reluctant acknowledgment in south Korea that Korea's futures will involve heterogeneity and difference. With democratization in south Korea, the increasing possibilities for open discussion and debate have also led to remarkable ambivalence about whether this openness will diminish the power of the state to enforce homogeneity. In light of the conflict between homogeneity and heterogeneity, unification discourses have to be analyzed for their disruptive effects.

The various chapters together also address a central problem in Korean society: the separation of people and state. This study examines the degree to which south Korea's conventional historical narratives have attributed responsibility for differences between the north and south to north Korea's late leader, Kim Il Sung, and more recently to his somewhat mysterious son, Kim Jong Il, and as a result have nearly erased the north Korean people from southern view. Indeed, few scholars address the social and cultural differences between north and south because they deny that there *are* meaningful differences, seeing almost all difference at the level of the state, and also because it is widely assumed that unification will result in the assimilation of the north into the south. From this perspective, north Korea is less a *people* than it is an illegitimate *state* vying for legitimacy against its southern brother.

Situating this discussion within a multidisciplinary literature on history, memory, and mourning, I suggest throughout the chapters that by postulating homogeneity—whether by steadfastly denying that there are any fundamental differences within the "people" or by arguing that there was absolute homogeneity prior to national division and that it is only since then that northerners and southerners have become different—south Koreans cannot mourn the loss of the homogeneous nation. Unable to mourn, south Koreans cannot negotiate with the (idealized) past, reconcile with the north Koreans, and begin to construct a more open and pluralistic society. As one result, unification is largely conceived in south Korea not as the integration of different identities, but as the southern conquest and assimilation of the north—in short, as winning the war.

In employing the concept of mourning, however, I am not suggesting in any way that Koreans have lost their nation or that unification is unrealistic or undesirable. Rather, I am pointing out that a central problem for south Korea is that it is uncomfortable with the present. National division is temporary—it is a death without a death— and so south Korean responses to national division and north-south differences contain elements of both grief and outright denial. Koreans cannot mourn the sundering of their nation because they also persistently maintain a vision and hope that the symbolic living and dead will be one again, that the homogeneous will be resuscitated from the heterogeneous. Representing north Korea and division in the south is a form of bereavement in which loss is denied.

In terms of the contest over legitimacy to which I have referred, Koreans from the north and the south have long insisted on a single legitimate history and future rather than multiple histories and futures. As one result, few writers in south Korea have approached the question of what sort of new and heterogeneous identity might emerge in a unified Korea. One of my central arguments is that the denial of loss is linked to an absence of thinking, writing, and debate about the destabilization of Korean identity. Throughout the text, I suggest that the trauma of division needs to be "worked through." Working through refers to the struggle to understand history and history's impact on the future. It also means balancing two tendencies in national trauma— protective numbing (for example, the Korean government's so-called pragmatic approach to north Korea) and disruptive emotions (for example, the student movement's so-called sentimentalist approach to north Korea)—and transforming the power of lost identity into creative literary and scholarly projects.

In focusing on how metaphors, conceptual oppositions, and psychological phenomena such as ambivalence and mourning are linked to contemporary unification discourses, I do not rule out more political or geopolitical modes of analysis; nor do I want to imply that my variously structuralist and psychoanalytic approaches have more explanatory power than an approach that more explicitly links unification discourses with colonial oppression. In fact, I would hope that the very different approaches of a number of scholars might yield similar conclusions, because this would strengthen each individual analysis. For example, I believe that many Koreanists might prefer to frame the contest between the two Koreas less in terms of the binary oppositions and Self/Other distinctions I employ and more in terms of a struggle between brothers, hierarchically related to each other in Confucian terms, over national legitimacy—that is, over the question of which of the two Koreas is the true, real, or legitimate one. This is a useful and accurate way of depicting contemporary discourses on Korean history that complements rather than negates a more structural analysis; for one thing, such a perspective might draw us much further into colonial and precolonial Korean history than I have attempted to go here, and since one might argue that Self/Other oppositions have little philosophical or ontological grounding in Korea, it establishes the cultural specificity of a Korean theory of legitimacy.

To establish my several claims, I analyze the various ways in which south Koreans represent north Korea in everyday conversations, school textbooks, public exhibition sites, writings by north Koreans who have defected to south Korea, and the discourses of activists who have traveled illegally to north Korea. Chapter 2 sets out the theoretical contours of my argument. By addressing south Korea's predicament of national identity in terms of unification as an idealized future, the chapter leads us to consider the pleasures of pursuing ideals and the displeasures, fears, and ambivalences that can be associated with the realization of the ideal. The chapter also contextualizes Korean identity politics within the ambiguities and fluidities of identity that are engendered in various modernities, not only Korea's. I pay special attention to Germany, as I do throughout the book, in part because studies of German modernity involve many issues that are central to the study of contemporary Korea—namely, unification, heterogeneity, and the Cold War—and in part because south Koreans themselves have in the past decade studied Germany intensively, often comparing Korea and Germany and exploring what the two nations might learn from each other.[2]

Chapter 3 extends the topic of ambivalence raised in chapter 2 to a 1993 exhibition in Seoul of north Korean everyday objects. Viewers show quite clearly that they simultaneously view north Korea as a place that has distorted Koreanness *and* as a place in which Koreanness has been preserved by communism. Communism, in other words, has changed much in north Korea, but it has also frozen in time many elements of Korean cultural identity that have been lost in the ever-changing, modernized, Westernized south. Through the tangible context of the exhibition, visitors give voice to a number of discourses on the saving or transforming of the north. These discourses are about denying the loss of homogeneity and wishing for the resuscitation of a more pure Koreanness that can be found in the north. The exhibition, then, serves as a lens through which south Koreans conceive of the problems of mourning. By illustrating how discourses on unification take shape through discussions of actual objects, the chapter lays the foundation for explaining in subsequent chapters the larger conceptual universe that informs viewer responses.

Chapter 4 focuses on the complex term *han* in order to establish a conceptual framework within which division and unification are framed. It is widely believed that unification will resolve much of Korea's *han,* or resentment, about division and other violations of Korean autonomy. Although it is a uniquely Korean concept, some aspects of *han* also bear a striking resemblance to what Freud termed "complicated mourning" and what some other authors have referred to as an "inability to mourn." This resemblance leads me to consider the relationship between mourning and unification in south Korea and to argue that *han* is in many ways a problem of mourning. That is, a central concern for south Korean identity politics is an inability, engendered in the conception of both *han* and complicated mourning, to recognize and adapt to loss. Just as complicated mourning inhibits the movement from a disabling grief to an adaptation to a new reality, so too does *han* potentially limit the ability to reconcile. Some variants of *han* and mourning lead to paralysis, attack, and emotional explosion as both personal and collective responses to loss, while others lead instead to creativity. Drawing on Korean scholarship on *han,* as well as Holocaust studies, I raise the question of how the aggressive potential of *han* can be converted into reconciliation and a recognition and "working through" of loss.

Chapter 5 concerns the idiom of family in division and unification discourses, focusing specifically on how north Korea figures into both pleasurable and frightening fantasies about the future of a unified Korea. The fantasies suggest that south Koreans have considerable ambivalence about whether unification will indeed resolve *han,* recover homogeneity, and negate prior loss. Ambivalence about unification emerges as south Koreans recognize, sometimes quite openly but more often in subtle, symbolically displaced ways, the irony that unification will disrupt the stability of the divided nation. The ambivalence is perhaps most salient in south Korean discourses about how the north Korean family may have changed. The conceptual distinction between people and state is essential to this problem. If it is only the state that has changed, then unification will reunite families; if the state has been able to fundamentally alter both people and values (and this is of course something most south Koreans I know want to deny), then unification may not unite divided families but only prolong the agonies of division and difference.

Chapters 6 and 7 are devoted to education at both the middle-school and university levels. Chapter 6 details some of the historical conditions that have given rise to certain kinds of discourses on the nation, as evidenced in ethics textbooks for school-age children, and it focuses in particular on a discernible movement in the texts away from the master narrative of Korean homogeneity and toward an understanding of cultural difference. The textbooks illustrate part of the new openness that is, paradoxically, an important factor in generating anxiety over unification and difference. Chapter 7 considers the ways in which dissident university students are implicated in the ambivalent process of historical representation as they become popularly characterized as north Korean "sympathizers." The central argument of this chapter is that the students and the government are complicitous in perpetuating a cycle in which homogeneity and heterogeneity, unification and division, mutually define each other in very conventional and routinized terms. What appears at first to be a revolutionary movement met with opposition from elites is yet another paradoxical means by which some south Koreans negotiate an increasingly unstable national identity (the homogeneous and unified nation). Student protests have certainly been valuable in facilitating numerous democratic reforms in south Korea, but at a more theoretical level student protests are also a means for struggling publicly with the uneasy opposition between unified and divided identities. The purpose of chapter 7 is not to illustrate the many ways in which individuals struggle and suffer for their country but rather to call attention to how systemic features of national division become implicated in student protests.

Chapter 8 continues the focus on dissidents by showing how they and government forces position themselves against each other in terms of a shared set of oppositions (between people and state, sentiment and science, truth and falsehood) that provides an additional conceptual framework for understanding south Korean ambivalence about unification, as well as by presenting some specific south Korean representations of ambivalence, in particular the travel accounts of three south Korean people who visited north Korea in 1989. The central question raised by the travel writings is: What is the best method of achieving unification? Does it involve the search for reality among the Korean people who live in a world in which the state has distorted that reality? Or are Koreans more likely to unify if they employ a dispassionate and scientific approach that privileges governments over people in the formation of a unified Korea?

Chapter 9 details the saga of the north Korean defectors, the role they play in the south Korean construction of north Korea, and therefore their part in the construction of south Korean identity. Defectors are very important to understanding south Korean attitudes toward north Korea and unification not only because they are, quite simply, north Koreans living together with south Koreans, but because the south Korean public watches them and listens to them on television and radio and reads their many written works. Moreover, statistics on the number and status of defectors become used in very political ways by politicians in south Korea to establish policy and perspectives on north Korea. Another reason defectors are important to this study is that they raise the subject of difference and heterogeneity that is so crucial to my argument that south Koreans' conceptions of sameness constrain efforts toward reconciliation and unification. Through a series of interviews with north Korean defectors living in Seoul, I emphasize the difficulty of reconciling south Korea's narrative of homogeneity with differences that have developed between the two Koreas in the last half century as well as differences within each Korea, such as between the southeast and southwest, elites and masses, students and police. The defectors also provide a better understanding of what a unified Korean society might look like. I should add that I do not consider the few south Korean defectors to the north that have been acknowledged by the south Korean government; I share south Koreans' lack of knowledge about these defections, and unfortunately my attempts to interview south Koreans on these defections were unproductive.

In the conclusion, chapter 10, I return to the subject of the Holocaust and Germany to raise questions about south Korean preparations for unification. I pay special attention to complicity and difference: Is there reason to suggest that the conceptual distinction between people and state in south Korea—a division that maintains the innocence of the north Korean people and the guilt of the north Korean state—will soon collapse? Will south Koreans be able to abandon the quest for assimilation in favor of the integration and appreciation of difference? I consider these important questions in the context of a recent exchange between Jurgen Habermas, one of the most vocal critics of German unification, and Paik Nak-chung, one of the most prominent Korean writers on unification and democracy.

PERSPECTIVE

At this point it is necessary to raise the issue of perspective. By perspective, I mean not simply the theoretical apparatus employed to guide the collection of interpretation of data, but rather the more general process through which authors and readers render complex and multidimensional experiences as texts. This process is important to describe, or, at the very least, to recognize as a central factor in the production of knowledge, because, as W. J. T. Mitchell has phrased it, "There is no vision without purpose" (1986: 38). This is a book about different ways of looking at the tragedy of Korea's division and the hope for its unification, and so it addresses and examines critically some of the structures of observation.

I begin with the position that representations are neither universally valid nor "authentic," by which I mean that knowledge and its images are constructed out of perspectives that are always partial, biased, and simplified reductions of more complex and nuanced phenomena. Studies of representation, however, and indeed nearly all forms of structuralism, risk focusing so much on symbolism and meaning that the people to whom the symbols belong, and who actually produce them, are nowhere to be found. Studies termed postmodern and infused with the jargon of literary criticism can appear as an intellectual game. This problem is most troublesome when it is created by authors who are not members of the society being discussed, who have not lived through the traumas whose representations they analyze, and who are, as one result, somewhat more emotionally detached from the issues at hand. While such authors, myself included, may profit intellectually from that detachment, sometimes being able to isolate certain data for analysis that others might take for granted, they have an extra burden to explain the value of their work, and to vigilantly consider the politically sensitive nature of their enterprise. Although this burden does not discourage me from working on unification issues, it does serve as a reminder that there are people living in Korea and elsewhere in the world who continue to suffer from the problems about which I am writing, and that readers may demand a more full explanation of my interests and motivations than they would demand from a native Korean.

I became interested in conducting research in Korea after I traveled to Seoul in 1990. Although I had been actively involved in research on ethnic relations in central Africa, I quickly became fascinated with the enduring division of Korea and the tenacity of north Korean communism in the midst of the "revolutions" of 1989, an age that many intellectuals called "the end of history" and that Germans have now termed the "turn" *(Wende)*. More specifically, I was interested in juxtaposing Korea to the African context in which I had previously worked. In northeastern Zaire I had lived with two groups of people who insisted that they were culturally, physically, and linguistically distinct from each other. Although they conceived of themselves as totally different groups while living in the most intimate association with each other, there was seldom any violence between the two groups. On the Korean peninsula, in contrast, two groups of people insist that they are culturally, physically, and linguistically homogeneous, and yet they are at war with each another. While the comparison between the two African societies and north and south Korea is obviously simplistic, this is the juxtaposition that stimulated my research and led me to explore the vicissitudes of north-south conflict in terms of homogeneity and heterogeneity. Indeed, such a formulation was a function of my lack of knowledge. And knowing little about Korea at the time, I asked some questions a true expert on Korea might not have asked.

This study subjects the well-worn terms of "division" and "unification" to what might, on the surface, be considered a naive or simplistic interrogation, to explore questions that might be posed only by the ignorant: Why do Koreans want to unify? Why is it so undesirable for Koreans to live in two separate countries? If the Koreans want to unify so much, why can't they do it? Why is it such a crime for south Koreans to travel to north Korea, and what is so threatening to south Korea about pro-north sentiments?

For many observers of Korea, these questions are much more likely to produce consternation than serious reflection. This is in large part because the answers are taken for granted. However, a concerted pursuit of these questions will necessarily draw us into an exploration of how unification and division appear in a variety of arenas of representation and how they are embedded in a complex and ambivalent struggle for national identity. I suggest this exploration will show how productive a critical examination of the seemingly obvious can be.

TWO

Nation, State, and the Idea of Unification: Speaking of the Unspeakable

THE TERM FOR UNIFICATION—*t'ongil*—is not employed only in contemporary or Korean contexts, and is not exclusively a political term. The term is used with reference to Germany, Yemen, and Vietnam (see Chun and Sŏ 1995) and to the ancient Three Kingdom period of Korean history *(samguk t'ongil sidae)*. The fragment *t'ong* is also incorporated into phrases such as "unification of political parties" *(t'onghap)* and "blending of primary colors" *(samsaek t'ongil)*. *T'ong* also denotes "standardization," such as "standardization of prices" *(Kagyŏk t'ongil)* and "standardization of the Korean alphabet" *(ch'ŏljabŏp t'ongil);* it is also employed in reference to the focusing of attention upon an object of scrutiny *(chŏngsin t'ongil)*. The term can even be used in reference to food, as when two or three different foods are deemed to be uninteresting when eaten alone, but, like rice and *kimch'i*, form a harmonious, complementary, and unified taste when eaten together. However, the most salient use of the word today is *nambuk t'ongil*, "unification of north and south," and the meaning is so powerful that it ramifies to a number of different areas of political and social life.[1]

Mention the word "unification" *(t'ongil)* and a flood of other concepts emerge in association with it: *chisang kwajae* (paramount goal), *tongjilsŏng hoebok* (regain homogeneity), *isan kajok chaehoe* (divided family reunion), *kungnyŏk pugang* (greater and more powerful nation), *chayŏn kaebal* (development of natural lands), and *tŏburŏ sanŭn sahoe* (literally, "living together society"). To this small sample of an enormous field of discourse one might also add the Korean words for "democracy" *(minju)*, "freedom" *(chayu)*, "security" *(anbo)*, and "prosperity" *(pŏnyŏng)*. German unification may have dampened some of the more positive fantasies about unification, producing discussions focused more on policy considerations of different unification scenarios, yet few Koreans will ever publicly argue against unification. It remains a sacred and paramount goal—as sacred as the Korean people *(minjok)*; it is imagined to open up endless possibilities for wealth, the spread of Christianity to the north, and the ability to compete economically with Korea's old enemy and colonizer, Japan. This is especially true for younger people I have interviewed. The older people I interviewed in south Korea represent unification as an endpoint, something to achieve before death—it means the possibility of visiting their hometowns, even if only once, before death. For younger people, especially students, unification also appears as an event, but as a place from which to launch an autonomous and authentic Korean history.

Unification also implies the reconstitution of the nation, for the nation and state should be one in Korea, with a racially, culturally, politically, and economically homogeneous citizenry. This view is widely held by south Korean historians to reflect Korea's ancient history of unity, and unification discourses depend upon it. However, in a study of the philosophy of Korean oneness, Chói Min-hong (1984) has argued against this conventional way of viewing unification. He asserts that *t'ongil* refers to a multiplicity of different ideas, objects, and factors joining together into an undifferentiated whole. But he adds the subtle point that the concept of *t'ongil* has the authority to unify even those ideas considered by most to be irrational, and to establish compromise: "*T'ongil* makes differences confront one another directly in an effort to become one" (1985: 20). In other words, *t'ongil* does not have to refer only to national unification as it is often defined, in terms of assimilation and absorption, but it also can characterize efforts to find ways to achieve complementarities.

For Chói, unification ideologies must be linked with the philosophy of *han* (*han* in this case meaning "wholeness," "brightness," "oneness," as the word appears in terms like *Taehan Min'guk*, the

Korean-language word for "Republic of Korea"). Choi argues that *han* posits oneness with compromise, and cannot allow exclusion or self-righteousness *(toksŏn)*.

Henry Em, another author who has challenged conventional notions of Korea's ancient history of homogeneity and who has worked on the concept of *minjok* (the Korean nation) has pointed out the very modern construction of the nation as an ethnic, Korean, and abstract category (Em 1995). Em's position is that the concept of the nation, as a global ideological form, has been naturalized in Korea. According to this view, nations depend for their continued existence as seemingly "natural" entities on the production and reproduction of historical narratives of continuity and homogeneity, and so Korean national unification discourses must necessarily be resistant to narratives of discontinuity and heterogeneity. Drawing on Carter Eckert's argument about the modern origins of Korean nationalism, Em attempts to historicize the Korean nation by questioning the twentieth-century Korean preoccupation with situating Korean national identity in ancient times. In an analysis of the work of Sin Ch'ae-ho, often praised in Korea as among the greatest nationalist historians, Em shows the ambivalence and non-nationalist (indeed, anarchist) elements of Sin's ideas. These elements have been neglected by Korean historians, even the most radical, because of the "still hegemonic forms created in the West—a hegemony wherein the nation state appears as the only legitimate form of polity, and the illusion of a nation's necessary and unilineal evolution appears natural and common-sensical. Caught in this hegemony, even radical historians are unable to imagine alternative political forms, and Sin Ch'ae-ho's anarchist ideas are passed over as their reading focuses on the figure of Sin Ch'ae-ho as the 'revolutionary nationalist'" (Em 1995: 20).

Em also points out that the term *minjok,* among many other words widely believed to be purely Korean, is a neologism (minzoku) developed by the Japanese educator Kato Hiroyuki, the first president of Tokyo Imperial University, during the late nineteenth century. *Minjok* was then defined by Korean nationalist historians as a primordial and ancient concept in order to establish a contemporary national and ethnic identity that would serve as a counterhistorical narrative to those constructed by the Japanese. Em adds that, although the Korean script was invented in the fifteenth century, it became a "national script" only in the late nineteenth century. This is not to suggest that Koreans do not

have a long and unified history, only that the concept of the Korean
nation today as *minjok* is a contemporary construction. This perspective
creates a terrible problem for Korean unity. If Korea's past cannot be
characterized by *minjok,* then are there other concepts that can denote
Korea's historical continuity? Phrased more precisely, if Korea's premodern period was not defined by the nation or *minjok,* then how can
unification be justified?

It seems unreasonable to define a continuous identity through
centuries of Korean history with a single and contemporary construct.
Similarly, I find it hard to justify an argument that Korean national
identity has been marked by unity and homogeneity since there is little
evidence to suggest that such a utopian vision has been realized anywhere
in the world. If one believes that Korea has been unified and homogeneous
for centuries and has been faced with difference or *ijilgam* only in the
post–World War II era, then one must rely on the argument that Koreans
are currently betwixt and between, in a temporarily divided land waiting
anxiously for unification. An alternative perspective might allow for both
unity and heterogeneity. If one assumes that Korea has always been
heterogeneous, then it is still possible to conceive of a long-standing and
ancient history of Korean unity, albeit a unity that also can be characterized by heterogeneity and complementarity. The current heterogeneity
could be seen as just one figuration of a long history of difference.

At this point it is necessary to state that this book generally makes a
presumptive claim for contemporary difference between the north and
south without specifying what may or may not have constituted difference
in the more distant past; I am concerned with how people use the idea of
differences to construct a vision of the nation. Chapters in which I
approach policy issues and prescribe reconciliation through an understanding of difference—chapters 1 and 10, and chapter 8 on north Korean
defectors—require some closure on the idea that there are currently "real"
differences between the people of north and south Korea. However, I do
not take on this burden of closure, or request it of the reader, in chapters
primarily involving the analysis of representations. I am interested in
understanding how concepts of difference and similarity effect south
Korean perspectives on unification but I am not interested in attempting
to determine any sort of actual differences and similarities.

Discussion in Korea about different kinds of unification remains at
a very general level, and only in the past few years or so, as the two

Koreas negotiate food aid for the hungry north and investors are given clearance to invest there, has there been an increase in public discussion about the north Korean people. There is remarkably little discussion about the practicality of gradual border openings and contacts, such as those that occurred between the former West and East Germanys; each side's knowledge of the other made the conditions more favorable for unification. There is almost no debate today in south Korea about the possibility of the continued existence of two separate Koreas with a relatively open border. Although two Korean states might conceivably coexist peacefully along with family reunions, inter-Korean sports, art, and other cultural exchanges, south Koreans do not and cannot support the idea of a confederation, and they have only occasionally conducted policy work on a related commonwealth system as an interim measure. North Korea's plans have included confederation but have also involved the replacement of the south Korean regime and the removal of all U.S. troops from the peninsula. The south's disagreement is in part due to the fact that they believe that the nation and state must be one, that a confederation is not unification, and that north Korea must be totally absorbed into the south, its state destroyed, and its people assimilated.[2] But it must also be said that disagreement with the north Korean plan for a confederation is also due in part to the fact that it was put forward by north Korea, and south Korean national security laws prohibit south Korean sympathy with anything north Korean. A true cynic might suggest quite simplistically that in south Korea one of the greatest fears of a confederation is that north Korea might agree to it.

PEOPLE AND STATE

How should we interpret the south Korean position on the necessity of merging people and state? Choi Jang-jip (1993: 23) writes that immediately following national division, Korean nationalism "became transformed into a statism that privileged anti-communism over unification." National security laws and anti-communist statutes in south Korea continue to inhibit free speech (and press) about the north; south Korean governments have long bolstered their power by promoting a Cold War discourse that vilified the north as the enemy and thus justified a strong authoritarian state that censored the flow of information to its citizens. The philosopher Song Du-yul (1995a: 110) suggests that from the perspective of south Korea, the continuing conflict between north and south was, indeed, framed as anti-communism but has more recently emerged as specifically anti–north Korea. According to Song, the principles of communism are no longer south Korea's main enemy; instead, the relational principles between north and south have taken center stage. South Korea, according to this view, wants to destroy its northern enemy and is using anti-communism as an ideological weapon to achieve its goal.

It seems to me that Song is trying to make the point that south Korean intolerance of a variety of different political views is determined ultimately not by the national security laws but by the widespread sentiments that support the continued existence and exercise of the laws.[3] This is a situation well known to observers of Korea, and it is a mark of the degree to which south Korean identity is dependent upon the existence of its opposite, the enemy. I recently spoke with a Korean economist about the best-selling autobiography by the late defector Yi Han-yŏng, a nephew of Kim Jong Il's former mistress, Sŏng Hae-rim. When I expressed doubt about the veracity of some of the author's comments on Kim Jong Il's eccentricities, the economist became angry and suggested that I might be sympathetic to Kim Jong Il and the north Korean regime. In other words, one is either "for us or against us," with little room for debate, contest, or a middle ground.

While many people may not agree with Song and may classify him as a north Korean sympathizer (he is, after all, living in exile in Berlin), south Koreans have clearly waged their own propaganda war, seemingly unaware that they have won it. South Korea has wealth, international respect, and one of the highest literacy rates in the world; south Koreans continually make major contributions to all fields of humanity, from the arts to the basic sciences. But they have not taken their revenge against the north. Indeed, many policy analysts I have met in Washington are concerned that south Koreans may not be happy until the north Korean state is destroyed. And opposing this version of unification puts one at risk for being accused of opposing unification altogether.

Let us return for a moment to Choi's accurate comment that south Korea produced a "statist" nationalism. In part as a result of the south Korean government propaganda, the Korean-language literature on national division was influenced by the anti-communist notion that the

Kim Jong Il. (*Korea Today,* P'yŏngyang, DPRK.)

state is the sole independent variable in determining north Korean history. In south Korea, any suggestion that it is the "people" of north Korea who create differences between north and south might be considered an anti-national act because it legitimates the north as a distinct and separate nation. Why talk about the "north Koreans," or exhibit them as a separate people, when they and south Koreans are culturally one and the same? An additional problem has to do with the potentially tautological relation between people and state. If there is indeed a distinct state, might it also require a distinct civil society to support it? Or, conversely, might a distinct civil society require a distinct state?

Scholars have also been preoccupied with the state as the primary determinant of the nation. Although some social scientists recognize that the separation between state and society is a model to be explained rather than simply appropriated at face value as a valid analytical distinction (Koo 1993a), these scholars remain in a small minority. In a typical separation of nation (people) and state, the political scientist Glenn Paige accepted in 1970 that Korea was divided into two equally "matched" test groups that were then "subjected to different kinds of political stimuli. . . . Because of its high degree of social homogeneity, [Korea] offers the social scientist an instance of quasi-experimental conditions on a vast scale rarely observable outside the experimental laboratory" (1970: 152). In 1984 Kihl Young Hwan, adhering to the orthodoxy that state and society are distinct, and reaffirming Korea's myth of cultural homogeneity, quotes with approval an unpublished paper by the political scientist Kim Han-kyo: "Different patterns of development in two regions of Korea in the postwar years may be attributed to political factors. . . . Inasmuch as social and cultural factors could safely be assumed to be fundamentally identical throughout Korea at the onset of national division" (quoted in Kihl 1984: 5). And, in 1994, Yang Sung-chul wrote:

> For a long time, I have been advocating that the two Koreas are the best living laboratories for comparativists, be they political scientists, sociologists, economists or other social scientists. To compare two Koreas' political processes and economic performance is, for example, different from studying the same topics of two states. For one thing, if enormous differences exist in political processes and economic performance in both halves today, an explanation must necessarily lie in the two entirely different political and economic systems they adopted in 1948. In analyzing both Koreas' diametrically opposed political and economic realities, cultural and other non–politico-economic factors are mostly given or irrelevant, and they cannot be the main explanatory variables. (Yang 1994: v-vi)

The split between the people and the state has made it possible for south Koreans to develop a discourse about the north that attributes agency and power only to the state and explains differences between the north and south as products of one man, Kim Il Sung.[4] South Koreans have been able to emphasize the unity of the people by stressing the differences between the states and by assuming that in north Korea the state neither constructs nor is constructed by the people. As a result, the north Korean people have been virtually erased from south Korean discourse on the north.

우물 안의 국민들

"Frogs in a well." The north Korean people blinded by Kim Il Sung and Kim Jong Il. (Y. H. Kim, *Y. H. Kim's Editorial Cartoons*.)

Media critics in the more liberal Korean newspapers complain that, even today, when one occasionally hears something about north Korean people, it almost always comes from defectors, who are unequivocally anti-north, paint frightening pictures of the north (see, for example, An 1995), and wish to publicize their loyalty to the south Korean state; these defectors perpetuate the view that north Korean ideas and behavior are wholly determined by the actions and ideology of the Kim Il Sung state (Chói, Y. M. 1993: 9). It is only the rare defector who has the courage to write negatively about the south and somewhat positively about the north (Chang, Y. C. 1997). As one famous example of the synecdoche whereby north Korea is collapsed into the state, in April 1989 President Roh Tae Woo pardoned Kim Hyun-hee, the north Korean terrorist who was convicted of planting the bomb that in 1987 killed 115 passengers of Korean Air Lines flight 858. Roh said that Kim was an innocent victim of a state that brainwashed its people, and that responsibility rested with Kim Il Sung and Kim Jong Il (see Kim, H. H. 1993: 173).

THIN DISCOURSES

The people of north Korea are also absent from most south Korean fiction, although this is slowly beginning to change. Novels, poems, and short stories that fall under the category *pundan munhak* (division literature) seldom explicitly represent north Korea or the people of north Korea, but rather they dwell on the tragic consequences of division for south Korean life. There is an emerging literature, however, that explores north-south differences outside of Korea, or in the margins, such as in the demilitarized zone. For example, Kwŏn Han-sook's popular book *Inshalla* [Arabic. "If God be willing"] (1995) explores the complexities of a relationship between a north Korean man and south Korean woman when they meet in Algeria; Yi Ho-ch'ŏl's short story "Pánmunjŏm" (1988 [1961]) addresses similar complexities when a south Korean man and north Korean woman meet in the demilitarized zone; Chói Il-nam's 1989 story, "Kkumkilkwa malkil" (Dream-way and language-way) depicts a dialogue between a north Korean man and a south Korean man who meet in a dream in the demilitarized zone. Kim Chin-myŏng's suspenseful 1995 novel, *Kajŭoŭi nara* (Kajŭo's Country), set in Japan, humanizes Kim Jong Il by depicting his relationship with a south Korean student. In the context of north-south relations within south Korea, discussion and study groups are emerging to help defectors and other south Koreans learn about their differences and similarities—for example, the *nambukt'onghapkyosil* (south-north integration class) at Chungang University.

In addition, in the past few years some carefully selected radio and television broadcasts from north Korea have been aired in south Korea, including *Nambukŭi ch'ang* (North-south window) and *T'ongil chŏnmangdae* (Observatory of unification). This has given south Koreans a chance to glimpse some of the official images of north Korean citizens crafted by north Korea's state-run media. North Korean defectors also frequently appear on radio and television to answer questions about north Korea. Quite remarkably, in a 1996 television show entitled "*P'okso Taejakjŏn*" (Strategy for Laughter), two men both named Kim Yong, one a south Korean comedian and the other a north Korean defector and folk singer, appeared together to poke fun at the differences between north and south Korean people. The Korean Broadcasting System also intends to broadcast a serial drama, "Until the Azaleas Bloom," which depicts everyday life in north Korea. Such shows mark a profound shift in the manner in which the media represent the north Korean people, and this is likely due to the greater amount of freedom of speech Koreans have had since the election of Kim Young Sam. That these shows are unusual also reminds us how invisible the north Koreans really are in south Korea. Readers should recall that, whereas east and west Germans could often visit each other, send mail, and watch each other's television programs, most products of north Korea (magazines, videos, newspapers, books, and articles) remain classified in south Korea as *pimil* (secret) and are illegal; indeed, as of November 1997, bookstores continued to be subject to government raids in which security officials detain or arrest bookstore owners on charges of violating national security laws—that is, of selling books that are not sufficiently anti-communist or provide a considerable amount of information on north Korea.

The absence of images of the north and of the Korean War is remarkable for a country whose "paramount goal" *(chisang kwaje)* is the reunification of the nation. Nations often trace their histories and ideals persuasively through museums, exhibitions, ruins, and sites of pilgrimage and festival that contain the fragments of past tragedies. But in south Korea, visitors do not see bombed or burned buildings, preserved for memory, and except for some photographs, museums show few visible fragments of the Korean War. The south Korean government opened an exhibition specifically on the Korean War only in June 1994, as part of a large museum devoted to the long history of military conflicts that involved Korea within or outside the peninsula. In 1989, then-president Roh Tae Woo had attempted to pass through the national assembly a plan to build a large museum to the Korean War in It'aewŏn, but he was temporarily prevented by an outpouring of public opinion against its construction, expressed in various media, especially the more liberal newspapers and journals. A general war museum with one section devoted to the Korean War was eventually approved, and it opened on June 10, 1994, but the project is still a very contentious issue (Jager, in press).

My impression is that most north Koreans and south Koreans with whom I have spoken about national division and the Korean War are embarrassed by these phenomena—indeed, so embarrassed that many cannot even admit that the conflict resembled a civil war, instead arguing that it was a war between the superpowers played out at the expense of Korea—and this embarrassment actually extends to such things as north Korean terrorism and human rights violations. Many still feel that, for all the differences that have come about over the past forty years, north Koreans and south Koreans are both Koreans—one people, one race *(kat'ŭn tongp'o, hangyŏre)*—and so southerners feel simultaneously angered by the north Koreans and embarrassed by them. This is true despite the fact that there are few people in Korea today who can remember what a unified Korea looked like.

The shame over Korea's past was also evident in the public reaction to the proposed Korean War memorial, which some people felt would demean the Korean heritage by glorifying war and the military.[5] Moreover, many think of their country of citizenship not as a nation but only as one state (perhaps the only legitimate one) in a nation that is still one. Division is thus an aberration from more than "half of ten thousand years" *(panman'nyŏn)* of unity, as south Koreans describe the length of their history, as well as a non-Korean, imperialist, Cold War construction. They might look upon any exhibition of the processes and consequences of national division as an acknowledgment that the division is final. Because ruins invoke the past, any display or memorializing of ruins would transform what many feel is only a temporary division into a permanent one. In a sense that would be true, for in fact north and south Korea have not officially ended their civil war but only continue to recognize a 1953 armistice agreement to withdraw their military forces behind a demilitarized zone;[6] as Boyarin puts it in the context of political divisions in the Middle East, "This past which is not yet mastered is not over" (1994: 33). In other words, to deny the past forecloses the possibility of mastering it. In the context of Korea, to make monuments to the war, or to the lost nation, might be seen as establishing a false legitimacy and a false emplotment of Korean history.[7] Monuments and memorials might actually undermine the solid foundations of *illegitimacy,* that is, the illegitimate and temporary system of "two states, one nation."

The fact that there are so few memorials or monuments in south Korea is one symptom of a crisis in mourning. Although monuments usually suffer from the curse of state sponsorship—states sometimes make their most explicit claims for the nation's birth and righteousness through quite self-aggrandizing structures (Young 1990, 1993, 1994)—monuments nonetheless tend to unite the suffering of individuals into a collective symbol of shared history and loss: they are the social and public counterpart to individual and private emotional experiences. They complement private experiences by giving them tangible sociological referents. Monuments about loss also package the past concretely— one can, quite literally, walk away from them—and thus provide the possibility to break with the past even as their monumental form makes it sacred; they simultaneously mark both a merger of the present with the past and a movement away from loss toward the present and future. Monuments illuminate the differences and similarities between individual and collective psychological dynamics, and the degree to which they merge or diverge in different temporal relations. As Homans puts it, quite psychoanalytically:

> Monuments contain a psychological core: they are also mnemonic symbols. Experienced unconsciously as objects, the monument is a sort of compromise formation by means of which a group can unconsciously immerse itself in an experience of loss (loss of persons, ideas, ideals, or a lost "reality," such as when a traumatic disaster destroys many members of the group) but not directly feel the full force of the pain which the loss arouses. The group is thereby enabled to immerse itself in the past (the loss itself), move on into the present (the construction of the monument), and from there to release into the future (the ability to mourn and return to, or create a rapprochement with, the great necessities of life). (Homans 1989: 271).

The absence of monuments, conversely, suggests an inability to move beyond the past into a new form of identity. By supporting a myth of a recoverable homogeneity, south Koreans continue the fantasy of an eternal present—the present in which "I lived in the north" or "I was together with my family." Chapter 3 is explicitly about the process of mourning when identity is disrupted, as revealed in viewer responses to an exhibition on north Korean everyday life. The grief for the loss of the nation coexists in a profound and ambivalent tension with the outright denial of the loss. The exhibition appears as a kind of monument itself— it reveals the beginnings of a mourning process for its viewers—and thus helps to engage the question of Koreans' inability to mourn, and whether that inability limits movement away from the longing for the lost ideal and toward a new and unique national and cultural identity. One might argue, along with Homans, that monuments and mourning are inextricably related in terms of growth and adaptation, that "the ability to mourn foreshadows the advent of individuation because it is, in its simplest sense, the capacity to support oneself internally while recognizing in full conscious awareness both the collectivizing and individualizing realities within which one inevitably exists" (Homans 1989: 278).

The limitations and thinness of discourses on north Korea, difference, and unification are thus the result of a complicated set of factors and cannot be reduced to one or another central cause without dissolving into a nearly infinite regress: the absence of discourses that escape conventional binarisms can be attributed to a lack of scholarship, the scholarship to a lack of data, the lack of data to national security laws that limit academic freedoms, national security laws to division, and so on. Even if one were to establish a cause that seemed to carry more weight than others, contradictions in interpretation would arise. The regress might potentially end at the level of the international forces that are blamed for the division of Korea, but even the international intervention could be blamed on the colonization of Korea by Japan, and the colonization in turn blamed on a number of factors, including the weakness of the Korean king and state, and a sort of dependence complex *(sadae ŭisik)* that facilitated Korea's reliance on foreign powers and the granting of economic concessions to Japan, China, Russia, and the United States. Discourses on the north are more accurately to be seen as the consequence of all of these factors joining to disrupt Korean identity and engender the effort to repair it. The binarisms that make up so many unification and division discourses are part of large and old political struggles that feed back upon each other and escape easy explanation.

UNIFICATION AND MODERNITY: KOREA AND GERMANY

I want now to shift the discussion to the relationship between mourning and modernity, not only because this is an area in which there has developed a growing body of knowledge, but also because Korean responses to division and difference can be fruitfully situated in terms of broader global processes. I have already mentioned that I will argue that Koreans face a crisis of mourning. One reason why some scholars of nations and nationalism have turned to the concept of mourning in recent years is to analyze traumas and tragedies, especially those associated with "modernity" and other social transformations (see, for example, Winter 1995; Santer 1990; Ivy 1995; Caruth 1994; Crimps 1989; Phelan 1997). Eric Santner (1990) has written extensively on mourning in postwar Germany as the task of integrating the damage, loss, and disorientation of post-Holocaust Germany into a "transformed structure of identity." Jay Winter (1995) shows how, in western Europe, the production of monuments and memorials to World War I in a "traditional" or classical style (for example, romanticism, the invocation of late-Victorian and Edwardian values about duty, honor and masculinity, and sentimentality), was a reactive effort to create a language of mourning; public art that was highly traditional in character helped survivors of the war not only to collectively mourn the material and human losses of the war through shared aesthetic symbols that evoked a common past, but also to resist mourning the loss of traditions. By interpreting the war largely though traditional frames of reference, Europeans attempted to stall the ascent of modernism in art and literature (see also Reynolds 1996).

Marilyn Ivy (1995) has considered similar issues of the rhetorics of mourning, loss, and recovery in Japan's nostalgic search for authenticity. World War II left both Germany and Japan with an extraordinary amount of wreckage to work through: fascism, massacre, loss of human life, and loss of the war. And clearly, for both Germany and Japan, the problem of denial—Germans initially denying complicity with the Nazis and only later apologizing for the past and paying reparations to its victims, and Japanese persistently avoiding public and official recognition of their responsibility for or remorse about numerous atrocities (such as the Nanking massacre and the oppression of Koreans)—has been linked to an inability to work through national traumas and losses. Korea's need to mourn is different, of course, as it is linked to the losses Koreans suffered as a result of political and military upheaval: national division, divided families, the loss of autonomy, and so on. Still, one might be able to draw some parallels between tragedies in Germany and Korea in the sense that vast crimes against humanity were committed in both of these nations, in the former by the Nazis and in the latter by the Japanese. In addition, the people-state division that I have stressed as so important to south Koreans has been extraordinarily

important to Germans and Jews alike as they struggle with the complicated and sensitive issue of complicity—that is, with the idea that it was
the Nazi state and not the people who committed the crimes of war, and
that the German people were largely unaware of the Nazi state's mass
extermination of Jews.

Another, more general reason why scholars have embraced the
concept of mourning is that the loss of "tradition" is a central feature of
"modernity" in general and late-twentieth-century capitalism in particular. As Koreans move from the agricultural sector into urban areas,
peasants, the land, and "Koreanness" are conceived as a thing of the past.
Nostalgia for tradition is also a result of fundamental transformations in
the global economy, such as increased permeability of national boundaries and profound experiences of displacement. Koreans, of course,
conceive of themselves as displaced not only because the nation is
divided, but because Koreans have emigrated throughout the world. In
this respect, Koreans are a typically "modern" people, caught between
the displacements of the late twentieth century and the belief in the
uniqueness and coherence of their culture. As Koreans "globalize," as
Kim Young Sam's administration frames Korean modernity, they find
themselves threatened, fragmented, and disjointed, a condition popularly described in recent literature on social thought as "modernity."

In contemporary social theory, modernity is not to be confused
with modernization. Modernity is a subtler and more complex concept.
It is about shifting borders, fluid boundaries, and unstable identities.
Berman (1983: 15), for example, writes of "modernity" in general that
we all "find ourselves in an environment that promises adventure, power,
joy, growth, transformation of ourselves and the world—and, at the
same time, that threatens to destroy everything we have, everything we
know, everything we are." Giddens (1990) writes at length about the
gaps between culture, memory, and location, about time-space compres-
sion in the process of globalization, and he asserts that modernity
involves the loss of security, embeddedness, and identity.

Koreans' uncertainty about their national identity is thus not only
culturally distinctive but also part of a more general process of displacement and resistance shared by communities throughout the world. Yet
far from dismantling notions of home and homeland, these so-called
modern conditions of fluidity and uncertainty, in south Korea and
elsewhere, often give rise to a heightened awareness of the conflicts

between ideals and perceived realities, and people may respond to the threats against those ideals by objectifying aspects of their culture that need to be revitalized, a process seen in Korea in the celebration of the so-called *minjung* or folk culture. *Minjung,* a subject discussed here and there throughout this text but in greater detail in chapter 4, shows that Koreans have not accepted capitalism and consumerism without resistance—not surprisingly, since traditionalism and reaction seem to always accompany modernity. Conservatism and modernity play off each other as mutually defining temporal orientations in what Peter Osborne calls a "politics of time" (Osborne 1995).

Before moving to a more elaborate discussion of the relations between these concerns and Korean unification, let us first consider briefly how two nations, Korea and Germany, illuminate the ways in which discourses on borders and identities give rise to multiple and sometimes antithetical sentiments. In both parts of the world, borders become implicated in the ambivalence that characterizes the processes of "modern" identity construction and representation.

In Korea, unification efforts seek to resolve a complex history of simultaneous rupture and continuity involving enduring social and political contradictions that emerged in the colonial period, Cold War discourses, the creation of a border at the thirty-eighth parallel, Korean civil war, and an ideology of Korean cultural homogeneity. Each of these aspects of Korean history constitutes an important narrative of struggle for identity and political agency, and, most important, the recuperation of the borders (and borderlessness) that define a Korea in which south and north are again one.

Korean national division is itself a sort of dispersal and displacement, with unification as the idealized return. Unification is not only a metaphorical return, but an actual one as well: Koreans separated from their homelands in north or south will be able to return to them, and many overseas Koreans may decide to return to live in a unified Korea. Many Koreans hold that they are not truly at home; they are, in a sense, travelers waiting in a temporary location. But unification too is about dispersal and social transformation; it is about the disruption of what nearly every Korean has come to believe is distinctively Korean—the division, the homelands that cannot be returned to, the resentment that defines emotion, national character, and the enmity toward the "other." Unification replaces a familiar and lived sense of nationality with one that is familiar only to the extent that it has been imagined. For southerners now in the north, and northerners now in the south, the dream is to travel home; this home may be a single town or province, but for many Koreans the true homeland is not north or south but a unified Korea, a singular place to which they will all one day return. If unification is about regaining an identity, it is also about overcoming and rupturing an identity—that of division and displacement—and many Koreans experience extraordinary ambivalence when they try to imagine that process.

There are obviously strong concerns about the financial burden of unification, whatever scenario is imagined: military takeover, absorption, the total collapse of the north Korean economy. Many Koreans are also concerned about the monetary and human cost of possible military conflicts in the event that unification occurs through violent means (Jee 1994). There are some who want unification now and suggest that it is so important that Koreans must make whatever sacrifices are necessary; there are others who suggest that unification should come later, when the north Korean economy is stronger, and/or when the south Korean economy is stronger, in order to produce a "soft landing" that will not devastate Korea's economy, for if Germany could not cope with the economics of unification, how could south Korea, with its own economic crises, manage the impoverished and "backward" north? People also cite inevitable social problems such as selecting a new name and flag, labor competition and unemployment, the reclaiming of rights of inheritance to property, meeting up with children and with spouses from whom people were separated but never divorced, possible acts of revenge at the level of national and local politics, and the problem of what to do with the demilitarized zone (see Foster-Carter, 1994; Grinker, 1995b). Yet most people that I know and have interviewed in south Korea have argued that unification will have to entail considerable sacrifice (what Kim Young Sam has frequently called *kot'ongpundam,* or "sharing pain"). Moreover, unification is seen as the solution for a number of problems caused by division, namely, the national security state, authoritarianism, and severe restrictions on freedom of speech.

The literary critic Paik Nak-chung (1993a, 1993b, 1994) calls Korea a "division system," and this is a concept I allude to in later chapters. I shall discuss the idea at some length here because it highlights contradictions and difficulties that arise in division and unification discourses. Paik argues that the unwanted and undemocratic features of contemporary Korea—corruption, a national security state, and lack of freedom of speech, for example—have their roots in the systemic nature of division and dispersal. I interpret Paik's notion of division as a form of deep structure, especially since he argues that recent changes in Korean society and politics constitute merely surface transformations that do not alter the division system. The only significant changes that can be made in Korea—that is, those that are not products and facilitators of national division—are changes that result in unification. So deeply is division embedded in Korea that Paik suggests the system may persist even after political integration is achieved, albeit under one state (Paik personal communication).

Paik's notion of a division system has not produced lively debate in either the Korean- or English-language literature. Paik suggests that the reason Koreans have not embraced this concept is that the "sheer weight of the national security state" has suppressed debate (1993b: 72). I do not know exactly why scholars outside of Korea have not explored the concept more fully. This may be simply because few scholars have actually looked critically at unification from perspectives outside mainstream political science, because Paik's works have only recently appeared in English translation, or because the concept is potentially quite controversial. The division system is, indeed, a provocative concept because it raises some uncomfortable issues, one of which concerns the world system, and two of which concern the conventional ways in which south Korean governments have addressed the relation between division and national security.

As for the first issue, the division system suggests that south and north Korea are united not only in the division system, but also as a subsystem of a larger global political and economic system, of which the United States is the clear leader. This modernist and world-system approach, while intellectually satisfying for many scholars because it seems reasonable to assume that Korea and the rest of the world are embedded within a series of international transactions and systems, can be interpreted—falsely, I believe—to mean that Korea has no agency of its own to reconstruct Korea. The second issue is that the systemic nature of division suggests that unification and democracy are opposed to division and national security—that division demands a national security state with the accompanying state restrictions on democracy and on the realization of the people's will for unification. In the absence of true democracy, for which, in Paik's view, Kim Young Sam's republic (*munmin chŏngbu,* "people's government") does not qualify, division will persist. There seems to be no way out. Without unification there can be no democracy; without democracy there can be no unification. The third issue is that the division system suggests rather explicitly not only that north Korea is an internal feature of south Korean life (not an external "Other" to be managed), but that south Korea is an equal partner in contributing to the ongoing division. Such a proposition— that south Korea is partly responsible for Korea's failure to unify, and that, by extension, the seemingly obvious impermeable border between north and south is in fact permeable—is simply too radical a notion for many scholars of Korean politics.

The division system, as Paik describes it, is a subsystem of Wallerstein's world system; however, the north-south dichotomy also constitutes its own unique system—a *sui generis* system, as Paik has phrased it in numerous writings. Quite contrary to Paik's own self-conscious formulation of the systemic nature of division in Wallerstein's terms, the division system appears founded on a structuralist premise that the binary opposites of the northern and southern systems form the larger division system, and that the two systems pervade Korean identity politics. The system is so pervasive that it becomes impossible to escape from north-south conflict and the national security state that the conflict entails.

But Paik enshrines the people-state opposition that I find so intellectually troubling. Within the system, Paik argues, the north and south Korean populace is opposed to the northern and southern system (1995: 180), a system that was "established by the intervention of outside powers" (1995: 150). This opposition is consistent with his argument that Koreans are homogeneous—as he puts it, the two Koreas are already unified on the basis of ethnic, linguistic, and cultural homogeneity. Paik's formulation thus requires that the people and states be diametrically opposed to each other. Indeed, it seems an insurmountable logical dilemma to argue that homogeneity and a system of division can coexist, unless one also wishes to argue that the division system is only operable at a single level, the level of the state, and not at the level of the people. Even if one were to argue that the system is operable at multiple levels, Paik is clearly ascribing agency only to one level, that of states. The state is the agent of division, while the people remain unified victims.

I would suggest that the binary oppositions between north and south are indeed pervasive, but to define Korea as a division system is to focus our attention primarily on the question of what precisely in south Korea is functioning to maintain rather than to subvert or complicate the oppositions. The answers to this question lead, not surprisingly, to the state. Such a perspective would be incompatible with the proposition that Korea is confronted with the fluidities and ambiguities of modernity. Indeed, Paik's system assumes that division and unification, too, are binary opposites and thus, to some extent, stable entities. Nor does the concept of the division system address the question of what in south Korea can be done to change the binary so that it is defined less by hatred and fear. This is where the concept of mourning becomes useful: mourning leads us to consider how ambivalence enters into binary oppositions, subverts their stability, and provides possibilities for creative resolution. It is the inability to mourn that can result in the reaffirmation of binary opposites.

Germany's simultaneous nationalism and Europeanism is also a good case for illustrating the contradictions that arise in division and unification discourses. In an essay on German film maker Edgar Reitz's successful TV series *Heimat* (Home), Morley and Robins focus on how Europeans in general, and Germans in particular, attempt to resolve what they see as a central tension of modernity between (figurative) homelessness and home (1990: 19). At the same time that Germans claim membership in a wider European union, two processes contribute to a backlash against the foreign *(fremde)*, the emigrant *(die Weggegangenen)*, and the American: globalization and a nationalist effort to release Germans from the psychological weight of Nazi history. In the first instance, Germans address their fears about the degree to which the European Union will mute the development and representation of national cultures, for it is in nations, Morley and Robins suggest, not economic or regional unions, that people feel most at home. In the second instance, Germans seek a renewal of German culture without fascism or imperialism, and also without emigration, Americans, or imported non-German popular culture. Reitz's drama of German history opposes emigrants (mostly men) to villagers *(die Dableiber,* mostly women) who remain at home, thereby valorizing the home as a domain of family, reproduction, and hearth and setting the stage for the denigration of the foreign, the un-German, the mobile. In his own writings on the series, Reitz describes one of the main male characters as a "real American": "a man without a home, without roots, a sentimental globetrotter" (quoted in Morley and Robins 1990: 10). The anti-Americanism can be understood as a rejection of modernity, of involvement with other cultures, and of the assimilation of non-German popular culture as a way of forgetting or repressing fascism. Reitz says:

> Nazism, the war . . . the defeat and its aftermath . . . produced a homelessness . . .in the feeling of a loss of "right" to a homeland . . . even language no longer provided a 'home'. Even the image of Germany in the post war period was part of this uprootedness. America [was] represented, for example, by the White House, England by Buckingham Palace . . . France by the Arc de Triomphe . . . Germany, however, (was always) represented by its division, above all by the Berlin Wall, marking the absence of certainty about home: Separation, expulsion, exile. (Quoted in Morley and Robins, 1990: 12)

Reitz's laments about homelessness and searches for a home raise the question of whether it is possible to live in a modern condition without a home, a center, a place or idea to which to return. Morley and Robins suggest that, given the mobile conditions of modernity, it is no longer possible to construct an exclusionary and defensive homeland (1990: 19-20), that people everywhere must learn to live within traditions of displacement and accept as an enduring reality the tension and double consciousness evoked in Senocak's poem about Germany, "Doppelmann:"

> I carry two worlds within me
> but neither one whole
> they're constantly bleeding
> the border runs
> right through my tongue.
> (Quoted in Morley and Robins, 1990: 20)

What the authors do not venture is an answer to the question of whether it is possible for people to maintain such an ambivalent existence without seeking its resolution or negation. It would be clearly unacceptable in south and north Korea, where unification and the recovery of homogeneity are sacred goals and where heterogeneity is a pejorative concept. One of the purposes of this book is to suggest that we draw our attention not solely to a world of displacement or a world of defensive homelands, but to the ambivalence people experience in relation to the coexistence of multiple worlds and to the destabilization of identity that results from displacement. It is a given that we live today in a world that is both with and without borders, where inward-looking social movements exist alongside outward-looking ones. But for most people, life is characterized by the tension between the two extremes, and conventional typologies of diasporas and other displacements of people and identities that focus on dreams of travel and return often do not take into account the extraordinary ambivalence many members of such communities feel about their displacement. The anthropological task is to identify the manner in which ambivalence becomes culturally patterned in specific times and places, to explore how, in the context of modernity, various forms of displacement—diaspora, transnationalism, migration, and unification, among others—engender symbolic struggles for identity. In the next chapters, I explore how unification, and the ambivalent identity struggles it involves, is culturally patterned in a number of different contexts in contemporary south Korea, and how these patterns relate to the theme of loss and mourning. As Santner suggests, the danger of modernity is not that it signifies the disintegration of a utopian world, but rather that it destabilizes the structures that were "good-enough" for both defining identity and healing the wounds opened up by the past (1989: 127).

Zeno's Paradox:
Unification, Modernity, and Ambivalence

Korean ambivalence over unification appears metaphorically at the end of the recent and well-known movie *Sŏp'yŏnje*. Song-hwa meets her brother, Tong-ho, for the first time in decades. Along with their father, who had adopted the two unrelated orphans, they had lived as wanderers, traveling entertainers performing *sŏp'yŏnje*, or Western School, a form of *p'ansori*, traditional Korean singing arts and storytelling. After years of searching, and following their father's death, Tong-ho finds

Song-hwa living on a remote farm, blind and poor. He introduces himself only as someone interested in playing the drum while she sings. As they begin, she recognizes his familiar drum and is moved to perform with the highest passion. Through their music, they release their *han* ("resentment," a concept explored in detail in chapter 4), the suffering of their lives, and for one night they come together through the performance. In the morning, the brother leaves, perhaps never to see his sister again. They part without ever speaking of their lives or identities, as if, one reviewer of the film wrote, "they were afraid of spoiling something they finally attained—the *han* which made them suffer so much and yet was the source of their vitality and strength" (Kim-Renaud 1993: 114).

Sŏp'yŏnje is a story of a divided family that sustains its ideals only by embracing the pain of life as fate. For Yi Ch'ŏng-jun, the author of the book, *Namdo saram* (Southerners), from which the film was adapted, pain and suffering in general, and hardship that is unarticulated and unexpressed in particular, constitute the reality of life and can serve as a life force (see Choi, J. B. 1993: 12; Kim, C. H. 1994: 206-207). This is a notion of hardship consistent with the assertions of *minjung* theologians that *han* can be sublimated as a generative and dynamic force for achievement, moral action, and revolution (Suh 1983: 63). For Suh Nam Dong, *han* "signifies the reality of the *minjung*'s, [masses'] experience." In order to endure their fate, the brother and sister must maintain their reunion as an almost spiritual one, as if an ordinary dialogue would harm the true reality of their relationship; they keep the relationship pure and perfect and control the release of *han*. The idealized relationship is not one of happiness or of nostalgia, in the way in which that term is often employed—memory without the pain—but rather one of suffering, as they long for a relationship always in the process of becoming, never fully realized. Yi does not explicitly say that the brother and sister can serve as a metaphor for north and south Korea, or for Koreans as a whole, but certainly Koreans can be conceived as wanderers in search of a lost homeland/nation. Moreover, the image of two separated siblings has frequently been employed in south Korean literature and political discourse to represent national division. In the epilogue to his 1993 short story "Hüin ot" (White clothes), Yi implies such a relationship when he says of *Sŏp'yonje,* "Were brother and sister to embrace or touch each other, they would be destroying, taking away, each other's homeland [*kwihyang*]" (1993: 285).[8] He follows this statement immediately with a discussion of unification and urges Koreans not to "push too hard," because they may not be ready for their dreams to shatter.

Yi's sentiments echo the extraordinary ambivalence of south Koreans toward north Korea about which I write in the next chapter (see also Grinker 1995a). Like the idealized, unspoiled relations between Song-hwa and Tong-ho, the idea of a homogeneous and unified Korea might be more appealing than actual unification, which would mean that people would live side by side, together with all the local politics and pain of everyday social life. The undivided nation lies in the realm of the imagination and the ideal, and the movement of this idealized identity into the realm of practice is fraught with uncertainty and fear.

Turning to south Korean representations of the north Korean state, there seems to be little confusion about its nature: the north Korean state is false, even evil, and it stands as the major obstacle to unification. The confusion emerges when it comes to the people of north Korea. South Koreans know little about them and consequently often locate them in a liminal space between essentialized identities. They are variously primitive, authentic, machinelike, blind, and innocent—brainwashed by the north Korean state, as embodied by Kim Il Sung and Kim Jong Il. At times, they are construed as "more Korean" than south Koreans, and at other times as needing to be saved by south Koreans and by Christianity. On other occasions southerners see north Koreans as purer *(sunsuhan)* than they are;[9] at yet other times they are seen as different, or even unnatural *(ijil)*.[10] The ambivalence is sufficient to make some people wish, quite heretically, that national division will continue for many years to come.

Unification is an idealized vision of homogeneity in a world of rapid historical changes, travel, and globalization. In social theory, globalization is often conceived as a homogenizing process, but the opposite holds in Korea. Homogeneity is all the more elusive as Koreans forge transnational relations that create differences rather than similarities, including the hyphenated identities of the Korean diaspora: Korean-Canadians, Korean-Americans, and so on. Another reason, related to the first, is that the south Korean media report extensively on all the vicissitudes of German unification, and to a lesser extent on unification in Yemen and Vietnam. Despite the many acknowledged differences between the political, economic, and social processes of Korea and these other nations, analogies continue to be drawn. In their work on Germany, for example, south Korean journalists focus negatively on a concept of difference, heterogeneity, and foreignness *(ijilgam),* and on the fear that the *ijilgam* between Koreans from north and south will be even greater than that between east and west Germans. As one author notes, east and west Germans could, at least, write letters to each other, and watch each other's television programming and thus minimize the potential for a divided (German) consciousness *(ŭishik tanjŏl)* to develop (Yi, C. W. 1993).

In a fascinating remark that echoes the end of the film *Sŏp'yŏnje,* Yi Chong-woo, an engineering student in Berlin, writes to the readers of the conservative journal *Pukhan* that many west German people had east German "pen pals" to whom they had written for years. With unification, the need for such letters diminished, and they now "miss the old compassion they shared with their east German brothers and sisters." A German unity was held together precisely because they could not meet each other (Yi, C. W. 1993: 171). A third reason, less salient than the others, is the fear, expressed in some of my interviews with college students, that unification, in any form, might not realize true homogeneity because it would be distorted by the state—in other words, governments would shape unification to fit their own needs rather than those of the people. Such a position can be justified by Korean history; after all, says historian Choi Jang-jip, "The vigor and energy for reunification, which came from the bottom, has been continuously co-opted from above by the state elites" (Choi, J. J. 1993: 49).

Ambivalent discourses on Korean identity often frame the search for the "real" or "true" Korea. Since I began doing research on Korea, I have been struck by the frequency with which unification is associated with concepts of truth, and especially with the words *silje* (reality) and *hyŏnsil* (practical reality). These terms form the conceptual foundation of a large number of south Korean texts that address national division and unification policies. They occur so often that in a later chapter I ask the reader's indulgence in some linguistic clarification, a clarification I make despite the fact that it will undoubtedly raise many questions and disagreements from scholars with Korean-language skills and fieldwork experience that exceed mine. At this point I wish only to point out that in texts that deal specifically with unification, division, and south

SPEAKING OF THE UNSPEAKABLE   45

Korean policy toward north Korea, *silje* and *hyŏnsil* can refer to north Korea's "true" intentions, the privileged position of the truth of diplomacy over sentiment, the reality of Korea as a unified nation, the actual conditions of democracy or communism, or the realities of the world that the north Korean government hides from its citizens. Among the most often discussed realities in texts that deal explicitly with unification are homogeneity and unity, because they are so desired and so elusive. The goal is to move from the world of "dreams" to the world of "reality."

Although many Koreans may hold that some reality can be found, interviews and literature abound not with affirmations of its discovery, but with the need to discover. As with the resolution of resentment, or *han*, reality is something one works toward (or perhaps even against), for it is the desire for discovery that motivates people to endure personal and collective tragedies. A conception of the real as unobtainable invokes a paradoxical subject-object relation. No matter how close the subject gets to its object, the object always remains inaccessible. This inability to attain, or perhaps the wish not to attain, is paralleled in some psychoanalytic discussions about the inability of the drive to attain the goal. The parallel to psychoanalysis, and the reason why I make special note of it here, also raises the point that pleasure is found not primarily in fulfilling a desired end but in trying to fulfill it. People may hold themselves from their destination in the service of their pleasure. In explicating Lacan's work on the subject of the relation between desire and reality, Slavoj Žižek draws an analogy to the *Iliad*'s tale of Achilles' fruitless chase of the tortoise. Although Achilles is faster than the tortoise and can certainly overtake him, Achilles' speed is always too slow or too fast. What would lie beyond the goal? Žižek writes:

> The goal is the final destination, while the aim is what we intend to do, i.e., the way itself. Lacan's point is that the real purpose of the drive is not its goal (full satisfaction) but its aim: the drive's ultimate aim is simply to reproduce itself as drive, to return to its circular path, to continue its path to and from the goal. The real source of the enjoyment is the repetitive movement of this closed circuit. (Žižek 1991: 4-5)

This is Zeno's paradox. We can never reach a place because we are always reaching the places on its path: the real goal of desire is not one particular place but the infinite number of points along the way.[11]

The conditions of inhabiting the path for the sake of the goal and of not obtaining the goal for the sake of the path are highlighted by Freud in a little-known essay entitled "Disturbance of Memory on the Acropolis."[12] When Freud traveled to Athens in 1904, at the age of forty-eight, he arrived at a destination he had longed for but for neurotic reasons had prevented himself from reaching. When contemplating his visit, at the age of eighty, he could think only of the difficulties of getting there. The Athens and Rome he idealized from illustrations did not, for Freud, actually exist, and he sought repeatedly, through his resistance to travel there, to repudiate reality. Upon arriving at the Acropolis, Freud experiences the feeling "What I see here is not real" (1936: 243). He calls this feeling "derealization," by which he means, first, that the ego defends itself against the real external world, and second, that the psychological constitution of interactions with this world is continually shaped by painful, historical (repressed) memories. Derealization emerges from a silent pain; it falsifies the past and present in the service of unarticulated, unconscious conflicts. In the end, Freud relates his resistance to travel to his guilt from going so much further in life (and space) than his father, to his transcendence of the hardships and limitations of his own father. As Freud himself states it, "filial piety" destroyed his ability to enjoy Athens. Yet writing the essay helped Freud work through his ambivalence in a creative and therapeutic manner.

For Freud, the real cannot be the destination; it is rather the movement of his life in the direction of reaching and then transcending his father's achievement. Because the Acropolis is an endpoint, it cannot exist. Indeed, its real existence might render his life meaningless, for if the goal is truly attained, what else is there to live for, to travel toward? His travels, construed as actual or metaphorical, are not simply movements from one place to another but imaginary trajectories of space and difference. Travels can be tropes of the Self, the home, imagined communities and identities, visions of the past, present, and future; they can involve encounters with the Self as much as with the Other. Thus, for example, Roland Barthes echoes Freud when he characterizes his desire to inhabit visited and photographed landscapes as *heimlich*, homeliness, "the return to the maternal body," one's originary homeland (Barthes 1981: 40). Chapter 8, on south Koreans who visited north Korea, deals explicitly with how travelers and traveling can become metaphors for shifting social and political boundaries.[13]

The quest for Korean unification is a desire to return home, to discover an originary and autonomous identity. Paradoxically, however, a unified Korea also threatens much of the only world most Koreans have ever known, a world in which they are a divided people whose paramount goal is to be unified. If Korean political identity can be characterized by its incompleteness—the self-conscious definition of the nation as anticipatory—then the search for unification places south Korea in an uncertain position in a series of oppositions: between real and unreal, between people and state, between unification and national division. These oppositions reflect not only the contest for legitimacy between south and north, but also underlying uncertainties and ambiguities about national identity, the future, and the journey toward a unified Korea; they also frame the imaginary travel of southerners to the north and northerners to the south, and more specifically of people who originally came from hometowns they have been unable to visit because they are located across the border. Such imaginary travel involves attempts to subvert the oppositions, crossing both a temporal and spatial border, beyond division, the Korean War, and the Cold War, and beyond the thirty-eighth parallel. The oppositions are symptoms and ramifications of division. Ambivalence emerges in positions along a continuum that pulls and antagonizes, as Koreans simultaneously denigrate and idealize particular aspects of the nation and project their ambivalence against the blank screen called north Korea, a screen made blank not only by north Korea's efforts to insulate the country from the rest of the world, but by south Korea's as well.

I want to emphasize that ambivalence, as I use the concept, is not really about indecision in a choice between two stable desires (wanting unification or wanting a continued division) and between two stable identities (a unified Korea or a divided Korea), although people may certainly experience their ambivalence in this way. The deeper or more latent problem, I believe, is how to find a fixed or continuous identity in a world in which there are no such identities. This is a project, I ought to stress again, that is not unique to Korea, although it appears in Korea in historically and culturally specific ways. Rather than view attitudes toward unification and north Korea as defined by conflicting desires—because this formulation would imply the existence of stable identities—I find it more accurate to think about south Korean attitudes in terms of disruptions. When south Koreans look at the north and imagine unification, these sights (or sites) threaten to violate the stability and order of the world in which most living south Koreans have been raised. In this respect, then, it is unification, not only division, that destabilizes identity. Both division *and* unification threaten the national myth of homogeneous belonging, and this is why, I believe, south Koreans do not want to know much about north Korea, and why for south Koreans the north remains, for now, only in the world of dreams.

THREE

NORTH KOREAN EVERYDAY LIFE ON DISPLAY

> It is the place where the spectator, presenting himself as spectacle, will no longer be either seer *(voyant)* or voyeur, will efface within himself the difference between the actor and the spectator, the represented and the representer, the object seen and the seeing object.
>
> —Jaques Derrida. On the concept of the festival. In *Of Grammatology.*

UNIFICATION, as I have mentioned, can be a euphemism for conquest, a gloss for winning the war.[1] In this section on a south Korean exhibition, I elaborate on the ambivalence with which south Koreans talk about north Korea. The ambivalence is the offspring of contradiction, as south Koreans idealize the nation as homogeneous and yet recognize that it is not, and as they view themselves as similar to the north and yet profoundly different from it.

At times the discourses represent north Koreans quite negatively as people who, after years of indoctrination, have no freedom of thought and behavior; they appear uncivilized, inhabiting a time before progress and enlightenment. At other times north Koreans appear more positively as the prelapsarian or primordial Korean before the fall of the south into the evils of modernity. These contradictory images are revealed in those infrequent spaces and times when south Koreans are permitted, or permit themselves, to imagine the north and unification. One might expect that ambivalence and the uncertainties associated with it could promote creative understanding of the Korean peninsula and discussion and debate about alternative paths to a future Korea. Such a process would be indicative of a collective mourning of the nation. Indeed, postcolonial critics (see Bhabha 1994) frequently argue that ambivalence is the space of subversion and creativity. In the Korean case, however, ambivalence is expressed either in the stultifying apathy and frustration of Koreans who believe Korea has perhaps irrevocably lost control over its destiny, or in aggressive criticisms that attack the north Korean state, and sometimes the south Korean state, as enemies of the people.

One of the reasons why ambivalence produces or reaffirms opposition rather than subverting it can be found in the idea of a complicated or unsuccessful mourning. Ambivalence that remains unexamined or that has not been worked through may lend itself to mutually exclusive oppositions, such as good and evil. For example, south Koreans' demonization of the north Korean state as evil puts on hold the difficult task of working through some of the psychological and moral dilemmas of division and unification. In the short term, the moral clarity of opposition can be comforting (Lambek and Antze 1996: xxviii). Another approach, to be addressed in this chapter, leads to the concept of mimicry outlined by Homi Bhabha in his essays on postcolonialism in South Asia (1994). Bhabha has argued that emergent subjectivities are found in the interstices of binary conceptual categories. He highlights the case of the Anglo-Indian who mimics the colonizer and thus inhabits ambivalent and powerful liminal spaces between essentialized identities. The ambivalence of mimicry lies in the colonizer's attempt to sustain a subject of both sameness and difference, an Other that will become like him but not too much like him.

Mimicry has implications for the study of colonial relations in situations historically different from the Anglo-Indian case, and even in contexts such as south Korean representations of north Korea, in which those relations occur entirely on an imaginary plane. In some south Korean representations of north Korea we find evidence of a similar thought process in which south Koreans imagine the north Korean as mimic, as an "almost south Korean." In south Korea mimicry leads to ambivalence but not to liberating possibilities for vision, subversion, and creation. In some respects, relations of mimicry between north and south appear in south Korea as the inverse of Anglo-Indian relations. In India, the Other moves in the direction of the colonizer, from an initial difference toward sameness. In Korea, north and south move apart from an initial sameness toward difference and symbolic domination. As the two Koreas diverge, south Korea takes on the role of metaphorical colonizer to north Korea as metaphorical Other. Another reason for the perpetuation of opposition lies in the imaginary nature of the north Korean mimic. Given that there is an almost total absence of knowledge in south Korea about north Korean everyday life, what we might call mimicry in the Korean context lies wholly in the imagination and is not grounded in any actual social interactions between north and south. Unlike Anglo-Indians, who are real people engaged in processes of mimicry and resistance, the north Korean is imaginary, a projection of and by the south. Precisely because there is no real agency behind this imagined subject, it is not surprising that it ends up repeating rather than breaking down the binary oppositions represented in the south.

My treatment of north-south opposition here turns about an exploration of ambivalence in a popular exhibition in Seoul entitled *Pukhan saenghwal* (North Korean lifestyles). For viewers, the exhibition is a powerful display of north Korean objects that gives rise to multiple and antithetical feelings and contradictory sentiments. One reason for the exhibition's enormous popularity is that strict south Korean security laws continue to prevent south Koreans from discussing openly the topics of north Korea and unification; politicians, students, and intellectuals who discuss unification issues, the reunion of dispersed families, or the sending of condolences to north Korea after the death of Kim Il Sung continue to be subject to harassment and arrest. Seldom do south Koreans have an opportunity to view representations of the north Korean people, and I do not know why the Korean government permitted an exhibition on north Korea that made possible a public context for discussion and debate about north Korea and unification. Regardless of the reason, the exhibition indeed offers south Koreans a distinct time and place for representation and discussion. It thus opens up a liminal space that lies out of the ordinary structures of south Korean daily life. Viewers, now numbering in the millions, appropriate the exhibition as a context in which to articulate conceptions about north Korea and unification. Their responses to the exhibition offer a window upon, and also help constitute, a wide range of discourses about the differences between north and south Korea.

The subtext of the exhibition is Korean unification, and this subtext evokes the difficult question for viewers of how north and south Koreans, in all their similiarity and difference, will be integrated into a future unified Korea. The subtext is made possible by the exclusion of Kim Il Sung and Kim Jong Il from most of the exhibition. Given that the vast majority of public representations of north Korea have concerned these two men, their absence is striking. It brings into relief the people-state opposition that is so central to unification discourses. [2]

The exhibitors explicitly claim in writing that the exhibition promotes unity—that by showing the objects of real people, viewers will begin to feel a common humanity with the people of the north, and thus subvert the Cold War essentialisms of the good south and the evil north. The exhibitors hope that viewers will imagine north Koreans as mimics on whom are inscribed various markers of Koreanness. However, the actual effect of the exhibition on viewers does not conform to the exhibitors' intentions. The north Korean mimic is a reflection not of a monolithic south Korean identity but of portions of a complex identity. The mimic brings only certain elements of south Korean identity into relief, and these are then open to critical examination as discrete elements of identity.

In imagining the north Korean people, south Koreans empower themselves through a vision that subordinates the north and separates it from the south: south Koreans believe that through the exhibit they can see north Korea, but they also imagine that the north cannot see them. This vision is, indeed, one of the primary appeals of the exhibition: the invisibility of north Korea and its consequent visibility only in the materials displayed to the south Korean public at the exhibition. One of the pleasures of·the exhibition lies in the south's dominating gaze over the north, the "right of sight" (Alloula 1986: 5) that viewers claim for themselves and deny to the north. A colonial quality to south Korean discourses on the north further complicates the drive to represent new relations between the two Koreas. Although these discourses are not directly modeled on any particular colonial experience, they incorporate several discursive features common to many colonialisms. North Korea has, to some extent, been appropriated by south Koreans not simply as a tragic land of lost relatives but also as a demonized Other to be saved, converted, and occupied. For example, south Korean viewers argue explicitly for the absorption of north Korea into capitalism, Christianity, and modernity. In these representations, north and south are conveyed through oppositions between diachronic and synchronic history, capitalism and communism, Christianity and heathenism. We thus add to the north Korean construed as mimic of south Korea a south Korean mimic of the colonist.

The metaphors that people employ to give meaning to their emotional and intellectual reactions to the exhibition shape south Korean discourse on the loss of the idealized homogeneous nation. South Koreans grieve this loss of the nation but assert that the grief will end at unification; consequently, their grief is problematic, and even contradictory. Because national division is not a final or single event but an ongoing rupture with no clear end in sight—as I phrased it in chapter 1, division is a death without a death—south Koreans envision an end to it. Unification becomes the endpoint of the suffering entailed by division, a denial of the threat of loss. Discourses on the saving, transforming, or appropriating of the north are thus discourses about how the loss can be denied. In that imagined world, heterogeneity must be transformed or converted into homogeneity. The assumption of conversion stands as a central obstacle to the incorporation of south and north Koreans into one another's societies.

In the remaining pages of this chapter I analyze the structure and organization of the exhibition and two sets of conceptual oppositions attributed by viewers to relations between north and south Korea: diachronic versus synchronic histories, and the saved versus the unsaved. Viewers critically examine their own past and future identities, as well as those of north Korea and a future unified Korea, by variously affirming and confounding these oppositions. Over and over again, visitors' descriptions of the north move between concepts of sameness and difference. But in doing so, visitors introduce into their discourses on the north patronizing and divisive colonial metaphors that move away from reconciliation and closer to discourses of conquest.

THE INVISIBLE NORTH

In an interesting passage in his book *Mŏrirŭl ppanŭn namja* (The man who washes his hair), the north Korean defector and folk singer Kim

Yong recalls the barber who used to cut his hair: "*Ajuma* worked at the Taedongsang barber shop. . . . She had the title 'people's barber' [*inmin ibalsa]* granted only to the most skilled. If I went to the shop and found she wasn't there, I would return home. She was a really nice person" (Kim Y. 1992: 25). The passage may not strike many readers as unusual, but to south Koreans, who are unnaccustomed to reading about contemporary people from the north, it is remarkable. The Korean graduate student who referred me to the passage could not explain exactly why she found it remarkable but simply said that it was perhaps the first time she had read an author so plainly and informally describe a person from north Korea. She was surprised to read the familiar term of address for women of one's mother's generation, *ajuma,* seldom used by south Korean (or north Korean) writers to refer to north Korean women. "I see [the words] *pukhan yŏsŏng,*" she said, "but not *ajuma.*" She said, in English, that she was "touched" and "moved."

An experience the following year with another Korean graduate student was equally enlightening. When a north Korean diplomat telephoned me in my absence, the graduate student working in my office answered the telephone. When I returned, she took a deep and audible breath and said with an excited smile, "I talked to a north Korean on the phone. I took a message for you. He was just a regular person."

Such wonder reflects a central problem in south Korean literature on north Korea, and the reason why *Pukhan saenghwal's* glimpse of north Korean everyday life is so popular and pleasurable. Although numerous books have been published in south Korea on Kim Il Sung and Kim Jong Il, their domestic and foreign policies, and their creation of a political cult, the publications rely so heavily on the analytical distinction between state and society, and the assumption that society is an epiphenomenon of the state, that the north as a totality, including ordinary citizens, has become nearly invisible.

Not surprisingly, with this absence in south Korea of images of north Korean everyday life, an exhibition entitled *Pukhan saenghwal* opened to a good deal of fanfare and newspaper coverage. First shown at the Midopa department store in Seoul in June and July 1993 and subsequently moved to a more permanent exhibition site in Taejon, the exhibition includes a large assemblage of photographs, posters, and postcards of the north Korean wilderness, a film describing the history of north Korea, a model apartment, and nearly two thousand separate items from north Korea, including canned foods, jewelry, books, toys, clothing, and batteries. Within three weeks of its opening in Seoul, attendance had surpassed an estimated 200,000 persons, and almost every newspaper and television news program in the country had run stories asserting that the exhibition portrayed the *silsang* (reality) of north Korea. The June 29 issue of *Hanguk kyŏngje* reported that the exhibition would show the *silsang* of north Korea, and the July 1 *Seoul Sinmun* was confident that the displays would help south Koreans "correctly" *(paro)* "regain" *(hoebok)* knowledge of north Korea lost during forty years of national division.

The Midopa department store prospectus, produced in large part by the *T'ongilwŏn*, the government branch devoted to analyzing and developing unification policies, and submitted to the government's intelligence service, *Anjŏn Kihoekpu* (Agency for National Security Planning, or ANSP), months before the exhibition opened, predicted that the exhibition would show the truth *(silje)* about north Korea, highlight the "humanity" of the north Koreans, and promote "greater public support" for unification. An article in the ultraconservative journal *Pukhan* (Chin 1993: 136) linked the exhibition to a specific social movement, *Pukhanŭi-silsangŭl-paro-alja-undong* ("the let's get to know the true picture of north Korea movement"), and noted that the exhibition would help to soothe *(tallaeda)* the nostalgia *(hyangsu)* of the *wŏlnammin* (southerners whose home towns are in the north). Major portions of the exhibition were designed by north Korean defectors, such as the north Korean architect Kim Yŏng-sŏng and especially the family of Kim Man Ch'ŏl, the first of only two complete north Korean famlies ever to defect to the south. That Kim Yŏng-sŏng personally designed a model P'yŏngyang apartment for the exhibition, and that his wife designed the apartment's display of household objects, led reviewers to praise the exhibition as providing *hyŏnsilgam* (a sense of the real or actual).

The "reality," as suggested by viewers whom I observed and with whom I recorded interviews (during approximately forty hours of "participant-observation"), is that the north and south are the same people occupying different historical spaces. According to this view, the north Koreans, marginalized from world and Korean history, inhabit the 1950s rather than the 1990s, their progress impeded and their true Koreanness submerged by the north Korean state. The temporal differentiation is framed ambivalently because the same qualities that mark a negatively idealized difference can also be idealized positively, or can be transformed into positive qualities through unification, conversion, and the penetration of capitalism into the north. For example, the north is highly valued for its purity because it is seen as fixed in time, and yet it is denigrated as primitive for the same reason. The exhibition thus constitutes a representational discourse that simultaneously perpetuates and muddles the oppositions between north and south. Before discussing these oppositions, however, it is necessary to describe the specific content of the exhibition. In the next section I describe some of the displays, outline their parameters, and suggest reasons why the exhibition's structure and organization motivated viewers to engage in certain discourses on division and unification.

THE WONDER AND RESONANCE
OF NORTH KOREAN OBJECTS

The exhibition consisted of a model two-room apartment, panels describing work and family life, photographs, posters and postcards, film, and about two thousand objects in common use in north Korean life. The model middle-class P'yŏngyang apartment contained photographs of Kim Il Sung and a loudspeaker through which praises to him would normally be broadcast. Panels along the wall near the apartment offered basic information about marriage practices, work schedules and salaries, the cost of foodstuffs, and the process by which someone acquires a job and an apartment. As a bonus to viewers who came during the first two days of the exhibition (unfortunately, before my arrival in Korea), Midopa hired some north Korean defectors to give guided tours and answer questions. In addition, early visitors could buy expensive bottles of north Korean liquor. Only a few visitors seemed to be buying while I was there, but many passed by the sales counter just to hold a bottle in their hand.

At the back of the exhibition, visitors also had the opportunity to watch a film produced jointly by the *T'ongilwŏn*, ANSP, and Midopa chronicling the political lives of Kim Il Sung and Kim Jong Il, with special attention to their violations of human rights in north Korea, international terrorism, and promotion of the worship of the two Kims, all interspersed with flashy advertisements for Midopa products such as stereo equipment and Mansport cologne. With the exception of the photographs on the wall of the model home, the film is the only site in which the Kims appear; the exhibitors do not link the film directly with the exhibition of everyday objects, and it appears more as an after-thought, placed at the end of the exhibition to remind viewers of north Korea's evils. Not surprisingly, the film portrays the Kims in a manner consistent with the anti-communism of the past forty years, differenti-ating sharply the communism of the north and the democracy of the south. Many scenes show speeches by north Korean students and political figures praising Kim Il Sung, spoken in a well-practiced rhythmic and theatrical style, like the recitation of poems or a chant. Interviewees referred to the sound as strange *(isanghada)* and disturbing because the speaker did not sound human; one viewer asked rhetorically, *"Saram sori majayŏ?"* (Is this a human voice?).

The major focus of the exhibition, and the part that drew the largest crowds, was the vast array of items displayed in glass cases. I was surprised by what I perceived as both their ordinariness and diversity, and yet viewers seemed to stare in fascination at an enormous range of goods that seemed no different to me from those one might find in the very store that housed the exhibition. I noted some of the objects on view:

> toothbrush, stethoscope, thermometer, after-shave lotion, door-knobs, locks, umbrellas, fans, chopsticks, knives, can openers, spoons, fishing rods, iron, telephone, strainer, dishes, glasses, con-tainers, blenders, skillets, orange and cherry syrup, *insam* [ginseng], *insam* tea, mineral water, Kŏngang brand beer, Ryongsŏng brand cola, washing machine, candy, tea, pipes, vases, eyeglasses, sunglasses, binoculars, pens, pencils, jewelry, books, children's toys (guns, tops, balls), batteries, shirts, skirts, pants, hats, socks, gloves, fur vests and wool coats, ice skates, roller skates, shoes, drums, electric guitars with amps, clarinet, oboe, flute, warm-up suits, men's ties, women's sweaters, scarves.

Korean visitors told me that these objects were quite different from anything one might find in south Korea. Why they thought so became a central problem of my research.

I spent most of my time at the exhibition observing viewers and sitting on a bench waiting for possible interviewees to sit down next to me. The long hours spent at Midopa gave me time for reflection, and on the second day I visited the exhibition, I made an association to the new Holocaust Memorial Museum in Washington, D.C., which displays piles of shoes and glasses that belonged to Jews who were exterminated during World War II. For reasons other than what the name for each separate thing signifies, or how the objects function in everyday life, these displayed objects enter into the dual phenomena of resonance and wonder, to use Stephen Greenblatt's words (1991: 43). The objects have the power to invoke highly charged symbolic and historical relationships, to freeze our gaze and compel us to see otherwise quotidian things as unique and worthy of display.

The resonance and wonder of objects is achieved at Midopa, as it is at the Hololcaust Memorial Museum, by a process of decontextualization and recontextualization. The placing of black leather shoes from north Korea on display, as in a museum, isolates them from their conventional paradigmatic and syntagmatic chains and thereby sets the framework for symbolic elaboration. The viewer believes these shoes to be different from other shoes. Although the viewer's own shoes are just one component of his or her own attire, the north Korean shoes, by being separated from the context of one scheme (an ensemble of clothes, or outfit) and recontextualized in another (the exhibition), become metonymically juxtaposed to other objects or sets of objects—for example, photographs, batteries, and musical instruments—that in everyday life occupy places in quite different syntagmatic chains. Therein lies the viewer's wonder. Decontextualization thus creates the possibility for the viewer to recontextualize the objects in the realm of individual fantasy and empathy—to ask, What were these people like? How would I have felt to be where they were?—and to make the fragments stand for a whole people.

As in many museum exhibits, viewers respond to the displays to the extent that they allow a displayed object to resonate, to "reach out beyond its formal boundaries to a larger world, to evoke in the viewer the complex, dynamic cultural forces from which it has emerged and for which it may be taken by a viewer to stand" (Greenblatt, 1991: 42). The Korean viewer associates the *Pukhan saenghwal* objects with both personal and national history: "These are the things of people who share my blood"; "The division of Korea is our people's *han*." The objects may evoke memories of the war, a lost or invisible family member, or a small detail of a way of life nearly forgotten, such as the scent of a flower; for one man, originally from the north, a soccer ball brought back a childhood memory of eating a crab. Few of the viewers whom I spoke to discussed any specific object in much detail; rather, they used the exhibition as a whole as a way to begin talking about the north and asking questions: How should I think about the north? How should I describe the north to my children? How is it that the north seems so different and yet we are one people? How is it possible that I am able to see these things? What would it be like to live together with north Koreans?

Exhibits, like mimicry, draw our attention to fragments, or collections of fragments, as constitutive of identities: the Dan mask that comes to stand for the Dan of Liberia; the collection of art from Liberia, Côte d'Ivoire, and Senegal that comes to stand for the people of West Africa, or the collection of art from Africa, New Guinea, and South America that comes to stand for the primitive. As Salman Rushdie notes in relation to partial recollection, "the shards of memory acquired greater status, greater resonance, because they were *remains;* fragmentation made trivial things seem like symbols, and the mundane acquired numinous qualities" (1991: 12, emphasis in original). Indeed, the Midopa display resembles exhibitions of "primitive" art and ancient societies and bears a curious resemblence to archaeological remains, the ruins of a past culture.

Like many exhibitions, this one succeeds because it reveals things that cannot otherwise be seen; these objects come from a virtually invisible land and are therefore unique in south Korea. The value viewers attribute to exhibited objects is thus linked to the aesthetics of appropriation. Numerous scholars have remarked that collections of so-called primitive art in nineteenth- and twentieth-century Europe became popular in part because the art had traveled so far, in time as well as space (Price, 1989; Steiner 1994). The two thousand items displayed at Midopa traveled farther than most south Korean citizens can ever go. In this regard, *Pukhan saenghwal* is a remarkable exhibition.

But I would suggest that beyond this aesthetic lies a more fundamental imaginative process in which north Koreans, and the objects made to represent them, are located in time. The next section addresses how viewers historicized the objects, and how this historicizing parallels broader south Korean discourses on Korean identity.

THE SUPPRESSION OF TIME

The most common impression of the exhibition expressed by my interviewees was that north Koreans were "still living in the 1950s or 1960s." One young woman in her twenties commented that the washing machine on display looked like a child's toy. Her female companion remarked, "Koreans used to live like this, but not anymore." On one Saturday afternoon the exhibition hall was filled with families, parents taking careful notes on the displays to help their children complete school assignments on the exhibition. I heard one woman, accompanying her son and grandson, emphasize to the boy how little space there was in the model apartment; she told him that although the model represented the upper-class residences of P'yŏngyang it reminded her of a small space in which she slept as a young child during the Korean War. In a parallel historicizing process, many viewers framed the objects in human developmental time. They talked about the childlike quality of the north Korean book jackets ("The title is mature, but it looks like a schoolbook") and the washing machine. Even the size of some of the objects was significant: for them, an accordion and electric guitar appeared small, and pots and pans seemed to belong to a toy kitchen. Similarly, a number of viewers employed a hierarchical metaphor of family for north-south relations, representing south Korea as the older sibling that must help or save the younger sibling who has lost his way or whose growth has been stunted by communism.

Embedded in the proposition that history is a process that can be stopped or continued is a primordialist notion that histories of authenticity are synchronic. According to this view, national identity runs in a continuous, and unchanging course through time, regardless of all the economic and political changes that may take place in history. Synchronic history is the history of the reproduction of identities. It follows that Korean school textbooks stress that Korea is unique, that it is one of the oldest, most continuous and most distinctive nations in world history. South Koreans also say that with such a long history as a unified nation, forty years of division are but a small blip in time. Synchronic history also locates the forces of change as exogenous. The threat to identity and nationhood therefore comes not from the people but from factors perceived as external, such as the state, the region, or the United States. Indeed, through a variety of political, academic, and literary movements (see chapter 7), many Korean students and intellectuals seek to preserve and continue an authentic past in which Koreans will be the agents of their own history.

The anti-historical theme was appropriated by many viewers not only as a way of criticizing the north Korean state but also as a form of self-criticism, a way of attacking historical changes in the south such as the growth of excessive consumerism and the emergence of a class order that includes the very rich and their children, the so-called *orenji jok* (literally, orange tribe), young men and women of Korea's "Rodeo Drive" in Apkujŏngdong.[3] That is, the north Korean people are viewed ambivalently in both a negative and positive light: on the one hand, they are automatons blindly obeying the north Korean state and living in the past; on the other, they are "more Korean," "less international," and less materialistic. Several south Koreans I interviewed regretted that, unlike north Korea, south Korea had become dependent on international powers *(sadaejuŭi)*, had lost the capacity for subjecthood *(chuch'esŏng)* and, interestingly, that south Koreans did not eat Korean food every day. South Korean parents generally complain that their children do not eat enough *kimch'i*, for in rejecting this national food they are losing their link to the nation (Han 1994). Food grown on foreign soil is symbolically contaminated and anti-national, whereas food grown at home is Korean and pure. In a paper on the relationship between food and national identity, Han Kyung Koo (1994) cites the recent popular song "Sint'oburi." In its emphasis on tradition, the song blends a lament on the loss of national foods and a lament on the loss of Korean names into a single narrative: the common name "Sŏn Hŭi" becomes the even more common, impersonal, and Westernized, "Miss Kim."

> Streets of Apkujŏng-dong, Kangnam-ku
> In what country are these streets?
> Where has Sŏn Hŭi gone?
> Why can I see only "Miss Kim" instead of Sŏn Hŭi?
> Red pepper paste, soybean paste, *kimch'i* [pickled cabbage], *kaktugi* [pickled radish]
> Do not forget, do not forget that
> You and I, we are Koreans
> Body and soil are one and the same
> Body and soil are one and the same.

Observers of south Korea bemoan internationalism, urbanization, the emerging class order, the destruction of the country for the city, and the widening gap between rich and poor.[4] A middle-aged physician who attended the exhibition remarked, "The north Koreans are more Korean [*sunsuhada*] but in the south we have been so corrupted by capitalism. People in Seoul are mean people, they push you on the street, they use *panmal* [literally, "half-language"] and only care about themselves. Young people don't know about commitment." On one occasion, similar remarks were made more specifically in reference to differences between north and south Korean marriage practices; south Koreans, according to one man, have made marriage into a commoditized and materialistic ritual (a sentiment expressed clearly in the data provided in Kendall's detailed study of south Korean marriage—see Kendall 1996). North Korea, in contrast, is thought to contain people untouched by the Korean "miracle" of economic development. As the exhibition's numerous photographs, posters, and postcards of wildnerness scenes tell us, north Korea has been unharmed by the industrialization of the south (the 1993 GNP of which was about fifteen times that of the north). History, in other words, may have given much to Koreans, but it has also taken away many aspects of "authentic" Koreanness. Ironically, this discourse is present not only in the south, where the *minjung* (masses, often typified by the peasant) are imagined as both inheritors and representatives of authentic Korean culture, especially songs, dance, and oral tradition (Abelmann 1993: 143), but also in the north, where, according to one expert on north Korean literature, north Koreans imagine Seoul to be a non-Korean "hell on earth" in which a mixture of languages is spoken, and they idealize the south Korean countryside as the land of good and true and pure *(sunsu)* Koreans (Myers 1994).

The idealized concept of *sunsu* (purity), along with the concept *tongchilsŏng hoebok* (recovery of homogeneity), emerged repeatedly at the exhibition. *Sunsu* is opposed to the pejorative word *ijil* (heterogenous, foreign, different), sometimes used in south Korea to refer to the differences between north and south Korea. *Ijil* refers to differentiation and heterogeneity, and its recent referent in much political discourse in Korea has been the inability of the two Germanies to dissolve their differences into a unified nation (Yi, C. W. 1993: 166).

Interestingly, viewers who were suspicious that the organization and content of the exhibition was government propaganda reinforced these arguments about difference, purity, and primitiveness. In contrast to most viewers, these men and women did not see the objects themselves as backward, but through the objects they maintained similar beliefs. There were some viewers, especially educated young men and women, who did not believe that the exhibited objects represented the *silje,* or reality, of north Korea. They said that the exhibition contained only what the government wanted them to see. However, they suggested that the south Korean government's intention was not to demonize the north, as it had done so often during the past forty years, but to show a positive image of the north and therefore promote popular enthusiasm for unification efforts. These viewers contended that the exhibition represented the *silje* only of the upper classes of north Korea and that the true or real north Korea was more pure, backward, and primitive than was suggested by the objects on display. They depicted north Korea as a place with an enormous gap between the rich and the masses, where the masses are so destitute that they cannot own musical instruments, have television sets, or washing machines. As one man put it, "I don't know who chose these nice things, but they are either what north Korea wanted us to see or what south Korea wanted us to see. And so it's not reality."

It is tempting to view these various discourses as simply ambivalent and to optimistically suggest that ambivalence will engender liberation from binaries. However, south Koreans frame the ambivalence within polarities. Certain characteristics, such as autonomy and purity, are at the same time negatively and positively valued, but regardless of their value they are meaningful in terms of, and in reference to, the oppositions between north and south, Self and Other. The exhibition serves as a mirror, reflecting back to south Koreans their own creation. South Koreans effectively create a north Korean mimic who is a partial mirror image, and therefore also a partial reversal, of themselves. It follows that it is useful to think of ambivalence not so much as a potential subverter of oppositions but as the *product* of oppositions. North-south oppositions are tendencies that pull in the direction of either side. One side may be dominant at one time and then be replaced by the other, but the point is that positions lie along a continuum. Thus, in the south Korean search for identity, the north Korean is not only denigrated; he also can emerge as an ideal formation, an Other, an "outside" (Laclau and Zac, 1994: 31) with which to identify. Phrased psychoanalytically, not everything that is projected as outside the self is reflected back. There remains what Lacan calls the "subject of the lack," that is, the asymmetry between what is projected and what is introjected. The gap between the two confounds the real—in Lacan's terms, disrupts the imaginary-symbolic universe (Laclau and Zac, 1994: 33)—and engenders ambivalence. In the next section, I suggest that one way in which south Koreans seek to resolve their ambivalence is to assume the metaphorical role of colonizer, transform the north, and reintegrate (unify) Self and Other. In doing so, they define and affirm north Korea's otherness.

CONVERSION AND COLONIZATION

I met one man at the exhibition who works in the boat construction business. He was born and raised in the north and writes poetry about reunification and north Korea. How, I asked him, will people who followed Kim Il Sung be able to live in a unified Korea? He answered only indirectly, and although he was clearly unsure about whether to identify himself as northern or southern, he initially took a position as a northern-er. "People from the north are so strong, but we won't become really important. Those of us who came to the south from the north have been successful, and many have been successful in the United States, but we have not been politically mobile here—especially those of us from Hamgyŏng province." He then identified himself as a southerner. "If it had been the other way around," he continued, "with the southerners going north, we would have died because people from the north every-where in the world are more industrious. Now the north Koreans practice Kim Il Sungism, but if they see Seoul, they will change right away." "Change to what?" I asked. "To capitalism instead of ideology" (sasang), he replied. Subsequently, I met this man at his home in Seoul; he took me to a window and pointed to some fruit sellers on the street below. "Those are the north Koreans. When they come here after unification, they will be poor. We will help them. Northerners are more industrious than southerners, so they will soon make a lot of money."

Another man I talked to, middle-aged but slightly younger than the boat builder, had come to the exhibition with his wife and his school-age nephew because the boy had to write an essay on the exhibition. When I asked the man what he learned about north Korea, he said: "I don't need to know anything more about north Korea. But my nephew is like most people in Korea. They don't know the reality [silje] of the Korean War."[5] He can see here that north Koreans are like the poor people in Seoul." How, I asked, will north Koreans fit into a unified south Korea? "Take a north Korean to Apkujongdong and he will say, 'Whaa! We were told that people in Seoul were miserable!' He will want to stay."[6]

Additional interviewees at the exhibition expressed similar perspectives on north Korea: that north Koreans are living in the past, that they have not progressed to the degree that south Koreans have, that they are poor and backward. At the exhibition, these viewers saw proof of the north's backwardness. What I saw as an ordinary shoe or battery, viewers saw as outdated. What I saw as a standard-size apartment, viewers saw as reminiscent of small, overcrowded living spaces during the Korean War. Yet these visitors also believed that north Koreans would quickly adapt to living in the south, or at least under capitalism, because they would be enamored with the wealth and would find a new religion, replacing Kim Il Sungism with Christianity. (If anyone doubts that capitalism and religion have a good deal in common, they need only come to Midopa, where viewers liken capitalism to conversion, enlightenment, and the saving of the [Korean] soul). The notion that north Koreans are a premodern people who would quickly be converted to capitalism suggests a view of north Koreans as having been fixed in time by the north Korean state; south Korea will someday release the people of the north, and in their freedom they will realize how blind they were in following Kim Il Sung and communism. That this unique exhibition about north Korea was held in a department store, where north Korean goods could be purchased, and where the documentary film footage was interspersed with advertisements, makes the juxtaposition of communism and capitalism so obvious that no one need worry about whether the capitalism of the south stands, like evangelical missionaries, ready to appropriate the north.

According to the views of many I interviewed, the people of north Korea must change, and this is asserted to be true regardless of whether the person believes that the northerners' true nature has been suppressed or whether their identities have been fundamentally transformed. The change is likened to saving, and one minister talked openly with me about his excitement at so many people to evangelize. "You cannot follow a false god, but [instead follow] our savior, Jesus Christ; northern people will find Jesus Christ," he said. Undoing communism also involves stimulating capitalism and markets. The boat builder mentioned above has joined with many of his fellow *wŏlnammin* to plan a postunification development project to open markets and build apartments, even vacation resorts, in and around his hometown in what is today Hamgyŏng-do, north Korea. (Alongside this man's intentions stand the huge Korean conglomerates, such as Samsung, Hyundai, and Daewoo, already competing with one another for future business in the north. In November 1994 the south Korean government agreed to permit direct south Korean investment in north Korea.)

The idea that north Koreans have to transform themselves, or be helped to transform themselves, is strikingly similar to the ideas of evangelists and colonists at the turn of the century, and it presents us with the disturbing recognition that a form of colonial discourse on unification is beginning to emerge. Discourses on the north recall two central themes outlined by Comaroff and Comaroff (1991: 59) in their analysis of British colonial discourse: the improvement of individuals in capitalist and "civilized" society, and the idyllic countryside. The first concept, self-improvement, refers among other things to British conceptions that the relations between individuals and groups in eastern and southern Africa prohibited progress; Africans, according to their view, could not better themselves because they lived in egalitarian societies in which extended kin drained the potential capital accumulation of any successful person. As in many societies, British capitalists and missionaries believed that a person could gauge self-improvement and worth by his or her *differences* from other people, including wealth, clothes and other personal adornment, and health. The homogeneity of the "faceless masses" of north Korea leaves little room for visible improvement unless individuals can emerge from those masses and participate in a capitalist economy with a market-regulated system of inequality. Moreover, improvement in the British colonies was dependent upon how well the British could expand, through literacy, the knowledge of the "isolated" Africans and lead them eventually to the salvation of spiritual and material accumulation. In both Africa and south Korea, it appears, civilization and progress became synonymous with capitalism and Christianity (Comaroff and Comaroff 1991: 70). I have commonly heard Koreans link unification to greater economic growth and spiritual progress of the entire Korean nation, through which Korea might become a leading force in global society, economy, and politics.

The second theme that the Comaroffs identify in British colonial writing is the urban longing for the country; not only as a road for further economic expansion, in which "all the 'country' will become 'city'" (Williams, 1973: 284), but as a return to the past. Speaking of the rapid industrialization of western Europe, they make this point:

> The contrast between the country and the city seemed, paradoxically, to be sharpening and disappearing at the same time. . . . The significance of the perceived opposition between the country and the city, then, grew in rough proportion to the breakdown of the ecological and social division between them. And as it did, it came to stand symbolically for the radical change of British society, picking out the counterpoint between mythic past and present reality. In this respect too the idealized countryside represented not only innocence lost, nature defiled; it also stood for the possibility of paradise regained. . . . In practice these dreams could not be realized in a greatly transformed England. But the open vistas of the non-European world seemed to offer limitless possibilities. (Comaroff and Comaroff 1991: 75)

The Midopa posters and postcards show natural rather than urban environments, mountains and rivers instead of factories and shipyards, flowers instead of people, and thus they parallel the idealized descriptions of the scenic north found in the memoirs of south Koreans who traveled to north Korea (Mun 1990; Im 1989, 1990; Hwang S. Y. 1989a, 1989b). These memoirs commonly depict north Korea, even P'yŏngyang, as the unspoiled country. One Korean professor who visited the north (Yi, S. W. 1988) describes it as an "incubator" that preserves the country *(shigol)* and the pure *(sunjin);* another professor who has been to the north says, "In a word, north Korea is *shigol*" (Cho, M. H. 1988). But these photographs show us not only a place that is pure and untouched, a lost and invisible land that needs to be seen, but also a land to be traveled to, appropriated, and perhaps occupied.

Janus-faced, the conversion of north Koreans looks forward to the transformation of north Korea but also backward to the recovery of a former and homogeneous "Koreanness." Korean identity would be resuscitated by unification. The north Korean people, long suppressed by the north Korean state, would quickly return to their former selves and would not be harmed by the corruption of capitalism. The parallel to Germany is striking: there, various scholars have embraced a distinction popularized by Peter Schneider between "nature" and "nurture" conceptions of the relationship between national integration and cultural differences in the two Germanies.[7] The first, a primordialist position, holds that national character is ingrained. Communism was a "freezer," Mushaben writes, and "once thawed out, [the historical characteristics and passions of east Germans] would presumably be reconstituted, taking up where they had left off as 'normal' Germans forty-five years earlier" (Mushaben 1993: 43). The converse of this theory holds that east Germans, like all people are socialized into social, political, and economic systems. If east and west Germans are distinct people it is not because identities have been submerged but because identities have been transformed. Whether one accepts that national identities are primordially or instrumentally constituted, Schneider's point is that east and west Germans are different. East Germans, according to another writer, Peter Bender, "were a product of their country to a greater extent than they wanted to be" (quoted in Glaser 1993: 69).

From this perspective, unification is the rediscovery of a Korean golden age when life and thought were Korean and pure *(sunsuhada)* and the land was unspoiled by industry. Photographs of north Korea's natural beauty reveal but at the same time withhold, for in offering only a glimpse of the north they perpetuate the invisibility of north Korean people and inspire the Seoul urbanite to fantasize about the idyllic and peaceful countryside. Even more troublesome, the city-country opposition risks becoming represented in patronizing terms similar to those of earlier colonial or Cold War discourse, or Pratt's notion of "anti-conquest," in which the conquerer clothes his paternalism as humanitarianism and brotherhood (Pratt 1992).[8] Rey Chow (1991: 90) writes, in the context of Orientalism, "We are thus confronted with what is perhaps the ugliest double bind in the history of imperialism: while the kind, personal intent behind many a missionary exploration of the 'Other' world must be recognized . . . such explorations are implicated in colonialism and neocolonialism" (1991: 90). It is worth pondering to what extent a colonial enterprise appears in the postcards sold at the Midopa exhibition that depict the paradise of the north Korean countryside. These postcards reveal and appropriate that which is supposed to be hidden from the viewer's eyes. In his analysis of French postcards of Algerian "harems," Malek Alloula writes: "Travel is the essence of the postcard, and expedition is its mode. It is the fragmentary return to the mother country. It straddles two spaces: the one it represents and the one it will reach" (1986: 4). Alloula further notes the importance of uncovering the dominating gaze of the postcard and its underlying hegemonies, because only then can we begin to argue against the stereotypes that are attached to the object and that symbolize the dominance of the seer over the seen.

THE PRODUCTION AND
COMPLICATED MOURNING OF DIVISION

Although Homi Bhabha's work, and the work of many postcolonial theorists, has focused primarily on histories of engagement between colonizer and colonized, metropole and colony—most prolifically in South Asian studies—*postcolonial* can refer to ongoing processes that occur even outside the conventional units of postcolonial analysis. The global ramifications of colonialism are wide-ranging and pervasive enough to permit postcolonial analysis not only of colonizer-colonized relations but also of relations within each of these groups, as well as of communities that were neither colonized nor colonizers. An important corollary of this argument against theory's somewhat narrow focus is that postcolonialism need not refer to conditions *after* colonization. One critic of postcolonialism has noted that when we orient theory around the temporal relations between colonial and postcolonial, or around the power relations between colonizer and colonized, we tend to overlook how other power relations, including hegemonic forms derivative of colonialism and imperialism, are implicated in post-colonial conditions (McClintock 1994: 296). We risk neglecting the "neocolonial" character of U.S. media, financial capital, and arms production, for example, and of exploitative relations within postcolonial societies and between postcolonial societies and their neighbors, such as between Indonesia and East Timor, or South Africa and Lesotho. McClintock thus writes: "It is precisely the greater subtlety, innovation and variety of these forms of imperialism that makes the historical rupture implied by the term

'post-colonial' especially unwarranted" (1994: 296). One salient continuity between the colonial and the postcolonial is the tendency for the
postcolonial subject to unwittingly repeat the discourse strategies of the
colonizer, even while carrying out the admirable work of decolonization.
Numerous ethnographies and historical analyses have taken as a central
topic the postcolonial appropriation of colonial models in South Asia,
Southeast Asia, East Asia, and Africa (see, for example, Cohn 1987;
Nandy, 1988; McVey, 1982; Anderson 1990; Paik 1993a, 1993b;
Grinker 1994). For Korea, Choi Chungmoo (1993) suggests that
opposition intellectuals in south Korea's *minjung* movement recuperate
the colonial process of othering while trying to represent those south
Koreans marginalized from and subject to the centers of economic and
political power.

Colonialism is not a thing of the past, for the past is still
happening. The same must be said about national division in Korea.
Although Korean and American history textbooks often objectify
division as an event that once happened, in Korea division is an
ongoing and creative process of remaking, remembering, and representing. Through *Pukhan saenghwal* viewers culturally pattern
national division and symbolically represent the loss of the north and
the hope for its resuscitation. For viewers, the exhibition stands for the
junctures and disjunctures of the Korean nation's past, present, and
future.

In the exhibition, the lost Koreans are brought back to life as
mimics, as fragments that can be construed as ruins of a sort that in their
return as converted north Koreans, point to a future in which Korea will
be unified. Ruins and commemorative constructions such as monuments and exhibitions do not always refer to the past or to the end of
something. They can refer to new beginnings or continuations. For
example, one can also imagine the *Pukhan saenghwal* exhibition occurring in a postunification Korea to memorialize, mourn, and perhaps
even resuscitate the people who had had a life in the north.[9] The
continuities and discontinuities between past and future can also be seen
in the television images from the Korean Brodcasting System's 1983
reunion telethon, in which several thousand Koreans held posters
bearing the names of missing relatives (Kim, C. S. 1988). The telethon
equated the memory and mourning of names and highlighted the
ongoing suffering of Korean national division: Korea's *han*.

The sort of remembering that goes on in an exhibition such as Midopa's resembles a complicated mourning not only in viewers' inevitably unsuccessful attempts to resolve loss and separation, but also in the expression of antithetical feelings, the love and hate that are directed at a lost love-object. In memory or in exhibition, north Korea, like the dead or lost love, becomes simultaneously an idealized and denigrated form of the self. Complicated mourning can sometimes be characterized by the survivors' identification with and internalization of the dead as part of themselves (Freud 1917). The internalization takes on a moral quality, and in cases of extreme ambivalence, aspects of a lost love may be internalized either in negative terms as a moral prohibition or in positive terms as an idealized object against which the mourner debases himself. Indeed, the south Korean images of the north shift back and forth between positive and negative idealizations. The north Korea of the Midopa exhibition is primitive, authentic, fixed in time, machinelike, blind, and in desperate need of being saved by the south. It is both authentic and not authentic, admirable and yet evil. South Korea appears as progressive, global, free, able to see, and yet in desperate need of rediscovering and reconstituting itself through the north. It is superior and yet in important ways inferior to the north. Although one set of descriptions refers to the north and the other to the south, the two sets of contradictory characterizations are dependent upon each other because they are part of the same fantasy, constructed in the same place and by the same people. When visitors, or exhibition panels, speak of the north, they are really talking about the south, for the "real" or "true" north is the reverse of the south, and therefore its reflection. Hence, the apparent contradictions in how south Koreans imagine the north come from more than simple ambivalence; they arise from both the powerful and, for the most part, conscious wish that the north and the south, the Self and Other, be one and the same, and from the difficult recognition that they are not.

One might suggest that south Koreans cannot truly mourn the north, for to do so might be tantamount to recognizing the total loss of the nation as it has been imagined. Mourning is highly desirable because it provides relief from some of the ambiguities and uncertainties of suffering, but it cannot take place without loss. However, south Koreans can practice a sort of anticipatory grief in which loss is contemplated and then denied, and in which the living seek to emancipate themselves from uncertainty. Although unification is the certain endpoint to the tragedy of division, it ideally involves the destruction of the various boundaries that currently separate north and south. Unification therefore also involves the destruction of current classificatory markers of difference between north and south, and the creation of ambivalence. In the imagined world of unification, a world in which ideally there are no differences, binary colonial metaphors of domination continue to separate north and south and provide a language with which to articulate confusion and ambivalence about the coexistence of sameness and difference. To some extent, *Pukhan saenghwal* can be seen as a temporary memorial to temporarily lost homogeneity. The displays analyzed in this chapter extend the discourse on difference into very concrete and specific terms and may thus serve to reinforce or intensify *ijil:* they constitute the representation, and therefore also the production and continuity, of a view of difference that is negative and unwanted.

LOSS, MOURNING, AND RESENTMENT: HAN

> When unveiled, the ambivalence [in mourning]
> does not disappear; it becomes that out of which
> we can make our histories so as to create the
> possibilities for change.
>
> —Michael Roth, *The Ironist's Cage*

ALTHOUGH THE MEANINGS OF KOREAN "MOURNING" will become clearer as the analysis proceeds, it is important at this point to provide some definitions, especially since the concept is psychological and is usually employed in psychological discourse to refer to the experiences of the individual rather than the collectivity. As I explained toward the close of chapter 2, the concept of mourning appears frequently these days in cultural studies and anthropology as scholars begin to explore more fully the culturally distinct ways in which people living in rapidly changing worlds respond to the loss of their ideals, but the methodological problems of using a term with explicitly psychological meanings are less often discussed.

Psychohistories have appeared in many formulations, from the Freudian post–World War II national character studies of Benedict and Gorer that posited essential national personalities as the outcome of childrearing practices, to the complicated works of Žižek and others in the late 1980s and early 1990s that locate ethnicity and nationalism in the traumas and antagonisms of early childhood separation, as it is uniquely defined by Lacan's theory of psychoanalysis and theory of ideology. Cultural studies that refer to the mourning, fantasies, grief, and ambivalence of a nation or other collectivity can be criticized for many of the same reasons that other forms of psychohistory have been criticized: for analyzing groups with concepts designed for analyzing individuals, for attributing a causal relationship between individual psychological processes and cultural patterns (that is, reducing culture to psychology), and for essentializing a national "character" in the face of tremendous social and psychological variability.

Yet all of these various psychological approaches to large-scale social processes are more or less vulnerable to the same criticisms. I want to stress that in this book I am not attempting to locate a modal personality, posit a group mind, or equate a specific agent with the abstract "ego" that so often comes to stand for the (liberal) individual in psychological accounts. Although I risk doing all of these things, my intention is rather to employ psychological and psychoanalytic concepts where they are analogically useful. I find that much of what I read in Freud's work on mourning, for instance, captures important aspects of some of the Korean discourses available to me and helps me to discern patterns that appear at the level of collective representation. In Korean discourses on unification, psychological concepts such as love, hate, revenge, and resentment—concepts that index internal psychological states—are frequently also present within collective representations, appearing there prior to analysis and thus demanding that our explanations employ a psychological terminology.

That a discourse on the loss of a loved one parallels a discourse on the loss of a nation—that people may explicitly say, for example, that they experience national trauma as the loss of a loved one or a part of their body—does not imply that the nation undergoes the same psychological processes as the individual, or even that the people who make that representation believe this to be so. What we will find in this chapter, through an examination of the Korean concept of *han,* is that this complex term expresses both personal and collective losses, violations, and consequent resentment—the tragedies of individuals and collectivities of different sizes and inclusiveness can all be represented with the term *han*—and also provides the victims with a means of representing and eventually resolving the resentment. *Han* and its processes of resolution thus resemble mourning too closely to be left unexamined.

The primary point of reference for my use of the term "mourning" is Freud's early definition of it as the loss of an abstraction (1917), an abstraction that could be a person but could also be one's country, liberty, or ideal. I do not find it difficult to argue, along with Freud, that the concept of object loss should be extended from the loss of persons, although of course in the Korean case actual persons as well as the nation have been lost, if not through war then through the enduring division of millions of families. Mourning is fundamentally about loss, and the data I will be analyzing concern the simultaneous loss of an ideal and the denial of the loss. Building on Freud's preliminary work on mourning, Heinz Kohut has described an element of mourning that he calls the process of "de-idealization" (1971). [1] The term refers to the process through which idealizations weaken or crumble. Although his work deals specifically with early childhood (pre-oedipal) unconscious issues of merger, loss, and the development of the self, the process provides a useful way to think about the relationships between mourning and adaptation to reality and between de-idealization and the loss not only of loved ones but of ideals, values, and traditions. The inevitable failure of the self (or, one might say, history) to sustain idealization weakens the self and leads to one of three possible results: "(1) it may move toward new knowledge of the self, new ideals and consequent new ideas, (2) the paralysis can persist, leading to apathy, cynicism, and chronic discontent, or (3) one may disavow the experience entirely and instead attack, often fiercely and rebelliously, the events or persons producing the de-idealization" (Homans, 1989: 23-28). De-idealization is thus similar to mourning but differs in some important ways. Most significant for my purposes is that de-idealization, as Kohut conceives it, can be productive, creative, and progressive, as opposed to the more limited role Freud's concept of "mourning" plays in repairing history's (reality's) damage to the ego. For Homans, nineteenth-century and turn-of-the-century social theorists such as Marx, Durkheim, Weber, and Freud lived and wrote within scientific communities that both consciously and unconsciously mourned the loss of primordial attachments to tradition, culture, spontaneity, and charisma. But these authors adapted to their de-idealization by constructing new forms of knowledge and intellectual inquiry.

The Industrial Revolution produced a mourning reaction to the increasing rationalization of "traditional communities" and their symbols.

For Weber, this meant the loss of the spontaneity and immediacy of religious cultures that had given way to disenchantment, bureaucratization, and calculation; even charismatic leadership had become routinized to the point of losing its affective and therefore political power. Freud and Durkheim also mourned the loss of tradition, and the new structures created out of their recognition and reaction to loss led European scholarship to new forms of social and self-understanding.

In commenting earlier on the history of psychological anthropology, I noted an opposition between individual and society because interpretations of the Korean word *han* also invoke a tension between the word's social and individual referents. This is an opposition that appears as well in the older forms of social thought mentioned above. Indeed, Homans's work shows some ways in which the concept of mourning can be linked up to both individual and collective experiences; these theorists' works were motivated by both personal and collective losses. However, the many differences between Durkheim and Weber's works notwithstanding, their structures were largely external to the individual. This is not to say that these authors neglected the individual. Quite the contrary. For Durkheim, especially, society could be defined only as a counterpoint to the individual, as the former shaped the latter into an epiphenomenal reflection of itself.

Freud's structure-building response was to shape a science that instead focused on internal experience and placed the individual at the center of a particular historical ontology that subordinated society to the individual. This historical process, which, in comparison to Weber's historical perspective, could arguably be called synchronic, is one in which the developing ego structures itself by internalizing and interpreting past experiences and meanings. Psychoanalysis moved science away from religion, so-called traditional symbols, and collective history, for these areas of human experience only obscured the workings of the mind and inhibited psychoanalytic interpretations. Granted, this reading of Freud, Weber, and Durkheim is itself framed in Freudian terms, but the point to be stressed here is that scientific advances emerged as a response to mourning, and that the various scientific perspectives reflected a tension between the individual and the group. Homans argues that the concept of mourning not only explains this tension as it appears in these authors' works but also provides an avenue for more broadly and theoretically linking individual and collective histories in other contexts as well.

The recent changes in thinking and writing about north Korea I note in chapters 2 (on the idea of unification) and 6 (on children's textbooks) may indicate the beginnings of a national mourning process—a process of mourning the lost hope that unification will mean a return to a prior undifferentiated union—but for the most part, contemporary south Korean history has been defined more often by paralysis (the hope for the recovery of homogeneity) and attack (demonization of the north as an enemy) than by movement and creativity. (How well north Koreans mourn the loss of Kim Il-sung remains to be seen and may pose a psychological problem analogous to the complicated relation between Germans and Hitler.) Not only have south Koreans' responses to division failed to achieve liberation from or adaptation to their (evil) object, the north, but they have also failed to establish that there has been a loss. In the introduction I phrased this denial as a death without a death, though it might also be called a "living death." As I put it in the previous chapter, it is as if many south Koreans were saying that north Koreans were frozen in time by national division and the north Korean state and are waiting for unification to defrost them. Indeed, most unification discourses in south Korea speak of "overcoming" difference rather than embracing it in more positive terms as diversity and strength. This suggests a complicated mourning of the losses suffered through national division.

Readers may object by citing *minjung* and other social movements in Korea as motivated by a collective mourning of the loss of tradition in south Korea. These movements are vitally important in south Korea, but as we shall see in chapter 7, which is devoted to students and student protests, there is good reason to doubt the creative, revolutionary elements of student movements, *minjung,* and another arena of protest, the mask dances. The ideology of homogeneity is as profound in many of these movements as it is at the level of government discourse and suggests that the recognition of difference and loss is a pervasive problem in south Korea, as perhaps it is in all rapidly industrializing societies.

DIVISION AND HAN

Once, when I advertised in a Korean newspaper for a research assistant, an elderly gentleman left the following message on my answering machine: "I am so happy to hear about an American professor who wants to learn about my country. I can teach you what you need to know. It is a word called *han*." Indeed, when I meet Koreans for the first time and explain that I am interested in learning about Korean culture, they commonly tell me that I must learn about the concept of *han* in order to understand what it means to be Korean.

For many people in south and north Korea, national division is widely characterized as Korea's *han*. The loss of autonomy due to past invasions and Japanese colonization has also created *han,* but division is a more immediate referent; division represents not only the (temporary) loss of the nation but also the two Koreas' frustrating inability to retrieve it. In contemporary south Korea the loss of autonomy is experienced largely in terms of division and in terms of the national security state that necessitates oppressive laws and makes south Koreans depend, to some extent, on U.S. military assistance. *Han,* in turn, is widely characterized as the essence of being Korean.

What are the meanings of this word that has become an aesthetic of Korean identity? Although *han* can be loosely and simply defined as "resentment," it requires an elaborate discourse to explicate it more fully. This chapter explores some of the uses of the term *han* as an idiom for conceptualizing and representing the tragedy of division and suggests that it poses both benefits and disadvantages for unification prospects. The term, as I show, is also directly related to processes of mourning. If we think of mourning as a kind of reconciliation, not with past traumas but with the ongoing strength of continuing traumas, then *han* itself represents the inability to mourn. *Han* refers to a consciousness of ongoing trauma and a lack of resolution and reconciliation. Paradoxically, however, *han* also provides a means of resolution, for the concept provides a path for the movement of the present into the past, and for a fresh and creative movement from the past and present into the future. The important question is whether this path can be identified and taken.

Han unites Koreans in a shared consciousness about their relations to each other and to the past. *Han* also relates to the future, since it is widely believed that Korean unification represents the resolution of the *han* of division. Yet division and unification appear to be beyond Korean control, and it is here that the issue of autonomy enters the picture. A common Korean perspective is that unification will resolve Korea's *han* but that currently there are political forces, within the two Koreas and outside of Korea, that make this resolution impossible. The frustration over not being able to resolve it builds additional *han,* reinforcing the frustration, and, some might say, making Koreans hate their perceived enemies, or at least those agents who are believed to be complicitous with division, all the more. Such feelings of hatred complicate the prospects for unification and reconciliation as peaceful and noncoercive, and so a circle of *han* continues. In this context, it is important to stress that it is unification and not peace that is most frequently cited by the people I interview as the solution to Korea's *han.* Discussions of peace almost always involve unification. But unification is not always or necessarily imagined as a peaceful process. War and the collapse of the north, both potentially involving a flood of refugees streaming to the south for food and refuge, are two of the many scenarios posited for Korean unification that do not involve peace. Indeed, *han* does not require a peaceful resolution, and some philosophers of *han,* while certainly not advocating violence, nonetheless would argue that *han* is best released through a violent explosion of emotion.

Han is a distinctive psychological concept. It refers to the heart and mind, to emotion and sentiment, to consciousness and mental states in general. It concerns frustration, victimization, and inferiority. *Han* is a complex of suppressed emotion, and it is so wide-ranging and significant that perhaps any definition will be simplistic. If the symbolic contours of *han* are undefinable, so too are the sociological contours, for it can be contained within individuals and within collectivities.

Han and its Variants

In everyday usage, Koreans employ the term *han* without specifying its particular import, and as a result people use *han* in very different ways. The literary critic Ch'ŏn Yi-du begins a comprehensive analysis of *han* with an illustration of the problems of meaning. In 1987, when the presidential campaign that ultimately elected President Roh Tae Woo was at its peak, one candidate said, "We must solve the *han* of those who fought for democracy." The next day, another candidate replied, "Politics is not a *hanp'uri* [a means of resolving *han*]; politics should be based on generosity and reconciliation" (Ch'ŏn 1993: 9). Clearly, the candidates were using *han* in very different ways. The first talked about solving *han* by realizing people's dreams for a truly democratic election, which in this case meant the election of a civilian leader rather than a military leader hand-picked by the incumbent; the second conceived *han* as revenge against past injustices, perhaps implying that his opponent would encourage aggressive actions toward the north or prosecution of corrupt politicians and military leaders. *Han* can thus be appropriated for many different contexts in which the speaker or writer intends to express regret, lamentation, and frustration over an inability to achieve something or redress a wrong.

Ch'ŏn elaborates several different kinds of *han,* which he separates into two categories, the dark and bright sides. The dark side consists of *wŏn* (enmity, vengeance), *wŏn* (written differently in Chinese characters and meaning "false accusation"), *sŏrum* (sorrow), and *t'an* (lamentation, regret, grief). The bright side consists primarily of *han* as *chŏng*— *chŏnghan*—by which Ch'ŏn literally means "attachment" but more generally means the conversion of resentment into creativity, love, and commitment.

The central feature of all of these aspects of *han,* bright and dark, is their capacity to constitute many different kinds of misfortune as a coherent set of sentiments and their temporal orientation toward the future resolution of those sentiments. In this regard, Korean tragedies do not "speak for themselves" but are always distilled, filtered, converted into something else; *han* is a culturally distinctive manner of conceptualizing and experiencing misfortune, but it is also a method for thinking about the relationship between historical experience and the future. It provides for sufferers a means of converting their tragedy into a dynamic and active process—whether externally through revenge or internally by self-reflection and the development of a new identity or art. This might also be explicated by saying that *han* expresses a continuous tension between enduring one's misfortunes and doing something about the misfortunes and the personal hardships and resentments that result from them.

The first kind of "dark" *han* Ch'ŏn considers, *wŏn* as enmity, is perhaps one of the forms of *han* easiest to recognize. It is commonly associated with the response to clear acts of wrongdoing against innocent victims. It has also been linked, more specifically, to the more liberal politicians in south Korea, who criticize conservatives for perpetuating a *han* of "reckless hatred" (Park D. U. 1996: 78) for the north. It is a sentiment that arises when it is impossible to take revenge against an offense. In some Korean translations of the Bible, "I will vindicate" is translated as "I will resolve your suppressed *han*" (Suh 1983: 58). The last words of dying victims in Korean translations of programmatic and stylized Hong Kong action movies are often subtitled as "Please, solve my *han*"—at which time a relative or apprentice goes off to take revenge; after having completed the act the avenger looks to the skies and says to the spirit of the deceased, "I have solved your *han*." Had the victims of an offense been able to complete their own act of revenge, they would not have developed *han*.

Wŏnhan as false accusation refers to the inability of a person to defend him or herself or take revenge against an offense to honor and reputation. Perhaps the most celebrated story of *wŏnhan* as false accusation is the mythical story of the sisters Changhwa and Hongryŏn whose deaths were caused by their evil stepmother: Changhwa was driven to suicide after being falsely accused of becoming pregnant, and Hongryŏn was drowned by an assassin hired by their stepmother. Unable to endure their *han*, even in their death, they appear as ghosts before the village judges. All judges but one die upon the shock of seeing the ghosts, and it is the surviving judge who exonerates them, frees them from their humiliation, and thus solves their *han*.

Han as sorrow, or *sŏlum,* refers neither to revenge nor humiliation but rather to individual sadness, what the poet Kim So-wŏl once called a "small mass" in one's heart *(sŏrumŭi tongi).* The significance and singularity of such a conception of *han* lies in its reference to individuals. Korean historians and philosophers have frequently referred to the *han* of the Korean people, the *han* of women, the *han* of slaves, or the *han* of laborers. Yet *han* as sorrow rests not in the community or in national tragedy, but in the individual heart.

For many Koreans, the essence of *han* is the variant sometimes referred to as *hant'an:* an unresolvable unhappiness and longing. *T'an* implies a sense of regret and weariness and is not necessarily created by an offense. For example, a woman's father may die in his eighties from natural causes, and yet she may still experience *han* and punish herself emotion-ally—not because her father's death is an injustice, but because she believes that she could have been a better, more loyal, more attentive daughter. This is certainly an example of complicated mourning, if not melancholia, inasmuch as the death is construed as a narcissistic injury that reveals the survivor's own failures. The similarities between *t'an* and melancholia are expressed in Kim So-wŏl's well-known, 1925 poem "*Chindalrae kkot*"

("Azaleas"), about a woman's contemplation of lost love. In the character's vision of loss, instead of trying to persuade her love to come back to her or expressing anger toward him for leaving, she anoints his path and refuses to cry, perhaps believing that she is to blame for his weariness.

> When you leave,
> weary of me,
> without a word I shall gently let you go.
> From Mount Yak
> in Yŏngbyŏn,
> I shall gather armfuls of azaleas
> and scatter them on your way.
> Step by step
> on the flowers placed before you
> tread lightly, softly as you go.
> When you leave,
> weary of me,
> though I die, I will not let one tear fall.
> (Translated by David R. McCann in Lee, 1990, p 29)

It is important to stress the frequency with which this poem (and others by Kim So-wŏl) is cited by Koreans as the exemplification of *han*. The poem draws our attention to a particular manner in which people conceptualize loss almost self-depricatingly as self-inflicted humiliation, a point that Oh Sae-yŏng (1976) makes with explicit reference to Freud's concept of unsuccessful mourning, by which I believe that he means melancholia: that *han* is an unresolved conflict between the impulse to long for someone and the impulse to feel anger and resentment toward oneself or the person who has departed. The result is that the sufferer renounces any act of revenge, believing that bitterness and lamentation toward someone or something exterior to one's self are futile sentiments that will achieve little. *Han'an* can be construed as an act of violence against oneself rather than against the true cause of one's suffering.

Two Genealogical Senses of Han

Oddly, Ch'ŏn's book contains no substantial description of two additional aspects of *han* that can be characterized as "dark": *han* as a sentiment that grows larger as time passes, and *han* as hereditary suffering. One of the more distinctive characteristics of *han* is that it can increase when unresolved and can be passed on to future generations. Abelmann argues that, in the context of *minjung* consciousness and the theological movement that employs the *minjung* as the central subject of emancipation and moral progress, *han* refers to a genealogy of hardship and struggle:

> *Han*, a central category in *minjung* theology, literature, and movements, in a single word connotes both the collective and the individual genealogical sense of the hardship of historical experience. It connotes particularly the accumulated anger or resentment born of this experience. . . . Its latency makes it powerful; when the experience, collective or individual is not the source of self-conscious action, *han* is only further "building up," becoming a greater force to fuel an eventual "blow-up." Indeed, in the very way that people talk about *han*, they talk about something that eventually explodes. (Abelmann 1993: 162-163)

Han thus has the capacity to grow and to be passed on to successive generations. For example, a colleague of mine from Seoul told me that in the 1997 presidential election he intended to vote for Kim Dae Jung of Chŏlla province (a province long neglected in this century by Korean presidents, none of whom have come from Chŏlla-do) not because of Kim's policies but because the people of Chŏlla-do have a *han* that has been accumulating for many generations; he made this point in the context of his own negative stereotypes about people from Chŏlla-do, "I don't like Chŏlla-do people but we need to resolve their *han* for the good of the whole country."

As time passes and more Koreans are born and die in a divided nation, the *han* of national division also becomes greater. As a form of grief, *han* thus has an unlikely analogue in one of the most visible constructions of national ruin in recent years, the American NAMES project AIDS quilt, which consists of thousands of panels, each designed and sewn to name and commemorate a family member, friend, or lover lost to AIDS. Every month more panels are added; similarly, at the Vietnam Veterans Memorial in Washington D.C., new names are engraved nearly every Veterans' Day. That the *han* of national division, the size of a quilt, or a list of names, continues to grow is a constant and tragic reminder that nations can also mourn the present and future, that commemorative constructions do not always signal the end of something past.

Ch'ŏn also does not elaborate *han* as a collective phenomenon, as it is so explicitly described by the *minjung* writers, such as Suh Nam-dong and the well-known poets Kim Ji-ha and Ko Eun, among others ("If you do not hear the sighs of the *han* of the *minjung,* one cannot hear the voice of Christ knocking on our doors" Suh, 1983: 68). Individual experiences can comprise the *han* of a collectivity, present and past. Thus, in reference to the death of a young female trade union leader, Suh writes: "[In her death] was concentrated not only the various contradictions of political and economic structures, but hers seems to be a death which *embodies the han of eight million Korean workers"* (Suh 1983: 56, emphasis added). He goes on to cite the poem "Slave Diary," by Yang Sŏng-wu, suggesting that *han* has been absorbed into the bodies of Korea's ancestors:

> Even though you survive for a million years
> like worms in dying petals;
> I will look down, waving my hands in the air,
> being torn like a rag.
> Even though you vanish as dew on a sword
> the blood scattered when you rolled and rolled;
> I will wet the scars of the swords, the gunshot wounds,
> wet your stained hearts
> as a shower falling down in May.
> Even though you thrash without stopping
> like the sleet in mid-winter;
> I will shout out
> breathing as roots of grass
> which sleep not under the ground. . . .
> Do you hear, you poets,
> the thick voice which echoes to the end of the earth
> hitting the air with fists,
> fists from inside graves,
> sorrowful graves of 5,000 years?
> (pp. 62-63)

The genealogical sense of *han* is well-suited to Christian theology because it links individual and collective moral action and is clearly oriented to a utopian future, as in this definition of *han* offered by the theologian C. H. S. Moon:

> *Han* is the anger and resentment of the *minjung* which has been turned inward and intensified as they become the objects of injustice upon injustice. It is the result of being repressed for an extended period of time by external forces. . . . Herein lies the complex nature of the *han* of the Korean *minjung*. As a people of a small and weak nation, they hate and resent the wrongs done to them by the surrounding nations whose might they cannot overcome. Yet although they do not know how their hopes might be actualized, being pressed by ever-increasing hopes for a free and just world, they cannot give up their yearning for a new future. Thus they are torn between hope and hopelessness. . . . *Han,* however, is a starting point for a new human history. . . . With *han* as our point of departure we begin to dream of a new, alternative future and to dedicate ourselves to the cause of making that future a reality. (Moon 1985: 1-2)

Likewise, *minjung* theologists often cite Kim Ji-ha and Ko Eun because these writers believed that *han* could form the dynamic for revolution—Kim suggesting that the tremendous power of accumulated *han* will lead to emancipation, Ko suggesting, in contrast, that revolution will be achieved by changing Koreans' ancient and "masculine" anger or hatred into what he calls a more feminine patient and self-controlled will (Lee J. H. 1994: 67-95; Ch'ŏn Y. D. 1993: 92-93).

The hereditary aspect of *han* is illustrated well in Kendall's work on shamanism in which she makes clear that the unresolved *han* of one's ancestors can be of great danger to the living, who may require a shaman's expertise to purify the household of illness and other sorts of misfortune (Kendall 1988: 8). In fact, when unmarried people die, it is often said that they have *han* because they never married, and that this *han* will be a danger to the living, especially to the fertility of the land. Their souls, like those of all people with unresolved han, are said to inhabit *kuch'ŏn,* a netherworld. For example, when the Sampoong department store collapsed in the summer of 1995, many of the employees and customers who died were single women. A community organization organized a mass spiritual marriage *(yŏnghon kyŏlhonsik)* for the souls of the unmarried dead.

Thus *han* is invoked frequently in individual narratives and life histories to underscore the degree to which one's ancestors' tragedies can continue to have an impact on how the living experience themselves in relation to their history, and, especially, how the living conceptualize the causes and consequences of misfortune in terms of the past. For example, in the following narrative a young woman tells me the story of a friend whose marriage deteriorated to the point that she was beaten and abandoned by her husband, yet she merges that story with an account of her friend's mother. The point I would like to stress here is that the daughter's *han* is not totally comprehensible to my interviewee without the additional understanding that she inherited an unresolved *han* from her mother.

> Mrs. Park was born the fifth child of a poor farmer in Ch'ungch'ŏng-do. Her father had some land but he did not work much. Her mother did all the work, and the husband fed her sons and not her daughters. All the boys went to a university but not the daughters; they had to stop at middle school. Mrs. Park was smart, and her elder sister worked at a factory to send her to high school. She actually got a scholarship to Ehwa and after that became a Northwest [airlines] flight attendant, and then a secretary to the ambassador of Canada. But she was never happy because her father kicked her mother out of the house. No one knows why. He said, "Your face makes me sick. Get out."
>
> [Her mother] now lives as a maid at a Buddhist temple in Anyang. Everyone told her to get divorced, but she wouldn't get divorce papers, wouldn't get a lawyer. One day she told my friend and me, "What will be different if I file for divorce? This is my destiny, to be kicked out of my house and sent to the temple." She was really miserable. She had no interest in getting her husband back, but she needed to have an identity, to keep her life moving. She is now even more miserable. Her husband even abandoned all the children except the first son. He used to say that his first son was his only child. Now the first one has abandoned his mother and the other sons do not see her either. My friend did not remain married like her mother, but she still had the same *han*. She contacted her father to

ask for some financial help, but he refused. She is now working for the Ritz-Carlton Hotel and she is well paid and lives on her own. She bought an apartment that has two rooms and wanted to ask her mother to come live with her. Her older sister told her not to do it. She said, "You're still young enough to get married again. If you take care of Mother, all our brothers will think you are now responsible for her, and what new husband would want to take care of his mother-in-law? Our mother would end up being abandoned three times—first by Father, second by you, and third when no one else in our family will take her."

My friend inherited her mother's *han*. She was beaten, suspected, verbally abused, and she is very sensitive—a *munhak sonyŏ* [a romantic; lit. "literature girl"]. She cries when she sees leaves drop in autumn or reads a greeting card. She is miserable like her mother. That is who they are.

Women also pass *han* to future generations as mothers-in-law. It should be pointed out that (perhaps not unlike in other societies in the world) relations between Korean women and their daughters-in-law are depicted in folklore and everyday conversation as filled with tension and conflict. According to one of my interviewees, a Chosŏn dynasty proverb states, *"Shiŏmŏni kubagŭn myŏnŭriga myŏnŭri kubagŭn puŏkkaega"* (the daughter-in-law treats the house dog as the mother-in-law treats her daughter-in-law). As she explained it, "The house dog becomes the object of *hanp'uri*. Everyone says they will not be like their mother-in-law, but then they think: 'I suffered for so long, someone else has to go through the same thing, otherwise I will be the only victim. It is not fair.'"

THE BRIGHT SIDE OF HAN

Where Ch'ŏn offers some of his most significant insights is in his emphasis on a "bright" side of *han,* and here his interests converge somewhat with the theologians' focus on *han* as an engine for creative, active, and positive struggle, and the psychoanalyst's emphasis on mourning as liberation and adaptation. For Ch'ŏn, *han* can lead a person to act sensitively and delicately toward the world (1993: 36). *Han* as *chŏng* (attachment)—*chŏngŭrosŏŭi han*—can refer to an attachment to nature, to art, and to love, most often experienced by the elite scholars or *yangban*, especially during the Koryŏ and Chosŏn dynasties. Unlike most commoners (*sŏmin*), some *yangban* did not work and thus were free to wander in the countryside and heighten their enjoyment of nature to the level of an art. But in their separation from society they sacrificed their families, and in some cases their personal well-being, for nature; therein lies their *han*.

Han is also a wish that can be transformed into a driving force to achieve a goal. For if one is able to truly resolve one's *han*, then one can reach a state of exuberance (*sinmyŏng*) and excellence in art and literature. Ch'ŏn articulates another transformation of *han* in his explication of a brief essay by the painter Ch'ŏn Kyŏng-cha entitled "*Han*" (Ch'ŏn 1993: 47). According to Ch'ŏn Kyŏng-cha's argument, *han* is the subject of art. Yet that artistic subject cannot emerge unless the artist first suffers an inability to express his or her thoughts and colors. This is a process reminiscent of the film *Sŏp'yŏnje*, discussed earlier, about a woman who performs *p'ansori*, a kind of Korean singing art. In the film, of course, *han* emerges in a different manner, not because of the *p'ansori* artist's own intentions but because of those of her adoptive father. Yet Song-hwa achieves her art because she has suffered so much, having been blinded by her father and having endured the rigorous training of a singer (at one point her father says to her, "If you don't [sing so hard that you] vomit blood you won't be a master of *p'ansori*"). Suffering not only becomes the subject of her art but paradoxically also provides her with a vehicle to express her suffering. Ch'ŏn cites the singer Kim So-hee, who trained the actress and singer who performed the role of Song-hwa: "*Han*, in a simple word, is *mŏt* [aesthetics]." (1993: 49). *Chŏnghan* is thus central to Ch'ŏn's discourse on *han* because he is critical of what he sees as a conventional literary emphasis on the dark side of *han*. *Chŏnghan* can inspire people to overcome their suffering without anger, violence, or revenge.

In contemporary Korea, such an inspiration to find the bright side of *han* is commonly found in political prisoners' retellings of their experiences of torture. One of Korea's most well-known political prisoners, the lawyer Kim Kŭn-tae (popularly called the "*Komun Pyŏnhosa*" [torture lawyer], because he has been tortured so often), who was released from prison in June 1988, told a reporter, "I feel it is my responsibility to overcome this [degradation], not only for my own salvation but for the sake of the Korean people. . . . " He added, "My human dignity was disintegrating. I was no better than an animal. I was naked, on my knees, crawling, I begged them to kill me. . . . I found the will to stand up again" (Chira 1988: 4). Kim emerged from his torture with an ability to speak generously about how to move the government in the direction of democracy because he had achieved a level of morality that transcended the fears, anger, and violence that characterized his torturers.

The Tale of Ch'unhyang

Although the *Ch'unhyang chŏn* (Tale of Ch'unhyang) is conventionally cited as an exemplar of women's fidelity and virtue, Ch'ŏn selects it for special critical attention because the heroine resolves her *han* not through force but through an individual and internal strength that converts *han* (resentment and grief) into *chŏng* (passion and love). Many heroines in Korean folktales rely on strong external powers to help them actively solve their *han*, but Ch'unhyang instead resolves her *han* through patience and self-control. In the end, it is her patience rather than surrender or physical power that saves her and brings her victimizers to justice. There are, of course, many versions of *Ch'unhyang chŏn*, but I focus here on the *p'ansori* version because it seems to have the fewest variations, and because it has been the subject of considerable scholarly attention. The story was first written down into the form of *p'ansori* in the late nineteenth century. It should also be added that *Ch'unhyang chŏn* has ordinarily been viewed as a story about fidelity and less often viewed through the lens of *han*.

In this well-known story about undying love and devotion in South Chŏlla-do, Ch'unhyang (the daughter of a *kisaeng*—analogous, though not identical, to the Japanese geisha— and a *yangban* man) and the *yangban* Yi Mong-ryong meet as Ch'unhyang walks with her maidservant *(momjong)* to a swing suspended from a tree. They quickly fall in love. However, while Yi travels to Seoul to take the national exams *(kwagŏ)* necessary for his advancement, the evil governor Pyŏn Hak-do attempts to seduce Ch'unhyang into serving him. She resists every effort at persuasion, including torture, responding to the governor's flogging by singing of her devotion to her fiancé. Each time she is beaten she replies with more poetry and resistance, making him all the more angry (see Lee, P. 1981: 257-284).

A powerless and lower-class woman, Ch'unhyang is expected to succumb to the governor. But for Ch'unhyang, what one might think would constitute *wŏnhan (han* as enmity*)* appears as *hant'an,* or lamentation, as she realizes she cannot take revenge. One night Ch'unhyang dreams that she travels to a mythical star called Chiknyŏsŏng, which Koreans have long believed symbolizes eternal love. This is the place where the mythical woman Chiknyŏ lives and from which she departs every July 7 to meet her love, Kyŏnu, who lives on a distant star (lit. Altair in the constellation Aquila). As several versions of the myth relate, Kyŏnu, who lived on his star, and Chiknyŏ, a woman who lived on earth, fell in love without permission from the god Okhwangsangje, the controller of the life cycle and afterlife. When Okhwangsangje became aware of their love, he was angry and separated them. Yet their love was so strong that, in sympathy, massive numbers of crows decided to link their bodies as a bridge across which the two lovers could travel to meet each other once a year. When Ch'unhyang goes to Chiknyŏsŏng, she is told that she lives on earth because her love for Yi is prohibited. Though she and Yi had once lived together, she hears, they must remain separated as a punishment for an unidentified and prior crime. If she is able to withstand her punishment, she will achieve prosperity *(pukwi)*. The god's warning inspires Ch'unhyang to remain patient and withstand the governor's cruelties.

In prison, Ch'unhyang sings two songs: "Mongjungga," about her dream of travel to Chiknyŏsŏng, and "Okjungga," in which she grieves over her predicament. The lyrics from these two songs express some contradictions in *han.* In the latter song, she pities her paleness and her filthy and disheveled hair, while in the former song she sings of her hopes for justice and the end of her suffering. Thus Ch'unhyang's *han* contains aspects of both surrender and anticipation. This is Ch'ŏn's primary point about the conversion of *wŏnhan:* that Ch'unhyang's positive sentiments were eventually able to overcome negative ones.

Not only is she able to withstand her suffering, but she also shows a desire for reconciliation and generosity. When Yi returns to Chŏlla-do as the royal inspector, saves Ch'unhyang, and imprisons the governor, she asks Yi to have mercy on him. "How could a virtuous woman be born without such hardships? Without Pyŏn Hak Do how could I have become a virtuous Ch'unhyang?" (Ch'ŏn 1993: 185). Thus she was able not only to convert her *wŏnhan* into *chŏng,* but she was also able to rise from a state of misery into a strong, reflective, and morally righteous woman.

Mourning and Melancholia

The bright side of *han* is thus linked to reconciliation, and to both melancholia and mourning. But what does reconciliation mean? Does it mean that one is no longer preoccupied with the past or does not think about the past? Certainly one could argue that the trials of the former Korean presidents Chun Doo Hwan and Roh Tae Woo, like the Nuremberg trials, were about reconciliation (not, of course, about forgiveness)—that they involved addressing the violence and inhumanity that accompanied dramatic historical changes—but it does not seem likely that as a consequence of these trials the past will be swept into a dark or seldom-visited corner of the nation (or mind). The division of Korea, like the Holocaust, will always be a part of those who are descended from it, even if there are war crimes trials after unification. This is the calculus for a theory of collective mourning: for mourning to be successful for a nation, the loss must remain conscious and be experienced as a loss in the external world.

Would war crimes trials suffice to release the accumulated *han* and facilitate mourning? The answer is no, if Germany is any indication. The Holocaust may have ended technically, and the Nuremberg and subsequent trials may have carried out some justice, but the burden of history continues. Mourning is not about closure as much as it is about working through trauma. As I noted in chapter 1, "working through" involves balancing two countervailing tendencies: the denial of the emotional dimension of loss in favor of an objective or detached perspective, and the overemphasis on emotion as definitive of the experience of loss. This is an opposition that the Holocaust studies writer Saul Friedlander has termed "protective numbing" versus "disruptive emotion" (1993: 130-131). For Friedlander, working through trauma also means resisting the temptation of closure.

Indeed, Jews and Germans continue to struggle with the past, as evidenced by the huge literature that continues to be published every year on memory, mourning, and the Holocaust, and especially younger Germans' resistance to acknowledging what their parents and grandparents may have done.[2] In 1996, newspapers throughout the world reported that newly released classified documents from World War II showed the broader complicity of the German people with Nazi war crimes (see Goldhagen 1996). As the author Peter Schneider framed the issue in an essay criticizing what he believes are exaggerated claims about this complicity: "I'm afraid we [Germans] cannot look for any lost or new identity. We have one and Auschwitz is a part of it" (Schneider 1996: 35). Indeed, opposition to German unification was framed precisely in terms of the Holocaust. Gunter Grass, one of the most vocal critics of unification, wrote that Auschwitz disqualified Germany forever from emerging again as a strong and unified nation-state (Grass, 1990: 122).[3] Coming to grips with the presence of a shameful ancestor is certainly different from working through the loss of separation. But both involve transformation of the self, a relinquishment of strict adherence to prior identifications, and a working through of the trauma.

Also in the German context, Alexander and Margarete Mitscherlich's *The Inability to Mourn* (1975) and Eric Santner's *Stranded Objects* (1990) highlight Germans' absence of a "sustained emotional confrontation" with the Nazi past (Santner 1990: 1). Both studies emphasize that mourning would have required a broad-based acknowledgment of German responsibility and complicity with Nazi crimes, as well as a forgiveness of those crimes. Neither of these phenomena began to emerge until the 1960s, and even in the late 1980s the so-called historian's controversy occurred over revisionist historians' attempts to rewrite the history of the Holocaust from a German national perspective. Much to the dismay of many, this perspective called for an empathic understanding of the Germans as victims, and even of fears and anxieties Hitler and his advisors may have experienced.[4] The Mitscherlichs and Santner suggest that this inability to confront the past has produced a paralysis of sorts, an inability to change and achieve an adaptive liberation from the object of loss. The second and third postwar generations share this burden of the past. Based on extensive psychological and interview data, both Santner and the Mitscherlichs suggest that parents were emotionally available to their children only to the extent that the children complied with their parents' defenses against guilt and complicity.[5] Like *han*, then, the German inability to mourn has a hereditary component and can be considered to have a coercive power over the emotional experiences of future generations.

Freud, of course, distinguished between two kinds of reactions to loss, mourning and melancholia. Mourning is linked to a sense of realism and attempts to reconcile with the past. But in melancholic reactions, individuals experience the loss of a loved one or an ideal as an impoverishment of the self. In other words, people grieve most for the part of themselves that was constituted by the deceased. Melancholic reactions, such as clinical depression and suicide, are often unconscious reactions to how loss has fragmented one's self. Mourning, on the other hand, is a more therapeutic reaction, a conscious awareness of the loss of an external other that was "loved for its own sake" (Mitscherlich and Mitscherlich, 1975: 27). Melancholia occurs when the personal losses are not consciously recognized but emerge only from the unconscious as debilitating forms of internal aggression. Freud says in reference to melancholia: "The object has not perhaps actually died, but has become lost as an object of love (e.g. the case of the deserted bride). In yet other cases one feels justified in concluding that a loss of the kind has been experienced, but one cannot see clearly what has been lost, and may the more readily suppose that the patient too cannot consciously perceive what it is he has lost" (1917: 155). I would emphasize the words "what it is" because I want to stress that a significant feature of melancholia is that loss is experienced at least on two levels, what one thinks one may have lost (one's father or mother, for example) and what is unconsciously lost (a part of oneself). This is one of the reasons why, as Freud tells us, the loss of the love object, through either death or some other experience, can be experienced as an abandonment and why hate is expended upon that object. However, since the object that does the abandoning is actually part of one's self, hate is thus expended upon the self through what Freud says is typical of melancholics: deep depression, self-torment, sadomasochism, suicide. The historian Michael Roth has summarized the differences between mourning and melancholia:

> [The mourner] gives up the world as it had been known, and gives
> it up piece by piece, slowly and painfully, until a connection with
> the world as it can be known is established as the period of mourning
> ends. The person in melancholy is lost to himself or herself; the work
> of melancholy is to preserve oneself *as* lost, as not worthy of being
> found. (Roth 1995: 195)

When melancholia and mourning are most complicated, individuals may seek to repeat the painful acts that first produced the loss (what Freud called "repetition compulsion"), often repeating the acts upon the self. Freud answered the question of why people would act in ways that make them suffer by arguing that the acts are actually pleasurable, perhaps because they help to punish the part of one's self that was lost, perhaps also because the repetition fulfills the unconscious desire to master and defy the loss. Recall Kim-Renaud's insightful comment that the brother and sister in *Sŏp'yŏnje* did not want to end their separation from each other because this would "spoil" their *han;* in "Azaleas," Kim So-wŏl's melancholic character appears to turn her resentment inward, inflicting punishment upon herself by blocking the expression of affect.

But as the Mitscherlichs show, melancholia does not have to exist when mourning fails. For the Mitscherlichs, Germans neither mourned nor were melancholic because they broke "all affective bridges to the immediate past" in the service of protecting themselves (and their children) from the potential catastrophe of a melancholic reaction. But this is not the only way in which people can avoid mourning and deny loss. Koreans have not severed their bridges to the past, even the immediate past, but this is in large part because they have denied loss and denied diachrony. The denial of loss has been inherited by successive generations, for they too have been appropriated into their parents' unmourned traumas. Korean lamentations about division and separated families are ambivalent and awkward because they simultaneously involve both grief and outright denial. The nation was lost, but this is only temporary, for the nation will be united again and homogeneity will be recovered. In this sense, the Korean War, communism, and the Kim Il-sung/Kim Jong-Il regime resemble a sort of freezer of Koreanness and Korean time. When the north Korean state dissolves, the Korean people, long suppressed in the north, will emerge again and take shape in the unified nation. This is a metaphor employed in Germany as well to repeat the people-state division, as in Ahrends's essay on Sleeping Beauty. In this sarcastic formulation, the people are submerged by the state, awaiting resuscitation from the west: "Sleeping for a hundred years in the enchanted castle, the sweet and dreadful dreams of those who lie there in "necessary" slumber, a slumber for which not they themselves are to blame but, rather, a general law of their existence, the magic spell, the system" (Ahrends 1991: 42).

In order to stave off melancholic reactions, it is often necessary for people to focus their energies indirectly or to "project" upon substitute objects. Rather than punish the self, one punishes a self that appears as other (as in an outside evil, such as the north Korean state), or alternatively one may focus energy upon instruments of narcissistic gratification, one of these instruments in south Korea being the concept of unification, another a synchronic conception of time. In any event, the inability to mourn is not a passive inability, but an active process of denial and representation. Homans's remarks about Germany's inability and Freud's ability to mourn are illustrative here:

> Both psychoanalysis and Nazism were confronted with the same rapid socio-structural change, the same experience of being uprooted precipitously from a religiously informed common culture and from the moral (self-control) and psychological (self-esteem) supports which such a culture invariably confers. In the face of this, psychoanalysis went one way (the ability to mourn), National Socialism another (the inability to mourn). Because they were capable of mourning the loss of the past, Freud and his followers were subsequently able to transform a devastating historical situation into an instrument for its investigation and into a mode of self-understanding which made possible the tolerance of the chaos, both inner and outer, which was in and around them. On the other hand, by denying the painful psychological consequences of the social and historical changes that were taking place—in other words, refusing to mourn—the German Nazis became intolerant of chaos. Instead, they sought to reinvent with great rapidity and astonishing creativity a total common culture in which a sacred symbolic structure overcame time, the sense of transience and diachrony. (Homans 1989: 338)

One could certainly argue that if Koreans have been able to limit the degree of melancholia they have experienced over the years, then much of this can be attributed to the denial of time: that division is temporary, unification eternal. Melancholy and mourning could also be avoided by viewing the north Korean people as simultaneously pure and pathetic, and by characterizing the north Korean people self-referentially as a way to criticize the south.

As we saw in the previous chapter, south Koreans sometimes represent north Koreans as a "purer" people, frozen in time by the north Korean state and unable to change through modernization. South Koreans, on the other hand, have suffered from consumerism and capitalism but can regain their Koreanness because it has been preserved in the north. In contrast, but also in complement, intense demonization of the north, though specifically a demonization of the state and not the people, has served the function of defining the south in quite positive terms, a comparison that became easier to make with the economic boom of the 1970s and 1980s, Korea's "miracle on the Han [River]."[6] South Korea's economic prosperity also provided an object of such worship and narcissistic gratification that it seemed implausible to conceive of a unified Korea in anything but the image of south Korea (see Santner 1990: 148, on an analogous reaction by west Germans in the postwar period, as they refused to dwell on the past). But this economic prosperity has produced, therefore, its own contradictions: on the one hand, south Korea has succeeded economically beyond most people's wildest dreams (and this sense of economic success remains even after the fall of south Korean currency in late 1997); on the other hand, unification stands to disrupt or at least temporarily set back the speed with which the south is growing, and therefore the object of what we might call south Koreans' narcissism. Unification will also require a reckoning with difference, especially different conceptions of history, and a direct confrontation, therefore, with south Korea's master historical narrative and mythology of homogeneity.[7]

When one looks at the literature available in south Korea on national division and unification its most obvious feature is absence: absence of debate and discussion about north Korea (especially before the late 1980s), absence of the north Korean people, absence of fictional or fantastic depictions of north Korea—that is, the absence of anything north Korean except for the north Korean state. This is a point I made in the preface and introduction and will return to again, because one of my central arguments is that the inability to mourn, as expressed through the denial of loss and the ambiguities of *han,* is linked to an absence of thinking, writing, and debating about the destabilization of Korean identity.

It seems reasonable to ask what might encourage thinking and writing about the north Korean people and about Korean identity more in Schneider's terms—as an identity that cannot be retrieved or regained, but that already exists and that will always include the division, the Korean War, and the crimes south Korea attributes to the north Korean state as some of its central features. Unification's status as a sacred goal has meant that unification has been isolated from the rest of Korean scholarship. As Maier has spoken of absence in German scholarship, "When some knowledge is put off limits and received traditions are shielded from objective reconsideration, we enter the realm of hallowing and sanctification" (1988:12). At the same time as knowledge about the north is inhibited for the sake of the sacred, the tendency to reenact and perpetuate the division is reaffirmed. The trauma of division cannot be mastered by putting off the work of mourning, by denying that division constitutes reality, or by controlling the degree to which division has become a stable and hegemonic component of Korean national identity. Rather, trauma can be mastered by recognizing that it is irreversible and by transforming the power of the lost identity into creative literary and scholarly projects.

Unlike the German and Jewish context, in which there have been concerted arguments against writing about the Holocaust, as Ellen Fine has put it, "for fear of betraying the sanctity of the subject" (1988: 42), the Korean context has offered few opportunities to establish such debate, or even to frame the absence of literature in similar terms. Because it is a sacred goal, there has been no explicit argument that one should avoid discussion of unification. Despite the fear among Germans and Jews alike, the literature on the Holocaust and Nazism is enormous, because even when people choose not to write about these issues, they write about having made the choice not to do so.

Is it simply that national security laws have prohibited extended and elaborate discussion of north Koreans and unification? Or is it something deeper, as for Holocaust victims, a fear that the imagination will contaminate the sacred nation, or, alternatively, especially for those who have never lived in a unified Korea, a fear that one does not have the right to speak for others?

Whatever the answer to these questions, it is probably not an overstatement to say that for most south Koreans today the idea of the north remains a vague constellation of concepts such as homogeneity, heterogeneity, communism, and democracy. The southern idea of the north shows us not only the lack of knowledge south Koreans have about the north, but also the lack of preparation for unification—emotional, social, scholarly, financial, and so on. It is this lack of preparation that makes it difficult for me to understand the words of so many people whom I meet in Korea who say that they are optimistic about the prospects for unification. In the midst of so much that is unknown, so much uncertainty, and nearly no dialogue at all with the north, it is sometimes hard for me to understand some of my interviewees' optimism about unification. Do they truly believe that their *han* will be resolved, or that the current north Korean government will collapse without another north Korean government taking its place? If mourning is about knowing what has been lost and what has survived, then Koreans have been unable to mourn. If mourning is about finding a language with which to express loss, the concept of *han* goes only part of the distance.

FIVE

DIVIDED FAMILIES

> The dream of the state is to be one, while the
> dream of individuals is to be two.
>
> —Jean-Luc Godard

I BEGIN THIS CHAPTER WITH GODARD'S JUXTAPOSITION of state and
individual, from his film *Germany Ninety 90,* written just as Germany
unified, because it leads us into the subject of unity and division. Social
theory has conventionally regarded individuals and states as perpetually
complementary and opposed in terms of merger and separation, identification and detachment. Individuals and states often seek to merge into
national singularities, whether through the image of a charismatic
leader, an idealized fatherland or motherland that replaces parent and
family as the primary object of love and identification, or through some
other political mechanism. It is the telos of statecraft to mute ethnic,
family, and other relations in the service of ties to the nation-state. In
specifically Freudian terms, the erotic instinct of the individual to
establish a "society of two" opposes the state's efforts to achieve a
totalizing unity. This is perhaps a problem for any superordinate entity,
but there is a peculiar situation in divided states. In those few political
communities conceived by their members as consisting of one people /
two states, or one true people / two false states, the energy of love and
emotion (or in psychoanalytic terms, the libidinal cathexis) is directed
not against the state but toward the idealized unified nation, the nation-
state. As the dream of the nation-state appropriates the drive, the unified
nation emerges as the symbolic union of separate, divided individuals.

In this chapter, I begin to explore south Koreans' record of their tragedy of national division to illustrate some ambiguities in representation that result from the people-state division. Through a variety of representational forms—art, poetry, schoolbooks, and everyday language and narrative, among others—we will see that the family has become a powerful symbol for the Korean nation, one that has a profound effect on the ways in which south Koreans conceptualize unification, but also that the family emerges as both isolated from, and yet also affected by, the state. The ambiguities appear most explicitly in south Korean discourses on the north Korean family, as south Koreans question whether north Koreans have remained similar to them or have changed forever. If it is only the state that has changed, then unification will bring families back together as they should be; if the state has been able to dramatically transform people and values—and this is something many people I interviewed want to deny—then unification may not truly unite divided families.

In other words, the separation of people and state takes shape in discourses on the family. These discourses, moreover, establish symbolic linkages between the nation and sexuality, the divided people of Korea and the trespassed and violated body. As we shall see, south Koreans hold that family relations have been disrupted by the division and by the power of the north Korean regime to destroy the family in the service of the state. Conflicts between state and family are, of course, found throughout the world, as states do dictate kinship practices. As John Borneman says in the context of a study on the former east and west Germanies, nation building and kinship and marriage are mutually constitutive, since nations succeed only when they are able to institutionalize conceptual apparatuses for shaping and understanding the family that are congruent with those of the state: "In this attempt to define, regularize, institutionalize, and normalize the domestic practices of the self, the state codifies the desires for specific kinds of relations and specific kinds of selves" (Borneman 1989: 59, see also Mosse 1985).

In south Korea, the state—usually the north Korean state—is often imagined as the enemy of the people, strategizing to establish patterns of belonging that strengthen the state and weaken individual and moral bonds.[1] The north Korean defectors, whom we will discuss at some length in chapter 9, and on whom many discussions of family are focused, personify this antagonistic relationship because they inhabit the ambivalent space between state and south Korean citizen. Betwixt and between, they are multivocal: although they give hope for a future unity and are on one level embraced as Korean citizens with a mixture of sympathy and curiosity, they are also viewed with suspicion. Alone in the south, the defectors become concrete examples of the much-feared dissolution of the Korean family, and reveal a central paradox whereby unification becomes represented as the reunion of families, and yet north Korea becomes represented as a place without families. Precisely because the defectors give both hope and despair about the resuscitation of sundered families, Koreans cannot mourn their lost relatives.

THE FAMILY AND THE NATION

> Being without ruler or father is the same as
> being barbarians and animals. How could men
> act like men and how could a state be state?
>
> —Statement by students of the National
> Academy in Seoul, on the eve of a strike in
> support of the king, 1873

In order to understand the culturally specific meanings of division, it will be useful to outline some general aspects of the Korean family, in particular the moral character of relations between agnates and the strength of blood ties. Although the general term for family in Korean is *kajok,* in Korean studies the term "family" has conventionally been used to translate the Korean word *chip,* meaning "home" or "household." Yet the sense of family extends beyond the house; "divided families" *[isan kajok]* include even second or third cousins divided from one another. Laurel Kendall writes:

> Household might be literally rendered in Korean as *sikku* (those who
> eat together, those who share a common domestic budget), but the
> word lacks the emotional resonance of *chip,* which connotes the
> physical structure of the house, and those who dwell there, those who
> once resided in the house, and, by very broad extension, all those
> who are (agnatic) descendants of a common ancestral house. . . . That

> married daughters or junior uncles might be called upon to subsidize
> the wedding of a daughter of the *chip* reflects notions of intimate
> kinship broader than any precise definition of "household" as a single
> domestic entity. (Kendall, 1996: 160-161, n. 10)

The strongest ties are those between parents and children; the moral relation between father and son, in particular, has been represented in terms of debt, devotion, and reverence. Roger Janelli and Dawnhee Yim Janelli have noted that during the early Chosŏn dynasty, the ideology of Confucian filial piety ordered all hierarchical relationships. Classical stories and oral literature contain tales of sons feeding their own flesh and blood to sick parents (Janelli and Janelli 1982: 50-51).[2] The relationship between fathers and their first sons is, of course, the most significant tie, for eldest sons not only provide direct lineal descent but also reside with their parents, care for them in their old age, and perform the ancestor worship rites; other sons leave and establish residence elsewhere, so they do not actually live with the ancestors or "gods" of the house. Unlike the extended sense of family throughout much of China, or the fictive kinship ties common to Japanese communities, the Korean family is more narrowly focused on actual bloodlines within a single lineage, both in terms of how a family is conceived and how a family carries out the social practices that continually define it.[3] Given the strength of lineal bonds and the emphasis on the actual display of loyalty within the family, the division of Korean families violates the conceptual foundations of that order. It is likely that this conception of the family predates conceptions of the Korean people as a "nation" in the modern sense of the term; as Carter Eckert writes, there was little pre-nineteenth-century sense of an abstract Korea: "Far more meaningful at the time, in addition to a sense of loyalty to the kind, were the attachments of Koreans to their village or region, and above all to their clan, lineage, and immediate and extended family (1991: 226-227).[4]

Given the importance of filial piety, it is perhaps not surprising that many south Korean discourses on division and unification are framed within the idiom of family. Koreans often construe division not only as the separation of the nation but also as the separation of families, and as a result unification is construed as the reunion of separated family members. The nation is the family writ large. Thus, although Korean division is sometimes represented in terms of land, or more literally the ancestor's land *(pundandoen choguk)*, the more conventional and primary representation is the division of people. Despite the fact that many whole families, or at least nuclear families, were able to flee together before the Korean War, an enormous number of people were separated from someone closely related to them. In both north and south Korea, separated spouses, sons and daughters, and brothers and sisters have had no chance to see each other, or even to contact or locate each other. Indeed, most know little or nothing about the whereabouts or condition of parents, siblings, and children over the past fifty years. The absolute lack of communication has meant that many estranged spouses, believing that their loved ones are still alive in the north, have not remarried (Kim, C. S. 1988: 4).

There are no exact or official figures on the number of south Koreans separated from their families, but one commonly hears numbers between five and six million. Official government statements that mention divided families often include north Korean families in their figures, thus doubling the figure to *il ch'ŏnman isan kajok* (ten million dispersed families), yet even then it is not known whether these figures refer to individuals or families. Whatever the positive outcomes of Korea's economic miracle in recent decades, little has happened to ease the ongoing suffering of the large number of dispersed families, and it is difficult to locate a realm of Korean life that has not been affected in some way by the dispersal.

Scholarly and government policy texts mention family and unification in the same breath, and literary, cinematic, and other artistic works often represent division and unification as the separating or reuniting of relatives. Chapters on north Korea and unification in schoolbooks at all levels of education focus on how the division and the war sundered families and created false or unnatural separations. In Korean everyday language, family division is represented as a deviation from the normal in the phrase "two bodies, one heart" *(momŭn tulirado, maŭmun hana)* commonly heard in discussions about unification. Recently, a similar sentiment has been expressed explicitly, and increasingly often, in artistic form as a body severed at the waist. In a 1993 painting by the artist Chŏng Pok-su, for example, entitled *Hanbandoŭi kkum* (Dream of the Korean peninsula), a man, woman, and child appear as a single body, with a map of Korea superimposed upon them. A snake, a common Korean symbol for wickedness, cold-bloodedness, and sexual temptation, divides the body horizontally in the shape of the thirty-eighth parallel. The woman's arm, appearing in the south, is red, while the man's arm and shoulder, appearing in the north, are blue, thus reversing the top-bottom juxtaposition of red and blue in the Korean flag (reproduced in Lee B. 1995: 106).[5] The reversal, like the merging of male, female, and child, suggests an ideal of oneness that would make divisions and differences irrelevant.[6]

The category of *isan kajok* (divided families) can include people who may actually be living within the same state but who have yet to locate one another; in fact, the term refers to anyone separated from his or her family after liberation, division, or the Korean War, no matter where the person is living. Indeed, in the absence of north-south negotiations that might have led to family visits, south Koreans focused their efforts more intensively on reuniting family members living outside of north Korea—in south Korea, Sakhalin Island, Japan, the United States, Canada, and Australia, among other places to which Koreans have emigrated. There are some estimates that about half of all Koreans living in Latin America, and a quarter of all Koreans living in the United States, are of northern origin (Abelmann and Lie 1995: 51-52, n. 7, 198-199; see also Light and Bonacich 1988; Kim, I. 1981), and there are many south Koreans who have relatives living in south Korea but have been unable to locate them due to the extensive dislocation caused by the division and war and a census registration system inadequate for locating people simply by name. Numerous Korean charitable organizations, in south Korea and elsewhere, including the Red Cross and provisional organizations of north Korea (founded and run by south Koreans of north Korean origin, people called *wŏlnammin*, or "people who came to the south"), have facilitated the reunions. If Koreans cannot truly know where their relatives are, or even whether their relatives are alive or dead, how can they mourn their loss?

Kim Choong-soon (1988: 111-112) has written on the challenges of the Korean Broadcasting System's 1983 reunion telethon in bringing together families living in the south. People held placards with information such as relatives' names and personal data (for example, "scar above left eye"). Split-screen television coverage permitted possible relatives to ask questions of each other. Kim estimates that among the registrants in the telethon more than 11 percent were reunited. For four and a half months, the program became a regular broadcast every Friday; it was at that time the most watched television program in Korean history and reunited an estimated ten thousand people with dispersed family members.

As one indication of the importance of divided families, schoolbooks for all levels contain passage after passage characterizing the *isan kajok* as a major national tragedy of division and describing how young people come to acknowledge their parents' or grandparents' suffering and are consequently motivated to work for unification. The following poignant story, as a typical example, appears in the fourth-grade, first-semester, elementary-school textbook entitled *Saenghwalŭi kiljabi* (Guide to Everyday Life), published in 1993 by the Ministry of Education. Stories such as this one are common to schoolbooks, but they are also not unusual in everyday Korean family discussions.[7]

A Wish

My father is a mailman. Some days ago, Father came back home very late at night. He was clammy with sweat and seemed tired.

"Father, why are you so late?"

"Well, there is an old man living in China who was separated from his family many years ago, and he sent a letter to his family here in Korea. It took me a long time to deliver it to the right place because the address wasn't right."

He held my hands tightly. His hands were colder than at any other time. Our family talked about the pain of separated families all night long.

Father said, "I hope I will be able to meet your grandmother in the north one day and deliver the happy news to my hometown that we are unified. I cannot understand why we can exchange letters and visit with people in China, a communist country, but not with our own people *[tongp'o]* of the same land and blood."

Father couldn't go on talking; he was thinking of his hometown again.

My father's hometown is Ch'ongjin, Hamkyongpukdo. His father came down to the south with my father during 6.25 [the Korean War] when my father was a child. My grandmother and the rest of the family were supposed to follow him right away but since the truce line was drawn they weren't able to make it. He separated from his family forty years ago, and for all that time he never even knew if they were dead or alive.

My grandfather died last year. From time to time, when he was alive, he would show us a picture faded and stained by the years and would say, "This is your grandmother. Isn't she beautiful? She may be pretty old now. She must have worked really hard with the kids."

My younger brother once asked him, "Grandfather, instead of looking at her picture, why don't you just go and get her? You prefer the picture to her?"

He answered, "I wish I could. Unification should come as soon as possible. I wish I could go and get her, but I cannot. There is a weight in the chest."

He rubbed my brother's back, and he cried all that day.

During the *isan kajok* program on TV a few years ago, we were up so late on several nights searching for Grandmother and the rest of her family, but it was no use. Grandfather had the picture of Grandmother in his hand when he passed away. The picture is now hung right next to Grandfather's portrait on the wall and underneath them is a telegram my father prepared: "Mother, we are unified now so I can go to the hometown where you live. Wait for me just a little longer. I'm running toward you right now."

The first thing Father will do after the unification is send this telegram. He still wears a hat with a white swallow design on it when he delivers mail from house to house. I wish the day will come when my Father will deliver a bagful of happy news to the northern *tongp'o*. When that day comes, Mother and I will buy some pretty postcards and send them to the children in Father's hometown.

There is a special pathos shared by all when people die without having seen their separated loved one, or to put it in more Korean terms, without erasing the longing or resolving the *han* (resentment) they experienced. One south Korean physician, Dr. Chang Ki-ryŏ, who had been given the nickname of the "Korean Albert Schweitzer"—

Schweitzer is a popular symbol of humanitarianism in south Korea (see
Linton 1989: 337-338)—for his lifelong commitment to serving the
poor, died on December 26, 1995, at the age of 86 without being
reunited with his wife. One obituary began with a lament that only now,
in spirit, has Dr. Chang gone to the north to rejoin his wife and five
children, for whom he had waited 45 years.

> He was a symbol of the divided family members *[nambuk isan kajok]*
> who never remarried because they longed for unification. Since the
> day he was separated from his family in 1951, he longed for the
> moment he could go back to his wife. At his home were placed two
> pictures of his wife. One was a young woman in her mid-thirties
> perhaps, and the other an old woman in the 1980s. His nephew, now
> living in the United States, had visited the north in 1991 and had
> brought this picture and a letter to him. Dr. Chang used to say that
> it pained him to see how much his wife had aged from raising their
> children alone. . . .
>   He once told me [the author of the obituary], "We are now
> both over eighty years old. We might not meet each other again. But
> after such a long time of being separated, how would it be different
> if I see her or not? She and I shared a real love and that love will be
> forever." . . . Maybe it was we who looked forward to their rendezvous
> with our hearts in our throats, even more than the doctor himself. . . .
> How many more divided family members will close their eyes
> without resolving their *han?* (Chang M. S. 1995: 2)

Despite the presence of the issue of divided families in schoolbooks
and in everyday conversation, the subject seldom emerges in my
interviews with younger people. However, elderly people—those who
remember their relatives, those who remember the war, and even those
whose relatives were not dispersed—are quick to discuss family as the
most important concern for north-south relations. At a *noinjŏng* (elderly
persons' center) in the industrial neighborhood of Taerim-dong, Seoul,
where I lived and conducted many interviews, discussions of family
quickly turned to characterizations of the north, as in the dialogue below
with Mrs. An, an 88-year-old woman originally from the northern
province of Hwanghae-do. She left Hwanghae-do for Seoul not long
after national liberation and during the war fled Seoul to move further

south to Taegu. As a result, she was initially separated from relatives both in Seoul and in the north—her brother remained in the north, her sister remained in Seoul until emigrating to Canada in the 1960s—but was later able to find her sister in Canada through mutual acquaintances. We spoke in Seoul in June 1993:

MRS. AN: I came from the north with my daughter when she was four years old. My brother died in the north, and I have a sister in Canada.

ROY RICHARD GRINKER: No one else?

MRS. AN: Yes, I have another sibling who could not come down from the north. I don't know whether he is alive or not. He should be eighty-two years old now.

RRG: Did you make any efforts when there was a program to find separated family members?

MRS. AN: I couldn't. Who could I talk to? Elderly people in the north die of hunger. There is nothing to eat there, right? My brother came down here [to the south] in one night because everything was taken from him and they [the communists] gave him no food rations.

RRG: Everything was taken from him?

MRS. AN: Yes, in the north they take everything from people. They are starved, starved. I mean really starved. What can they do, since everything is stolen from them? I am alive here and well because there is no hardship for me in the south. My brother must have died because there is no food to eat there. Life in the north is not even worth talking about.

RRG: If there is unification, perhaps you could find your brother.

MRS. AN: It would hard to find him, and he wouldn't be able to live that long anyway.

RRG: But if you could find him easily?

MRS. AN: I heard there is no use even if you used to have land there. I heard we can't get our land back even after liberation, I mean to say unification.

This interview, which I include here because it is fairly typical of other interviews I conducted, contains some passages that provide insights into how some south Koreans think about the north. Mrs. An's rendering of north Korea conflates present and past time so that at any point in her discussion, it is difficult to determine whether she is speaking of the north during the late 1940s and the Korean War, or if she is speaking of the north today. Indeed, for Mrs. An, as for many other interviewees, there is little difference between the two. North Korea exists in a state of frozen time. Relatives age and pass away, but the north, once presented in a south Korean television drama entitled *Tongt'oŭi Wangguk* (Frozen Kingdom), remains the same cold place where people starve, betray their relatives, and leave their children at day care centers while they work at factories. In fact, in a slip of the tongue, Mrs. An says "liberation" (which refers to 1945) instead of the intended "unification." Rather than attribute the slip to her age—since I have no reason to question Mrs. An's mental faculties—I would suggest that there is a logic to her words. Liberation, unification, division, the Korean War, divided families—these terms have to some extent become empty signs used in everyday conversation with little question, and they have been attributed meanings generalizable to all of post–World War II Korea. They are, in other words, all of a piece, woven together in a seamless historical narrative. Each concept in some way engenders the other, and each exists at a high level of abstraction. Because these are terms that have changed little in recent years, are seldom open to critical examination, and have therefore become routinized, it is not surprising that Mrs. An blends them together.[8]

Neither Mrs. An nor her friends and acquaintances in and around Taerim-dong think much about the complexities of unification; neither do they feel very optimistic about it. They have difficulty even imagining that they might one day go to the north to find their relatives or their relatives' offspring. Mrs. An, for example, may have little hope that her brother is still alive, but one might expect her to express a desire to know her brother's children. Instead, she expresses the resignation common to so many south Koreans who have long ago lost hope that unification would be achieved in their lifetimes. Such an apparent surrender relates to that category of Korean *han* called *chŏnghan,* a feeling of attachment and longing that nothing can replace. Because one cannot find the longed-for object with which to share one's *chŏng*, it "contracts" (according to Kim Dong-ree, "*chagi naeburo such'ukhanŭn*," quoted in Chŏn Y. D. 1993: 43) and remains inside, unexpressed. The misery of family separation, whether because of division or some other reason, can thus produce an attitude that resembles surrender, the belief that one must remain with one's misery as destiny. There is a pleasure to *chŏnghan* in the sense that it becomes a major constituent of identity, alongside woman, wife, or Korean, among other identities subject to misfortune. Such *han* can be characterized as the will to sustain a loss, to forfeit something out of respect for one's fate or for the sake of someone or something else. Some Korean writers (see Chŏn Y. D. 1993: 57, 63, 66) have argued that such an attitude is nihilistic *(hŏmujuŭi)* and reinforces the *han* of separation *(pyŏlhan)*, but the experience of such *han* is much closer to sacrifice than surrender. Here Freud's concept of mourning has to be relativized and made more complex, because in south Korea, "doing something" about one's suffering is not necessarily the culturally valued response to suffering.

One might, of course, question whether Mrs. An is truly resigned or simply ambivalent. For many south Koreans with relatives in the north, unification is construed as compulsory travel, or at least, some compulsory action in relation to the people or hometowns with which one is reunited. It is a desired goal that will also entail potentially unpleasant obligations. An emeritus professor at Seoul National University who had a wife and children in the north before the Korean War and eventually remarried and began a new family in the south is concerned about his obligations in a unified Korea. He said, "What about my wife and children here in Seoul? If I go to the north to see my wife and children there, how will they feel? My son here will no longer be the first son, and my wife [in Seoul] will be very upset. If I do not go to the north to see them and help them, my wife [in Seoul]—and other people too—will say, 'You are not a man.' In my heart, I want unification, but please, not during my lifetime."

In this narrative, the concept of unification emerges as a site for ambivalence and uncertainty, especially when Koreans contemplate the realities of a unified Korea. Unification thus stands as an ideal that cannot easily survive when subjected to practical considerations. As we shall see in the next section, these troubles are highlighted when south Koreans talk about north Korea and the imagined destruction of the family there. Thus, most important for this discussion is the fact that many of my south Korean informants appropriated the family as a vehicle for criticizing the north, albeit often indirectly, as when Mrs. An questions whether her relatives would even want to see her. This is an ironic point: Korean unification discourses are founded upon both family reunions *and* the belief that in the north the Korean concept of family has dissolved.

Southern Views of the North

Many south Koreans who imagine family reunions are afraid that their relatives in the north will not want to see them or will have forgotten the meaning of family. Such fears are supported by some of the information ordinary citizens receive about the north Korean state, occasional media coverage, and defectors' writings about north Korean social life. As a result, many south Koreans believe that the family has been all but destroyed in the north, in large part due to the practices of Kim Il Sung, who is well known to have substituted the state for the family. It is known, for example, that Kim Il Sung promoted loyalty among his government officials by appointing orphans to the most powerful positions; north Korean films and fiction have few father figures as central characters (Myers 1994); and north Korean defectors and captured spies have written that they were separated from their families in order to serve Kim Il Sung. In *The Tears of My Soul* (an English translation of *Ijen yŏjaka toego sip'ŏyo*, "Now I want to be a woman"), Kim Hyun-hee's account of her bombing of a Korean airplane in the late 1980s, her father, angry about his talented daughter's training as an intelligence officer, says, "You're not my daughter anymore. You belong to them." And later he says, "But it would be foolish not to acknowledge that, practically speaking, you are now the Party's daughter, not ours" (1993: 77).

   In another account of north Korea, the well-known south Korean actress Choi Eun-hee writes of her abduction and eight years of residence in north Korea, "I will never forget the images of housewives enslaved by work, having forgotten that thing called family *[kajokiranŭn kŏt]*, children who became like machines, deprived of the innocence of childhood. As I watched. . . . I thought they had lost the sense of family" (1988: 4; see also Shin S. O. 1988). Similarly, a 1989 study of anti-communist education

(Hwang I. S. 1989) shows that south Korean school textbooks have, for the most part, characterized north Korea as a place where people are forced to think, behave, and live in large groups, making intimate family life impossible. According to the textbooks' characterizations, which do not appear to be based on much data or first-hand knowledge of the north, children and their parents lead separate daily lives, although, to be precise, the textbooks explicitly say that children are "separated from their families" because they go to day care centers. In the event that children hear their parents say something negative about the government of north Korea, they are compelled to report it to their teachers so that their parents can be punished (Hwang I. S. 1989: 26). Family life and loyalty between parents and children are therefore represented in the books as something impossible for north Koreans to comprehend.

The folksinger and defector Kim Yong says that most north Koreans who live in provinces different from those of their parents visit them "less than once a year," and he points out that when he arrived in south Korea he had never before heard the words *ppuri* (roots, genealogy) or *pongwan* (ancestral home) (Kim, Y. 1992: 25, 263, 265-286). During a radio broadcast of his show *Namkwabuk* (South and North) in 1993 (a broadcast for which I was present in the studio), Kim answered a letter from a fan asking him why he hadn't married and if the north Koreans have a concept such as *sarangaenŭn kuggyŏngi ŏpda* (love knows no national boundaries). He reported that many north Koreans who had traveled outside of north Korea as students or diplomats and who had married foreigners were forced to divorce, even if they had children. All of these married people, he said, had become divided families *(isan kajok)*.

Many south Koreans have seen television interviews conducted at nursery schools and playgrounds in P'yŏngyang in which young children refer to Kim Il Sung as their father. In one famous televised interview repeatedly mentioned by my interviewees, a Japanese journalist approached a young boy eating a piece of candy his mother had given him and asked where he had gotten the candy. The boy replied, "From the Great Leader, my father." In fact, north Korean news media and creative writing contain few representations of teachers or father figures; Kim Il Sung (and, more recently, Kim Jong Il) appears only secondarily as a father figure, but primarily as a mother figure, his mannerisms described in literature as feminine, motherly, nurturing, and soft; his

Kim Il Sung as a parental figure. (*Korea Today*, P'yŏngyang, DPRK.)

face as indulgent, round, dimpled, and relaxed (Myers 1994). Both Kims are praised by the Korean Workers Party (Nodongdang) press for bringing abandoned or orphaned children from the countryside into the bosom of P'yŏngyang for sustenance. Kim Il Sung has often been referred to as *ŏbŏi*, a term that condenses "mother" and "father".[9]

Simply for lack of data from the north, I do not take up in detail north Korean discourses on the south Korean family. However, anecdotal evidence from north Korean newspapers I have read, as well as defector interviews and writings, suggest that the main argument in the north is that capitalism in the south has destroyed family solidarities in the service of money. It is, indeed, ironic that both southern and northern perspectives on the other argue that opposing ideologies produce the same result: one harms the family through loyalty to the state, the other through loyalty to capital.

To return to southern discourses on the north, the family is imagined to be further harmed by the fact that, because of national division, south and north Koreans cannot adequately perform funeral rites for their relatives across the border; north Koreans, it is widely believed, are prohibited from ancestor worship or tomb-visiting services (Kim, Y. 1992: 263-268). Burial sites are selected by the government, so people usually

Kim Il Sung with children. (*Korea Today,* P'yŏngyang, DPRK.)

cannot bury their relatives near other family members, near their home-towns, or at a place chosen as propitious by a fortune-teller. Defectors report an almost total absence of genealogy except in the most rural villages. Defectors also note that, for as long as they can remember, census registrations have excluded family history information. One of the few popular books on north Korean social life, *ŏ, kŭrae?* (Is that so?), based almost entirely on defector writings, states that the Korean Workers Party believes that genealogies are feudal, and that, as a consequence, north Koreans do not discuss their roots or *chŏnt'ong* (family traditions) and do not even have family reunions (Yi, P. K. 1995: 61, 64).[10] Similarly, in the 1996 revision of the second-year middle-school textbook on ethics, the Ministry of Education writes that in north Korea, "traditional ancestor services are believed to be vestiges of a superstition and feudalism, and so have been officially abolished" (p. 248).

It would indeed be difficult for many north Koreans to identify themselves genealogically, since Korean genealogies are written in *han-mun* or *hanja* (Chinese characters used in Korean writing). North Koreans do not know many *hanmun* and do not learn to write their own names in Chinese characters.[11] One defector, Chŏn ch'ŏl-woo (1994:

173-175), writes that when he applied for a residence identity card in Seoul, he was asked to identify his *pongwan* (ancestral home)—a question he could not answer because he had almost no knowledge of his lineage. Someone at the identity card office also named Chŏn suggested he take the same *pongwan* as he had; for the Chinese characters with which to write his name, he chose the most common characters for the sound of his name. Chŏn writes that "unification should be done while our parents' generation is still alive, or else they will die with the memory of the *chokpo* [genealogies] in their minds. If unification is achieved only for those who are now young and who know nothing of their *pongwan* or Chinese characters, then it will be almost impossible to reunite family members separated in north and south" (1994: 175).

The conflict between the vision of unification as the union of families and the belief that the northern family has dissolved—as well as the liminal (one might say "no-win") position of the defectors—is highlighted in a recent editorial in *Hanguk ilbo* on defectors to south Korea. The author comments on his concern upon discovering that a north Korean woman, Ch'oi Soo-bong, defected from her diplomatic post in Zambia (where, like north Korean diplomats everywhere, she was stationed without her children); he suggests that for north Koreans ideology comes first and family comes second:

> How could she leave her children in north Korea? It is against one's basic instincts because blood is thicker than water. Or perhaps, as with cults, ideology takes precedence over one's responsibility as a mother. . . . Until today, our greatest tragedy was the separation of families, but that separation was carried out by external forces. For us, the reunion of the separated families is the most important goal in our lives. Now the greatest tragedy is that families are making the choice to separate. (Chun, S. I. 1996: 12)

Despite the fact that it is the defectors who are responsible for circulating this information about the family (or lack thereof) in north Korea, they are also angry about the repercussions. Several of the defectors I interviewed in 1996 explained that they have been hurt by south Korean criticisms of their defections. Although they appear to be welcomed into south Korea and are cited as the evidence of the failures of the north

불초자(不肖子)

During a south Korean telethon to reunite sundered families, Korea's mythical ancestor, Tangun, takes Kim Il Sung and Kim Jong Il to task. (Y. H. Kim, *Y. H. Kim's Editorial Cartoons.*)

Korean regime, they are also criticized publicly—and more infrequently in private interpersonal confrontations—for an absence of *hyo* (loyalty and love for one's parents).[12]

In a television interview segment for the program *Ch'ujŏk 60 Minutes* (March 25, 1996), a segment that was never aired, the defector Kim Ho says that he has been told that he is not a *hyoja* (a man who has *hyo* toward his parents).[13] This is a very telling statement because it illuminates the irony to which I referred earlier. The defectors personify the vexing problem of a unification discourse that is founded upon reuniting something that may no longer exist. Kim quickly defended himself. He argued that north Koreans do have "a consciousness of *hyo*" and that most defectors left the north for the sake of their parents— to have stayed and been imprisoned would have increased the chances for their parents to be imprisoned, sent to a labor camp, or even executed. When Kim, a former logger in Russia, realized that he would be arrested for speaking negatively about north Korea, he decided his family would be better off if he simply "disappeared;" he hoped that a disappearance would spare his family.

The Korean War Monument Statue of Brothers.
(Reprinted with permission of Choi Young Jeep.)

If unification is construed as the recovery of the family, whether by
reuniting sundered families or by bringing north Koreans back into a
more Confucian kinship universe, then north and south are generally
construed in family and hierarchical terms as well, sometimes as siblings
and at other times as spouses. The most frequently used metaphor for
south-north relations is that between elder brother (the south) and
younger brother (the north), a metaphor that can easily be characterized
as patronizing.[14] The elder brother must save the younger brother, who
is astray in a world stunted by communism: historian Park Il Sung calls
south Korea an "older brother" who will lead and rejuvenate north
Korea, "the younger brother who is astray and ill" (1983: 206). The
same symbolism is represented in a statue in Korea's new war museum
entitled "*Hyŏngjeŭi sang*" (Statue of brothers), which depicts a south
Korean soldier (an older brother) embracing his younger brother, a
north Korean soldier he meets on the battlefield. In addition, on July 13,
1994, four days after the death of Kim Il Sung, *Hanguk ilbo* ran an
editorial saying, "We need to sympathize with and help the north
Koreans with the heart of an older sister."[15]

And in a funny photographic juxtaposition of Kim Il Sung and Kim Yong-sam, printed in the Korean-language newspaper *Korea Post* just as the two announced their plan for a first summit—a summit that never happened, due to Kim Il Sung's death—Kim Il Sung is dressed in a conventional Korean bride's costume adjacent to Kim Young Sam who is wearing a groom's costume. It would, of course, have been a major faux pas in south Korea to depict Kim Young Sam as the woman, but the point to be stressed here is that the two Kims are represented as marriage partners. I will return to the metaphor of the nation as spouse at the end of this chapter when I briefly consider Sheila Miyoshi Jager's argument that national division has become symbolically represented in terms of sexual violation.

UNIFICATION AND GENERATION X

If there is one concern that clearly dominates current south Korean discourses on everyday life, it is the failure of Korea's youth (the new generation, or *sinsedae,* sometimes now referred to as "*X-sedae*"—that is, "Generation X"— a copy of the popular American word for people in their twenties) to preserve conventional Korean values of loyalty, family, and community. As Nancy Abelmann has phrased it, "People bemoan the loss of *insim* (human feeling),[16] *chŏng* (human emotion), *yeŭi* (manners; propriety), and *kongdongch'e* (community), among others. Some of these losses have additionally been mapped generationally on the so-called *sinsedae* (new generation), a generation distinguished by its lack of restraint and respect" (n.d.: 2). I have heard older Koreans say that younger Koreans have little desire for unification or family reunions because they do not want to sacrifice for the common good. Unification might mean a loss of income, higher taxes, greater social obligations, and a general economic instability that the wealthy and the young do not want to accept. According to some of my interviewees, those young people, especially students, who are committed to unification are committed not for the sake of family, but for other reasons, ranging from their hope for an economic and political utopia to a desire for democracy, sovereignty, and the recuperation of Korean values lost during what students some-times refer to as the "American occupation." Though the students, like most Koreans, are committed to unification, they are often believed to be primarily devoted to the idea of the sovereign and united *kukt'o* (national

Kim Il Sung as bride and Kim Young Sam as groom in a computer-generated photo. (Courtesy of *Sisa Journal*, Seoul, Republic of Korea.)

land) rather than to people and community. Some older interviewees suggest that younger people fight for unification as an end in itself without really knowing what they are fighting for, thus positing an opposition between ideology and experience.

Older Koreans also criticize younger people as rude and say that they speak Korean poorly, know so few *hanmun* that they cannot even read the newspaper, and are interested only in American movies and music. To a certain extent, discourses on the young often replicate discourses on the elite or wealthy, because both are criticized for departing from "traditional" Korean ways, and because the most conspicuously wealthy Koreans are young people. The wealthy young in particular, pejoratively called *orenji jok* (or "orange tribe"), are said to spend too much money on entertainment and clothing, to engage freely in premarital sex, and to have little appreciation of how their luxurious lives were made possible by the suffering of their predecessors. During the south Korean economic crisis that began toward the end of 1997, older Koreans felt vindicated by the frugality campaigns; the entire country seems to have turned against affluence and consumption.

Different criticisms are leveled against students, student leaders (many of whom are no longer students), or younger non-elites, since students have over the years led a powerful drive for unification, democracy, and the revival of the Korean *minjung,* or masses (see chapter 7).[17] Student activists, among the most notable of whom is Im Su-kyŏng (who as a senior French major in Seoul went to north Korea in 1989, and who is discussed in more detail in chapter 8), have also spearheaded efforts to travel illegally to the north, violating draconian national security laws and sacrificing their own futures for the sake of unification. During the late 1980s a large number of students also traveled to rural areas to help the farmers (idealized as the true *minjung)* and to facilitate and participate in the revival of Korean traditions (in a movement called *nongch'on pongsah-waltong, nongch'onhwaltong,* or *nonghwal* for short, meaning "agricultural activities"; see Abelmann 1996). Although older Koreans may not criticize students for lacking a commitment to unification, they are nonetheless critical of the students' methods and frequently associate student activists (often pejoratively called *ppalgaengi chiptan,* or "reds," in the Korean press) with north Korean propaganda, Kim Il Sung, and *chuch'e sasang* (Kim Il Sung's ideology of self-reliance). While students advocate reconciliation, friendship, and exchange with the north, conservative and older Koreans often argue that south Korea needs to be so committed to unification that it uses its military force to destroy the north Korean regime, even if it causes great hardships or losses of Korean life.

Im Su-kyŏng, for instance, was the object of an enormous amount of vitriol suggesting that, by going to the north, she became a pawn of northern propaganda, hurt efforts toward persuading the north Korean people of their leader's evils, and thus contributed to the ongoing division of families. When she returned from north Korea weak from a hunger strike and was hospitalized in Seoul under high security that inconvenienced many patients and their families, the conservative media criticized her for dividing them and more generally criticized her for harming her own family's reputation and causing them distress. In the more liberal media, her trip to north Korea was construed not as a separation from her family, but as a separation from her lover, Yun Wŏn-chŏl, thus pitting the "modern" generation's devotion to romantic love against devotion to one's family. The journal *Mal* reproduced Im's passionate goodbye letter to her lover; and, in an extraordinary passage, the liberal paper *Hangyŏre sinmun* suggested in an editorial that Yun was so distraught that he could not celebrate Ch'usŏk (Korean Thanksgiving) with his family.[18]

These conflicts are highlighted in an illuminating 1988 Korean television drama entitled *Chae 3ŭi kukkyŏng* (The Third Border), based on the novel by Mun Sun-tae of the same title. The drama tells a story of three men originally from north Korea (Park Dong-sik, Yi Sang-wŏn, and Pae Ch'ŏl-do) whose incarceration in a prisoner-of-war camp at the end of the Korean War solidified their friendship but also ended in their geographic dispersal. Park chose the south, Yi chose nonaligned India, and Pae chose to return to the north to find his wife, Keum-soon, who, unbeknownst to her husband, had traveled south in search of him. Yi becomes an extraordinarily wealthy businessman in India, Park opens an electronics repair shop named Samwu (three friends), and there is absolutely no information known about the whereabouts of Pae. Park is consumed with nostalgia, a love of the past, the memories of his hometown, and the hope that he can return there in a unified Korea. The story centers around Yi's surprise visit to Seoul and Park's anticipation and excitement at the prospect of seeing his friend for the first time in more than thirty years. Park not only wants desperately to see the friend for whom he maintains his devotion and loyalty, but also to ask for his assistance in getting news about Pae for Pae's wife in south Korea. Always in the background, Park's activist son, Park Yun-ki, the first in the family to attend college, awaits trial in prison for violations of the national security laws.

The film is intended to illustrate that, much to Park's dismay, both Yi and Yun-ki appear to have little devotion to him and treat him with indifference and condescension. The former has no interest in helping anyone but himself and comes to Korea only to make money, not because he feels himself to be Korean; he is critical of Park for "living in the past" and says quite explicitly that he has seldom given any thought to the old days. Park's son can barely look his father in the eyes, saying only that the miserable days of the past are irrelevant to his work as a student and dissident. When Yun-ki is released from prison at the end of the film, Park and his wife try to greet their son and bring him home, but the son walks away with few words other than "I have more important things to do with my friends."

Park Yun-ki has committed himself to a vision of Korea that departs from that of his family; because his vision does not include any apparent loyalty to his father or concern for his father's suffering, he represents the stereotype of the young person who has lost the value of family, or *hyo*. He is the epitome of the elders' characterization of the *ppalgaengi*, or "reds," who disregard family in favor of communism. He views the past with derision and cannot see that unification and democracy are, indeed, both about the past—that they concern the resuscitation of a five-thousand-year-old nation that is the will of the people, sovereign and whole.

The Third Border does not privilege any particular position and, instead of simply depicting an irreconcilable difference between father and son, draws a parallel between them. Park and his son seem equally out of touch with the realities of their lives, and so are unable to achieve any substantive change. Their impotence stems from an inability to comprehend the present—one lives in the past, the other in the future— while Yi's callousness stems from a rejection of his place in a continuous, ongoing history.

THE TALE OF CH'UNHYANG: LOVE, SEPARATION, AND HAN

In sharp contrast to Park's son, famous figures in Korean literature and folklore unselfishly sacrifice their needs for their spouses and families. *The Tale of Ch'unhyang (Ch'unhyang chŏn)*, discussed in the previous chapter, is especially important in this regard because every Korean knows at least the outline of the story, and because it makes salient some of the central features of a sort of *han* (*han* as sacrifice) that I have been discussing in relation to divided families and lost loves. More specifically, the tale metaphorically represents the relation between family (and especially marriage) and national division. Ch'unhyang is the metaphor for the nation, violated by an apparatus of the state, while her devotion to her future husband is a metaphor for Koreans' devotion to family and national unity. The tale thus crystallizes the hardships of Korean history, the antagonistic relations between nation-people and state, and the process through which the nation becomes construed in terms of family, marriage, and sexual violence. For this reason, the tale has increasingly figured into student and dissident discourses on unification, as the separated lovers become a metaphor for north and south Korea, forcibly divided by an external or foreign male—in one case the evil governor, in the other, the American military. Another element of the Ch'unhyang story that needs to be highlighted is the ability of the oppressed lovers to wait for their inevitable union.

Before stressing the relations between Ch'unhyang and the family, I want to note that Ch'unhyang was able to rise from a state of misery and achieve a new strength out of her hardship. Jager (1996) asserts that Ch'unhyang is the ideal Confucian woman, and indeed this is how the story of Ch'unhyang has been commonly read. Jager analyzes the tale in order to demonstrate the degree to which the division of Korea has been symbolically linked with violation of the female body. However, it should be stated that while Ch'unhyang may be a good example of the ideal of a woman's ability to resist violation and to remain devoted to her husband, she is not the ideal woman in Confucian terms; indeed, she is construed as attractive in part because she does not conform to Confucian ideals. For example, Ch'unhyang is rebellious; some versions of the tale imply that she and her fiancé had premarital sex, or at the very least that she was sexually playful with him (not at all the Confucian ideal) in her mother's house (a site that could be attributed a variety of levels of respectability). Portions of one very modern version of the Ch'unhyang story contain explicit descriptions of sexual activity. In some others, Ch'unhyang is represented as ugly, Yi breaks off his engagement with her, and she dies without resolving her *han;* her soul then wanders around Chŏlla-do and makes the land infertile as an expression of her suffering, though she is later reincarnated and there is a happy ending. Thus the importance of Ch'unhyang may lie, mostly, not in her devotion to her future husband or in her exemplification of Confucian ideals, but in her ability to transform potentially paralyzing *wŏnhan* into patience, strength, and reconciliation. Indeed, it is this ability to find the high moral ground within a sea of violence and anger that makes some thinkers optimistic about south Koreans' capacity to eventually extend themselves to the north rather than absorb or attack the north in an explosion of *han* (Park D. U. 1996).

In focusing on Ch'unhyang, Jager makes a significant contribution by demonstrating a symbolic pattern of association between the nation and sexuality, of which the tale of Ch'unhyang is no doubt a part. Jager writes that "the figure of the anguished, lonely female, unduly separated from family and friends, is a ubiquitous presence in Korea" (1996: 4), and that the tale of Ch'unhyang established a genre tradition for representing the nation as a despoiled woman (see also Standish 1994).

Clearly there must be something powerful in the tale of Ch'unhyang that has helped it remain a favorite story for more than a hundred years. For Jager, the story's power seems to be in its juxtaposition of the elite governor (who symbolizes the foreign, and whom Ch'unhyang herself characterizes as somewhat non-Korean and without a love for the Korean people) with Ch'unhyang, a symbol of the people. Their relation is analogically equivalent to the juxtaposition of Korea and foreign nations in a long historical process of confrontation and resistance. Indeed, Jager argues that "resistance to the division, and the virtuous struggle for reconciliation that it implied, took the allegorical form of resistance to the foreign male" (1996: 13)—that is, the "foreign males" (the superpowers) who divided Korea. "Conjugal reunion, and by extension, national consolidation, could be achieved only if women adhered to the principles of Confucian virtue, that is, by faithfully awaiting the arrival of their (absent) husbands and resisting other (Western) men's sexual advances" (1996: 13). In another work, Jager also notes that the state's primary instrument of suppression against student protestors in recent years—tear gas—is widely thought to impair reproductive function, thus interrupting the normal continuity of life and blood (1994: 256). These arguments are supported by the data provided by Jager and by the easily recognizable association between division and familial separation illustrated in the first section of this chapter. Clearly, as I have noted, the public reactions in both conservative and liberal media to Im Su-kyŏng's travel to north Korea symbolically elaborated her transgression and separation in family terms, as Im and her family, patients and their families at the hospital in which Im was being treated, and Im and her lover, Yun, all came to stand for the divided nation. Im represents a form of suffering generalizable to the nation.

As Jager points out, the association between nation and sexual violence has been repeated time and again in various forms of Korean discourses—in abstract terms, such as in the tale of Ch'unhyang and in Confucianist writings on the necessary relation between proper conjugal relations and the well-being of the larger social order, and in a more concrete fashion, as in the characterization of Japanese colonialism, the division, the Korean War, and the presence of American troops in Korea, in terms of their actual sexual consequences: rape, the Japanese forced conscription of sexual slaves (the "comfort women"—see Choi, C.

1997), and the destruction of Korean "racial integrity" through the mixed-race offspring of Korean women and American men. These latter images have become important elements in student and intellectual support for self-reliance *(chuch'e)*, sovereignty, and autonomy *(chuch'esŏng)*, as well as in opposition to Korea's dependence on outside powers (*sadaejuŭi*, literally "the doctrine of serving the great [China]") (Robinson, 1988: 34).[19]

Indeed, it is here in the intersection between the nation and sexual violence that the family becomes so important. As Jager notes, there are many national communities throughout the world that have depicted violence against the nation in terms of violence against the female body, but in Korea there is a culturally specific pattern of construing sexual violence within the context of marriage. Jager shows that the contemporary significance of Ch'unhyang lies not only in marking the foreign and external as male but also in a particularly *Korean* narrative patterning of love, loss, and reunion. This is a pattern that can be seen clearly in dissident discourses that frame unification as a "coming home."

In this chapter, then, I come full circle, from a consideration of divided families as a primary representation of national division and cultural differentiation between north and south, to an exploration of the important concept of *han* and its relation to the role of marriage and separated families in the constitution of Korean nationalism. It comes as no surprise that the division of a nation will be associated with the division of the body or the division of the family; among the most powerful, familiar, and immediate experiences we have are the wholeness of our bodies and the merging of our individual lives with those of intimate family members. Symbolic representations always arise out of that which is closest to us. The intellectual challenge is to discern how these representations become part of a larger pattern of thought and practice and how that pattern affects political practices. The next chapters continue this exploration by bringing together the concepts described here with an analysis of school textbooks, student protests, and an account of three south Koreans who defied the national security laws to travel to north Korea in 1989 to promote unification, people who believe that they stand for the unity of the people against the division of the nation into two false states.

A number of anthropologists specializing in refugee studies have recently noted how the challenging study of "part-societies" or displaced communities brings into sharp focus the vocabulary of nationhood and national identity (Malkki 1995; Daniel and Knudsen 1995; Ghosh 1993; Krulfeld and Camino 1994; Harell-Bond and Voutira 1992). This and subsequent chapters clarify the complex ways in which attachments to the nation are construed in the highly symbolic and moral terms of violation. It is true that the defectors and the three travelers who defied the national security laws by going to north Korea all committed acts of transgression, but the very fact that they transgressed was predetermined by a prior transgression of wholeness: the division of the nation. Separation, division, displacement, and defection are violations of the conceptual order of wholeness, what Malkki refers to as the "national order of things," and unification is the conceptual response to those violations.

ELEMENTARY FORMS OF KOREAN HISTORICAL REPRESENTATION: SCHOOL TEXTBOOKS

Ah ah, how could we forget
The day our enemies trampled on our country
Blocking them with our bare fists and red blood
Stomping on the ground, shaking with righteous
    indignation
Now we will pay you back, our enemies of this day
We will run and run after the retreating enemy.
And our country and people will shine
When we defeat each and every man among our
    enemies.

          —Elementary-school song, South Korea, ca. 1970

Unification
We used to be one
Spoke the same language
Had the same customs
Respected the same ancestors
If we could meet, we could be
Friendly right away
But we just envy the birds
Flying between Paekdu and Halla mountains

        —Children's song from *Ppo ppo ppo*, 1996

"Under the leadership of Kim Il Sung and his comrade Joseph Stalin, northern communists invaded the south on June 25, 1950, and started the Korean War." The statement is, for nearly all south Koreans, an unquestionable truth. So in 1996, when a television program designed for toddlers and elementary-school-aged children aired a special feature on the Korean War and yet failed to clearly place blame on the north, some people were outraged. After all, first-grade textbooks, as late as 1989, argued that the north Koreans were cold-blooded killers who continue to show no remorse for their deeds and will do anything to communize the whole peninsula. 1996 elementary and middle-school textbooks—perhaps the most propaganda-free textbooks ever assembled in south Korea—explicitly say that the north started the war. Moreover, even high-school level textbooks perpetuate the conventional historiographic myopia by focusing attention almost exclusively on the events of that one day, June 25, rather than viewing the war as part of a complex series of social, economic, and political transformations beginning at least during Japanese colonial rule at the start of this century.

Yet the construction of nationhood is as much a process of forgetting as it is remembering; it is a process of filtering, condensing, and organizing the complexities and uncertainties of history into the well-bounded and highly specific terms that constitute national narratives: dates, periods, actors, and plots, among others. There is an additional but related aspect of forgetting, however, that extends the point that nations are invented traditions (Thom 1990: 31), namely, the capacity "to forget to remember" (Bhabha 1990: 311). The danger of memory—and more specifically of creating new memories or altering memories through revisionist historical scholarship—is that it shows that nations are composed of fragments. Nations, one might suggest, would not be nations if they embraced revisionist or competing histories; nations are partialities made to appear total, yet when that process is unmasked, certainties become uncertainties, truths become contingencies, the natural becomes the cultural.

A south Korean journalist named Cho Sŏng-kwan published an article in 1996 in one of the most popular monthly magazines in south Korea, *Wŏlgan chosŏn*, in which he argued that the televised children's program, aired on June 25, the day the war had begun in 1950, was guilty of revisionist history. The producers and writers represented the war and its effects in perhaps the simplest terms possible and emphasized brotherhood in the future instead of resentment in the past. In fact, this emphasis parallels that of the most recent school textbooks in south Korea. But the program struck to the heart of some people's concerns that Korea is forgetting its old history and creating a new and subversive one, that young people have little awareness of the suffering of those who produced the great country in which they are being raised, and that, as a result, north Koreans will escape paying for their sins. Indeed, in August 1996, President Kim Young Sam blamed the violent student protests (widely characterized as pro-north) on the educational system, saying that educators were not providing students with the proper guidance. He argued that south Korean schools, and especially universities, had failed to provide their students with an appropriate ideological and philosophical education (Korea Herald, Aug. 22, 1996, on-line edition), and that as one consequence students were becoming increasingly pro-north. Thus, the children's program could not be reconciled with south Koreans' continued and widespread resentment toward the north, a resentment that often takes shape in discourses on education.

For my purposes here, the program and Cho's response to it resonate with a number of themes central to this chapter: children's textbooks as an institutional framework for nationhood; the potentially coercive role of education; and the relations among education, the demonization of north Korea, and Korean unification. The program is also linked with the difficult question of how south Koreans can overcome their resentment and reconcile with the north without violating the various spoken and unspoken rules prohibiting statements that are "pro-north." Will reconciliation demand the passing of the older generations who experienced the war or who were educated with propaganda? Or will the younger generations wish to keep things as they are? With these themes and questions in mind, I take a closer look at this children's program and then look at how the treatment of unification, division, and the differences and similarities between north and south Koreans in elementary and middle-school textbooks has changed over the past thirty years. It will be apparent that the textbooks are increasingly less focused on the Korean War and more focused on difference, heterogeneity, and the social and cultural dimensions of unification. But at the same time that the texts have become more open to the idea of heterogeneity and have become increasingly less anti-communist, they continue to explicitly support the south Korean state and to present north Korea only in vague terms.

PPO PPO PPO AND THE KOREAN WAR

The children's television show *Ppo ppo ppo* opened with a group of young
boys and girls singing a song called "T'ongil" (Unification). At the center
of the ornate set was positioned a large pink heart, fractured down the
middle; the left side contained the syllable *T'ong-*, the right side *-il*.
Following a short English lesson, the scene shifted to three people sitting
outside a museum and talking about the Korean War, or, as it is conventionally called, "6.25" [June 25, 1950]. The speakers are two unnamed boys
(played by grown men) who for simplicity's sake I will call Sang-joon and
Kyŏng-ku, and an adult emcee, whom I will call Ŏnni. One boy is dressed
in lime-green traditional Korean boys' attire; the other is dressed in a very
contemporary manner, in black pants, combat boots, and a white T-shirt.
Ŏnni appears in sneakers, a flowered T-shirt, and overalls.

> ŎNNI: Today's subject is 6.25 [June 25]. Do you know what it is?
>
> SANG-JOON: 6.25—it sounds familiar.
>
> KYŎNG-KU: Yes, that's the day a war started.
>
> SANG-JOON: Yeah I think I heard about it from my dad.
>
> KYŎNG-KU: Who fought with whom?
>
> ŎNNI: I knew you didn't know!
>
> KYŎNG-KU: Then why did you ask me?
>
> ŎNNI: Just to see how much you knew about 6.25.
>
> SANG-JOON: Why should I know about it; it happened a long time
> ago.
>
> KYŎNG-KU: That's right. 6.25 has nothing to do with me. It's not
> even a holiday.
>
> ŎNNI: Come here, I'll teach you.
>
> [The scene shifts to the two boys standing before the tombstones of
> soldiers at the national cemetery; they read the names solemnly, one
> by one.]
>
> ŎNNI: These are people who died for our country.

[The two boys look surprised.]

BOTH BOYS: All these people?

KYŏNG-KU: I will take back what I said before.

SANG-JOON: Me too.

ŎNNI: Listen carefully, I'll teach you. [Camera moves to a display narrating the war.] The war between north and south started at dawn on 6.25.50. Within three days, southern soldiers lost Seoul to northern soldiers. Foreign countries sent their troops to help the southerners, our military soldiers joined with the foreigners. They fought the northerners and pushed them. Our soldiers went so far north they could even drink water from the Amrok river. Then the Chinese started to help the northerners. Huge numbers of Chinese soldiers organized and came down to help the north. At night, they played flutes and drums and the sound made our soldiers realize how many Chinese there were; every night people could hear Chinese soldiers playing music and that sound was scarier than the gunfire. That's why our soldiers came back to the south. A truce line was drawn in the middle of Korea.

SANG-JOON: It is a sad story.

KYŏNG-KU: It is a real war story. It is thrilling. Please tell me some more.

[ŎNNI appears upset.]

SANG-JOON: Are you upset [Ŏnni]?

ŎNNI: Yes, I am. Because you both seem as if you are listening to a myth [*yetnal yegi*], but this is a true story. And as you know, the south and north are divided by the truce line.

KYŏNG-KU: But we haven't experienced a war.

SANG-JOON: Yeah, that's why we don't know anything about the war.

ŎNNI: Okay, follow me.

[The three go to the war displays at the new national war memorial museum. They, and the audience, can hear the sound of gunfire, the shoutings of soldiers. The scene shifts and the boys are shown examining a statue of two soldiers, one from the north and one from the south, in an embrace.]

KYŎNG-KU: So you're saying that in our hearts there is a true love of brotherhood *[hanhyŏngje]* and blood *[hanpitchul]*.

SANG-JOON: If unification is achieved, I want to hug my north Korean friends.

ALL [in an embrace]: Me too, me too, me too!

The journalist reacted bitterly to the program. He argued that it was "too neutral and objective," in particular in its use of the equivalent terms "northern soldiers" and "southern soldiers" to describe the military. Cho writes that the program gives the message "that 6.25 is a war that happened between north and south and that it is no longer important to define who invaded whom first. As the northerners and southerners are the same people, we have to reconcile with them for unification" (1996: 2). Such a characterization, he says, might be found in a "third country" such as Canada or Australia, but should not appear in Korea. Cho reproduced his conversation with the writer of the program, who, he stressed, was a young man in his mid-twenties.

CHO: Why didn't you use the word *namch'im* [southern invasion] or *ch'imryak* [invasion] to explain the origin of 6.25?

WRITER: How could I use such political terms on a children's program?

CHO: North Korea's "invasion" is not a political expression but a historical truth.

WRITER: Since we said the north came down to the south before the south went to the north, don't you think that children will infer the appropriate sequence of events?

CHO: No one can understand how 6.25 happened if you say it that way.

WRITER: Frankly, the word *namch'im* is too difficult for young children.

CHO: Then you could say that they came down first or attacked first.

WRITER: I thought it was not that important. The main focus of this program was to produce the very feelings one gets looking at the brothers statue,[1] to express the will for unification.

Later, Mr. Cho interviewed the producer, who is also young, and the writer together.

CHO: What was the intention of the 6.25 special?

PRODUCER: With the exception of Independence Day, 6.25, Constitution Day, and March 1 Movement Day, *Ppo ppo ppo* does not air special features. In the case of 6.25, I wanted children to remember that we experienced a terrible war and to emphasize its dangers—so that we don't have another war, and for the sake of unification.

CHO: But if you want children to know that we experienced the war, don't you think that the program should be based on historical facts? Why didn't you, at least, use the expression "north Korean communists?"

PRODUCER: Well, why didn't I use it? I don't know. Maybe I didn't think it was a good expression. I thought it was not necessary for it to be in the script when I checked it for the last time.

CHO: By using the terms *namhangun* [southern soldiers] and *pukhangun* [northern soldiers] in the same line, you put them on an equal footing and made the war neutral.

PRODUCER: Well, maybe, yes.

CHO: Do you think you, as a representative of Korea's *[taehanmin-guk]* broadcasting company [sic], should take a neutral and objective position to explain the origin of 6.25 and neglect to use the terms "communist," "southern invasion," or "invasion"?

PRODUCER: I don't know much about that. I gather you saw the entire program. I focused more on the matter of unification, which is why I ended the program in the way I did.

CHO: Perhaps there are some children who learned about 6.25 for the first time through this program. Is it right for you to teach them about 6.25 without giving them clear answers about the origin of the war?

PRODUCER: So, you are saying that I have a responsibility to mention clearly that 6.25 happened because the north invaded the south.

CHO: Of course. Without a clear explanation of its origins, it seems irrational to talk about the need to recover homogeneity and achieve unification.

It seems to me that an assumption underlying Cho's argument is that no discussion of homogeneity can take place without first accepting that it is the north, rather than the south, that has deviated from Korean homogeneity. "Achieving unification," then, refers to the need to assimilate the deviant north into the south.

Cho could not reconcile *Ppo ppo ppo*'s neutral representation with the view that the north violated the south. *Ppo ppo ppo*'s neutrality brings to mind the intriguing cover of volume 1 of Cumings's *The Origins of the Korean War* (1981), which reproduces Picasso's 1951 painting *Massacres en Corée*, in which children and pregnant women stand defenseless as robotic soldiers prepare to follow an order to kill. Much to the dismay of the communist groups for which Picasso was an emerging hero, and which had hoped this new work would indict the Western world, the painting does not depict the identity of the aggressors or victims. It is an appropriate piece for Cumings's book, since he does not assign blame to some agents while exonerating others, instead locating the origins of the war more diffusely, primarily in the revolutionary struggles and socioeconomic transformations of the five years between liberation and the outbreak of the war, and secondarily in the anti-Japanese resistance during the colonial period. For this reason, the book had a powerful impact on Korean historiography (Em 1993), although it was received with reservation and criticism by all but the most progressive academics in Korea. Even today it is difficult for scholars in Korea to explicitly agree with Cumings's arguments without risking their careers, for Cumings says that the question of who started the Korean War cannot be answered and should not even be asked (1990: 619, 621).

EDUCATION AND POLITICS

In light of the need to allocate blame, it is all the more impressive that the school textbooks in 1996 allocate so many pages to reconciliation and so few to criticisms of the north. The 1996 ethics textbooks, for instance, make it clear that the north Koreans continue to hope for unification on their terms, that is, according to the ideology of Kim Il Sung, yet the authors implore the readers not to focus exclusively on negative valuations of the north. They also draw readers' attention to some of the complexities of the period between liberation and the war, including the often confusing roles of Seoul, Washington, Tokyo, and Beijing in the construction of Korea's greatest tragedy. In the second-year middle-school ethics textbook, students are, remarkably, asked to empathize with the north Koreans, to see everyday life from the point of view of a north Korean.

There has been considerable movement over the years in Korean school textbooks, from the unabashed anti-communism of the 1960s and 1970s to the more tempered and neutral assessments of the 1990s that permit interpretation and even ambiguity. These changes are important because they are *official* changes; because all school textbooks are sponsored, edited, selected, and standardized by the Ministry of Education, the views represented in the textbooks are sanctioned by the government.[2]

Of course, no one can know how the textbooks will change in the near future. On the heels of the student protests of August 1996, President Kim ordered the Ministry of Education to pursue a framework for a new "ideology" *(inyŏm)* because, as he pointed out, the standardized anti-communist education had not corrected the students' inclination for the leftist politics of "the enemy" (*Hanguk ilbo,* Aug. 21, 1996, part 2, p. 4). Whether this is simply political rhetoric or will actually result in specific changes to curricula remains to be seen. This first democratically elected administration in south Korean history may continue to support democracy, but perhaps not too much democracy. Textbooks, especially those at the elementary and middle-school levels, continue to be carefully regulated by the government.

The purpose of this chapter, however, is to go beyond merely identifying education as an instrument of power or coercion to identify breaks and continuities of historical representations of north Korea and unification, and to show how these representations have been patterned in ways similar to representations in the realms of south Korean life discussed in other chapters. Since I have been arguing that south Koreans are increasingly aware of the possibility of Korean heterogeneity and the dissolution of the strict people-state division that supports the concept of homogeneity, I am especially interested in illustrating how young children are beginning to be exposed to narratives that reflect ambivalences about unification.

Early educational texts are of special interest, not only because their clear language gives a false impression of simplicity and closure, but also because they so explicitly articulate the ideological foundations of unification and division discourses. The texts are patterned along many of the same oppositional lines between state and people that can be seen in interviews, literature, defector narratives, and, especially, south Korean representations of Kim Il Sung, Kim Jong Il, and north Korea. Moreover, textbooks provide one of the most obvious vehicles for making particular historical narratives into "doxa" (Bourdieu, 1977), that is, narratives that become so taken for granted that they are seen as neither heterodox or orthodox (words that suggest alternative narratives) but natural and true.

In more general terms, then, this chapter concerns the importance of education as an instrument for the formation and reproduction of a particular and doxic vision of nationhood. Emile Durkheim long ago stressed education as a site for the production of nations and called on states to use education to create social solidarities. Therein lies a disturbing paradox of liberal political philosophy: states ideally represent the will of the people, and yet states take on the role of producing nations— homogeneous social organizations, communities of like-minded citizens. Why is it necessary for the state to take on the role of constructing the very "we" it is supposed to represent? Or, put more specifically in the context of education, why is it necessary for the state to educate the people if the state is supposed to be the creation of the people?

Ernest Gellner has answered that education, or what he calls "exo-socialization," is indispensable to the function of the nation-state:

> But some organism must ensure that this literate and unified
> culture is indeed being effectively produced. . . . Only the state can

> do this, and, even in countries in which important parts of the
> educational machine are in private hands or those of religious
> organizations, the state does take over quality control in this most
> important of industries, the manufacture of viable and usable
> human beings. (Gellner 1983: 38)

Whereas in prenationalist, pre-eighteenth-century Europe, "culture"
(for Gellner, the values that supported local agrarian social orders) could
be reproduced through a small number of educated specialists, or simply
within the family, nationalist and industrial Europe needed to reproduce
itself as a mobile, standardized, and unified culture, through a central
and generic education. Thus,

> the imperative of exo-socialization is the main clue to why state and
> culture *must* now be linked, whereas in the past their connection was
> thin, fortuitous, varied, loose, and often minimal. Now it is unavoid-
> able. That is what nationalism is about, and why we live in an age of
> nationalism. (Gellner 1983: 38, emphasis in original)

Gellner's view is quite explicitly ideal; some might say it is utopian. He
conceptualizes the nation as an instrument or machine that produces
the conditions necessary for its continued existence. The argument is
not dissimilar to Durkheim's idea that education does not necessarily
take on the power of the state, for the state and the educational
system that reproduces it are ideally the image and reflection of
society—though for this argument Durkheim has been often criticized
(Lukes 1992). For in actual practice, education transmits ideologies
that are never neutral; they will benefit some people and some classes
more than others, and they may be active agents of oppression. Thus,
more recent scholars have analyzed teaching in more Marxist terms as
symbolic violence (Bourdieu and Passeron 1977: 5) propagated in the
service of elites and the state and rationalized in nationalist terms as
necessary for the preservation of culture. Bourdieu and Passeron note
that education becomes linked with law and order, and they cite a
conservative critic of education: "The task of the teaching profession
is thus to maintain and promote order in people's thinking, which is
just as necessary as order in the streets and in the provinces" (Gusdorf,
cited in Bourdieu and Passeron 1977: 70).

Different states or governments do not simply make different kinds of schoolbooks, writing more democratic texts as their governments become more democratic. I think we can assume, to some degree, that different historical and political conditions make possible different kinds of texts, with new periodizations, plots, metaphors, mediums of expression, and concepts. New political tendencies can materialize within the classroom and make education a vital site for the production of nationhood. While I am not prepared to make an argument about whether the textbooks are actually successful in creating particular ideologies or reproducing the goals of the state, I am prepared to show how the textbooks resonate with the other discourses described in the various chapters of this book.

HISTORICAL REPRESENTATION

We are all one
One heart
We are one
I am one
We are one
Like drops of water make a river
If you meet me we will become one
Where the river flows
Ah
Into a wide sea with blue waves
You and I makes us
We are one
Your heart,
My heart
All one heart

—*Urinŭn modu hana* (We are all one), in
Saenghwalŭi Kiljabi (Guide to everyday life),
fourth-year elementary-school text, 1993

For the purposes of this chapter, it is not necessary to plunge into the extensive literature in the field of education on how schools and schoolbooks serve as an instrument for the production, reproduction, and transformation of shared knowledge. This is a literature that extends back to Plato's *Republic*. Nor is it necessary at this point to address in depth the recent debates in the United States on "cultural literacy" (Hirsch 1987). There is also a significant literature dating from the 1950s and 1960s on the extent to which state-sponsored education could promote particular kinds of economic and political changes in developing countries, or in rural regions of developed countries (Inkeles and Holsinger 1974), but I am not attempting to argue that Korean schoolbooks have a specific influence on Korean students. Rather, I am suggesting that the schoolbooks are part of a larger process of producing a particular set of south Korean discourses of nationhood. I assume that there is a significant relationship between nations and texts, and more specifically between the material included in schoolbooks and the way educated citizens come to think about their nations. Even if one does not wish to accept Benedict Anderson's argument that the nation is a modern consequence of print capitalism (Anderson 1991 [1983]), it is difficult to reject the proposition that there is a relationship between what people read and what they think. And since this is a book about what south Koreans think about north Korea and unification, it must also be about the ways in which they learn about those topics. (The next chapter will address some of the ways in which students at the university learn to *unlearn* the material they encountered in elementary, middle, and high school.)

Perhaps the most central vehicle for teaching elementary-school and middle-school students in south Korea about the value of the Korean nation, the tragedies of Korean division, and the hopes for unification is the subject of ethics *(Tŏdŏk)*.[3] Ethics textbooks normally consist of chapters on community life *(iut saenghwal)*, democracy, national development, and the people's will for a peaceful unification.[4] Most of the chapters in some way stress the need for south Koreans to develop a consciousness of independence and democracy and to build a distinctive national identity. Particularly in the textbooks of the 1960s and 1970s, the authors view these aspects of nationhood largely with reference to north Korea, which, it is argued, is not independent, democratic, or distinctive. It is instead seen as a failed imitation of socialism, which is in itself seen as a failure. Thus a significant portion of any ethics book is devoted to defining south Korea as north Korea's opposite, and this is achieved by demonizing the north in quite dramatic terms, as a land of robotic communist cult-members who blindly follow Kim Il Sungism's drive to communize the entire peninsula.

These features of *Todŏk* textbooks have to be placed within the larger context of Korean historiography. In portraying the history of south Korea in terms of its opposite, historians reveal the extent to which their own writing is historically embedded. I should stress that I am neither a historian nor a specialist in historiography; I defer on many historical questions to others far more knowledgeable than I am. However, in order to comprehend the school textbooks, it is also important to place them in the context of Korean history, and so I ask the reader's indulgence in a brief overview of some aspects of Korean history writing.

The writing of history in Korea has been inextricably tied to a history of domination—in particular Japanese colonization and imperialism, and to a lesser extent the relation of the superpowers to Korea's ongoing division, as well as a perceived neocolonial American imperialism. As a consequence, historians have struggled not only to write their histories but also to write *against* histories that they believe were distorted through the colonial lens of power and control. Of Korean historiography, Kenneth Wells says, "The chief concern is with the proper or preferred responses to colonialism and imperialism," and that therefore Korean histories are imbued with metaphors of power (1996: 1). Such a historical project is not surprising since, as part of a systematic oppression carried out by the Japanese, Koreans were denied access to their own history, a history they could neither construct nor learn. One of the central goals, then, of postliberation (post-1945) Korean history has been to illuminate the ways in which the writing of history during the colonial period was influenced either directly by Japanese scholars and Japanese-trained Korean scholars, who conveyed a particular political agenda that muted Korea's creativity and historical dynamics, or indirectly by scholars whose visions and interpretations were largely constrained by the overall context of colonialism. In contrast to Japanese historians, Korean historians would seek to represent Korea as situated within a dynamic process of "internal development" *(naejaejŏk palchŏn).*[5]

Historians during the colonial period, for example, Ch'oi Namsŏn, Mun Il-p'yŏng, and (perhaps most influential) Sin Ch'ae-ho, struggled to construct histories that would locate Korea's roots in a specifically Korean history; this included efforts by historians to figure

Korea's ancestor Tangun into a contemporary historical narrative, and to reject Confucian elements of Korean culture as Chinese (that is, foreign) or repressive and incompatible with the Western ideals embraced by many Koreans (Robinson 1988: 35). As I mentioned in the introduction, Carter Eckert and Henry Em have both investigated the modern origins of Korean conceptions of the national people or *minjok* and have shown that far from being an ancient concept, the term *minjok* was appropriated by nationalist historians as a counterhistory to the Japanese version. *Minjok* became the most fundamental concept for defining the Korean people as a continuous and ancient nation. For this reason *minjok* has become an essential component not only of historical representations in history books of all kinds, but also of nearly all unification discourses.

It should be mentioned that in north Korea, too, foreign influence is extirpated from schoolbooks, with special attention to ancient history. But the north Korean historians go further by claiming a number of independent inventions—for example, of bronze culture during the ancient period of Kochosŏn (a dynasty that collapsed in 108 B.C.), the existence of an independent state called Nagrang (running from the second century B.C. to the third century A.D.), which was wholly distinct from the well-known Chinese commandery, with its capital in P'yŏngyang (Ch'oe 1981, 1976), and the discovery of Tangun's tomb.[6]

Therein lay a central contradiction in Korean nationalist thought: at the same time Koreans sought to emphasize their historical autonomy they also sought to integrate themselves into what some Korean intellectuals perceived as the enlightened, global, scientific, and secular West. The contradiction is embodied in the short-lived but important Independence Club *(Tongnip Hyŏphoe)*, a nationalist reform movement founded in 1896 to strengthen the nation, encourage political participation by the masses,[7] and develop a nation in the form of a Western ideal.[8] At the same time that Koreans sought to establish a distinct history, the occasional Marxist perspective also appeared during the 1920s and 1930s, not so much to address the conflict between elites and peasants but to place Korea in the trajectory of Marxist historical dynamics (most notably, Paek Nam-ŭn in the 1930s).[9] In other words, Marxism could not see Korea as the stagnant civilization described by Japanese historians (Kang, H. H. W. 1974); from a Marxist perspective, not only was Korea moving away from feudalism, it was also therefore part of an evolutionary process shared by societies throughout the world. It is ironic that much of contemporary south Korean historiography is directed toward a similar idealization of Korean traditions in the resuscitation of the concept of *minjung*—a pure folk culture untainted by foreign influence—since the *minjung* movement valorizes so many aspects of Korean tradition, such as shamanism and other folk customs, that nationalists during the colonial period denigrated as backward or irrational.

For much of contemporary Korean history nationalism has become the central trope of recovery for Korea and the new lens through which Korean history is to be viewed. Criticism of the value of nationalism in Korea became tantamount to criticism of Korean culture as a whole. As a result, nationalist histories begun during the colonial period continue to be linked with much of contemporary south Korean historiography. To a certain extent, then, the anti-foreign sentiments expressed during the 1980s and 1990s in the student movements have their roots in a long-standing nationalist tradition constituted in large part by Korea's relations with other countries. Although there is certainly a considerable amount of debate about precisely when Korean nationalisms began to emerge, the relationship between Korea's tragic history of subordination and Koreans' current search for sovereignty is discernible no matter where one locates its origins.

As one consequence of Korea's history of subordination, nationalist discourses throughout the twentieth century have employed the term *sadae*. Before the turn of the century, the term had referred to relations between Korea and China (literally, "serving the great"), but with the emergence of the early nationalists and the anti-foreign perspectives they advocated, *sadae* became a pejorative term that implied Korea's dependence upon China and, by extension, other foreign powers:

> Thus, beginning with the Independence Club, *sadae,* formerly a neutral term connoting the nature of Korea's status vis-a-vis China, took on an increasingly pejorative tone. *Sadae, sadaejuŭi* (the doctrine of *sadae*), and *sadae ŭisik* (a *sadae* mentality or consciousness) became synonymous with dependence, subservience, lackeyism, or toadyism in the eyes of nationalists. Nationalists hurled the charge of *sadae* at conservative officials who rejected new ideas as heterodoxy and defended Confucian orthodoxy as the basis of traditional society.

By 1900, the use of classical Chinese as the official form of written communication was linked to the issue of cultural dependence. (Robinson 1988: 34)

Some scholars have blamed *sadae ŭisik* for Koreans' inability to resist Japanese colonization (Em 1993: 452). The linkage between *sadaejŭui* and contemporary political perspectives is made explicit by Korean historians who have appropriated Sin Ch'ae-ho's juxtaposition of *sadaejuŭi* with a concept of autonomy and self-reliance *(chuch'e)*. In both south and north Korea, critics have charged that the other lacks *chuch'esŏng*, meaning autonomy and agency. Readers familiar with Kim Il Sung's politics will recognize the word *chuch'e*, but it should be pointed out that the word predates Kim Il Sung's use of it, and as Henry Em (1993) notes, the fact that Shin established the opposition in his writings permitted south Korean historians to talk about *chuch'e* without necessarily being accused of sympathizing with Kim Il Sung, or having to accept his particular socialist discourse on *chuch'e*.[10]

Em groups the major historiographic positions into (1) the orthodox-international view, (2) the liberal-international view, (3) the critical-domestic view, 4) the critical-interactive view, and (5) the heterodox-international view. Although these views do not correspond neatly to any specific time period—for example, the orthodox view was popular in the 1950s and has persisted to this day, whereas the critical-interactive view emerged during the 1980s and has coexisted with other views—the rise of more liberal views paralleled the rise of the student movement in the 1980s. Increasing democratization has also heightened the number of different historical voices present in south Korean scholarship. As the schoolbooks will show, the orthodox position may have persisted, but the other positions are also apparent. For example, the 1996 schoolbooks emphasize heterogeneity between the south and north Korean people, something that would have been unthinkable years ago and that has caused concern in the south Korean government. As I have already mentioned, the increasing liberalism of the schoolbooks and the dissolving boundary between people and state presented in them has led to a backlash against the schoolbooks, as conservatives fear that the students will be indoctrinated incorrectly.

The first label, what Em calls the orthodox-international view, is a gloss on official south Korean history, in which the division of Korea is seen to be a product of Soviet (and, more precisely, Stalinist) goals to communize Korea. In other words, Kim Il Sung and his colleagues were Soviet puppets.

The second view, the liberal-international view, is a bit more liberal, suggesting that although the division was caused by international forces and not by Korean agency, both the United States and the former Soviet Union are equally to blame. In other words, the division of Korea was a product of the Cold War.

Proponents of the third view, the critical-domestic view, attribute some agency to the Korean people but continue to place the primary responsibility on the superpowers for taking advantage of Korea's internal conflicts between a gradually polarizing right and left. This view aims to show more of a dialectic between Koreans and the superpowers, yet it perpetuates the separation of people and state; according to these historians, Em writes, "like any other nation, Korean society had had its class conflict and political differences, but as for the division of Korea and the Korean War, the Korean people must be seen as victims who were caught up in a maelstrom not of their making. Although it was Kim Il Sung who started the Korean War, he could have done so only with the consent of Stalin" (1993: 455). This view merges well with the arguments of student protestors that the division and the war could not have occurred without some complicity on the part of Korea's elites.

Among the various views outlined by Em, the fourth view, the critical-interactive view (corresponding to what, in Korean, would be called *pokhapron*),[11] has perhaps the most scholarly appeal and yet is politically one of the least satisfactory. In this view, the Korean War was not simply a battle in which Koreans were caught in the crossfire of Soviet and American competition, nor was it simply a war in which the superpowers took advantage of Korean internal divisions; instead, it was a civil war with a complex constellation of actors in which the superpowers and Koreans were all responsible. According to Cumings, one of the supporters of this view and perhaps also one of its greatest influences, the origins of the Korean War can be found in the social, economic, and political transformations that took place primarily during the years 1945-1950, but also in the preceding years. For within those five years, Korea struggled with the legacies of Japanese rule and the social and economic contradictions within its own civil-state/ peasant-lord relations. *Pokhapron* conveys a sense of the complexity of the issues involved not only in the Korean War but perhaps in any war; yet the Korea of 1945, after 35 years of brutal colonial domination, was especially chaotic and unstable. This perspective portrays the Korean War as a civil and revolutionary act that emerged from the conflicts inherent in the complicated mixture of class, politics, and ideology in postliberation Korea. As Cumings writes, "the opening of conventional battles in June 1950 only continued this war by other means" (1981: xxi). *Pokhapron* perspectives have never become particularly popular among Korean historians and politicians, primarily because the theory does not place blame squarely on one party, and by not doing so it can appear to let north Korea escape responsibility for starting the war.

Partly in response to *pokhapron,* a new historiography emerged in the 1980s and 1990s. Em refers to this fifth view as the heterodox-international view, although it is most commonly and most simply termed *chuch'eron. Chuch'eron* denies that the Korean War was a civil war and proposes instead that the true culprit of the postliberation years is the United States. Bringing back Sin Ch'ae-ho's opposition of *chuch'esŏng* and *sadaejuŭi, chuch'eron* proponents argue that Korea has, for more than 50 years, been in a state of dependence, or *sadae,* with the United States; that the division would never have taken place without American support of right-wing nationalists (many of whom have been labeled pro-Japanese, or Japanese collaborators); and that the real cause of the Korean War was a hitherto invisible war between the *minjung* (masses) and U.S. imperialism. Not suprisingly, *chuch'eron* became a favorite perspective among student organizations, many of whom embrace the manner in which *chuch'eron* shifts responsibility away from Koreans (north Korea) and onto those who are thought to continue to deny Korea its sovereignty. In an essay on tropes of romance in unification and division discourses, Jager writes that *chuch'eron* invigorated romantic depictions of the north and south as lovers struggling to overcome divisions imposed from outside (1996: 7).

Clearly, each of these historiographic positions demands far more elaboration than can be undertaken here, and the boundaries between the positions are not as clear-cut as the classification might suggest.[12] However, this outline of historiography may help us to conceptualize the relationship between school textbook historical representations and dominant themes in the work of professional historians. After all, it is professional historians who write the school textbooks. In fact, it could be argued that the complexity of professional writing, with all of its caveats and intertextual references, obscures the assumptions and biases of official histories. They are uncovered, or one might say distilled, in schoolbooks because the histories have to be framed in the most accessible and simple terms for children in the third, fourth, and fifth grades of primary school. Indeed, the *Ppo ppo ppo* segment on the Korean War brought the theory of *namch'im* into much sharper relief than would have been possible in a history intended for an academic audience. It is, in fact, the raw, pure assertions embedded in *namch'imron* that evoke such powerful responses. We might refer to the schoolbooks as "elementary forms" of Korean historical representation.

THE TEXTBOOKS

It is done. Unification.
What is done? The mountain ranges.
That's right, our mountain ranges.
It is just one range, a range.
It is done. Unification.
What is done? The rivers.
That's right, the rivers in our country
Meet in the sea.
It is done. Unification.
What is done? The flowers.
That's right, in the spring the flowers
Bloom together.
It is done. Unification.
What is done? The birds.
That's right, in Korea [P'aldo Kangsan]
They fly freely.
Unification, unification.
Only we remain.
Only people remain.

—Unification is Done, in *Guide to Social
Life,* fourth-semester elementary-school
text, 1993

First Reforms (1945-1963)

Given the profound ramifications of Japan's 35 years of domination of Korea, it is not surprising that the focus on independence in ethics textbooks is linked to the south Korean state's efforts at decolonization.[13] The first ethics textbooks in Korea, entitled *Kongmin* (Citizen) in 1945, and later, between 1946 and 1957, called *Sahoe saenghwal* (Social life), replaced the Japanese *Sushin* books that had been standardized for the Korean students who attended elementary schools under colonization.[14] The adoption of these new textbooks for the opening of Korean schools following Japanese colonization thus constitutes the first reform of the school textbooks. By 1997 there would be five more reforms (the sixth currently in the final stages), each reform corresponding roughly to changes in the government or constitution—one reform when Park Chung Hee took power, another when he established the Yusin constitution, another when Chun Doo Hwan took power, and so on. It should be pointed out that no substantial changes are made in the schoolbooks during the years in between reforms.

At the time of independence, only about 30 percent of school-age children were enrolled in primary schools in the south, and less than 5 percent attended secondary schools (Yang 1994: 768). Under the guidance of the United States Army Military Government, the Council for Korean Education adopted John Dewey's educational philosophy— that education should be a natural development of learning to master experiences, not the memorization or compilation of massive amounts of information. Toward this end, textbooks, especially ethics textbooks, were developed to stimulate the growth of a national spirit. All the books were designed to follow the resolutions adopted by the Chosŏn Kyoyuk Simŭihoe (Council on Korean Education), a council of private educators who sought to reorganize education so that it would be under more local control; the reorganization never succeeded and during the 1960s and 1970s public education was almost completely absorbed by the Ministry of Education (Linton 1989: 280-281). One of the resolutions covered by the ethics books read "In order to strengthen ethnic consciousness *(minjok ŭisik),* the Council would develop materials for teaching Korean history and geography that reflected the Korean spirit" (quoted in Linton 1989: 281). Ethics books focused on Korean habits, customs, and proper manners and highlighted the careers of noble characters in Korean history. The textbooks called this spirit an ideology for the "love of country and people" *(aeguk aejok sasang)*. The authors of these books spent little time on contemporary Korean history and seldom mentioned division.

With the increasing tensions on the peninsula and then the devastating Korean War, educators began to focus intensively on the question of how to prevent education from being used as a tool for political indoctrination. Section 1 of Article 5 of the 1949 Education Law, for example, reads: "Education shall be carried out in accordance with its original purpose and shall never be utilized as an instrument of propaganda for any political, partisan, or other personal prejudices" (quoted in Yang 1994: 755). Following the Korean War, however, fervent anti-communist passages were included in the ethics textbooks at all educational levels. Anti-communist education also took hold at a time when the number of Korean students and the number of educational institutions increased dramatically. The ethics textbooks during the period immediately following the Korean War armistice in 1953 (and continuing through the 1970s) were sometimes simply titled *Todŏk* (Ethics) but were also given titles such as *Pangong Todŏk* (Anti-communist ethics) and *Sŭnggong* (Defeating communism).

Second Reforms (1963-1972) and Third Reforms (1972-1981)

Elementary-school curricula during the second educational reforms (1963-1972) were designed so that anti-communism would have a place in every field of study, including biology (the role of anti-communism and democracy in developing a healthy mind and body) and mathematics (in which problem sets sometimes used numbers of anti-communists or infiltrators to demonstrate mathematical principles and functions). The other major emphasis in Korean education was modernization, a process that, the textbooks suggested, could not go forward without democracy and the people's trust in their government. Political indoctrination was especially salient in the third textbook reforms (1973-1981), begun just after Park established the Yusin constitution. Beginning in this period of authoritarianism, anti-communist fear and propaganda, teachers and students were prohibited from saying anything that might resemble an anti-state sentiment or sympathy with the north.

The intensity of anti-north sentiments expressed in these books, as well as the simplicity of the orthodox-internationalist view that the north Korean elites were Soviet puppets, can be startling to readers unfamiliar with the anti-communism of the Cold War. In a book published for second-year elementary-school students in 1965, entitled *Sŭnggong* (Defeating communism), the opening pages depict north Koreans, both in north Korea and as spies in the south. One illustration, with the caption "North Korea today," shows a younger brother expelling his older brother from the house for not being a member of the Party. This is a powerful image since it explicitly says that political ideology has taken the place of family ties; that the younger brother expels his older brother is an even greater violation of the structure of Korean family hierarchy. The next page depicts a soldier executing a farmer, with the caption "People are killed like this for being 'counterrevolutionaries.'" The next pages consist of illustrations under the heading "Frightening spies," intended to teach young people how to detect communist infiltrators. Thus, there is a drawing of a man in a trench coat and fedora secretly listening to the radio (the caption reads: "Listens to radio secretly"), and a drawing of the same man at an airport terminal ("Travels here and there without purpose"). He also appears in the mountains ("Whispers secretly deep in the mountains") and standing next to a group of citizens with his head turned to one side ("Eavesdrops").

The textbooks produced through the late 1970s also included stories of spies who, upon entering south Korea and seeing that they had wrongly believed south Koreans to be impoverished, decide to defect, pay for their crimes, and commit themselves to saving the "pitiful north Koreans" from the communist party. As paranoid as such illustrations might seem at first glance, over the years there have been several "infiltrations"—terrorist acts, kidnappings, assaults, and spying incidents—carried out by the north against the south. In early 1968, less than three years after the publication of the 1965 edition of *Sŭnggong*, north Korean commandos attacked the Blue House (the presidential mansion) in downtown Seoul in an apparent attempt to assassinate President Park Chung Hee. And, of course, a north Korean submarine carrying armed commandos was found off the coast of south Korea in September of 1996, and the commandos fled into the countryside to escape capture.

The books were, however, not intended only to alert south Koreans to the presence of infiltrators, but also to strengthen the government. Indeed, various presidents of south Korea have made political use of north Korean aggression by arguing for a strong national security state. In the story that follows the illustrations of north Korean spies, entitled *Tariwa tuk* ("The bridge and the riverbank"), a young boy watches as a flood washes away a bridge linking two south Korean provinces, Kyŏnggi-do and Kangwŏn-do. Villagers report the disaster to the government authorities, saying that they do not have enough of their own money to rebuild it. The government builds a new and stronger bridge for the people and rebuilds and reinforces the riverbank, and the boy thinks that without the government's help the river might have risen above the bank and destroyed the village.

This is an interesting story precisely because it is not explicitly anti-communist or anti-north. The story is certainly about fear, about forces beyond people's control, but it does not oppose individual/corporate action to collective/socialist action, and it is not explicitly pro-democracy. The moral of this story, which might well have appeared in north Korea or in any other country regardless of whether it defines itself as socialist, communist, or capitalist, is that the people need their government. Other schoolbooks contain stories about how the government and its soldiers have contributed to the success of the people without the people's awareness; the purpose of the story is to make the reader aware.

The most common characters are children the readers' age whose teachers or parents show them evidence—through stories or, especially, through visits to cemeteries—of how south Korea has achieved its state of well-being. In the 1965 second-year *Todŏk* text, for instance, in a story entitled "Kidnapped father," students read about a boy teased at school for being fatherless, and yet his father was a government official who had been kidnapped by the north Koreans. In several stories, including the story of the bridge mentioned above, memory of the past is represented as an internal experience, something not collectively shared and acknowledged but individually conceived. In "The Restaurant," a boy eats a delicious lunch with his uncle at a gourmet restaurant but feels angry about the division of Korea and empathy with the poorer north Koreans when his uncle tells him that north Korean children cannot enjoy such meals. Walking home, he tells himself that he will one day rescue the north Koreans from the communists' hands. In another chapter, entitled "A Hospital that [tries to] Cure Only with Words," a northern boy who is gravely injured when he saves the life of an infant in a burning house is treated with iodine because, the students are told, this is the only medicine available in north Korea. A student who hears the story tells himself how lucky he is to live in the south.

Perhaps the most famous story in the schoolbooks that relates directly to north Korea, and which appears during the second reform, is the tale of Yi Sŭng-bok, a boy who died in 1968, allegedly at the hands of north Korean infiltrators. This is a story that was perpetuated as true and was included in elementary-school *Todŏk* textbooks from 1968 until it was removed in the sixth revision, in 1996. The story first appeared in the newspaper *Chosŏn ilbo* on December 11, 1968. In the 1974 fifth-year *Todŏk* text, a whole chapter (pages 67-74) is devoted to him, with the story title "*Urinŭn kongsandangi sirŏyo*" [We don't like the Communist Party]:

> Sŭng-bok, I still hear your voice singing like a swallow, but where have you gone? We will take revenge for you when we grow up.
>
> One day in December 1968 at Soksa elementary-school in Kwangwŏn-do, thousands of adults and children burst into tears at the memorial for a young boy named Yi Sŭng-bok. North Korean infiltrators stoned him to death and then mutilated his mouth as the sentence for the crime of saying that he did not like the Communist Party. The memorial address was interrupted because so many people were crying. The service was held for Yi and his whole family, who were then killed when north Koreans infiltrated Ulchin and Samch'ok in 1968.
>
> The surviving father and brother could not bear to come to this sad service, attended by thousands of villagers and students. The students crying before Sŭng-bok's coffin were filled with a heartfelt desire to destroy the communists. Sŭng-bok was just nine years old, in the second grade of elementary-school. He lived happily in a house with his father, mother, an older brother, and two younger brothers. No one could ever have imagined what would happen on that dreadful day. It was about eight-thirty at night when five infiltrators entered the house. The soldiers put the children in different rooms and ordered the mother, who was making *meju* [fermented soybeans] at the time, to feed the men. When they pointed a gun at her heart,

she said, "But I have no rice." In response, the infiltrators said, "Then prepare some corn for us." Everyone was motionless and trembling with fear. They searched the house; one went to the yard and grabbed a chicken, another went to the garden to get some corn. All the while, they tried to promote the Communist Party. Sŭng-bok could not stand the propaganda and shouted, "I don't like the Communist Party." "What?" an infiltrator said, "I will teach you how to speak." The infiltrators took him outside. His mother cried, "He is just a little boy. Stop!" An infiltrator standing near her hit her in the shoulder with the butt of the gun, and she fell. The children begged them not to hit their mother. They grabbed at the infiltrators, but the infiltrators had no sympathy. They took everyone outside and began to stab them with knives. Then an infiltrator took a knife, mutilated Sŭng-bok's mouth, and stoned him until he was unconscious. Then they stabbed him.

This powerful story has been taught to young children in Korea for years as a true story and is one of the clearest examples of how the government used a tragic event to promote anti-communism. Little could be as perfect for anti-communist propaganda than a story of an innocent boy whose simple statement, an exercise of free speech, resulted in the brutal execution of him and his family. In 1995 and 1996 two journalists reported that the story, as it appeared in the paper and in the schoolbooks, was distorted. It appears that there was a boy named Yi Sŭng-bok who was killed by infiltrators in December 1968, but the police and the military had not permitted journalists into the area in which he was killed until well after the story had been published in the newspaper. Furthermore, neither the police nor the military filed reports that detailed the specific interactions between the infiltrators and Yi Sŭng-bok and his family, and the survivors were not present at the home during the crisis.

The story has now been removed from the textbooks, but one wonders whether the journalists' revelations will have any effect on anti-north sentiments. I suspect not, as the comments of one young woman I interviewed suggest: "[The] Yi Sŭng-bok [story] may not be reality, but it really could have been a reality." The story's veracity is thus irrelevant because the meanings of the story, and the assumptions that underlie its widespread use, have in no way lost their strength and immediacy in south Korean society. Yi Sŭng-bok's actions and words, and the tragedy that befell him, represent the morality of the south Koreans, the south Korean future as embodied in its children, and the immorality of the north Koreans. The reason this story appeared in textbooks on ethics is precisely that it valorized in very clear and simple terms a standard of moral conduct defined as anti-communism.

The role of the government in protecting the people was reinforced not only by heightening fears about north Korean infiltration, but also by emphasizing the power, sophistication, and bravery of Korea's military. Since military service has long been mandatory in Korea, many children learn to respect soldiers through personal experience with uncles, cousins, or brothers who fulfill their military obligations, as well as through textbooks. Moreover, since the primary contemporary event addressed in ethics textbooks is the Korean War, soldiers occupy a prominent place in the Ministry of Education's presentation of Korea. It should also be noted that classroom exercises have long focused on appreciating the military, sometimes through essay writing and often by helping children find penpals in the military. A long-running television program in Korea *(Pedalŭi kisu)* that aired on Saturday afternoons focused quite positively on soldiers' everyday lives. Whereas the Yi Sŭng-bok story normally appeared toward the middle or end of the school books, the first chapters usually detailed the achievements of the military. In the 1966 *Sŭng'gong* book for the third grade, chapters one through four are devoted to the southern military, chapter five to the north Korean soldiers who have defected to the south, and chapters six and seven to the respect and worship of one's ancestors, especially on Memorial Day, when Koreans honor men killed in battle. The books say that the south Korean military sank fleets of north Korean ships with only one shot and assert that, due to the shortage of aircraft designed specifically for bombing missions, some south Korean soldiers fighting during the Korean War had to drop bombs with their own hands.

In these books, north Korean elites are increasingly denigrated not only as puppets but also as having appropriated Soviet-style government to transform the Korean people and culture. Indeed, in these books, when it comes to family and the worship of one's elders, the north Koreans appear to have lost the Confucian ethic of respect. In the 1966 edition of *Sŭng'gong*, Kyŏng-sik, a young boy from north Korea, watches as the north Koreans take his grandfather away because he is too elderly and so of no use to the Party. The elderly man is called to an investigative office of the Communist Party, where he is accused of being a counterrevolutionary *(pandong)*. Kyŏng-sik's grandfather replies: "I don't know if I am *pandong* [half-something] or *wandong* [whole-something]." The ensuing miscommunication over the homonyms between the confused grandfather and the angry investigator leads to the investigator's final and frightening words: "Do you think our country should practice social work? A country does not need old people like you, we need healthy young people. We cannot feed old people who don't work." The text continues, "No one knows where Kyŏng-sik's grandfather was taken. Kyŏng-sik has been waiting for his grandfather to come home. Will he come tomorrow? Kyŏng-sik cannot even count how many years he has been waiting. Even today, he may be crying, waiting for a grandfather who will never come back." (p. 22-23).

A 1965 fourth-year *Todŏk* text includes additional commentary following the Kyŏng-sik story:

> No matter how old you are, everybody should satisfy their own quota [in north Korea]. That is the only way they can manage to live, day after day. The society in which you educate your children, in which you save your money, is scarcely a dream in their socialist country. Even though you work hard in your younger days, your property will never be yours for it can always be taken. This is communist society. Even a parent's warm love cannot give children delicious things to eat and nice clothes to wear. You study whatever they tell you to study. This is their plan and so-called *choguk* [motherland] construction. We should save our northern compatriots suffering in horror and insecurity and bring them into the arms of freedom. (p. 24)

Fourth Reforms (1981-1987)

It is important to mention that, despite government interference in education, schools were able to select from a variety of different schoolbooks, at least until the late 1970s. These included some books published by presses other than the government press, *Kukjŏng Kyo-gwasŏ*. For ethics classes in 1964, for example, schools were permitted to choose among seven different books sanctioned by the government. Not long after the *Yusin* constitution, however, the system changed, and schools had to select from the books published by the Ministry of Education. This still holds true for both public and private schools. It should be noted, however, that teachers have some freedom to select additional reference books to accompany the government texts. These are sometimes published by the government but are frequently put out by a variety of academic and university presses.[15]

At the same time, the older and more variable titles had given way to the single title *Todŏk*, with ethics one of the nine major fields of study (the others were Korean language, social life, math, science, physics, music, painting, and practicum). This is certainly not to suggest that anti-communism disappeared, only that it was subsumed under the more general category of ethics. Beginning in the early 1980s, with what was then the fourth reform of school textbooks since 1962 (the end of Park's regime and, therefore, also the end of the *Yusin* constitution), a variety of virtues *(Tŏk)* were included in the books, the anti-communist sentiments were toned down somewhat, and there was an increase in memorization drills. By this time, the Dewey-inspired general education had been to some degree abandoned in favor of repetition and memorization—what Dewey might have referred to as indoctrination. Rather than prepare students to become "universal men" (in Dewey's terms), the schoolbooks had become quite blatant instruments of state propaganda. Students were not encouraged to think for themselves or to explore alternative interpretations of historical events. The high-school entrance exam questions from 1987 that I have seen illustrate the limitation on interpretation. Here are some examples:

Question: Why might the north Koreans want to build a dam at Kumgang mountain?

A. To prevent future floods

B. To use it as a military facility

C. To divert water for agricultural use

D. To develop tourism

[The correct answer is B.]

Question: Why would north Koreans want to carry out land reforms?

A. To establish a stronger political base for the party

B. To collectivize agriculture

C. For farmer ownership

D. To isolate middle-class farmers

[The correct answer is A.]

Question: What is the best description of north Koreans' daily life?

A. They are permitted to build a happy life

B. People are forced to entertain themselves

C. Individuals have few freedoms

D. They are free to develop their own talents

[The correct answer is C.]

The amount of information on north Korean society and politics included in the middle-school texts used by the students who took this exam was minimal, and the information itself was superficial. Although the anti-communist rhetoric had been softened, the images depicting a people oppressed by their dictator had become more pronounced. Instead of the usual illustrations, photographs of parades and large statues and murals of Kim Il Sung showed how north Koreans were required to worship him, and instead of the focus on communism, the texts paid more attention to Kim Il Sung and the manner in which he "blindfolded" the north Korean people. The north Korean people appear often during these years as innocent victims, and, although in these revisions the word "puppet" was dropped with reference to Kim Il Sung, the whole nation of Korea continued to be characterized as the victim of Soviet foreign policy.

The central feature of these books is the intensive focus on the allocation of responsibility for Korea's tragedy of division. It is impossible to assess whether these textbooks succeeded in convincing students that the Soviet Union and Kim Il Sung were to blame, but the books clearly and sometimes quite persuasively make the case that the *people* of north and south Korea had little to do with the division. One scholar criticized the schoolbooks during the 1980s for failing to educate students (Hwang I. S. 1989: 50-55) and based her conclusion on her own survey of high-school and university students. She showed that the older the student, the more likely he or she would be to see the division as the shared responsibility of the superpowers. Hwang suggested the schoolbooks failed because students later changed their minds and saw division and the war differently. I would disagree with Hwang's logic, since at the very least the students appear to have been successfully taught about the concept of blame, and more specifically that blame must be placed outside of Korea (or more precisely outside of the people of Korea), and instead on the United States, the Soviet Union, and Kim Il Sung as an extension of the Soviet Union.

Fifth Reform (1987-1996)

The fifth reform of the schoolbooks, established in 1987 and extending to 1996, attempted to focus less on the differences between north and south Korea and more on what were considered to be very contemporary issues with global significance: sex discrimination, changing sex roles, pluralities of religion, and the international image of Korea. Although there had been relatively few changes during the fourth reforms, carried out during Chun's presidency, Roh Tae Woo's foreign policy demanded more radical changes in the content of schoolbooks. Roh's 1987 "northern diplomacy," like West Germany's *Ostpolitik*, was aimed at dramatically ameliorating the Cold War enmity and improving overall ties between socialist and democratic-capitalist regimes. As a consequence of the policy shift, Roh's administration ordered textbook writers to delete direct criticism of north Korea and socialism, as well as any unconditional praise for capitalism. The texts focused much more intensively on brotherhood between the north and south and on the inevitability of unification. Many of the passages are quite sentimental in tone, as students declare their commitment to love their compatriots in the north.

With an ever-increasing Korean diaspora population, the books place more emphasis on overseas Koreans, either directly, through stories about Korean children in the United States and Canada, among other places, or more indirectly, through stories about Koreans who were tragically separated from their families, hometowns, or country. The purpose of including these stories is not only to teach Korean students in Korea about the diaspora, but also, and perhaps mainly, to teach Korean children outside of Korea. Throughout the world, overseas Korean parents purchase Korean schoolbooks so that children can learn about their country with text and images provided not by their new home overseas but by Korea. Hence the following story in a 1993 fourth-year elementary-school *Todŏk* text, in which a Korean-Canadian travels to an idealized Seoul to discover the beauty and goodness of his homeland:

> The airport [in Seoul] was clean and neat. I was comfortable. I took a cab to the hotel. The scenery was beautiful. The Han River was clean, the roads were lined with flowers. When I got to the hotel, I had a big problem. My wallet was gone. At that moment, the taxi driver ran after me. "You left this in the taxi!" He wiped the sweat from his brow and smiled. I tried to give him a reward but he shook his head and said, "It was my duty." (p. 94)

In the 1993 first-semester fifth-grade *Todŏk* book, in a passage about Koreans living in Japan, a young boy named Min-gyu learns that hundreds of years ago the Japanese stole enormous amounts of fine pottery from Korea, and that they were so greedy they even forced Korean potters to move to Japan. Today, the story tells us, there is a gravesite in Japan for Korean potters who were unable to return to their country: "This is a place where the spirits of those who were kidnapped and forced to mold pottery now sleep." Following the story, the authors ask, "Now that we have acknowledged the spirit of the potters, what should we do? What can we do for overseas Koreans?" (pp. 137-142).

Whereas the middle-school books from the third reforms contain almost nothing on sentiments of brotherhood toward unification, fifth-reform middle-school books emphasize the need to develop trust and minimize difference between north and south. Korea needs to unify, according to the 1975 middle-school texts, because there is the "fire of war around the country," because there are "communist invaders" nearby, and because "unification is the most important goal." The 1975 books also note that south Korea is "economically crippled" by the division, that the north wants to communize the south, and that Kim Il

Sung and his party have made north Korea a "living hell." In the 1993 second-year middle-school *Todŏk* text, a chapter entitled "The Will for a Peaceful Unification" begins by noting the barriers to unification. Difference and distrust must be minimized, north Korea's communist ambitions must be reduced, and the international environment has to be mature enough to accept a unified Korea. Even though Korean unification is an internal matter, the authors write, Korean unification will affect other countries in the region and throughout the world, and it should always be remembered that Korea was divided by the superpowers. Unification will be achieved, the book continues, as long as Koreans approach it step by step with patience and effort and accept unification as the assignment of their generation.

This is not to suggest that these schoolbooks completely avoid demonizing the north. In a text for the very youngest elementary-school students (second semester, first year), entitled "Paron Saenghwal," the chapter on national holidays for north Korean children opens with a photograph of north Korean people standing in a long line for food distribution. A photo of south Korean children playing happily appears on the adjacent page.

Sixth Reform

The sixth reform, only just beginning to appear at the time of this writing, is even more progressive in the sense that many of the old anti-communist stories that had endured every other reform have now been completely abandoned. For example, the story of Yi Sŭng-bok has been eliminated; at the middle- and high-school levels, children will be taught about gradual approaches to national unification, and new chapters on communism that attempt to be value-neutral will be inserted. Currently there is no framework in Korea to retrain teachers. However, the Ministry of Education has promised to institute two model schools to train teachers in the new curriculum; the ministry has also promised to promote writing competitions on the subject of unification, and to provide a greater diversity of educational materials, including some north Korean literature and film (*Hangyŏre sinmun* Feb. 26, p. 2). As I have mentioned above, President Kim Young Sam also seriously considered a seventh reform of all schoolbooks, with a special emphasis on increased criticisms of the north.

Let us look at some of the differences between books of the same title and grade level published in 1993 and 1996. In the 1993 edition of the third-year, first-semester elementary-school *Todŏk* text, the chapter on unification spirit, "*Han'nara Hangyŏre*" ("One country, one people/ race") appears at the very end of the book, just after the chapter on the Korean War. Unification is juxtaposed to the war as its opposite. In contrast, in the same book published in 1996, the chapter on the same subject and with an almost identical title appears between chapters on community service and love of country, thus situated as a part of general Korean ethics; indeed, the 1996 book does not even contain a chapter on the Korean War. Although the war is mentioned from time to time, there is no use of the term "invasion" and no statement about how the war began. Of special interest is that the chapter title has changed from "*Han'nara hangyŏre*" to "*Hangyŏre han'nara*" (One people/race, one country). My guess is that the editors reversed the phrases to appeal to overseas Koreans, for whom their biological and historical Koreanness may be a more primary constituent of identity than nationality and citizenship, as well as to encourage people in south Korea to conceive of Korea as a larger entity that embraces diasporic Koreans.

As for the content, the first pages of the two chapters are identical, but the subtitles are different; whereas the 1993 book contains the subtitle "Truce Line" (pp. 122-128), the 1996 book reads "Memorial Day" (pp. 67-75). Moreover, the sections contain different stories:

"Truce Line" (1993)

We have been living on this land for a long time. This land is the home cultivated by our ancestors. The shape of the country some-times resembles a tiger or rabbit. China and Russia lie to the north, and Japan lies to the south. We who have been living here are the same race, with the same ancestors, language, eating and sleeping habits, and behavior. This is why no matter how far away we might travel we will easily recognize a Korean when we see him. Until recently, we could travel anywhere in this country. People born in the north could visit their relatives in the south, and people born in the south could visit their relatives in the north. But an unfortunate thing happened. Even though we are one country, one race, and desperately want to see one another, we cannot come and go as we please. It is because of the truce line. The truce line separates the south and north. It is a wall in the middle of our country, a wall we can never get over. Separated family members cannot meet each other. Let's learn how the truce line was drawn, and let's think about the problems we've had because of the division.

"Memorial Day" (1996)

Today is Memorial Day. Every year on this day our family visits the national cemetery to pay our respects to my grandfather's tomb. He died during 6.25 [the Korean War]. *Halmŏni* [grandmother] woke up before anyone else. She dressed in a white *hanbok* [traditional Korean dress] and my sister and I raised a flag to half mast. It was very crowded at the cemetery even though it was so early in the morning. We laid Chrysanthemums on the tomb and made a silent bow. *Halmŏni* didn't say anything, but she cried. On the way back home in the car, *Halmŏni* grabbed my hand; with eyes wet from tears she told me that if there had been no 6.25, I would have been a special part of my grandfather's life. Let's learn more about the difficulties our grandparents experienced during the Korean War.

The most striking difference between these stories is that the latter focuses on collective suffering while the former is a far more neutral consideration of "basic facts." The latter story is about emotion, sentiment, and the pain of division, whereas both the content and tone of the former have to do more with the facts of division. The difference, a day of remembering versus an actual structure, reflects a difference in the kind of reaction the stories stimulate. The focus on memory in "Memorial Day" demands the reader's empathic understanding and imagination: to imagine one's national community through this child, for the child could be anyone, boy or girl, from any region of post-war Korea.

Both the 1993 and 1996 second-year elementary-school *Todŏk* books contain sections on unification. The 1993 section, entitled *"T'ongilŭl ŭihan chase"* (Attitudes toward unification), is included in a chapter entitled *"P'yŏnghwa t'ongil ŭi ŭiji"* (The will for a peaceful unification), which concludes the volume; the 1996 section devoted to unification, *"T'ongilŭl ŭihayŏ heya halildŭl"* (Things we have to do for unification) is contained within a chapter entitled *"Nambukhanŭi t'ongil chŏngch'aek"* (Unification policies from both south and north), and is followed by an additional chapter on Korean and non-Korean heroes. The 1993 chapter begins with a focus on the barriers to unification: the first is a lack of trust and homogeneity between north and south, and the second is the fact that north Korea has not given up its desire to communize the south. In elaborating additional barriers, the text stresses that, although unification is an internal Korean matter, it cannot be achieved until the international community is ready for it. Overall, the text suggests that unification can be achieved only if Koreans approach it gradually, as a slow, step-by-step process combining patience and a persistent vision for unity and sameness. The role of the government is stressed repeatedly, whereas in the 1996 text, as I shall show, the focus is more on the citizen.

Like other books, the 1996 text attempts to strengthen the state, but it goes about this task by emphasizing the role of the citizen in refraining from explicitly political action. The chapter as a whole comprises sections outlining the history of south and north Korean policies and plans for unification, but it culminates with a portion of text on the differences between the individual and the citizen. Individuals need to think about the differences between the south and north, understand that there will be financial and social burdens associated with unification, and try to understand the perspectives of the north Korean people. Citizens *(kukmin)*, however, need to work with the government, support its policies, and wait. Both of these units, the citizen and the individual, appear as somewhat passive; the message is that Koreans are contributing to unification as long as they prepare themselves for the sacrifices they may need to make and trust that the government is doing everything in its power to bring about unification. The categorical distinction between individual and citizen is obviously problematic (where is the boundary between individual and citizen?), but the passages, in general, fit well with the government's need to discourage young people from taking unification efforts into their own hands. As the chapter ends, the authors encourage students to think about the complexities of their feelings about the north. Students are asked to "escape from prejudice, ignorance, or simple sympathy *[tansun-han tongjŏngsim]*." It concludes, "We have to understand [the north's] life and consciousness. If we do not know this, we may be disappointed from the moment we start living together with them."

The degree to which the 1993 and 1996 books mark a change from past education about north Korea is highlighted by comparing them with middle-school books from the mid-1970s. In these earlier texts, there is virtually no discussion of individual attitudes, as students are very bluntly told that unification is necessary to end war and to stop communism. The authors do not ask the students to learn about north Korea, only to fight against it. All responsibility for division is placed on external forces (Kim Il Sung being defined as external) and all responsibility for unification rides on the south Korean people's and government's ability to stand firm against the violence of the north.

In 1996, however, in the second-year middle-school *Todŏk* text, we find the following sentence: "The tragedy of our divided land did not come from the strategic interests of the United States and Russia, but from us *[han minjok]*" (p. 215). The authors also ask the question "Would we have been divided if there had been no interference from the superpowers?" Throwing some light on the potential problems of communication between northerners and southerners, the book asks: "If you had a discussion with a north Korean middle-school student who claimed that 6.25 was started because the south invaded first, what would you tell him, and what would be the rational basis of your argument?"

In this book, a considerable amount of space is devoted to differences between north and south Korea —the authors seem to think that south Koreans should know more about north Korean life. It is certainly widely understood that south Koreans know almost nothing about north Korean people: surveys administered to high-school students show that few students knew the national flower of north Korea, the names of north Korean universities, the exchange rate of the north Korean *wŏn,* or the north Korean national treasures, among other things. Although it is certainly possible that students feigned ignorance for fear that knowledge about the north might incriminate them, my own conversations with students confirm how little they know. It is unclear how much teachers know about the north since their survey responses are even more likely to incriminate them. A recent survey of high-school and junior-high-school teachers indicates the teachers' own lack of knowledge about the north (Yi, S. K. 1994), but given the national security laws that prohibit direct contact with north Korean materials the answers have to be placed in their political context. Not surprisingly, only a handful of teachers claimed ever to have seen any part of *Nodong sinmun,* the daily paper of the government in north Korea, which is "classified" in south Korea; of those teachers who said they used north Korean "materials" in their classes (which meant secondary sources in south Korea rather than primary north Korean materials), the majority (58.3 percent) relied on classroom visits by defectors.[16]

In the text, the differences between north and south Korea are termed *ijil* (the word I have described as having a negative connotation) and grouped under the categories of language, tradition/national holiday, unification policy, and work ethics, among others. As for language, vocabulary differences are listed under six categories: identical words with different meanings in the north and south, different words with identical meanings in the south and north, words that were once dialect that have become standard language in the north, foreign words that have become standard language in the north, north Korean pronunciations of foreign words, and aggressive and offensive words that have become integrated into everyday language.

There are so many vocabulary differences between north and south Korea, in fact, that there are efforts underway to publish a unified dictionary of the Korean language. The middle-school book lists only a few words in each category. (For example, *ŏbŏi*, "parents" in south Korea, is used only for Kim Il Sung in north Korea; "bathroom" is *wisaengsil* in north Korea, *hwajangsil* in south Korea; "milk cracker" is *uyukwaja* in north Korea, *adongyong kwaja* in south Korea; "geese" is *kaesani* in the north, *kŏwi* in the south; "lettuce" is *puru* in the north, *sangch'u* in the south; "barley rice" is *kkangboribap* in the north, *k'ongboribap* in the south; "lunchbox" is *kwakpap* in the north, *tosirak* in the south. The authors then ask the students: "What are the merits or weaknesses of the north Korean language *[pukhan ŏnŏ]*? How can we overcome the heterogeneity of the language *[ŏnŏ ijilhwa]*?

On the subject of unification policy, students are asked to think about its complexities. For example: "To understand the true meaning of unification, let us study how we became divided. First, the land was divided; second, the people *[minjok]* were divided; third, the south and north developed different systems. When we think about division we have to think about these three aspects. Therefore, if unification is intended to solve division, does unification necessarily have to change all three of these aspects? And does unification mean something different for each of these aspects?" (p. 252). A section on Germany raises questions, but does not provide answers, about how Korea can learn from Germany's unification process. Of special interest is a statement that the end of the Cold War may not produce unification in Korea, that "the northern system may remain for quite a long time," (p. 257), but that the end of the climate of hostility between the superpowers should lead to a more open and cooperative north Korea. This focus on cooperation rather than unification is consistent with recent government efforts to mute the call for a fast unification and instead to promote "gradual unification by agreement" *(habŭie ŭihan chŏmjinjŏk t'ongil)*.

At this point in the schoolbook, the authors introduce a brief history of unification policies, with the central argument that while policies may have changed over the years, the government's commitment to unification through peace and democracy has remained stable. What is most remarkable, however, is that the textbook not only remains somewhat neutral in its treatment of south-north conflicts over unification policy, it almost totally ignores the decade of the 1970s—the decade that saw the most significant demonization of the north. The spin of the book, therefore, is reconciliation, and this is complemented by the authors' mention that the north Koreans provided some aid to the south in the 1980s. The final section of the third-year *Todŏk* text's chapter on unification turns back a bit, however; it is intended to be critical of the north, but the criticism is leveled scatalogically:

> Let's look at an example of the individual's responsibility in north Korean society. In the north, an individual is nothing more than a government employee, so they do not feel a duty or responsibility to work creatively on the tasks given to them by their superiors. The following conversation took place between a Chinese university professor and a north Korean farmer:
>
> PROFESSOR: Why don't you work harder?
>
> FARMER: Sir, no matter how hard we work, it brings nothing more into our mouths. Everyday I urinate three times and defecate once, and that's my whole day. We used to watch each other, long ago. . . . We no longer report on someone's lack of revolutionary spirit like we used to. In the middle of the workday we have a break to urinate and defecate; we work an hour, then waste an hour saying that we're

going to the bathroom. This way we can use up a whole day.

Through this slice of north Korean life, as reflected in this conversation, let us try to imagine how we will live together after unification. (p. 276)

Still, the focus on difference is astonishing in comparison to previous textbooks, as students are asked to imagine that a unified Korea will not be a homogeneous Korea and, by implication, are asked to share the burden of understanding difference.

In sum, then, the textbooks have come a long way, especially if one considers humor as indicative of a step toward making north Korean difference more comfortable to south Koreans. There was nothing funny about north Korea in past years. But the humor provides some distance, a way for south Koreans to feel superior without feeling hatred. What the textbooks cannot address, however, is the question of how the *ijilgam*, the sense of difference, will be reduced; more important, perhaps, is that the textbooks do not address the question of why south Koreans must assume that *ijilgam* is a bad thing. Indeed, the bulk of scholarly writings on education are explicitly about shaping curricula to more efficiently recover national homogeneity. For instance, although recent scholars might argue against the simple demonization of north Korea and idealization of the south in the older schoolbooks, they still argue that it is the schools' responsibility to make sure that students know both that north Korea is an eternal part of Korea and that it is a dangerous place.

To recapitulate my argument: the primary instrument for producing this constellation of south Korean nationalist visions—the myth of homogeneity, the belief in the state as the fundamental evil in the north and benefactor in the south, and the absence of north Korean people in south Korean discourses on the north—is the south Korean government, which, in its efforts to legitimate itself and maintain its power, has contributed to the demonization of the north and only reluctantly accommodated efforts at reconciliation. These visions emerge clearly in the schoolbooks, where indoctrination is simple and efficient. However, educators are also beginning to advocate more thorough teaching on north Korea, and this has already resulted in the establishment of a kindergarten curriculum, published by Poyuksa, to teach about north Korean geography. Lee Yong-hwan explains:

The so-called unification education [t'ongil kyoyuk] was directed to infuse students with the idea that the north is a hell under the control of Kim Il Sung and a group of aggressive and greedy comrades who want to communize the south. But educators made their point without providing a full explanation of why we have come to believe this about the north, or referring students to additional sources on the north (Lee, Y. H. 1993: 184).

Lee cannot, of course, say that north Korea should be viewed positively, but neither does he want to cast aspersions. He advocates more detailed education about the north and defends this view with data from a survey about which the reader is given little information. In his survey, carried out among sixth-grade students at a school in Inch'on, unification appears as an abstract and general subject: 12.8 percent of students could identify the geographic location of north Korea and 38.7 percent thought that the north and south spoke different languages; yet 94.4 percent believed that the Korean War was caused by the communists' invasion of the south, and 75.7 percent said unification was necessary. I cannot find the figure of 12.8 percent credible without more detailed information on the survey; the figure is so low as to be bizarre. However, I do find it important that Lee chose to write about the survey. From his point of view, educators must teach about north Korea, not indoctrinate people into demonizing an abstract Other. Lee has also proposed a number of practical projects. These include creating academic competitions between south Korean teams, each of which would represent a particular north Korean school, city, or region; eliminating all anti-communist poster competitions and replacing them with unification contests; building a north Korean folk village in order to understand the lives of north Koreans; building a classroom savings account for unification; and writing letters to north Koreans with the same names as the students.

These are similar to the recommendations made repeatedly by other educators, and they all point to the poverty of south Korean education on the north, a poverty that will not be ameliorated under current political conditions. How can teachers be expected to teach about north Korea when there are no materials at hand—when the teachers themselves cannot learn about the north except through the limited information provided by the government, and the occasional book or speech by a defector? The comparison between Korean and German division on this front is striking when one considers how much more Germans knew about each other than the two Koreas know.

But I would also suggest that were south Koreans to know much more about the north than they do now, the wish for unification might not be so salient. If north Korea exists in south Korea in the realm of desire, nostalgia, tradition, and the past, then its existence depends largely on absence. Through their texts, the government instills in youngsters a strong desire for unification, and yet it is the government that also prevents them from fulfilling it. As we have seen, the government uses schoolbooks as an instrument of power that presents two narratives: the narrative of difference that demonizes the north, and the narrative of sameness meant to promote unification. As the schoolbooks' contents begin to escape the grasp of state power by moving toward reconciliation, and potentially also toward the erasure of the opposition between sameness and difference, the reins are pulled in.

SEVEN

DEMOCRACY AND UNIFICATION: STUDENT PROTESTS

> Korea has been known as a land of scholars. And just as some countries may be said, broadly, to specialize in some particular sphere of learning and culture, so Korea in the past "specialized" in scholarship. The Italian, for instance, loves not song and music more than doth the cultured Korean love the things of the scholar. He is an artist in scholarship.
>
> But to be a scholar, one must be educated. An educated Korean, however, is a unit of protest and resistance against Japanese tyranny in Korea, since education—particularly modern education—breeds thoughts and ideals that deny the right of one nation holding another in political serfage.
>
> —"The Claim of the Korean People as a Nation," Petition from the People of Korea to the Paris Peace Conference, 1919.

IN THIS CHAPTER I look at the collision between dissident university students and the government as yet another example of how difficult it is for south Koreans to escape the hegemony of the binarisms of unification and division, south and north, people and state. As we saw in chapter 6, these oppositions ramify to many aspects of Korean education. The oppositions are also given explicit and vocal expression in student protests.

It is necessary, at the outset, to emphasize how remarkable it is that students have been able to dissent at all. It is not easy to be admitted into a university in south Korea, especially into universities in Seoul. University students have gotten to the university because they performed extremely well on their elementary-, middle-, and high-school exams, exams that require a very comprehensive and detailed knowledge and memorization of the content of state-sponsored schoolbooks. The students of the most active period of dissidence, the 1980s, were educated with the most explicit anti-communist propaganda. Perhaps it may appear easy for some students to rebel against an educational system that is so coercive, but it is also difficult to rebel against something that has been part of one's consciousness for more than a decade.

Equally important is that by dissenting, many students who represent their families' hopes to rise on social and economic ladders hurt not only their own potential for social and economic success but that of their parents as well. The conflicts between university students and the police, or in many cases between university students and their universities, may also be seen as conflicts internal to the students: they are fighting with themselves against the perspectives and information they were forced to learn in order to get where they are. They are also fighting with themselves over an illegitimate national identity as a divided people that they have inherited, in large part through their education, but which they also believe is a violation of the proper national order.

Student protests appear as acts of great personal courage and have the potential to assert the rights of the people to represent themselves. On the surface, it also appears that the protests function to divide the people and the state rather than to facilitate the negotiation of a preexisting divide. But the collision between the students and the police is more dialectical than divisive. The students stand between opposed social and cultural categories and use their position to create a playing field on which opposed forces can confront and construct each other in dialectical fashion. The state and the people are indeed conceptually opposed, but the students (who claim that they represent the people) mediate between them. What appears at first to be overt conflict is yet another paradoxical means by which an unstable national identity is negotiated and a long-standing structural tension between the concepts of people and state is mediated.

Like most south Koreans, student protestors do not see themselves as having arrived at an endpoint of nationhood and national identity; they are travelers in a temporary location looking in different directions—positively toward the ideals of purity, Koreanness, and Korea's natural and unspoiled beauty, and negatively toward the impure, Westernized city. The oppositions of the pure and impure, the country and the city, and tradition and modernity represent a theme of conflict we follow throughout this study. They are salient within discourses that separate people and state, such as those of the *minjung,* or masses. The *minjung* are idealized as more pure than those Koreans who have Westernized and who have co-opted the political language and practices of colonial (Japanese and American) and postcolonial (American and south Korean governmental) agents.

The oppositions appear not only in what the students say and do but also within official government discourses, in my interviews with exhibit-goers, and in the writings of dissident travelers to north Korea described in other chapters in this book. Student-movement discourses on oppression, particularly those that valorize the folk, dovetail with south Korean discourses on north Korea, as north Koreans are widely idealized in terms reminiscent of the folk. It is partly for this reason that student protestors are often labeled pro-north. In protesting, they denounce some of the most obvious features of authoritarianism and praise the qualities of Koreanness shared by the folk, and therefore also by the north Korean people as they are envisioned.

By looking at the protestors, for example, one can gain access to an important element of Paik Nak Chung's concept of the division system, namely, the tension between unification and democracy. As I mention in more detail later, much of the conflict between students and government forces is a consequence of disputes about the term "democracy." For the state it may mean free elections, while for the students it may have more Marxist overtones of the mobilization of classes oppressed by an elitist, authoritarian state. Democracy, from the students' perspectives, often refers to revolutionary change and reconciliation with the north. As students protest for democracy and seem dissatisfied with what the government believes are true democratic reforms, such as free elections and freedom of the press, the students also appear to move closer to reconciliation with the north and to reject south Korean government anti-communist propaganda. The closer they move toward reconciliation, the more they appear to be revolutionary, anti-capitalist, and pro-north, and the more the government finds it necessary to restrict democratic freedoms. The ironic result is that the government reaffirms division and the national security state—that is, restrictions on democratic freedoms—as necessary for preserving democracy and capitalism, that is, for preserving the distinctiveness of south Korea that the students are believed to threaten. In other words, the closer one gets to the north and unification, the more south Korean identity—as a divided people, as a capitalist people defined in opposition to a communist state—risks being erased. The students are a fulcrum through which south Korea's struggle between division and unification is exercised.

Three related themes converge in student dissidence: liminality, purity, and ritual. The students are ambiguously positioned and therefore open to symbolic elaboration along the purity-impurity continuum; as we shall see, their symbolic power is then organized, muted, and controlled through a ritualized form of protest. Herein lies a central feature of all intermediate spaces for rites of passage: its occupants are structurally invisible, and as a result they are endowed with symbols drawn from the realm of the divided, the incomplete or the external. The students are symbolically dangerous, and I say "symbolically" because I am in no position to argue that they could do any real damage to themselves or the nation if left alone. Moreover, the classification "student" is non-specific. Some but not all students are protestors, and some but not all protestors are pro-north sympathizers who threaten "law and order." Moreover, there is variation even within student groups; different students have used different methods of protest, ranging from shouting to suicide and other forms of violence.[1] Even those students who seek to threaten the nation will eventually occupy a legitimate and fixed category of person in Korean society. There is also a profound difference between students who attended the extraordinarily politically active campuses of the 1980s and those who attend universities in the 1990s. Student activism in south Korea is a moving target, always changing and unstable, and for this reason it is very difficult to attempt to characterize it. Some students and observers of the student movement have told me that during the 1980s particular popular songs, slogans, and dances were often short-lived, disappearing quickly only to be replaced by new ones. Student activists might leave south Korea for one or two years to study in the United States and return to find student movements with which they are unfamiliar.

At the time of this writing, student activists form a much smaller fraction of the total student body as compared to the 1980s, and public perceptions place student activists more at the margins of the university. Students are widely seen as having "achieved enough," and many people argue that students have to move on with their lives, and that to remain active in the student movement is anachronistic. Yet the symbolic valence of the students and student protestors continues to be extraordinarily salient and powerful in Korea irrespective of their sociological contours. The fluidity and instability of the category "student" or "student dissident" produces an anxiety of sorts, the kind anthropologists have typically associated with category violations—things, events, or ideas that defy classification. In addition to being liminal, students represent the future—a frightening proposition for some people perhaps, since the students, and by extension the future, cannot be essentialized, predetermined, or controlled. If they represent the future, then they cannot be revolutionaries or guerrillas; for these terms imply an external and "impure" threat to a self-sustaining system. Rather, the students continue to be an integral part of a long-running drama in which the students and the university provide a stage for Korea's contradictions and paradoxes and for the contemplation of Korea's possible futures.

The students serve this role because they do not fit into certain comfortable categories. They are neither workers nor elites, neither children nor adults. And although they are south Korean, in many ways they look politically like north Koreans. Indeed, a key activity of student dissidents during the 1980s was to promote illegal travel to north Korea. The university gates establish the ambiguity, setting the campus apart from the city—the "real world," as it is sometimes phrased in imitation of the American idiom. Jager notes that for student activists, the gate itself marks a symbolic boundary between the less polluted, healthier, inside world of the students and the polluted, ill, outside world of the city and the government (1994: 224-25). Although this symbolic value did not prevent students from protesting against their universities (especially during the 1980s), the campuses became powerful sites for learning and for unlearning the propaganda of the elementary- and high-school years.

In addition to being spatially and developmentally liminal, students are also situated ambiguously in the narratives of Korean history. Student protests appear to be of recent origin, and yet they are of long standing, clearly traceable to the Chosŏn dynasty and to the Confucian ideal of students and scholars as the "guardians of state virtue" (Eckert et al.1990: 353). Protests are revolutionary in character, and yet they are explicitly acts of memory and ritual reenactment; they appear to be directed in opposition to political currents, and yet in many ways they reinforce conventional Korean historical and national representations.

In this chapter, I suggest that precisely because of their intermediate (and unique) position, students are able to articulate (and symbolize) some of the central contradictions of contemporary Korean politics and are therefore well located to express the complications of mourning. To some extent, the protests provide a means for students to individuate, to establish identities separate from those dictated by the government or by parents, and more precisely to reconcile their new or emerging identities with their pasts. Although their identities emerge within the context of the divided nation, recognizing that their identities are embedded within division can help students to both recognize and move beyond the past. If the university is a transitional space, it can also resemble a transitional object that facilitates the articulation and negotiation of future, potential spaces.

In addition to noting that the students are engaged in a process of working toward the future, it is also important to state that the students are deeply involved in the past. Student protests are as much about working through the traumas of the past as they are about resolving those traumas in the future. In this respect, the task of government and the task of student dissidents do not seem that far apart. Indeed, despite the fact that students use the protests to symbolize their own separation from and union with the past, a process that foreshadows the ability to mourn, the students become caught in the same web of conflicting significations as the government. Together, the police and students play out a long-standing Korean drama of negotiating political and cultural identity in the face of trauma, a drama framed in terms of an opposition between the people and the state. One might even assert, more boldly, that the police and the students are on the same side.

Before proceeding, I would like to stress that I do not specifically take up the platforms of student groups, such as their increased calls for greater democratization or the expulsion of American forces. These elements have been addressed in great detail by other researchers who have focused specifically on the student movement (Jager 1994; Kim D. J. 1991; Park B. C. 1995; Jang 1994; on the Christian elements of the student movement, see Jager 1994: 69-99; Riew 1985). I am more concerned here with the degree to which activist students, increasingly lacking popular support (for reasons to be discussed later), remain central to south Koreans' struggle for national identity at the level of representation. Students in general, and student demonstrators in particular, become powerful symbols for an imagined community between division and unification. I would also like to acknowledge the great difficulty of speaking of "the students" as if they were a homogeneous entity, when only a minority of students actually participate directly in demonstrations. Moreover, there are many student movements, just as there are many nationalisms and democracies. However, I also want to emphasize that there are numerous structural similarities among student activist ideas and practices. Even if a comprehensive and comparative history of the student movements of south Korea has yet to be written, the available data and literature do point to some general patterns in south Korean student activism, patterns that appear frequently in a host of discourses on unification, as well as in discourses of nonactivism.

STUDENT MOVEMENTS IN SOUTH KOREA

> —Although we live in many different social associations, the most important is the state.
> *Sahoe* [Society], fifth-grade textbook (cited in Linton 1989)

The history of student movements in Korea is not well documented, for many of the same reasons that the scholarly tradition in south Korea for studying anything that might resemble an anti-state discourse is so poor, as I have noted. What is quite clear, however, is that scholars and students have long been invested in articulating Korean national identity. There is some evidence that students during the early Chosŏn dynasty protested against extreme tendencies toward Buddhism or Confucianism. Kim Doh-jŏng, a historian of student movements, notes that in 1519, when a young official named Cho Kwang-jo was purged during Confucianist reforms, students forced their way into the king's residential grounds to proclaim Cho's innocence (1991: 89). There is more evidence of early activism before the turn of the century. In 1873, during Kojong's reign, students at the National Academy of Seoul called a strike in support of the king and his state and against a critic of the government, Ch'oe Ik-hyŏn. Ch'oe had leveled harsh attacks against the government, saying "The people [have become] fish and meat, and morality has been destroyed" (quoted in Palais 1975: 184), and although he was supported by the king, who praised Ch'oe's honesty, a significant number of officials resigned in protest or were exiled by Kochong. The students protested, demanding the return of the leaders and punishment for Ch'oe. Kojong ordered the students back to school and expelled those who refused. In another incident during the 1870s, students at one of the first private schools in Korea to offer Western curricula—the Paechae school—threatened to march on government schools unless the Ministry of Education allowed them subsidies and agreed not to discriminate against graduates of nongovernment schools.

One of the earliest nationalist demonstrations took place in Tokyo, on February 8, 1919, when 600 members of the Korean Youth Independence Corps *(Chosŏn Ch'ŏngyŏn Tongniptan)* demanded independence from Japan. Like many others to follow, the demonstration had a considerable impact on students in Korea, especially those working to develop active independence groups (Lee, K. B. 1984: 341). The next month, students and intellectuals joined large numbers of people from various walks of life and began a mass demonstration for Korean independence at Pagoda Park that spread throughout the country and eventually involved the participation of perhaps two million Koreans (Lee, K. B. 1984: 344; Lee, C. S. 1963: 114-118). The participants were predominantly farmers, but many students, such as a high-school girl, Yu Kwan-sun, took active leadership roles. Yu was arrested and later executed by the Japanese. Although the protest, known as the March 1 Independence Movement, was crushed by the Japanese, it encouraged further resistance and led to the establishment of a provisional government in Shanghai, under the leadership of Syngman Rhee.[2] This government published the *Tongnip sinmun* (Independence news), a daily newspaper that served as the unofficial organ of the Independence Club (Lee, K. B. 1984: 303), and sent a representative to the Paris Peace Conference in 1919.

Education was of special interest to the Koreans who attended the conference. The sixteen-page memorandum produced there ("The claim of the Korean people as a nation") noted Japan's total control over education in Korea.[3] The statement, part of which appears as the epigram to this chapter, is also an explicitly nationalist document, as the Koreans say clearly that scholarship is a major feature of their national identity. But Korean history could not be taught in the schools. And at any rate, the number of students permitted to attend school was quite small—according to the conference document, in 1917 only 86,410 Koreans out of a total population of 16,648,129 were enrolled in schools of any kind, and of these, only 745 were in graduate or professional schools. After 1943, all Korean students were conscripted into the Japanese army (Robinson, in Eckert et al. 1990: 321).

Despite the fact that students during the Chosŏn dynasty were protesting aristocratic or royal injustices, students during the 1980s and 1990s would instead view the anti-Japanese struggle of the early twentieth century as a primary starting point for their movements, and this is perhaps the main reason why student struggles in Korea have been explicitly nationalist in character. The choice of the anti-Japanese struggle as a starting point is not surprising, since scholars during the Chosŏn dynasty were *yangban,* aristocrats who may have protested here and there but seldom questioned the social order, because the social order was designed in their favor.[4] Indeed, during the student strike of 1873 noted above, students passionately defended the state against an official's criticism of its moral foundations, for to criticize the state was tantamount to attacking their father.

As part of this historical genealogy, student movements have secondarily viewed themselves as the inheritors of the spirit of the anti-establishment, anti-foreign *Tonghak* (Eastern Learning) rebellion of 1893-1894, a movement that occurred prior to Japanese colonization. As one consequence, student activists have been far less concerned with general ideological formations, such as Marxism or communism[5]—thus remaining relatively independent of communist organizations—than they have been with articulating a nationalist project that draws on the national spirit of the *minjung*, exemplified by the peasant and the particular discourses of resistance associated with the *Tonghak* rebellion.[6] Usually less interested in advocating one or another institutionalized ideologies in the abstract, they make specific demands such as the expulsion of U. S. forces from Korean soil and the immediate unification of the country.

In the second half of this century, the students almost single-handedly overthrew President Rhee's autocracy and his Liberal Party *(Chayudang)* in the April 19, 1960, uprising. Widespread corruption, the so-called 3.15 election fraud, and police brutality produced massive student demonstrations in Masan, Pusan, Taegu, and elsewhere. There were also prior protests as a result of Rhee's attempts to thwart the campaign of a vice presidential candidate, Chang Myŏn. According to the *Chŏndaehyŏp* student organization's official history, Rhee forced students to attend school on Sundays in February 1960 so that they could not participate in the rallies for rival parties (*Chŏndaehyŏp*, 1991: 19). On April 19, after the discovery of a deceased high-school boy named Kim Chu-yŏl in the harbor at Masan, apparently killed by riot police, students from Koryŏ University and other campuses marched throughout Seoul demanding Rhee's resignation. Hundreds of students were killed by riot police, while the military observed events at a distance. On April 26, exactly one week after the onset of the riots, Rhee resigned from office, bringing to a close the First Republic of Korea. The uprising also marked the continued strength and efficacy of the students as the nation's moral conscience, and because the students had been supported by the vast majority of the Korean people, the uprising also invigorated the prospects for democratization. April 19 is today a day on which students gather together to march not only in commemoration of the 1960 uprising, but also to reaffirm their role as protectors of the people against government excesses.

Student activism, though not new, blossomed in the postwar period, in part because of the corruption of the state in what was ideally an emerging democracy, but also because the number of students, educational institutions, and urban dwellers increased rapidly. In fact, the number of institutions of higher learning doubled and student enrollments increased twelve-fold in the period between 1948 and 1960 (Eckert et al. 1990: 354). For instance, in 1948 there were 7,819 Koreans enrolled in colleges or universities, whereas by 1964 there were 142,629; the number of high-school students increased during the same period from 84,572 to 1,066,247, and elementary-school students from 1,366,024 to 4,626,297 (Oh, B. H. 1975: 116). As Eckert notes, however, employment for all of the new graduates was hard to find, urban living was financially unrewarding, and the students vented their frustrations on elites as well as on their own educational institutions.[7] This is important to emphasize, for despite the fact that the campuses were symbolized as sites of purity, the university administrations and staff frequently became objects of protest (especially at national universities such as Seoul National University, in which the professors are technically government officials). Many students sought their education instead in the student underground movement—primarily in study groups called "circles," in which students read and discussed books that had been banned or censored by the government, as well as student movement literature and pamphlets. Furthermore, despite the figures on increases in the number of young people pursuing higher education, social mobility was limited by gender, class identifications, family background, and regionalism. This was true especially for women; very educated women did not necessarily find good jobs or "marry up," and this lack of mobility certainly played an important role in increasing disaffection among young people.

Student participation in politics remained vigorous throughout the era of Park Chung Hee's dictatorship as well, as students advocated democratic reforms in all areas of life. Ironically, the achievements of the 1960 uprising were followed by the rise of the most authoritarian administration in south Korean history (Lee, N. 1991: 212). Under Park's regime, professors were compelled to convey pro-government views, and this led many students to begin protesting directly against the universities. Students were required to enter the military, and Park's constitutional reforms, especially the *Yusin*[8] constitution (revitalizing reforms), established in October 17, 1972, when Park declared martial law, led to a number of mass protests: in 1972, for example, students demonstrated against *kyoryŏn* (student military training) for the sake of campus autonomy; in 1973, students led the *Minch'ŏnghakryŏn* incident (short for *Minju Chŏngryŏn Haksaeng Yŏnmaeng*, or Democratic Youth Students'

Union); in 1975, a student from Seoul National University, Kim Sang-jin, committed suicide by disemboweling himself as an act of protest; and in early October 1979, in a Pusan and Masan demonstration known colloquially as *Pu-ma Hangjaeng* (Pusan-Masan Disturbances), student protests against the government and for the reinstatement of then-opposition leader Kim Young Sam into the national assembly led to major disagreements between Park and the director of the KCIA (Korean Central Intelligence Agency), Kim Chae-gyu, on how to handle the situation. Historians have conventionally assumed that the conflict between the two provoked Kim to assassinate Park later that month.

The Yusin constitution, which became invalid only with Park's violent death on October 26, 1979, had given the president broad powers that included dissolving the national assembly, declaring martial law, banning all political activities, and making any criticism of the president a criminal offense.

> By the Yusin period, the anti-Park student opposition had already accumulated a decade of experience, punctuated by dramatic and prolonged episodes of violent struggle, as in 1965, against the ROK's normalization treaty with Japan, and again in 1969, against the constitutional amendment for a third-term presidency. Yusin gradually galvanized the student movement and kept it at an intense pitch. By 1979, the movement had begun to assume the character of an underground institution in South Korean society, with its own extensive organization, heroes and martyrs, patois, and culture. Works by dissident musicians, writers and other artists, together with the artists themselves, became icons of the new subculture and gave it both emotional strength and intellectual substance. (Eckert et al. 1990: 386)

Student participation in politics was crystallized as well by the increasing regionalism between east and west, exacerbated by Park's neglect of the Chŏlla provinces, and the students were now joined in support by the emerging middle class and urban intelligentsia, which had previously remained on the sidelines of political culture. In addition to the regional imbalance in economic development, industrial development under Park was concentrated in a small number of heavy industries. The huge conglomerates *(chaebŏl)*, such as Samsung, Hyundai, and Daewoo, continue today to control much of the wealth in Korea, although their executives have increasingly been subject to Kim Young Sam's anti-corruption campaign, and many have been convicted of bribing former presidents Roh Tae Woo and Chun Doo Hwan. Much of the increase in student activism occurred as a result of Koreans' struggles against such big money. While the elites prospered from the *chaebŏl*, laborers struggled to earn substandard wages under miserable conditions, and when they protested, they were beaten, imprisoned, and tortured. The tedious and usually unsuccessful drive for labor unions in Korea faced overwhelming opposition and was pushed forward only by remarkable acts of students and union leaders, such as Chun Tae-il, a garment worker at Seoul's Peace Market who self-immolated in November 1970 as a protest against Korea's treatment of laborers.

Choi Jang-jip writes that Chun Tae-il's death was a turning point in the student movement (1993: 33-34). New dissident groups, clubs, and circles were established, and they joined with each other to oppose the Park regime. The students also became further involved with labor, spawning two distinct lines of dissent. While some students (who became known as *hakrim*) concentrated on political demonstration as a way to stave off the government's anti-democratic crackdowns, advocating a "political struggle first" policy, others (specifically, a group that became known as *murim*) advocated a policy of *hyŏnchangron*—educating workers in night schools, mobilizing union movements, and spending time in the factories (Lee, N. 1991: 216). The latter direction, stimulated directly by the death of Chun Tae-il, continued in the 1980s in student agricultural activism *(nonghwal)*, to be discussed in more detail below. Under the influence of liberation theology, churches became increasingly involved with student organizations and helped to produce a rich literature on the relation between the people *(minjung)* and the teachings of Christ. Hagen Koo notes:

> One important consequence of Chun's suicide was its impact on intellectuals, students, and church leaders. It awakened them and made them realize where society's most serious problems lay and how strategic the labor movement could be for their democratization struggle. Student-labor linkages began to develop during this period, as did the labor involvement of activist church groups. Thus economics and politics became closely entwined to shape the character of the working-class activism to come. (1993b: 139)

The church was particularly active in the mid-1980s, when a religious organization investigated the death of a Seoul National University student, Park Chong-ch'ŏl, who had been arrested in the search for student leaders. The student organization *Chŏndaehyŏp* credited the pastors for revealing that the police had suffocated Pak and crushed his windpipe during the interrogation (1991: 26).[9]

Returning to the topic of unification, student protesters continued to advocate democratization during this time, but not as an end in itself; rather, democracy was the necessary first step to unification. Vincent Brandt has written that the concept of democratization for many students during the 1980s was a vague and abstract term denoting the whole process of the resolution of injustices, from the oppression of labor to national division. More specifically, he notes, "the term 'democracy' is a kind of code word that encompasses two principal meanings from the student perspective: 1) egalitarianism—a major concern with the equitable distribution of wealth and power; 2) the mobilization of the masses, i.e., raising the consciousness and releasing the energies of the oppressed classes in order to bring about fundamental structural change" (1991: 15). Similarly, J. O. Jang writes, "Every discourse producer in each stream [of the student movement] used the master frame 'democracy' to justify actions and rhetoric, regardless of whether or not they were aware of a particular meaning of democracy" (1994: iii).

The focus more specifically on democracy was in part because these activists truly believed that democratic reform was the natural precursor of unification, but also because the overwhelming anti-north sentiment in south Korea (reinforced by actual cases of northern infiltration and terrorism) could not permit much sympathy for unification discourses that advocated reconciliation or appeasement, or that acknowledged anything good in the north.[10] Anti-north sentiment did not facilitate the public, middle-class support on which the students had come to depend. Perhaps the most well-known case of student protest for democratization is the Kwangju uprising, during which students staged massive protests against Chun Doo Hwan's coup but also made explicit their anger and resentment at the U. S. military occupation and the economic injustices of the south Korean government and the large conglomerates. After Kwangju, students power was enhanced, in part because of the increase in public support.

At this point the students were strong enough to begin calling for greater efforts toward unification. Statements regarding unification linked unification and democracy, suggesting that the two were inseparable—with unification would come democracy, and with democracy would come unification. Between May 17 and May 27, 1980, in perhaps the most ghastly police response in Korean history, about two thousand students (according to most accounts—although government numbers are usually under a thousand) were massacred in Kwangju, Chŏlla province. The government denied that they had murdered anyone innocent and launched an effort to tighten security and limit individual freedoms. An enormous number of political prisoners were taken during the early and mid 1980s, and the vast majority of them were students. During Chun's administration, more than a hundred thousand students were expelled from institutions of higher education.

As I noted, Kwangju only reinforced the students' opinions and helped consolidate popular support for future protests. My interviewees who attended college during the 1980s in Seoul report having seen horrendous photos of the corpses of student protestors such as Yi Han-yŏl and Pak Chŏng-ch'ŏl, who, it is widely believed, were tortured and murdered by the south Korean military. Many Korean students believed that the United States had turned a blind eye to Chun's dispatch of troops to Kwangju (Eckert 1990: 379), and that at the very least it was obvious that the U.S. government supported Chun's presidency. By the time the Kwangju massacre occurred, most student activists believed that the United States had contributed to the military and authoritarian rule of Chun's predecessors as well (Shin 1995: 521-522; see also Kim, D. J. 1991: 456-486). Soon, cases of political violence and torture became widely known, and Chun's support began to disappear. By 1987 the United States had begun to pressure Chun for civilian reforms, and forces within the Korean government itself were recommending some sort of resolution of popular dissent on the eve of the 1988 Summer Olympics, to be held in Seoul; moreover, student protests had so intensified, and popular support was so widespread, that even white-collar workers and housewives joined in student demonstrations. Chun had little choice but to accept new presidential elections, albeit with his handpicked successor, Roh Tae Woo, as the leading candidate.

After Kwangju the students organized as they never had before; indeed, there were so many protests it was reported that in 1987 the highest income in the country was received by the primary manufacturer of tear gas (Ogle 1990: 99). By 1985 nearly two dozen universities had joined together to form a national federation of students (*chŏnhakyŏn*) and a related committee for the "Three People's Struggle" (*Sammint'uŭi*, also known as PD, "People's Democracy," or *Minjungminju*). The committee was dismantled quickly by the Korean government, but this action only stimulated the students to establish more, and increasingly militant, political wings of the federation. One branch, the "Self-directed struggle for democracy" (*Chamint'u*, also known as NL, "National Liberation," or *Minjokhaebang*), popularized Kim Il Sung's ideology of self-reliance among other student groups, arguing that while south Korea was a colony of foreign (U.S.) imperialists, north Korea had achieved its independence from imperialism (not to mention feudalism).[11] NL asserted that the current state of Korea was *sikminji panchabonjuŭi* (literally, "colonial semicapitalism"), by which was meant that south Korea appeared to be a capitalist society, when in fact the vast majority of capital was distributed to and controlled almost exclusively by the large conglomerates.

On August 19, 1987, a portion of *Chamint'u*'s members established *Chŏndaehyŏp*, the National Council of University Student Representatives, a group that included more than a hundred universities and colleges (*Chŏndaehyŏp*, 1991: 37). The organization, later to change its name to *Hanch'ongnyŏn* (Korean Youth Federation), became the most powerful activist group in Korea and has been the major sponsor of student demonstrations throughout the 1990s. *Chŏndaehyŏp* was an explicitly feminist organization as well, tracing much of its inspiration to Yu Kwan-sun, the high-school girl who had been executed by the Japanese during the March 1 movement, and choosing to send the female student Im Su-kyŏng, rather than one of the male leaders of the organization, to north Korea. *Chŏndaehyŏp*'s charter clearly states that the organization opposes all forms of male oppression and subsumes under "male" the U.S. military presence in south Korea. The group split into two major factions in 1990, those advocating Kim Il Sung's *chuch'e* ideology and those seeking national sovereignty, unification, and democracy without Kim's particular version of self-reliance, and it is the former that has been the most vocal in recent years.

The Korean government has seized on the advocates of Kim Il Sung's *chuch'e* (self-reliance) ideology as the essence of student protesters.

Despite the early moves of Kim Young Sam's administration to open up a dialogue with the students—Yi In-mo, an unrepentant communist political prisoner, was sent home to north Korea, and Han Wan-sang, the former vice minister of unification, met with student leaders—the ruling party soon chose to end compromise and begin a full-scale assault. Some schoolteachers have been arrested for saying overly positive things about Kim Il Sung: people who offered condolences to north Korea following Kim Il Sung's death were arrested; and, in the summer of 1996, the assault became violent. On August 28, 1996, Kim Young Sam's minister of justice promised to destroy *Hanch'ongnyŏn,* since, according to Kim Young Sam, the student movement was no longer "pure," no longer represented the legitimate concerns of the past, and was directed by the north Koreans through secret faxes and telephone calls. The government called the students terrorists, guerrillas, and "leftist revolutionary forces." Most Koreans and every political party, including the opposition parties, appeared to support the crackdown.[12] Opposition to the students increased significantly in 1997 after June riots ended in the apparent beating death of a young man interrogated by *Hanch'ongnyŏn* on suspicion that he was a police informant.

Beyond being held accountable for violence, *Hanch'ongnyŏn* is criticized for appropriating Kim Il Sung's rhetoric, honoring *chuch'e* ideology, and denying the south Korean government's unification policy in favor of Kim Il Sung's confederation system. It has been argued that the organization itself has become communist, because sections of its charter parallel those that appear in the north Korean constitution and in the North Korean Workers Party rules (Yoo 1996: 70-71). An advisor at a Korean think tank designed to develop strategies against the north *(Taepuk Chŏllyak Yŏnguso)* has argued that south Korea must outlaw all pro-north organizations, remove all "leftists" from politics, strongly encourage schools to prevent students from becoming protestors, intercept all "behind-the-scenes" maneuvering by north Korea, and abolish the passivity of authorities, parents, families, schools, and corporations toward the students (Yu, D.R. 1996: 86-87). By "behind-the-scenes," Yu refers to his citation of more than 200 fax or telephone correspondences between *Hanch'ongnyŏn* and north Korea's *T'ongil Chŏnsŏnbu* (Unification Front Department), as well as other organizations such as *Pŏmch'ŏnghakryŏn* (north Korea's pan-youth students' union) and the north Korean government's office of social and cultural affairs *(Sahoe Munhwabu).*

While representatives of the opposition, such as Kim Dae Jung and his staff, also condemned the students, they also criticized the Kim Young Sam administration for overreacting to the students and for once again proving that, as one official I interviewed put it, Korea has no "discussion culture," or room for active debate. Opposition leaders feared that the government's response to the students would reverse the course of democratization and post - Cold War politics and would prevent the government from looking critically at itself (see Hŏ 1996: 278-283; for a different view from the ruling party, see Kim Y. C. 1996: 272-277; and, for a view from the student movement, Chŏng 1996: 12-13). Indeed, in December of 1996, in a predawn meeting without opposition leaders present, the south Korean ruling party passed new legislation to return to the Korean intelligence agency (ANSP) many of the powers it had during the height of the military dictatorships.

Students in Korea today find themselves in an uncomfortable position of power: they have the power to achieve wealth, status, and social mobility for themselves and their families, as well as the power to disrupt and disappoint their families by violating their expectations. In contemporary south Korea, parents dream of having a child enter the university, because university degrees are a ticket—for some the only ticket—to a higher social status. Many students struggle between ideological commitments and the wish to fulfill their families' desires. The two do not always conflict, but for some the ideological commitments involve protests and other activities that threaten students' futures and the reputations of their families. They see themselves as inextricably linked to their families and to other Koreans, and yet as autonomous subjects; they see themselves as linked to the past, but also as deserving of something different and better than their predecessors.[13] This concern is an expression of filial piety, one of the most distinctive features of Korean culture, as described earlier in the chapter on families. (I take up the relation between students and their families more fully at the end of this chapter in a brief discussion of a recent novel about students.)

It may seem odd to some readers that the president would posit such things as "pure" and "impure" student movements. Yet, as we have already seen, the trope of purity occurs often in Korean discourses on identity and is possibly more salient today in the era of globalization, as many Koreans fear that their traditions are threatened by the emergence of a global monoculture. By drawing on the trope of purity, Kim separates the students from the internal dynamics of south Korea, as well as from the continuities of Korean history, and classifies them as external to Korean society. From the perspective of the government officials who commented so harshly on the 1996 Yonsei riots, these are not the scholars about which Korea's representatives to the Paris Peace Conference in 1919 wrote so passionately; rather, these are students tainted by foreign—north Korean—ideas. And they are students who have become increasingly violent, thus, for Kim, crossing the boundary from student-citizen to terrorist. In so doing, they have also crossed the boundary (figuratively and, sometimes, as in the case of people such as Im Su-kyŏng, literally) from behaving like south Koreans to behaving like north Koreans. In short, discourses on the impurity of the student movement provide an indirect way of marginalizing, externalizing, othering, and even demonizing both the students and the north. Abelmann has commented on how the idiom of purity has been applied to the students in past years: "'Impure' students threatened national security, while pure students were training to become the minds of the body politic and the engineers of economic development" (1996: 122).

It is ironic that President Kim employed the opposition between the pure and the impure, since this is exactly what the students do when criticizing the government as a puppet of American imperialism. The terms of the discourse are shared, as if each side is looking at itself in a mirror. In the next section, we see that the discursive equivalence between the two is highlighted in their mutual performance of protesting and policing. Without the students, the police would have fewer chances to enhance the authority of the state and to make the argument that strong government and the national security state are necessary; without the police, the students would likely become simply another voice struggling to be heard in the national assembly, with no need to use firebombs, rocks, or steel pipes. The police and students continually construct each other as opposed forces. And this is why the question of what would happen if the students protested and no one interfered is ludicrous: the demonstrations are organized against the police as symbols of the state, with the knowledge that the police will arrive as expected.

THE RITUAL OF STUDENT PROTESTS

I don't trust purity. You throw a firebomb to
look for your purity. A Buddhist self-immolates
to reach the purity of nirvana. Marx's proletari-
an revolution was supposed to produce ideological purity. Yet it brings only chaos.

—Cha Tae-soo, in Kim Ha-ki's
Flying Without Direction

Jager (1994: 218-265; 1996) describes the spatial and temporal structure of student protests and government response as repetitive and
ritualized. Jager has theorized the ritual components of student protests
more fully than other scholars, but she is not alone in framing the
protests in terms of ritual. A quick glance at any of the English-language
Ph.D. dissertations on the student movement published in the last
decade reveals a consistent use of the terms "ritual" and "ritualized."
Authors also use words such as "cycle," "pattern," and "model" to
underscore their arguments that, despite the apparent spontaneity of
student passions, or the apparent wildness that government forces wish
to highlight, there is a discernible structure to student protests.

We have already noted that Jager identifies the university gate as
the boundary between an inside world and an outside world, and that
the students stand in a liminal position between countervailing forces. A
more thorough analysis of students might explicate the many ways in
which they stand between tradition and modernity, Korea and the West,
childhood and adulthood, past and future. The gate distinguishes
campus from city, a terrain of tradition (scholarship) from capitalist
culture. Moreover, during their demonstrations, students explicitly
represent the nation in terms of a violated body (Jager 1994: 221). The
nation, in these terms, has been wounded violently; it is often a family
that has been sundered or a woman who has been sexually violated.

Not only do students occupy a liminal position, but they must also
actively negotiate between opposing tendencies:

That the central arena of struggle and debate between students and
the West took place at the university gate was directly related to the
ambiguous nature of the university itself. This is because the univer-

sity served as *both* the locus of change and the locus of tradition. Thus, while students were being transformed by the university into Korea's "modern" and enlightened citizenry, they also fought the terms of this transformation on the battleground between the city and the gate. The seeming contradictions of these ideological perspectives betray the ambiguous nature of nationalism's project: the selective appropriation of the West and the simultaneous safeguarding of one's essential identity. (Jager 1994: 235)

Demonstrations often begin as students collect in front of their respective academic departments and then join in larger groups while singing songs about unification, the preservation of faith in the country, and the need to fight against state oppression. Songs link the Korean nation with one's love or lost love (Jager 1994: 245). Following the singing, student leaders ordinarily direct the groups into marching columns, and they proceed to the campus center. There the students sit in semicircular rows and cheer the arrival of other students. The leaders speak, direct chants and hand gestures, and later follow the students in dance. The content of the speeches and chants concerns not only love but also indictments of the American military occupation and previous military dictatorships, and praises for the students who championed the April 19, 1960, uprising and other protests. In the protests described by Jager, the students generally move together, arm in arm, toward the university gate, where many students are already waiting, having collected rocks and made firebombs. Students and police ordinarily wait on either side of the gate and then at some point begin to exchange fire: the police launch tear gas, the students hurl rocks and firebombs. Eventually the tear gas proves overwhelming, and the students disperse into the campus or into the city, chased by the police.

The spatial organization of student protests symbolically enacts a process of unification within the gates (as the students assemble) and of division when they clash with the government (when the students disperse). What is less obvious is the degree to which the groups cohere in terms of memory. For Jager, the drama of the protest (ritual) is the collective repetition and remembering of the past. The remembered past is a history not only of student struggles, but of the importance of students and scholarship to Korean identity. The students remember the long history of Korean struggles for sovereignty in the face of countless invasions over the past half a millennium, as well as the recent history in which Koreans continue to suffer from national division, the Korean War, and all of their sequelae. The demonstrations thus carry out one of the most universal tasks of ritual: the narration of history.

To elaborate on Jager's work, I would suggest that the demonstrations are meaningful not so much because of what the students actually say, but because what they say, and do, is repetitive and expected. Clearly, much of the content of the speeches is about historical change and the need to overthrow the past in favor of a new, autonomous, and democratic future. And indeed, student protesters have had near-revolutionary success in bringing about social and political changes. However, we have already seen that despite the passion with which demonstrations are carried out and the spontaneity that can ensue from that passion, the protests are nonetheless routine. The overall behavior, moreover, is consistent not only with general expectations of how students, and young people in general, act or represent themselves publicly, but also with the role of students and scholars throughout Korean history. I wonder how students might be perceived if they abandoned their protests completely. They might even be compared to the apathetic and wealthy youth of Apkujŏngdong called *orenjijok* who are widely criticized for caring for neither kin nor country. In other words, the students, by virtue of their youth, are playing an important, and one might say conventional, role in Korean society.

The process by which the two sides construct each other is highlighted in a number of arenas in popular culture, one of the clearest being Pak Kwang-su's well-known film *Ch'il-su wa Man-su* (Ch'il-su and Man-su). In a brief analysis of the film, Abelmann (1996: 40-41) points out that while Ch'il-su and Man-su, two men in their twenties, have no intention of being politically active, their drunken yelling atop a skyscraper in Seoul becomes interpreted by the people below as political dissidence, and their bottles of liquor are believed to be Molotov cocktails.[14] They cannot understand why the people below are concerned because from their perspective, they are simply getting drunk. As Abelmann puts it, "The film is an ironic parable in which protest is quite literally fabricated by the forces that suppress it" (1996: 40). Police, government officials, and the military are mobilized to suppress the imagined labor strike, and as the intensity of the confrontation increases, Ch'il-su and Man-su are drawn into the government's projection by complying with its need for confrontation. Although their voices are inaudible on the street below, the two men begin to complain about the state. As the police climb to arrest them, Ch'il-su jumps to commit suicide, thus ending the dialectic.

It is significant that their voices cannot be heard. This is, no doubt, a metaphor for the relations between people and state in which the people, here represented by Ch'il-su and Man-su, cannot be heard and must instead adopt the discourse of those who dominate them and who continually reproduce themselves by inventing dangerous objects that must be repressed. Clearly, Ch'il-su and Man-su are not revolutionaries, although the people below want them to be, but neither are the students I have been discussing in this chapter revolutionaries. They are not permitted to be. Their voices, too, remain silent as they are drawn into the state apparatus for creating and then controlling protest.

In a similar manner, Snyder (1997a, 1997b) draws on Abelmann's analysis of tenant-landowner negotiations (Abelmann 1996) to suggest that south Koreans commonly pattern conflict and articulate grievances by precipitating the appearance of crisis. In a place such as south Korea, where communication across hierarchical boundaries is constrained by linguistic markers for respect and status, one cannot easily express grievances. The power relations between faculty and students, parents and children, and landlords and peasants, restrict the ability of the disempowered to represent their demands and also restrict the ability of those who are empowered to solicit or listen to demands. Communication emerges when a crisis occurs that requires the joint attention of the parties involved. Negotiations are then moralized, as in the opposition between people and the state, or the philosophy of *han*. Moreover, leaders of negotiating parties often feel compelled to make their positions extreme, not only to ensure the ongoing need for negotiation, but also to prevent the groups they represent from fragmenting. Drawing on Snyder and Abelmann, we might even argue that the student protests and the clashes that ensue are to some extent necessary for communication between students and the government. Indeed, Ch'il-su and Man-su and the government speak to each other only when the government precipitates the crisis and then searches for a way to resolve it. Ch'il-su and Man-su's innocent screams become framed in both extreme and moral terms.

Paik Nak Chung's comments on student dissidents can also be read as a criticism of the students' inability to achieve "true revolution."

Although Paik has applauded the degree to which the students have effected democratic reforms, he remains critical of many of the so-called radicals for becoming stymied in short-term routine projects that have further marginalized the students and that have not addressed the longer-term concerns for creative action, reconciliation, and unification. Paik describes the three national assignments that the Korean people wish to achieve as unification, democracy, and autonomy. All the various scenarios of unification and change on the Korean peninsula are directed toward reaching these three goals, but the political perspectives that have been offered in support of reaching them fail because they do not address the systemic nature of division. For example, the unification theory supported by the PD ("the people's unification theory," *minjung t'ongilron*) contends that there should be *sŏnminju hut'ongil* (democracy first, unification later). This theory is inherently flawed, according to Paik, because it envisions a national project as a series of consecutive and well-bounded events or sudden occurrences (1994: 27). It also resembles much of the history of official unification discourses, which have advocated capitalist development first and unification later. Another wing of the student movement, the NL (National Liberation), declares "*sŏnt'ongil huminju*" (unification first, democracy later) and so suffers from the same problems. (However, it should be noted that the latter position is, by far, more controversial since it suggests the possibility of a non-democratic unified Korea, a situation that would violate the constitution of south Korea). Democratic reforms initiated since 1988 have made possible greater freedom to discuss unification in public, but for Paik the various dissident political wings, namely the PD and the NL, have not progressed beyond their simple slogans. Paik believes that it is necessary to view unification and democracy as inextricably related.

In addition to seeing the students as unable to reach beyond the limitations of their previously defined role, one might also see the students as players in a ritual of rebellion. A ritual of rebellion is an anthropological classification of those rituals that appear to subvert hierarchies but actually reinforce them. Rituals of rebellion ordinarily are not explicitly about reaffirming hierarchies, but they nevertheless have a stabilizing function. Hierarchies are contested in all parts of the world through a variety of different media, some overt and some covert, some obvious, and others so symbolically powerful or unconscious that they are difficult to discern. Although student demonstrators express their anger, resentment, and frustration as subordinates, this manifest content also structures their sentiments in a specific ritual form that mitigates the potential for radical consequences. The demonstrations subvert hierarchy, but they do so in a structured and formal manner that also helps to define the government as the students' political opposite.

The status quo is reaffirmed precisely because the contest compels its participants to articulate the hierarchy through its opposite. I am not suggesting that the students are not effective in achieving many of their manifest goals or in effecting long-term political reforms. Rather, I am suggesting that, far from being "revolutionary," the students are enacting a long-running drama that mediates the underlying structure of opposition. The act of mediating is the very act of purity that former student leaders such as President Kim Young Sam are now mourning as lost.

Subversions of hierarchy are most explicitly attempted in three related arenas of symbolic representation: first, in the *nonghwal* (agricultural action) movement, in which students travel from urban areas to live with farmers; second, in the folk theater and mask dances intended to convey many of the messages of student movements; and third, in the frequent articulation of *minjung* histories by students and scholars within student movements. These three arenas are interwoven with each other, so much so that one could make the argument that their analytic separation is a distortion, though perhaps necessary for their explication. *Nonghwal,* folk theater, and student demonstrations each contain elements of the other, and so there are no clear-cut boundaries to be found between them; for example, student demonstrations and *nonghwal* workers invoke shamanic rituals, and folk theater productions incorporate idioms of peasant tradition (Kendall 1996: 78). Each also involves attempts by predominantly young people, mostly students, to locate national and personal identity in the folk, and by implication to locate false or temporary identity in the state. These are *movements,* literally and figuratively, because they represent real and imaginary travel and return in both geographic and temporal terms. The imaginary travel leads participants into a symbolic world that is strikingly similar to a world sometimes occupied when imagining the north: an unspoiled land and time of pure Koreanness, a world away from the city and the West, the nonautonomous government, and the elites.

NONGHWAL AND FOLK THEATER

We all have something in common. We have
inherited *ŏpbo* [in Buddhism, retribution for the
deeds of a former life] from the preceding
generations. We thought our conflict with the
older generations was just a generation gap. But
we shouldn't have to suffer from their problems.
We should stop the chain here. And I don't want
to be defined by ideology or any group [-*kwŏn*].
I want to change naturally and instinctively.

—Chŏng Taŭm, in Kim Ha-ki,
Flying Without Direction

Although the students have often been successful in gathering public
support for their pro-democracy protests, they have had less success in
achieving their goals in the areas of agriculture and factory labor. Many
students have been extraordinarily frustrated when their own high energy
and enthusiasm is sometimes met with resignation, cynicism, and passivity. Yet if the move to facilitate labor union activity and to educate peasants
about their marginalization has done less for the laborers and farmers than
many had hoped, it has done much for the students themselves. *Nonghwal*
programs have meant that students in institutions of higher education, the
vast majority of whom live in Seoul, could challenge the myopic perspectives of urban and campus life, extend public sympathy for their positions
to the countryside, and, through their own sympathies with the farmers,
attempt to subvert the hierarchical relations between urban and rural
areas, and between the southeast (from which most of the presidents of
Korea have come) and the southwest (an agricultural region more
underdeveloped than any other part of south Korea). Moreover, in the
valorization of the folk, they challenge the hierarchical relation established
during Korea's economic expansion between the "backward" peasant and
the "progressive" capitalist. While many Koreans might easily be embarrassed by international media images of Korea as "traditional" or rural,
many students express pride in the strength of the masses to continue
Korean traditions and criticize the elites of government and industry for
depending on foreign ideas and capital. (It remains to be seen how the
elections of Kim Dae Jung, from the oppressed Chŏlla province, which

occurred at the time of this writing, will influence student activism in the southwest).

The word *nonghwal* is a condensation of the longer phrase *nongchon pongsahwaltong*, meaning "agricultural service activities." An outgrowth of earlier movements in the 1970s to popularize a national student summer service *(chŏnguk taehaksaeng hakyaeyŏnhap pongsatan)* and of sporadic student service in rural villages dating back to the 1950s, *nonghwal* is a very general term that can refer to a range of different activities. Whereas in the 1950s student activities were directed more at a broad "enlightenment" *(kyemong)* and "guidance" *(chido)*, the *nonghwal* of the 1980s were directed more specifically at a number of different services, hence the use of the term *pongsa* (service). Kangwŏn University conducted a survey on *nonghwal* in 1981, well before *nonghwal* participation reached its peak in the late 1980s (Kangwŏn University 1982). In a sample of 612 students from Kangwŏn University who joined *nonghwal* teams, the vast majority of students (about 80 percent) worked directly in agricultural activities by laboring in the fields; 12 percent worked in medical service in the rural areas, building wells, septic tanks, sewers, and operating mobile public health centers; 4 percent worked in education; and the small remainder worked in family planning and nutritional guidance.[15]

In the most comprehensive English-language treatment of *nonghwal*, Abelmann (1993, 1996) illustrates how students became disaffected with the programs because they established a hierarchy between the students as "teachers" and the farmers— between those who were enlightened, and those who needed to have their true consciousness illuminated. As a result, many students intitiated a "new *nonghwal*" movement, one aimed more at a dialogue between students and farmers than the unidirectional approach of past years in which students viewed themselves as providing services to the farmers. Abelmann cites one publication in which the new dialogue is clearly explicated:

> Students, through a comprehension of the realities of farming villages, will personally experience the reality of their colonial territory-homeland, and build an emotional link with farmers. . . . While farmers, through [their contact with] the students will plant a consciousness to become the masters of society and get connections with students. (Agricultural Action Resource collection statement, 1987: 1, 4, cited in Abelmann 1993: 132)

For the purposes of our consideration of education, one of the most important functions of the students' efforts toward establishing a dialectic between themselves and the farmers is that these efforts, like all activities within student movements, involved a rejection of their earlier education. University students argued that they had to "unlearn," by which they meant they had to become conscious of the ways in which the government sought to indoctrinate them with a particular ideology. Like university students everywhere, perhaps, educated Korean men and women emerged as critical thinkers questioning the ideas they had taken for granted. Even today, Korean university professors are seldom questioned openly and are widely venerated. But in student "circles," or study groups, men and women read Marx, Lenin, and Gramsci and there pose questions that are deemed inappropriate in a classroom setting.[16] Abelmann writes of the extraordinary resentment experienced by Koryŏ University students when they learned that Kim Song-su, the founder of the university, had collaborated with the Japanese and had played a part in the oppression of some farmers in Chŏlla-do. She quotes a student on Kim Song-su:

> "How could an enlightened smart person tell people to do and fight for the voluntary Japanese military units... ignorant citizens believed this . . . and now Roh Tae Woo who participated in the coup d'etat [by Chun] and Kwangju still runs for president, calling himself a regular guy [*pot'ong saram*]; is it so easy to become a great person? If *he* is a great person, *who* will try and become a great person? . . . When I hear male students who study [in the student movement] say that the people in North Korea live well and fully, I doubt them. . . but since I have seen the distortion and hidden facts [in south Korea] I'm not really so surprised. In Junior High we were asked to write down what we knew about north Korea; I wrote, 'corn meal soup [i.e., no white rice], forced labor, and reds catching flies and killing them' . . . how deplorable that I wrote that about people of the same nation."
> (Abelmann 1995: 134)

One result of this student's education, then, is to make her react negatively against the reality she had taken for granted. Like other students, she is ashamed to have been indoctrinated, to have supported historical representations she now knows are false. Many students describe *nonghwal* as a reawakening, an experience that reveals to them the masks covering the realities of the human condition in Korea, and this includes north Korea. Thus, as this student's statement implies, images of north Korea form a central battleground for conflicts over the representation of reality. As was shown in the analysis of school textbooks, north Korea becomes a primary object of south Korean historical narrative, and it is from the subject of north Korea that discussions of south Korean identities—democracy, capitalism, and progress—emerge.

Mask dances and folk theater are an outgrowth of students' attempts to resuscitate the folk *(minjung)* culture exemplified by the farmers (and more indirectly exemplified by the *Tonghak* rebellion) and within which, it is widely believed, lies the spirit of the Korean people. It is not uncommon for student demonstrators to wear the style of clothes preferred by farmers, to perform traditional rural songs, and to travel to farms to work and live for a time. Such an idealization of the folk is common to nationalisms throughout the world—in this case, it is as a reaction against globalization, Westernization, and what is often conceived as a neocolonial American presence in Korean affairs. Abelmann defines the *minjung* movement of which these activities are a part as a struggle to revive and identify with the "people"; she writes, "the *minjung* movement refers to the theories, idioms, and strategies by which a community of activists sought to evoke and mobilize people broadly perceived to be dispossessed, and hence the rightful subjects of history and agents of political transformation" (1993: 119). Wells classifies the *minjung* movement as "interventionist," because it challenges official history; as a community of sufferers, because its adherents have been oppressed by those in power and yet strengthened and defined by that very oppression; as "predictive," in that the *minjung* are proper subjects of history and will serve as the agents of the Korean unified nation in the future; as being dedicated to unification as Korea's paramount goal; and, finally, as a culturally distinctive historiography (Wells 1995: 12-14) (on the last categorization, see the previous chapter).

University mask dance drama groups, established in the late 1960s as a central part of the student movement, and professional theater groups enact this constellation of features. They generally depict characters who resist the powers of oppression and marginalization. Choi Chungmoo describes the formation of an early mask dance group, the Malttugi Association, established in 1967 and named after a slave character who ridicules the *yangban*. Comparing the mask dance to the subversion of the moral order, as elaborated in Bakhtin's well-known work on traditions of carnival (1984 [1965]), she writes:

> In this style of theater, the slave, Malttugi, ridicules the ruling *yangban* class (aristocracy) with exuberant, bawdy puns and obscenities, using bodily substrata, and defames the very authority of the rulers. The lowly slave also profanes the sacrosanct Confucian morality of the *yangban* and exposes the falsity of their moral superiority, the foundation of the existing class hierarchy. By way of poetic transgression, the drama suggests the possible *reversibility of the hierarchical social order.* (Choi, C. M. 1995: 110, emphasis added)

In other words, the mask dance resembles a ritual of rebellion that turns the conventional social order on its head, claims equality for all, and makes possible new (bodily) pleasures and political organizations. Choi believes that the mask dance opens up an "alternative epistemological space" (1995: 117) that provides opportunities for students to join together for a common national project. But this does not mean that the mask dance functions to alter the social order. In another work, Choi also argues that in a new people's theater genre called *madangkŭk*, a pure, united, postcapitalist history can be made:

> It appropriates a shamanic ritual format so that ancient time, space, and characters can be freely exchanged with those of the present through the mechanism of ritual ecstasy. . . . The polysemous layers of metaphor invested in *madang guk* [sic] have enriched and elevated the popular movement from the pursuit of a romantic revolution as well, and this has fostered in the movement a great staying power (Choi, C. 1993: 93).

In this utopian vision, *madangkŭk* "is a site where this utopia is to materialize through a carnivalesque communal festival and through a collective struggle against the ruling bourgeoisie as the commoners of the pre-rupture period are imagined to have carried it out" (Choi, C. 1993: 92).

I would hesitate to accept wholeheartedly Choi's comparisons to carnival—a classic ritual of rebellion—because it obscures the functionalist role such rituals play in preserving the social order. Read as part of the broader cultural patterns of south Korean social life, the ostensible "carnivalesque" reversals of hierarchy are, by Choi's own characterization, similar to rituals of rebellion. These are rituals that appear to be transformative and yet often function sociologically to reaffirm the existing social order, and function psychologically as a release of frustration and resentment. By drawing an analogic equivalence between carnival and Korean folk theater, Choi unwittingly suggests that the folk theater contributes to the continuity of the existing social order. Indeed, among the most important lessons learned in the wake of anthropology's historical turn are that history is not only about change but also about continuity, and that acts of resistance frequently reinforce preexisting systems (Jager 1994: 175-176).

MINJUNG

> The *nonghwal* paradox is that, while the "subjects" of production, farmers, have turned away from "traditional" culture, students have been maintaining it.
>
> —Nancy Abelmann

I have already defined the concept of *minjung* to some extent above. A very detailed English-language treatment of the concept of *minjung* can be found in Kenneth M. Wells's collection, *South Korea's Minjung Movement* (1995), and in Nancy Abelmann's *Echoes of the Past, Epics of Dissent* (1996). There is also a rich literature in Korean on *minjung* theology, *minjung* (and *minjok*, or "national") *literature* (Paik 1994), and *minjung* arts (Choi, Y. 1994; *Hyŏnsilkwa parŏn*, 1990), and to the extent that *minjung* has become a social category in recent historiography, there is an important literature in the field of history (see, for example, Song K. H. 1989; Pak H.1988). Student demonstrations, the mask dances, and *nonghwal* can all be seen to cohere around the very powerful and populist concept of *minjung*, a term that has defined much of south

Korea's recent dissident movements, and that quite clearly demonstrates the relation between student activism and historical memory.

The *minjung*, as has been already noted, can be defined in the simplest terms as the people or masses, idealized as the farmers, peasants, or laborers. Although there is disagreement in Korea on whether the *minjung* constitute a "class" in the Marxist sense of the term (Shin, G. W. 1995: 514-515), the *minjung* and their suffering are in large part defined by their relations of production (Wells 1995: 13).[17] There are, of course, other terms for the "people," in particular *inmin* (used in north Korea) and *kukmin* (citizen, used in south Korea); indeed, although the word *minjung* was used by national liberation movements during the colonial period, these other terms were used far more in the period between the onset of division and the student activism of the early 1960s. *Minjung* became the term of choice, to some extent, because it had been employed during predivision days, especially by the anti-Japanese resistance.

Within the *minjung* lies the resentment or *han* not only of the current structural domination by elites in south Korean society, but also of the longer span of Korean history in which the people have been marginalized from and dispossessed of the centers of economic and political power and agency. The so-called *minjung* movement consists of scholars, students, theologians, and others who call for a Korean history in which the *minjung* will be the agents (or subjects) of history. Much of the spirit elaborated by the *minjung* movement can be located in the *Tonghak* rebellion of 1893-1894, either because the rebellion exemplifies that spirit or because it is considered the actual birth of a *minjung consciousness* (Abelmann 1996). The participants in the *Tonghak* movement handed down their spirit, their *han,* and their identity to the farmers of contemporary Korea, who are the proper subjects of history and who can properly carry on the revolution initiated during *Tonghak.* *Minjung,* in these terms, is thus far more than a class, and more than a revolutionary agent. The *minjung* are, in some sense, more pure than those Koreans who have Westernized and co-opted the political language and practices of colonial and postcolonial agents. The *minjung* movement, then, is more than a call for a transfer of power to the oppressed; it is a historiography, a way of rewriting history, of giving a particular past an authority in the present and future. This is an authority greater than that of the West. In Abelmann's treatment (far more elaborate than that presented here), *minjung* is conceived as a mode of resistance in, at least for analytic purposes, both cultural and political terms: in cultural terms, it represents a way of life, a possible national culture defined by a distinctly "Korean" village socialism; in political terms, it refers to the role the *minjung* might assume in national politics (Abelmann 1993: 143-144).

Minjung thus stands for people who are inheritors of the past and yet live in the present; the student activists position themselves between the *minjung* and the rest of the nation, as well as between the present-day government and the early-twentieth-century anticolonial intellectuals' *minjung* movement, to some degree translating the experiences and spirit of the *minjung* into contemporary political and literary discourses.[18] Through *minjung,* folk theater, and *nonghwal,* students thus attempt to reverse their indoctrination by the state, to reduce their dependency on foreign powers, to resuscitate a lost past embodied in a marginalized segment of Korean society, and to realize a future in which a more pure Korean spirit, living within the *minjung,* can take hold.

It is perhaps wrong to try to determine whether a *minjung* actually exists. As many writers have noted, *minjung* is a very abstract concept—a consciousness rather than a sociological category. Its importance lies in the ability of people to use the idea to stimulate creative struggle, not in whether the concept is held to correspond to an objective unit of reality. Certainly, there can be little doubt that the *minjung* are a discursive product of contemporary politics, defined so that they can be appropriated for particular political strategies. This is a process highlighted by Choi in a critique of the *minjung* movement's strategy to authorize itself as the representative of an oppressed people. She suggests that there is a colonizing, patronizing element in *minjung* discourses that alienates the *minjung* from the process of self-representation:

> In order to prepare (educate) people to assume a role in revolution, these intellectual representatives of *minjung* attempt to instill a new epistemology and raise historical consciousness. In other words, the agenda of the representatives of the people is to shape the people they are representing; this implies the process of othering, while

>   simultaneously representing and constructing "the people." (Choi,
>   C. M. 1993: 97)

Although the intention of the *minjung* representation, as Choi notes, is
to reverse the trope of the peasant, usually denigrated as an uneducated,
backward element of Korean society, into an idealized epitome of
"Koreanness," the idealization masks the degree to which intellectuals
are actually classifying and appropriating, and thus intellectually subor-
dinating for their own purposes, a group of people who may not classify
themselves in the same terms. These followers of *minjung* culture are
predominantly urbanites who worship and celebrate themselves by
borrowing from and reaffirming a folk culture that to a large extent they
themselves have actually designed in the process of building a new
nationalism. Many students have taken this kind of criticism to heart,
and, along with many other factors, not the least of which is the
democratization of south Korean politics, this is one reason why the
popularity of *minjung* discourses is in decline. It should be mentioned,
too, that *minjung* literature has been redundant in its message, themes,
and plots, despite the attempts of creative writers to produce a rich
language in which to frame *minjung* perspectives. This routinization
may also have contributed to the decline.

Minjung, nonghwal, and folk theater are thus part of the process
through which young people struggle with identity. They try to define
their own identities through the detour of the other, both in space (by
traveling on *nonghwal* projects) and in time (by idealizing the *Tonghak*
peasant and idealizing the contemporary peasant as being continuous with
Tonghak). They are also serving to give voice to the society at large; this is
a role they have had for much of contemporary Korean history, and there
is no evidence to suggest that it will cease simply because of the election of
Kim Young Sam. An opinion that student protests are anachronistic
would have to be based on an assumption that the students' primary role
is to effect change. But while they may effect dramatic structural changes
in Korean society, and while this may be their manifest purpose, it is not
necessarily their latent function. They are serving as mediators, as voices
for the articulation of the instabilities of south Korean identity. Students
are in a good place to take on this role in part because, as students, they
are already liminal and structurally unstable.

A LITERARY PERSPECTIVE ON STUDENTS AND DIVISION

> The film could be called: "The Children of
> Marx and Coca-Cola." Think of it what you
> like.
>
> —Jean-Luc Godard., Masculine *
> Feminin: 15 Acts

In the final section of this chapter, I want to explore a recent south Korean novel, Kim Ha-ki's 1993 *Hangnoŏpnŭn pihaeng* [Flying without direction], which highlights the power of the university to shape personality and political consciousness, but which also leads us to see student activists not as renegades, guerrillas, or ideologues, but as people caught up in a web of conflicting representations. The anthropologist Cho Hae Joang has described some of this complexity in her stimulating two-volume 1992 study of students of social theory at Yonsei University in Seoul. In this work, Cho explores how the educational process and the students' personal experiences resonate with each other. Cho had expected her students to fit her stereotype of Yonsei students: well-positioned young men and women, Korea's first "socially stable" *(sahoe anjŏng)* generation, raised in cities to be good middle-class, forward-looking capitalists. Yet she found instead that the students conceived of themselves as continually linked with the past, to feudalism, the chaos of liberation, and the division of families. Some students identified themselves first and foremost as sons and daughters of people who had lost their hometowns (Cho, H. J. 1992: 126-127). With regard to actual school activities, some students felt liberated by the freedom of discussion in student "circles," while others felt oppressed by them and tried to escape ideological conflicts (1992: 131); however, they were fairly united in expressing the need to unlearn the canons of political ideology drummed into them during their primary and secondary school years. As the epigraph to the fifth chapter of her book (1992: 125), Cho thus offers a sarcastic poem, part of which reads:

> Teacher, don't ask us questions that are not in the book.
> Teacher, we were happy to memorize the canon.
> Afflicted high-schoolers? No, afflicted universities.

Give us order in an authoritative voice.
Tell us what the problems are, and give us the solutions too.
We don't want to see reality.

As we shall see, not only do students want to acquire the eyes with which to see reality, but they also want to learn to see more clearly just how they are connected with their pasts.

Flying Without Direction is a bildungsroman *(sŏngjang sosŏl)* about a young woman and several of her classmates, all of whom come from very different backgrounds and yet join together as student activists. More specifically, however, the novel enacts the drama of maturation as a search to distinguish falsehoods from realities. There is no "true crime" committed by students or police, since they are all integral parts of the same system of reality distortion. It is a system that produces political difference, a system within which the students, their parents, and the police are each both victimized and complicit.[19]

In presenting a view of students as embedded in a system of representation, Kim departs from the more ordinary depiction of student-parent relations that we saw in *The Third Border*. Recall that the young Park barely speaks to his father and appears to be so blindly committed to the student movement that he is unwilling to engage in a dialogue or express ambivalence about his project and its ramifications for those around him. He gives no indication of a desire for reconciliation, and so the condescending message, allowing no room to share or debate ideas and feelings, is all that remains: "Father, you and your generation are wrong; you do not understand the needs of this nation." In contrast, in Kim's novel—a novel that is different from many, since representations of students in literature have been rather one-dimensional, conforming to government restrictions on literature that might appear to be sympathetic with the students, and hence "anti-state"—Kim offers the students' perspectives. The conventional superficial characterization of students cannot convey their powerful emotional commitment to their causes or their willingness to risk their futures (and sometimes their lives) for the student movement. In his novel, Kim moves beyond an examination of students as a collectivity to illuminate the complexities of particular lived realities.

Although the students depicted in *Flying Without Direction* hold some divergent views, they all share profound conflicts and uncertainties about their participation in student activism. The central conflict that unfolds is not between the students and others but within the students themselves as they struggle to balance their commitments both to political causes and to their families. Once again, we see how political discourses oppose politics and the family. The novel opens by depicting the protagonist, Chŏng Taŭm, as an innocent, a young woman as yet unable to objectify herself as a "student" or "laborer" in contrast to other categories of person. Ambivalent about seeking a higher education, she waits so long to leave her home that she must rush to take the entrance exam on time. Unable to find a taxi, she flags down a kind policeman, who offers to drive her to campus. Kim No-kyŏng, a student activist, blocks the vehicle from entering the sacred *(shinsŏnghan)* grounds of the campus. The scene marks the opposition of police and campus, with Chŏng as mediator. In the context of a long history of conflict between students and police, the whole scene seems incongruous, and yet it logically marks Chŏng's passage into the new world of the university.

If Kim's characters are complex, it is in large part due to their complicated backgrounds and relationships with their families. Indeed, each student represents an individual who is in some way tortured—or, one might say more benignly and precisely, *constituted*—by his or her own parents. These are not students who achieve autonomy from their parents; these are students who gradually come to realize that their parents are a central part of their identities and life courses. Despite their independence of thought, they eventually end up identifying, and in different ways reconciling, with either their parents or the perspectives on Korean politics their parents represent.

Unable to endure her abusive marriage, Chŏng's mother leaves her four children and travels to Japan to become a bar hostess (though it seems uncertain whether her employment is voluntary or coerced by illegal recruiters). A welder whose small salary gives him just enough money to get drunk, Chŏng's father appears as a cruel figure who beats Chŏng's sister until she must escape to a life of prostitution in an area of Seoul frequented by American GIs. At school, Chŏng befriends a number of people, especially a computer expert named An Kyŏng-tae. An's mother defected to north Korea, while his father lives an ascetic life in the forest making traditional writing brushes and eschewing all modern technology. Chŏng also meets Kim No-kyŏng, the student who had initially stopped her and the policeman from entering the university. He is a remarkably bright man—he received the highest score on the entrance exams—and he leads a student activist group that Chŏng eventually joins. He has no knowledge of his biological father (who impregnated his mother out of wedlock) and very limited knowledge about his social father, a man born mentally retarded who was falsely accused by Kim's mother, and the village community, of raping and impregnating her. Chŏng also meets Cha Tae-su, an attractive man who is classified as *orenji jok* (a rich, young, urban elite who demonstrates his wealth through conspicuous spending and dating). He rudely addresses his father, a pastor, as "religious fanatic" *(chonggyoae mich'imsaram),* and his wealthy mother, who made her fortune selling to developers land she had inherited in Kangnam, as "lucky wife" *(pokpuin).* Cha's best friend, Nam Yi-bŏm, is even wealthier. His social father is a director of one of the *chaebŏl,* his biological father is a convicted and unrepentant communist.

As their university life evolves, all the students acknowledge that they are forever connected to their pasts. Chŏng Taŭm thus says to Yi-bŏm and Kyŏng-tae, "We all have something in common. We have inherited the deeds and retributions *(ŏpbo)* of the preceding generations. We thought our conflicts with them were simple generation gaps. The basic point I am making is that we suffer because of them. We have to cut the chain now, and stop passing on such suffering" (Kim, H. K. 1992 vol. 2: 92). The words ring true for them. Early in the novel, Yi-bŏm discovers that his true father is a political prisoner, and that both his mother and father had been communist partisans before and during the war. Kyŏng-tae, whose mother defected to the north, is followed and eventually detained by government agents convinced that he had secretly traveled north to see her. Yi-bŏm's interactions with his father are strained and pregnant with contradiction; his (formerly communist) father wants him to be an anti-communist, yet at this point Yi-bŏm has no clearly defined political views other than the anti-communism he learned at school. His father urges his son to pursue a romantic and liberal social life and yet asks him to join the military or at least the Korean equivalent of the ROTC; he urges Yi-bŏm to appreciate all that he has done for the family and yet admonishes him to uphold the family's precept *(kahun):* "Never look back." Yi-bŏm soon visits his grandfather in the countryside, a man estranged from his son. Although his grandfather will not reveal the truth of his grandson's birth, Yi-bŏm notices the family precept in his grandfather's bedroom. It reads: "Review the past and learn the new."

Other figures are equally shrouded in layers of misrepresentation. For example, a student leader, Cho Yang-tal, is in fact a CIA informant whose American contact is married to a Korean woman so artificial and pretentious that she is almost comical (her hair is dyed, her face is heavily made up, her body is adorned with jewelry, and she owns a German shepherd named Manhattan). A particularly militant female student, Wŏn Tong-suk, turns to violence after discovering that her father, an outspoken professor and media figure advocating fidelity and other virtues, has been carrying on a long-standing sexual relationship with a neighborhood shop owner. Wŏn is physically weak but proclaims that her true self emerges when hurling firebombs.

Despite the fact that the students collectively appear to fight against American imperialism, anti-democratic government practices, and the division of the country, at the individual level they are fighting against the constitutive role of their pasts, including their university experience. It is not simply that some of the students detest their parents; rather, they resent the power of the intergenerational linkages. In the end, nearly every student reconciles with his or her family, either by acknowledging the parents' limitations, or by accepting compromise. Even An Kyŏng-tae's ascetic father eventually says that he would like to visit a city. And, with the help of Chŏng, Nam Yi-bŏm seems at peace with the idea that his biological father is a communist (coming to terms with the fact that, as Godard might say, he is a child of Marx).

Along with their relationship to their parents, the students wrestle with their role as activists. At times they believe strongly in the causes of the student organizations, while at other times they reject the activists as blind and unpatriotic ideologues—ironically, this is a conventional and popular criticism of student activists. Their ambivalence is palpable. The struggle to acknowledge that one's father is a communist, to experience ambivalence about the ineluctable continuities of history—these thoughts are all, to some extent, metaphors for Korea's struggle with its past. Each of these young people inherits the legacy of Korea's division and war in very distinct ways, thus showing how powerfully Korea's history ramifies to individual lives. It would be far too simple to say that these students are revolutionaries. It would be more accurate to say that they appear to be revolutionary because they stand between the past and the future and are therefore symbols of the potential for both continuity and change, as well as the positive and negative aspects of both of these directions. Kim Ha-ki's students realize where they stand, but they are uncertain as to which direction to fly. Are there some perspectives that are more true than others? How can they be sure that their own views on the past and future are not perpetuating the hegemony they believe they are fighting against? Toward the end of the novel, Chŏng Taŭm sums up many of the sentiments experienced and expressed by the other characters when she attempts to persuade Yi-bŏm to visit his communist father in prison. Whether Koreans like it or not, she seems to suggest, they are faced with perspectives on the nation that appear real or true when, in fact, they may be as arbitrary as the thirty-eighth parallel or the border between south Korea's southernmost provinces:

TAŬM: Have you considered that [your father] is a victim of the division?

YI-BŎM: Isn't that too generous, to simply call him a victim? He came to the south with a particular purpose [as a spy].

TAŬM: Is there a bigger difference between north and south than between Kyŏngsang-do and Chŏlla-do? Think about who drew the line at the thirty-eighth parallel, and why we haven't been able to achieve our paramount goal of unification [for almost fifty years].

YI-BŎM: So you want to talk about foreign powers again?

TAŬM: Not really. No matter how strong they are, we could unify if we were strong enough. The real problem lies within us. Anti-north sentiments, our consciousness of division, these have become a kind of myth inside of us. Division has replaced *Tangun* [Korea's mythical ancestor]. Anti-communism is a fixed national policy that gives people anti-north sentiments as an a priori experience. But if we look carefully, can't we see that our division consciousness emerged at the same time we started drinking Coca-Cola? Illusions and falsehood separated Kyŏngsang-do and Chŏlla-do, north and south. It broke the Korean identity. Division will end only when the myth ends as well. (Kim, H. K. 1992: vol. 2, 262)

Kim's portrayal is fictional, but this does not mean that it is false. In fact, his portrayals will no doubt ring true for many who know student activists well. Student activists are not anarchists, they are not terrorists, and there is no such thing as a pure or impure student movement. Students give voice to the conflicts and uncertainties of a nation whose citizens continue to undergo rapid historical change. Sometimes these changes conflict with each other. The reduction of authoritarianism, for example, can lead to heightened fears about the ability of the state to defend the country, and yet governments with great authority inevitably risk being nondemocratic and corrupt. Or, as another example, anti-north sentiment can heighten the sense of need for a U.S. military presence in south Korea, and yet the more the United States participates in south Korean's defense, the more south Koreans talk about their loss of political autonomy. I should even mention that, although young people represent the vanguard of modernization and globalization, they are also criticized for straying too far from tradition. These conflicts and contradictions are a part of historical change, as south Koreans struggle for a national identity in a changing world complicated by national division, democratization, and industrialization. The message that students present is that south Korea has a crisis of identity, a crisis that any rapidly changing society experiences, and this is a message that Korean students gave during Japanese colonization as well. I would not anticipate that student demonstrations would end after unification either, for then there will be a crisis of identity at least as profound as that afflicting south Korea today.

The next chapter takes up the theme of the boundary between north and south Korea in the travel accounts of three south Korean dissidents who decided to step over the false border, and in some conservative responses to their illegal travel. What we find is that, although south Korean administrations have long argued that the border is indeed absurd and one not of Koreans' own making, the border becomes real when it is threatened.

DISSIDENCE AND
BORDER VIOLATIONS

THUS FAR, this book has sought to characterize south Korean discourses on north Korea and unification, and certain absences of discourses as well, in terms of a process of complicated mourning. The complications arise in the challenge of recognizing what may have been lost during national division, and they are a product of discourses on similarity and homogeneity. One of the most important components of mourning processes is ambivalence—the coexistence of or oscillation between conflicting sentiments and perspectives about that which is lost or appears to be lost. In this chapter on border crossings, I argue that south Korean ambivalence about division and unification emerges in part as the search for a "real" or "true" Korea—a unified Korea—but that this search cannot succeed. To support this argument, I address the ways in which ambivalences about national division and unification are symbolically patterned in south Korea, and how they become constitutive of Korean conceptions of the reality and authenticity of the Korean nation, and of attempts to deny the loss of homogeneity.

By focusing on illegal border crossings, I hope to highlight the power of division to sustain itself. The three people about whom I write here—the late Mun Ik-hwan, a famous and very popular pastor in south Korea; Hwang Sŏk-yŏng, a well-known and respected author in south Korea, and Im Su-Kyŏng, a student activist—all did what many south Koreans can only dream of doing: they went to north Korea. Yet by going to north Korea, these people were considered traitorous and dangerous to the welfare of the nation and the process of unification. Why would a few people crossing over a border that is by all Korean accounts a *false* border elicit such a strong reaction? What is so wrong about traveling across the border? And why are "authorized crossings," in which investors, diplomats, or Red Cross officials cross into the north, not met with the same negative public reaction?

Mun, Hwang, and Im illuminate for us some of the uncertainties and ambiguities of unification discourses. They stand for the unity of the people over the state, and yet, at the same time, they are often perceived to have unwittingly supported the state division by becoming pawns to north Korea's propaganda, and to have hurt themselves and their family's reputations for the sake of ideology or nationalism. It is not that these sorts of people—students and the non-government political leaders often called *chaeya insa*—are so different, in terms of their general values and aspiratons, from those Koreans who articulate official policy, but rather that they bring into relief the incompleteness of Korea and so are easy targets for resentment. It is safe to say that most Koreans do not like to see themselves as partial, and yet that is what they are beginning to believe themselves to be.

Themes addressed in this chapter recall those addressed in chapter 3 on the 1993 exhibition in Seoul of north Korean everyday life, since the exhibition served as a form of imaginary, symbolic travel. The exhibition also brought up the subject of ambivalence about travel. The discourses described here about actual cases of travel to north Korea bring out aspects of ambivalence about north Korea and unification that I have only touched on in previous chapters, and they illustrate some of the different ways in which ambivalence is rendered in narrative: the concept of homogeneity, the search for the real, and a major political cleavage that turns about differing conceptions of reality.

SWALLOWS OF THE SPRING

> Smelling boiled eggs, this is what the nation
> means, to be able to discern truths without
> thinking.
>
> —Hwang Sŏk-yŏng

In late March 1989, many of the largest newspapers in south Korea, such as *Tonga ilbo, Hanguk ilbo,* and *Chosŏn ilbo,* ran articles, editorials, and letters critical of the illegal travel of the Reverend Mun Ik-hwan to north

Korea. In discussing these criticisms, I do not mean to validate them and give them further voice; rather, I want to analyze them to find out why they were so negative. The media coverage, in particular, tells us a great deal about how states, in coordination with newspapers, seek to reinforce the people-state opposition and to frame debates about north Korea and unification in terms of an opposition between sentiment and science, that is, between the passions of "children," as the state would like to define many students and dissidents, and the objectivity and maturity of "elders," as the state would like to define itself.

Mun, a well-known and popular political and religious figure in south Korea, frequently arrested during the 1970s and 1980s for his opposition to the government, defied strict south Korean national security laws that prohibit south Koreans from going to north Korea. Mun justified the trip by appealing to his commitment to promote unification through actual interpersonal contact, and by stressing that all Koreans belong to both north and south. As he explained in his account of the ten-day voyage, "I am a part of my country from Paekdu mountain in the north to Halla mountain in the south" (Mun 1990: 107-108). Mun says that he crossed the border so that he might understand north Koreans not through propaganda or rumor, but, as he said, with "my own eyes and heart" (1990: 107). Korean observers of Mun's visit were at once confronted with an unpleasant ambiguity of travel: movement that is both transgression and desire, movement that is both a leaving and a return. Mun compelled people to negotiate the public and normative desire for contact between south and north Koreans and to consider how subverting official policy can make contact possible.

Mun insisted he was not leaving a place but rather going toward one: Korea. Despite the fact that Mun was, and remains even after death, a person of extraordinary popularity and renown, media reaction to his trip was blistering. Editorials in *Tonga ilbo* on March 27 and 28, 1989, referred to Mun's visit as "illegitimate," "risky," and "dangerous" and called Mun himself a "dangerous figure." Some authors stressed that his visit resulted in "instability" and "despair" in south Korea. *Hanguk ilbo* ran a cartoon on March 28 illustrating Mun competing as a runner, but taking an illegal shortcut in order to beat his rivals. The caption read "Foul!" *(Panch'ik!)*. In that same issue, an editorial criticizing Mun's idealism read, "The cold reality *[hyŏnsil]* is different from the world of dreams and poetry." One writer angrily scolded Mun, asserting that the road to unification was not a child's "dream road" but a road of "reality" (Chung, D. Y. 1989: 5). A poll conducted by Sŏgang University of the general population and published in *Hanguk ilbo* on April 4 asserted that 66.8 percent of Koreans considered Mun's trip to be "wrong," 20 percent thought it was "good," and 13.2 percent thought that a value could not be placed upon the trip until a later date. I do not know if this poll or others were biased in favor of the government's enforcement of the national security laws; what is significant to me is not the poll's results but only that the poll was given a good deal of press coverage and therefore had a large audience.

There were similar responses to travels to north Korea, in the same year, by a college student, Im Su-kyŏng (a representative of *Chŏndaehyŏp*, National Council of Student Representatives, now called *Hanchongnyŏn*, the National Federation of Student Councils), and a noted writer, Hwang Sŏk-yŏng. Im's stay in north Korea, from June 30 to August 15, became a cause célèbre that summer, as south Koreans were variously outraged and fascinated by her violation of the national security laws. While the north Korean media embraced Im's visit as heroic, the south Korean media leveled furious attacks against her during her trip and after her return. South Korean media reactions, almost universally negative, were supported by large numbers of critical letters to the editor by south Korean citizens. When, in August 1989, Im entered the hospital weak from the hunger strike she had called in order to compel the Joint Security Area to allow her reentry into south Korea through the demilitarized zone, many people complained publicly that she was no different than any other Korean, that she deserved no special treatment, and that security at the hospital inconvenienced the other patients and their families. One might well suggest that her presence at the hospital was construed as separating people from their families, symbolically linking her to the separation of families by national division. Hwang, whose time in north Korea overlapped with Mun's, remained in north Korea for five weeks (March 20 - April 24) and was also subject to intense criticism. All three travelers faced interrogation and arrest in the south, and were imprisoned as the result of their actions. Im spent many months in jail, and Hwang spent three years in hiding in Japan and Germany before returning to south Korea in 1993 to stand trial.

One reason why Koreans were so angry at these individuals is that each challenged the categories of dialogue and debate. Like must always meet with like: the people of one state cannot meet the government of another, for to do so would threaten the integrity of administrative hierarchies and national boundaries. Voyages such as Mun's, Im's, and Hwang's implicitly threaten the separation between people and state.[1] This is why various border crossings that have occured over the years, under the auspices of the south Korean government, have met with much less outrage. When south Korean organizations deliver food aid to north Korea, south Koreans travel to the north but they do so with the blessing of the south Korean state. While many politicians and journalists have criticized south Korean assistance to north Korea, the object of debate is the assistance and not the crossing of the boundary.

The opposition between people and state articulated in the criticisms is consistent with the oppositions articulated by *minjung* nationalists in their arguments that unification will be achieved by the masses, not by the state. Moreover, Im and Hwang's accounts of their trips, published in the magazine *Shindonga* (Im 1990; Hwang 1989a, 1989b), employ categories to explain their crossings that bear a striking resemblance to the public reactions. Both invoke oppositions between individual and collective, thought and feeling, real and dream. Both focus on how their experiences in north Korea revealed the reality of feeling as well as the "false dream" that thought and ideology (read: the state) can lead to national unity. If the criticisms asserted that the state must take priority over the people in the practice of a north-south dialogue, Hwang and Im say that the people must take priority over the state, and emotion must take priority over thought and logic. Thus the state "thinks," it makes ideological claims, and it depends for its actions on formal methods of diplomacy. In contrast, these authors say that when they arrived in the north, they ceased thinking and began, instead, feeling. Im reports that when she met north Koreans she felt their breath, heard their *han*, and sensed their grief.

Hwang's memoir is especially aimed at making salient the truth or reality of feeling. In making such linkages, he is consistent with his previous writings, such as *Kaekchi* (Strange land), *Samp'oro kanŭn kil* (On the road to Samp'o), and *Hanssi yŏndaegi* (Chronology of the Hans), in which he links national strife with the range of human emotion. Indeed, his participation in the *minjok munhak* (national literature) was founded upon a belief that Korean writers must represent the tragedy of national division and promote unification. And they must represent the tragedy not from the point of view of elites, but from the view of the masses, or *minjung*. In an interview published in the journal *Shindonga*, Hwang tells the senior editor: "The reason why a division writer exists is to devote his literature, his body and soul, to the fight against the absurdity of division" (Hwang, S. Y. 1989b: 265; see also 1989a: 244). Hwang contends that his travel resembles the swallow whose flight tells us that spring (unification) is coming to melt the frozen land (of division).

In order to promote unification, Hwang posits several oppositions between the desirable and the undesirable. He favors the senses over thought, emotion over logic, heart over head, nature over culture, primordial essence over temporariness, and the *minjung* over elites: "This time I will hold the people of the north passionately and, like a blind man who extends his trembling fingers, groping for his long-lost flesh and blood, I will touch and feel the reality of the north" (Hwang, S. Y. 1989a: 256). Touching facilitates emotion, diminishing the possibility that thought, ideology, and logic will suppress his oneness with the north. When Hwang lands at Sun'an airport in P'yŏngyang, a girl who meets him with a bouquet of flowers appears as his own daughter; when their cheeks meet, he is unable to restrain his tears. At this moment in the interview text, the editor, Chun P'yŏng-woo, adds the parenthetical note that he also has begun to cry, and that Hwang appears to him as a boy. Hwang then lists a series of additional hugs and tears, culminating in an embrace with Kim Il Sung. For Hwang, action comes not from thought but from emotions he cannot suppress or control: "From the beginning I treated them [north Koreans] as my heart commanded, thinking that the very nature of humanity *[ingan-simsŏng]* is most important of all. In some ways, they looked more innocent and disinterested than us [south Koreans]" (1989a: 256).

Indeed, within the first several pages of Hwang's memoir, we encounter the senses. He tastes the simple truth of Korean history in a boiled egg; he cannot sleep because birds *(sotjŏk sae)* cry loudly outside his hotel room, evoking the *han* he has inherited from his ancestors; he smells the distinctive odor of north Korean soil; and he becomes aware of the essence of being Korean in the touch of his compatriots' embraces, kisses, and handshakes. Hwang sees the reality of Korea with his eyes both open and shut; either way, he sees flowers, rocks, rivers, and mountains, and they are as they were when he was a child living in what today is called north Korea, "as in the faded color pictures I have" (1989a: 289).

Hwang invokes a heightened sense of purity in his descriptions of north Korea. The food is unpolluted, and women are beautiful without wearing makeup or elegant clothing. He refers to Ch'oi Yŏng-hwa, an elder north Korean poet with whom he meets, as so pure and simple *(sunsu)* that he "takes candy from children." In that imagined action, Ch'oi is doing nothing wrong; he is so pure as to exist prior to morality. Hwang describes the childlike weeping of Paek In Jun (the chair of the Chosŏn Arts and Literature Organization) during Paek's remarks about division.

Moreover, north Korea is characterized as maternal; it is not only the land of his mother, who was born and raised in P'yŏngyang, but constitutes a symbolic mother of all Koreans. Indeed, both Hwang and Mun stress that Kim Il Sung himself is maternal, and he appears continually in these memoirs embracing the two writers, holding their hands, and weeping with them. He is also depicted as bringing families together, and as bringing orphans from the countryside to P'yŏngyang for feeding and care. In this regard, Mun's and Hwang's depictions of Kim Il Sung parallel north Korean propaganda. For example, in one passage Hwang tells the story of how the daughter of a woman arrested for theft pleaded with Kim Il Sung to reunite her family. Kim blamed the community for having failed to eradicate the disease of criminality and released her. Hwang also writes that Kim Il Sung personally demanded that a photograph of the whole family be sent to him so that he could be sure that the family had been unified. Mun stresses that Kim is committed to unification far more than he is to resolving class conflicts, and so on at least three occasions, Mun refers to Kim as a nationalist as opposed to a socialist (1990: 100, 101, 104).

Along the same lines, north Korea is naturalized; it is described by the travelers as a land of unspoiled and scenic beauty. Mun tells his north Korean guides that photos of Paekdu mountain are becoming increasingly popular in south Korea, and that these photos demonstrate that the Korean people's basic emotions cannot be forever swayed by ideologies and doctrines.[2] Hwang spends much time trying to locate a rock on a particular mountain, a rock against which he and his father used to rest on long walks in the country. He climbs the mountain, just as he did when he was a boy, and discovers that the rock is still there: nature, unchanged.

Although less focused on the senses than Hwang's, Mun's work also highlights the emotions involved with division and imagined unification. He describes attending a school specializing in music, drama, and gymnastics where the students peformed a theatrical sketch. Although Mun at first suspects this to be propaganda, he takes off his sunglasses and sees the students "as they really are." In one classroom, a third-grade girl, a second-grade girl, and a first-grade boy perform a skit in which they talk about mailing letters. The second girl asks how she can mail a letter, and the first girl tells her to affix a stamp to the envelope. When she responds that this will not work, the boy seems confused. "You see," she says, "the letter is for my grandfather who lives in Kwangju [in south Korea]. We cannot go there." At this point, Mun impulsively jumps into the skit, saying, "Give me your letter! I'll give it to your grandfather. I've come here to make a world in which you and your grandfather can meet" (1990: 83). All the children break into tears. Preempting his critics, Mun says that even if the crying is trained and practiced rather than being a spontaneous outpouring of emotion, the students are certainly receiving training for unification.

In positing the various oppositions discussed above, the voyages of Im, Mun, and Hwang bring into relief an opposition salient in many contemporary discourses on unification and posited explicitly by the south Korean government itself. The opposition can be framed as a conflict between pragmatic (hyŏnsiljŏk) and sentimentalist (kamsangjŏk) approaches to unification. Although Kim Young Sam (1993) has implored people to abandon sentiment as an avenue to peace and to embrace a "scientific," "realistic," and "empirically verifiable" unification process, creative writers, academics, and students privilege the heart over the mind, feeling over logic, as a way to discover reality and to initiate a unification process that is the will of the people rather than the state.[3] Historians also use the opposition to characterize people-state conflicts in previous administrations. Chun Duk-ju (1994), for example, attributes the weakness of Chang Myŏn's second period as prime minister (1960-1961) to the influence of student and other radical kamsangjŏk t'ongilron (sentimentalist unification theories). He holds that sentimentalist opposition compelled Chang to abandon an important aspect of Syngman Rhee's prior aggressive policy of pukjin t'ongil (northward unification)—the threat that if the north did not hold free, democratic elections, the south would use military power to make them do it.

What is meant by "reality"? Two words used to refer to reality, *silche* and *hyŏnsil*, are often interchangeable, with the subtle difference that the former most often refers primarily to facts and truths, while the latter refers to actual circumstances: for instance, "Although it is true *[silche]* that Korea is one nation, the reality *[hyŏnsil]* is that Korea has two states."[4] While the terms are usually employed to refer to facts, details, and circumstances rather than visions, prospects, and hopes, in unification discourses they are also used for more abstract purposes. (This is especially true of *hyŏnsil*, which is often opposed to an abstract term, *isang*, "ideal").[5] *Silche* and *hyŏnsil* can refer to north Korea's "true" intentions, the privileged position of the truth of diplomacy over sentiment, the reality of Korea as a unified nation, the actual conditions of democracy or communism, or the realities of the world that the north Korean government hides from its citizens. Among the most often discussed realities in texts that deal explicitly with unification are homogeneity and unity, because they are so desired and so elusive.

The position of the so-called sentimentalists, who search for reality in feeling and emotion, is often seen by the more conservative south Koreans as naive if not potentially traitorous. In 1989, while Im was still in north Korea, a reader of *Tonga ilbo* wrote that he wanted to admire Im and to love her courage. But, he said, the heart and passion *(yŏljŏng)* cannot achieve unification. He went on to say that while he understands her passion, reality and passion are two very different things (Kim, D. M. 1989: 11). Some weeks later, on July 27, 1989, *Tonga ilbo* wrote its own criticism, saying in an editorial that "simply comparing [Im] to a lamb and emphasizing sympathy and obligation toward her by priests ignores two million other Catholics' opinions about unification. What we must do is overcome the sentiment *[kamsang]* and transform sixty million Korean's wish for unification into realistic *[hyŏnsiljŏk]* efforts." Fantasies of the north, the editorial continued, "cause worry and cannot constitute a real unification movement." The pragmatists see in sentimentalism an unacceptable criticism of south Korea and a hubris whereby the people assert their will above that of the state. In fact, as one clear expression of how concepts of reality separate the two sides, pragmatists employ the term *isang* (ideal) to denote the future conditions or ideals that sentimentalists refer to as *silje* (real).

Sonu Chong-wŏn's essay is also worth quoting at length because he makes it clear, albeit unintentionally, that for the pragmatists, the sentimentalists come to stand for north Korea as a whole:

> In dealing with unification, our nation's sacred goal, sentimental passions and excitement are prohibited *[kŭmmul]*. . . . The safest way to guarantee our nation's happiness is to implement scientific and reasonable unification policies. . . . Sentimental *[kamsangjŏk]* unifi-cationists have common characteristics: they lack confidence about our own system, and they are ignorant of north Korea's strategies. Kim Il Sung's communism is not orthodox. It is pagan and poison-ous. It is dangerous for these sentimentalists to think we'll achieve unification just because we have the same blood. . . . That kind of dangerous sentimentalism is injurious to unification. Unification cannot be achieved with excitement *[hŭngbun]* and fervor *[hyŏlgi]* but only with systematically verified scientific policies and conse-quent reasonable and legal processes (Sonu 1993: 19-21).

Sonu directly links the sentimentalists with Kim Il Sung and thus draws a parallel between pragmatist-sentimentalist relations and south-north relations. The parallel seems justified to many writers on unification not only because the sentimentalists are sympathetic to the actions and policies of the north, but also because, like the north Korean govern-ment, the sentimentalists often speak in ideal and emotional terms. Indeed, since the Korean War and partition, a central area of policy concern for the United States and for south Korea has been the problem of how to engage north Korea in a discourse of "rational pragmatism" (Jee 1994) rather than to accommodate the ideological and "sentimen-talist" terms of discourse offered by the north.

Thus, in opposition to the pragmatic representation of Im and others in the conservative media, the more liberal media, especially *Hangyŏre sinmun*, characterized Im's travel to the north in quite sentimental and emotional terms. Jager (1994: 147-150) describes how some media construed Im's travel less as a separation from her family than as a separation from her lover, Yun Wŏn-chŏl. In doing so, the liberal press paralleled the more conservative media representations of Im as divider of families, but it differed in important ways, for Im came to stand not only for a larger national concern but for love and the separation of loved ones. Im became a hero, like Ch'unhyang, separated from her lover for the sake of higher virtues, in this case the reunification of Korea; thus Jager quotes *Hangyŏre sinmun*: "Her countenance exudes in its appearance the whole tragedy of a people divided for almost half a century" (Jager, 1994: 148).

In their focus on science or sentiment, the "pragmatists" (as they call themselves) and the "sentimentalists" (as the pragmatists call people such as Mun, Hwang, and Im) both surely risk making similar errors. They may produce exaggerated and self-serving representations of north Korea that exacerbate internal tensions in south Korea over unification policy. The "pragmatists" clearly wish to perpetuate images of north Korea consistent with conventional Cold War demonizations of communism. So, too, do the "sentimentalists," in their own truth claims, risk ignoring fundamental social, economic, and political differences that make unification an extraordinarily complex issue.

Of special interest to me is the question of whether these opposing sides can be balanced, for this is what would be necessary in a process of working through the trauma of division. The opposition suggests a fragmentation of historical consciousness into two movements toward closure and certainty. If, instead, unification remained more loosely defined, more indeterminate and fluid, one wonders if the so-called violation of borders would produce such excitement.

FROM HOMOGENEITY TO HETEROGENEITY

The author of a recent essay on unification says that Koreans have a "homing instinct" *(kwisobonnŭng)* that will lead them to unification (Koh 1993: 68).[6] To unify is to return home. So far in this chapter, I have examined some of the ways in which some south Koreans frame their perspectives on returning home as the search for reality. For people such as Hwang, unification quite literally means the return home to his birthplace. Although unification and the recovery of homogeneity ostensibly remain the paramount goals of the south Korean people and state, they remain elusive. Yet elusiveness itself creates desire—in the Korean case, a desire that partially eases the pain of past losses and separations and gives reason to endure. Unification is a metaphor for the return home, an ideal that always awaits.

South Korean ambivalence about unification and north Korea emerges in terms of a general cleavage between those south Koreans who search for reality through sentiment and feeling and those who search for reality through doctrine, logic, and formal methods. The ambivalence is discernible not in the perspectives of individual writers, such as Mun, Im, or Hwang, but in the larger collective division they articulate between sentimentalists and pragmatists. It is possible that the master narratives are changing, and anecdotal evidence from scholars working in Korea indicates that many people are beginning to discuss more explicitly the potential problems of unification, including the possibility that Koreans will never arrive at the ultimate "reality" of unification, even if north and south Korea officially join together as one nation, one state. A "wall of the mind," as Germans describe their own heterogeneity these days, may persist long after the demilitarized zone has been dismantled and the troops have retreated. For now, the divided nation serves as an integral element of south Korean identity. South Koreans define themselves in terms of, and in opposition to, the north. But this politics of identity cannot sustain itself if challenged by the muddle and practices of everyday life—the dialogue into which the blind *p'ansori* singer Song-hwa and her brother Tong-ho of the well-known film *Sŏp'yŏnje*, discussed in the introduction to this book, refused to enter. Such a dialogue would create a completely different relation and would not constitute the real. We know that there is no conceivable real, except an illusion, presumed to exist, when all we can ever speak of is a reality constituted by our own perceptions, a utopia—literally, "no place."

The elusiveness of the real is apparent if we return to the analogy to Achilles made in the introduction to this book and imagine that Achilles ultimately captures the tortoise. The relation between the two would be forever altered; the captive would no longer be desired solely as an object but instead for whatever its new relation to its owner entailed: a use value transformed to an exchange value, from an imagined relation that is entirely narcissistic to one in which subject and object become enmeshed in a network of intersubjective associations (Žižek 1991). Therein lies a frightening change: moving from an ideal that sustains to a real that engages in the complexities of actual social exchange.

Nostalgia is the mourning of inauthenticity (Stewart 1993: 23). The longing for unification is a utopian longing, and yet we know that utopia can exist only in the present—as narrative, as discourse, as the text of fantasy. Unification would not be utopian if it appeared as lived experience; nostalgia, as Stewart tell us, is a sadness without an object.

THE DEFECTORS

> Most people have been brainwashed since the
> day of their birth so that even though they may
> be miserable they believe that Kim Jong Il will
> save them. I was one of these people. I guarantee
> you there is no defector in south Korea who did
> not weep when Kim Il Sung died.
>
> —North Korean Defector in Seoul, 1996

MUCH OF THIS BOOK HAS BEEN CONCERNED with the predicament of
Korea's myth of homogeneity and the inability of south Koreans to come
to terms with difference. I have framed this inability in terms of a crisis of
mourning. The myth of Korean homogeneity is a myth about the past, a
golden age to be recovered rather than mourned. The myth is one that
cannot be reconciled with the heterogeneity that exists now, and that
almost certainly existed in the distant past. North Koreans will never be
replicas of south Koreans, any more than one would assume that poor and
rich south Koreans, male and female south Koreans, or Koreans from the
southwest and the southeast are identical to one another. Obviously
similarity and difference cannot be quantified, but we can study how
concepts of similarity and difference influence policy, sentiment, and
expectation. For example, if south Koreans continue to expect that
unification will produce homogeneity on the peninsula, little attention will
be given to establishing long-term policies on the social costs of unification.

While this argument may appear, at first glance, to be like pouring
water before there is even a fire, the range of possibilities for social

conflict is staggering. A unified Korea may confront widespread discrimination, massive unemployment, political clashes including revenge attacks, and an overburdened legal system handling land claims and other disputes. South Koreans may want to address these issues only as they appear, but it is usually wiser to address emerging crises on the basis of a well-considered and coherent policy, rather than on the basis of quick reactions. My argument is that south Korea has not prepared for unification, and that the defectors are a model for the potential costs of unification, whatever the peace dividend. As I inquired earlier in this book, how is it possible that the north and south will be integrated harmoniously when there are so many cleavages within south Korea itself, cleavages that are exacerbated by the lack of interest in or acknowledgment of diversity?

In recent years, south Korean experts on north Korea and unification have focused almost exclusively on nuclear proliferation and the Geneva Agreed Framework, food shortage and famine, and speculative and anecdotal evidence about Kim Jong Il's political stability. The experts explore these areas at the expense of more long-term and fundamental issues of social and political integration. Unification prospects are most often framed only in economic terms and are seldom linked to social issues. A common perspective on unification goes something like this: if north Korea is made more economically healthy, then unification is less likely; yet, if the north Korean economy collapses, then unification is more likely to occur but with devastating effects. Helmut Kohl's administration in west Germany framed German unification strictly in material terms, and this is one reason why Germans did not foresee the widespread costs and dissatisfaction with unification.

There are many ways to approach the subject of unification costs. One may consider them in purely economic terms, focusing on unemployment, the decisions that must be made about restructuring labor and infrastructure in the north, and the preparation of the south Korean economy to deal with north Korea's overproduction in certain areas (such as heavy machinery) and underproduction in others (such as valuable minerals). One might also consider that, despite many south Koreans' worthy goal of achieving a unified society whose economic and defense policies will be independent of foreign powers, the complexity and costs of unification will inevitably require some outside assistance, even if only in the form of an international financial mechanism. But unification costs can also be considered more generally in terms of potential social costs, and here the defectors are especially useful.

This chapter describes the general condition of north Korean defectors: the laws that serve them, the process they undergo as they are integrated into south Korean society, and the problems they confront. I believe that defectors tell us far more about the potential for a difficult and complex unification than they do about current events in north Korea. Yet the defectors I know who have been interviewed by American and Korean government officials, as well as scholars working on north Korea, tell me that they are seldom questioned about their lives in south Korea. I think this is a mistake. Most defectors I know are not doing well in south Korea. In a recent survey conducted by the Unification Ministry, north Korean defectors report great difficulties with everyday life, especially with communication, finding and keeping jobs, and finding marriage partners (Lee, W. Y. 1997). In addition to feeling socially isolated, they feel they are discriminated against. Some believe they are treated worse than foreign guest workers. Many are distressed by what they perceive to be a general south Korean view that nothing in the north is worth preserving. When they do not achieve economic success in the south, they become anxious that they will have nothing to show their north Korean relatives for the pain they caused them by defecting. They are accused in south Korea of having no sense of loyalty to family. And of course, even raising and thinking about families is quite different in the north and the south, and this is a subject about which defectors are continually reminded. North Koreans do not keep genealogies or worship ancestors as south Koreans do, and south Koreans do not have the *t'akaso*, or day care centers, that north Koreans have. The differences between north and south Koreans, as we saw in an earlier chapter on divided families, are used against the defectors.

DEFECTOR LAW

Until July, 1997, defectors from north Korea to south Korea were administered under the Korean Protective Law for North Korean Defectors *(Kwisun Pukhan Tongp'o Pohobŏp)*, item number 4568 in the Republic of Korea document "Territory beyond the military demarcation line" (revised June 11, 1993). The law, to paraphrase, serves the purpose of providing "protection" for compatriots who have defected from the territory above the military boundary *(kunsa pungyesŏn ipuk chiyŏk)* to south Korea as they resettle and make their livelihood, until the achievement of a peaceful unification. In July 1997, the law was replaced by the "Law regarding the protection and resettlement of north Korean escapees" *(Pukhant'aljuminŭi poho mit chŏngch'akjiwŏne kwanhan pŏpryul)*.

However, the 1993 and 1997 laws serve only those north Koreans for whom the minister of health and social affairs has submitted a successful petition for protection *(poho sinch'ŏng)*. In other words, not all north Koreans who want to defect are permitted to defect. There are certainly political prisoners in south Korea *(mijonhyang changisu)*, some of whom are north Koreans who have refused to abandon their ideological commitments to the north. Many politicians speculate on the number of political prisoners in order to exaggerate the number of north Koreans who want to defect; the purpose of the exaggeration is to heighten south Koreans' fear of mass defections, as well as their hope for the end of the north Korean regime. Indeed, opposition party leaders have occasionally suggested that defections themselves are selectively revealed at times when the south Korean government wants to deflect attention from other issues, such as government corruption and other scandals.

There is some disagreement on the actual number of people who have been permitted to defect. Numbers are seldom revealed by the government, and so estimates vary. One government official who is in frequent contact with about a hundred defectors gave me the number 560 in March 1996; the same month, a television program, *Ch'ujŏk 60 Minutes,* gave figures that totaled about 400. Seo Dong Ik cites the figure 738, which he asserts is from the *Kwisun pukhan tongp'o* registry and represents the number of defectors since the truce agreement between the north and south on July 27, 1953 (1996: 50). According to Seo, this number is quite different from the smaller numbers cited by the Ministry of Defense, the Agency for National Security and Planning, the Ministry of Health and Social Affairs, and private think tanks. The differences, Seo suggests, are attributable to different methods of tabulation, and to the fact that none of the agencies know how to account for defectors who have died since 1953. If one includes all defections, he says, the number may be as high as 1,000.

In an October 1 article in *Hanguk ilbo* entitled "*Saship kunyŏn ihu pukkwisunja ch'ong 616 myŏng*," the newspaper writes that the National Board of Unification's report on defectors gives numbers for defections between 1949 and August 1996. According to the report, which was submitted to the National Assembly on September 29, 1996, the number of north Korean defectors to the south totaled 616: 241 from 1949 to 1960, 146 from 1961 to 1970, 31 from 1971 to 1980, 64 from 1981 to 1990, and 134 from 1991 to August 1996. These numbers are not totally consistent with those cited in September 1996 by *Chugan hanguk* (*Hanguk ilbo*'s sister magazine), which gave the number of 613 defectors between 1953 and June 1996. The *Hanguk ilbo* report also states that between 1,000 and 1,500 people escaped from the north and are wandering around Russia or China; thus, according to the board, the number of defectors is likely to increase if and when these north Koreans find their way to an embassy. Moreover, the board reports that since the armistice, 3,738 south Koreans were kidnapped by the north, and that all but 442 were eventually returned to the south.

At any rate, all of these numbers seem very small given the fact that there are nearly thirty million north Koreans and that Korea has been divided for more than fifty years. Also, these figures are a small fraction of the German defections during their division. Even if one includes *t'albukja* (people who escaped from the north and are still in a third country), the number would probably not rise above two thousand. (Most researchers assume that the vast majority of *t'albukja* have already contacted south Korean embassies abroad, and that the south Korean government is therefore well aware of the figures.) More important for many observers of Korea is not how many defectors there are, but rather the rate of increase in defections, and the kind of north Koreans who choose to defect.

Many Koreans in the government and in the media say that the rate of defections has increased dramatically over the last decade, and perhaps this is true in terms of the percentage of the total number of defections. In tables 1 and 2, I cite two sets of figures, those provided by my source in the government, and those provided to the public on *Ch'ujŏk 60 Minutes.*

TABLE 9.1

STATISTICS ON DEFECTIONS NUMBER OF DEFECTORS BY YEAR:	
1/97-12/97	65
1/96-3/96	19
1995	45
1994	50
1993	8
1992	5
1989-1991	28
PERCENTAGE OF TOTAL DEFECTORS ACCORDING TO YEARS OF DEFECTION:	
1980-present	13 percent
1970-1979	18 percent
1960-1969	35 percent
1954-1959	29 percent
1945-1953	5 percent

Source: Figures provided through personal communication
with anonymous official, Ministry of Unification,
Republic of Korea.

The most significant increase in recent years was in 1994, when 23 north Koreans working in miserable conditions in Siberia defected. The 23 loggers constitute about half of all defections in 1994; of these, 8 defected in August 1994 through the United Nations High Commission on Refugees. There was also a small increase in defections by north Korean foreign students in eastern Germany following the collapse of the Berlin Wall. Yet the most defections continue to come from China. This will probably continue to be the case for some time because the other popular site for defections, Siberia, has become less accessible to north Koreans since north Koreans violated deforestation agreements with Russia and, as a result, lost clearance for logging (*Korea Times*, Jan. 31, 1997). For reasons I do not know, the majority of defectors in the 1960s and 1970s came from the northern provinces of Hwanghae-do and P'yŏnganbukdo, whereas during the 1990s the majority of defectors come from either P'yŏngyang or Hamgyŏngnam-do. Defections do not appear to have been planned through any organized system (like an "underground railroad"), although it has become clear that a December 3, 1996, defection of a

TABLE 9.2

CH'UJŎK 60 MINUTES STATISTICS ON DEFECTIONS	
NUMBER OF DEFECTORS BY YEAR:	
1986-1990	46
1981-1985	16
1976-1980	20
1971-1975	11
1966-1970	102
1961-1965	44

Source: *Ch'ujŏk 60 Minutes*, March 25, 1996,
Korean Broadcasting System.

woman and 15 of her family members from Hamgyŏngbuk-do was facilitated by her father, Ch'oi Yong-do, a Korean-American dentist living in New York City (see Yun, S. H. 1996: 3).

In conversations with both government officials and journalists, I commonly heard that even if the numbers had not increased dramatically, the incidence of high-level defections had increased significantly. For example, in 1994, Kang Myŏng-do, the son-in-law of then north Korean prime minister Kang Song-san, defected, as did Cho Myŏng-ch'ŏl, north Korea's chief of construction. In 1995 there were defections by Yi Min-bok of the Institute of Agricultural Science; Oh Su-ryŏng, a wealthy businessman; Ch'oi Chu-hwal, a high-ranking military officer; and Ch'oi Se-ŭng, a foreign currency dealer. In January 1996 there were defections by diplomats posted in Zambia (the third secretary, his wife, and a security guard), and later in 1996 an air force captain who flew his MiG jet into the south. One of the most highly publicized defections was that of Song Hye-rim, Kim Jong Il's former girlfriend and the mother of some of his children, who had been living off of north Korean money in Europe. This defection, however, appears to have been a hoax, and it was a major embarrassment to the Korean media who reported it as well as to the newspapers worldwide that reproduced the story.[1] Sŏng Hye-rim's nephew, Yi Han-yŏng, defected much earlier to south Korea, but his mother and aunt have not defected or sought asylum. The most remarkable defection occured on February 13, 1997, when Hwang Chang-yŏp, one of the highest-ranking north Korean officials, a close advisor to Kim Jong Il, and an architect of the *chuch'e* ideological system, reported to the south Korean embassy in Beijing for asylum. Several television commentators said the defection was tantamount to "Jefferson defecting from the United States of America."

The vast majority of defectors are men who defect in their late teens or twenties, although there are about 20 women who have defected, most with a family member, as in the case of Kim Man-ch'ŏl and Yŏ Man-ch'ŏl, both of whom defected with their wives and daughters. (Yŏ Man-ch'ŏl's first daughter, Yŏ Kŭm-chu, has, in fact, become increasingly vocal to the media about the plight of defectors.) Most recent defectors cite "political reasons" as their motivation. By this, they mean that they had in some way violated anti-state laws, by either speaking out against the north Korean regime, defacing an image of north Korean leaders, or committing a felony such as fraud or theft. Others say they defected because of an unwitting mistake—for example, accidentally receiving Voice of America broadcasts, committing an error in the construction of a building, being a member of a military group whose leader (and therefore the entire group) was convicted of a crime—that would have led them and their families to be imprisoned. Unlike early defectors from the 1960's, they tend not to cite general political reasons such as "discontent with communism" or "hatred of the north Korean system, a pattern shown by researchers at the National Unification Board; the reasons given for defection seem to correlate well with the years during which the defections took place (Lee, W. Y. 1997). According to my source in the government, only a small percentage of defectors cite economic reasons for defection, although this small figure is probably due to the fact that few nations, including south Korea, consider economics to be a legitimate excuse for asylum.

I would stress that none of these figures should be taken too seriously, as they represent trends only and are culled from my interviews and from the media. It is also difficult to believe the figures cited for settlement payments. According to article 4 of the 1993 defector protection law, defectors are provided settlement payments necessary for them to "preserve" their livelihood. This means that a wealthy defector will be paid more, and a poor defector paid less, the settlement payment being calibrated to the defectors' prior economic status in north Korea. This is a decision made by a special committee *(Kwisunpukhan Tongp'o Poho Wiwŏnhoe)* that reviews the petition by the minister of health and social affairs. The settlement payment law stems from an earlier law, established in 1962, and commonly referred to as *kukka yugongja mit wŏlnamkwisunja tukbyŏl wŏnhobŏp* (special law to protect those who contributed to the country). This law, which divided defectors into three grades according to prior rank in north Korea, was replaced in 1978 by a law referred to as *wŏlnamkwisun yongsa t'ŭkbyŏlposangbŏp* (special law for brave soldiers). The new law divided defectors into five grades and included special attention to medical assistance, education, welfare payments to elderly people and infants, and assurances about a minimum space (15 *pyŏng*, approximately 530 square feet) for housing. In 1993, during the Kim Young Sam administration, this law was replaced by the *kwisunpukhantongp'o pohobŏp*, a law that significantly reduced the payments; it was designed in anticipation of greater numbers of defections but was explained publicly as an attempt to make the defectors more self-sufficient. As one result of the attempt to reduce financial payments to defectors, the 1993 law deletes all uses of the phrase "special compensation law for defectors" in favor of the more general "protective law for the honorable treatment of people of national merit," and it also deletes most uses of the word "defector." The word *poho* (protection) is substituted for *posang* (compensation) in both the 1993 law and the 1997 law.

In addition, however, extra monies can be granted according to the value of information (such as state secrets) or equipment (such as an airplane or firearms) brought to the south. The bonus compensation has produced great wealth for some defectors. The defector Yi Ung-pyŏng, for example, who flew to south Korea in a fighter jet, purportedly received the equivalent of about $300,000 U. S. in his choice of cash or gold bars as reward for his defection, and I have also heard rumors that he received about $125,000 additionally for the jet. In September 1996, a journalist quoted the pilot Yi Ch'ŏl-su, who defected in May, 1996, by flying his MiG jet into the south, as saying that he received a settlement payment of 430 million *wŏn* (about $537,000). Non-military defectors seem to fare less well. For example, when Kim Jong Il's ex-girlfriend's nephew defected in 1982, he received either 7 million *wŏn* (approximately $9,000) or 17 million *wŏn* (approximately $22,000), depending upon which report one believes (Yi, C. H. 1996: 4). As I mention in greater detail below, the settlement and compensation monies are the major point of conflict among defectors and between defectors and the

TABLE 9.3

DEFECTOR OCCUPATIONS	
Civil servants	19
Employed by nationally owned corporations	13
Employed by banks	24
Teachers	2
Soldiers	1
Physicians	4
Employed by private corporation	203
Small business owner	44
Farmers	1
Homemakers	14
Unemployed	202 (perhaps higher)
Others	34
TOTAL = 561 (tabulated from March 1996)	

Source: Figures provided through personal communication with anonymous official, Ministry of Unification, Republic of Korea.

government. As one result, gossip and rumor inflate the figures for the wealthy and deflate them for the poor. The lower-paid defectors accuse the higher-paid defectors of lying about their knowledge of north Korean military and politics, and they also accuse the south Korean government of discriminatory practices.

According to most defectors, officials, and journalists with whom I spoke, about half of defectors are unemployed. However, the most recent statistics, cited in *Chugan hanguk* (September 5, 1996: 32-25) indicate an unemployment rate of about 36 percent.

Nearly all defectors are given some sort of education, job, or job training by the Agency for National Security and Planning (ANSP), the Department of Labor, or the Ministry of Health and Social Affairs (MOHSA) soon after the defection. Employment is guaranteed by article 8 of the 1993 law, education by article 9. According to article 5, sections 1 and 2, any former north Korean military staff or government official who chooses to enlist in the south Korean military or serve in the south Korean government will be appointed to the equivalent level he or

TABLE 9.4

FINANCIAL SUPPORT TO DEFECTORS (IN THOUSANDS OF WON)					
YEAR	FINANCIAL SUPPORT DETAILS				
	Total Sum	Resettlement	Medical Assistance	Housing Assistance	Education Assistance
1993	941,649	317,102	—	522,500	102,047
1994	2,139,576	759,310	210,000	1,084,384	91,556
1995	753,633	218,654	245,000	192,000	97,979

Source: Yi, C. H. 1996: 12

she held prior to defection (a path taken by some high-ranking defectors, such as the colonel Chŏng Nak-hyŏn, the squadron leader and pilot Yi Ung-pyŏng, and the major Shin chŏng-ch'ul); section 3 also provides for promotions to a higher level if the defector, having met the provisions of the first two sections, contributes greatly to the national interest. Medical assistance is also provided under article 10 of the 1993 law for the defector and his dependents in south Korea (see table 4). As indicated in table 4, the figures for which come from MOHSA, the resettlement payments in 1993, 1994, and 1995 totaled 1,295,066,000 *wŏn*, or about $ 1.5 million. This is a very small amount of money, given the size of the south Korean economy, yet the compensation for defectors remains an important issue in Korean political debate.

Also of concern to the defectors is the short time period in which they are expected to settle into south Korean life (table 5). All defectors are initially placed in government shelters, ideally for one month but often for as long as eight months. The 1997 law extends this to one year. The law stipulates special attention to "false defections," and the need to house "escapees" in protection facilities built and managed by the Ministry of National Unification. I have been completely unable to determine what transpires in the defectors' lives during that time period; despite the fact that many defectors are quite willing to talk to me, and to speak with some intimacy, they all say that they are strictly forbidden to discuss their initial half year after defection. I can only surmise that the initial period is one of intense and frequent interrogation and "reeducation" (according to one informant, there is a four-month course) in order to ensure that the defector is neither a spy nor a terrorist. (The recent revelations that a history professor at Seoul's Tanguk

TABLE 9.5

SUPPORT OPERATION CHART					
STEPS	SENIOR AUTHORITIES	JOINT AUTHORITIES	ACCOMMODATION FACILITIES	PERIOD	OTHERS
Protection management	MOHSA	• ANSP • Police • Board of National Unification	• Short-term accommodation facilities	1 month	
Primary education on adaptation into society	MOHSA		• Short-term accommodation facilities	1 month	Inclusive of employment guide and counseling
Job training	MOHSA	• Department of Labor	• Short-term accommodation facilities	12 months	
Employment assistance	MOHSA	• Department of Labor	• Job training centers • Short-term accommodation facilities	12 months	
Resettlement support	MOHSA		• Short-term accommodation facilities	12 months	
Further management	MOHSA	• NSPD	• Job training centers • Place of residence (Public rent house)	12 months	
Support for social adaptation, education, and mental stability	MOHSA	• Police • Local government body (local social welfare center)	• Place of residence (public rent house)	24 months	

Source: Yi, C. H. 1996: 25

University, Chŏng Su-il, is a north Korean spy who secretly entered south Korea more than a decade ago, and that a prominent former Seoul National University professor, Ko Yŏng-bok was a north Korean spy for nearly thirty years, will no doubt increase the attention given to defectors). My sense is that the south Korean government is attempting to improve the early experiences of some defectors, since special attention has been given in the 1997 law to building protection facilities separate from the current facilities constructed and managed by the Agency for National Security and Planning (formerly the KCIA).

According to the defectors with whom I spoke, they were given some tours of Seoul, factories, and farms outside the city just before their release and placement into housing. Job training lasts about six months, and those whom the government cannot place in jobs are directed to one of more than 300 social welfare centers in the country, 89 of which are in Seoul. Upon release, the defector is assigned a personal security officer, who keeps in close contact with the defector for a period of at least two years. Indeed, policemen accompanied some of my interviewees, saying either that they were the defector's "older brother" (an unintended pun for an Orwellian "big brother"), or that they were there to protect the defector from revenge attacks by south Koreans. The "policeman," as he is known, not only accompanies the defector on interviews, speaking engagements, or domestic travel, but he also assists the defector in his or her daily life. For example, it is the policeman who initially arranges for the defector's employment, mediating between the workplace and MOHSA. To some extent, the company selected has no choice but to hire the defector, although there is some freedom to fire them for incompetence. Since most defectors do not want to perform manual labor, few know English, and none know many Chinese characters, they experience numerous work problems, and some are fired if they do not quit first.

At this point, let me note that remarkably little has been written about the defectors. Although defectors have written books and articles about their own experiences, the only substantial or scholarly works I know of written by nondefectors are those by Oh Hye-chŏng (1995), Yi Chŏng-hoon (1996), Yun Yŏ-sang (1994), and Min Pyŏng-ch'ŏn (1980), and most of these are unpublished manuscripts. Most of these authors relied on surveys to assess the defectors' adaptation to south Korean life. The picture they present of a people struggling with an uncertain identity and future is worth thinking about because the defectors may reflect, in microcosm, the future of north Koreans living in a unified Korea. I chose not to conduct surveys and instead engaged the defectors in long (one- to three-hour) interviews in which I asked them to provide their own questions, and in which I encouraged them to talk about whatever they liked.

Oh Hye-Chŏng surveyed 44 out of 120 defectors she initially contacted; all of the 44 defected after 1980 and represent a variety of occupations and classes, as well as a variety of different home provinces in north Korea. Of these 44, about 80 percent are men. Oh makes it clear from the beginning that she wants to highlight the cultural differences *(munhwajŏk ijilgam)* between north Koreans and south Koreans because, she suggests, it is the cultural differences that pose the greatest challenge to re-creating a unified society.

All of the 44 receive money from either employment, MOHSA, or both. Four (5 percent) receive less than 500,000 *wŏn* ($625) per month, 14 (32 percent) receive approximately 1,000,000 *wŏn* ($1250) per month, 6 (13 percent) receive between 1 and 1.5 million *wŏn* ($1,250 to $1,875), 7 (16 percent) receive more than 1.5 million *wŏn*, and 12 people refused to report their monthly income. Most of the defectors I interviewed claimed that they were given far too little money, yet when I asked why they needed more, they replied that it was in order to be at an equal level with the other defectors. They also said that they would have been happy with the money if all the defectors had received the same amount. They continually compare themselves not to other Koreans, but to other defectors, and they actually argue that they do not need to have more money in order to live well. One man who complained about not having enough money said that he cannot spend the money he has: "Once I got my TV and some other appliances, there is nothing left to buy. I only need a few shirts and a suit, and I can eat pretty cheaply at any restaurant." The same man was critical of the few defectors he knew who were extravagant in their spending.

Oh (1995) classifies the 44 defectors according to a very common economic unit used in Korea, *Aengel kyesu* (Engel's coefficient). This figure refers to the income a person spends for food products divided by that person's total disposable income. The proportion of expenses, that is, Engel's coefficient, will decrease as total income increases. Oh's figures and her classification of the various coefficients are reproduced in tables 6 and 7. It is clear that there is a wide array of incomes, extending across the class markers of low, middle, and upper class. Five of the defectors she interviewed can be considered extraordinarily wealthy.

In large part, the jealousies and criticisms among defectors I interviewed derive from the fact that they have frequent contact with one another. Most defectors are close only to other defectors, and because the government officials in charge of the defectors want to centralize them, they ordinarily live in the same apartment complexes.

TABLE 9.6

ENGEL'S COEFFICIENT	
COEFFICIENT	DESCRIPTION
Over 55%	Minimum standard of living *(ch'oijŏ saenghwal hangye iha)*
50%	Able to survive *(saengjoni kyŏu kanŭnghan chŏngdo)*
45%	Able to remain in good health *(taso kŏngangŭl yujihal su itnŭn chŏngdo)*
40%	Unable to provide secondary education for one's children *(chanyŏege chungdŭngkyoyugŭl sik'il su ŏpnŭn chŏngdo)*
35%	Comfortable, with few financial worries *(Kŏkjŏng ŏpsi p'yŏnanhan)*
30-25%	Wealthy *(puja soridŭlŭl chŏngdo)*
Under 25%	Super-rich *(aju sangryu saenghwal)*

Source: Oh, H. J. (1995:22)

In addition, they belong to defector organizations designed, organized, and run by people who defected in the 1960s or who came to the south during the early turmoil of division. (However, these groups are *not* the same as the voluntary organizations of *wŏlnammin*, which are mostly provisional organizations in the south for north Korean localities.) The defector organizations, supported by the government with sentiment if not with finances, are mainly social clubs that provide friendship, gossip, and everyday information about such things as jobs, health care, and educational opportunities. According to the heads of a large defector organization with whom I met in 1996, their group was established by former president Chun Doo Hwan as a "voluntary organization" *(chayul Tanche)* that was, in fact, not voluntary. The defectors are required to belong to an organization of defectors, of which there are now several.

The largest defector organization is called *Sungŭi Tongjihoe. Sungŭi* comes from the Chinese character meaning loyalty, praise, or respect, and *tongji* means "colleague," "comrade," or "friend." The organization was named in 1982 but was actually formed under another name *(Myŏlgongŭihoetang,* or Anti-communist Organization) in 1965 under Park Chung Hee's administration. At the same time, Park had established a national veterans' administration department *(kukka wŏnho ch'o)* within which there were several welfare sections. In 1968, all

TABLE 9.7

DEFECTOR'S CLASS DISTRIBUTION
(BASED ON ENGEL'S COEFFICIENT)

Engel's coefficient	Number of defectors (%)	Social class (%)
Over 55%	7 (15.9)	Lower class 14 (31.8)
50%	7 (15.9)	
45%	2 (4.5)	Middle class 7 (13.7)
40%	1 (2.3)	
35%	4 (6.9)	
30-25%	6 (13.7)	Upper class 11 (25.1)
Under 25%	5 (11.4)	
No answer	12 (27.2)	
Total	44 (100)	44 (100)

Source: Oh, H. J. (1995: 22)

defectors who had joined the voluntary organization were told to join the new *Kwisunja Tongjihoe* (Defectors' Organization) contained within the *wŏnho ch'o*. The name changed again under Chun Doo Hwan to *Sungŭi Tongjihoe* when the organization was removed from the veterans administration and placed within the ministry of health and social affairs. *Sungŭi Tongjihoe* is now affiliated not only with MOHSA but also with the *kyŏngch'al ch'ŏng* (police department).

According to my informants within the organization, it now operates in relative independence from the government, and this has actually been somewhat detrimental to defector morale. In the days of greater government interest and intervention, they suggest, they had numerous opportunities to discuss their needs with responsible government officials, to arrange better employment opportunities, and to discuss what the defectors might do to help unification efforts. In fact, the defectors were important enough to the government during the 1970s that officials responded positively to a strong defector lobbying effort to provide special protections. According to the 1972 amendment of the special protection law, for the first time all defectors would be guaranteed free housing and employment. As the president of *Sungŭi Tongjihoe* put it: "We were treated like national heroes;

President Park called us all *yongsa* [brave soldiers]." Under Kim's
administration, what the *Sungŭi Tongjihoe* president, along with many
south Koreans, calls the "people's government," defector resettlement
payments have decreased from an average of 40 to 50 million *wŏn*
($50,000 to $60,000) to 7 million *wŏn* (less than $9,000), and instead
of being assured a free apartment with a minimum size of 15 *p'yŏng* (a
small apartment by Korean standards; this figure would also include
balconies, as well as hallways and other common space outside the
apartment), the defectors are now assured only a payment of ten
million *wŏn* toward the rental fee of an apartment. The decrease in
housing funds is significant given that many 15 *p'yŏng* apartments cost
approximately 20 million *wŏn* in key money. Key money payments are
made prior to the rental; one then occupies the residence without
additional fees and receives the original payment upon leaving the
residence. Many new defectors must rent by the month, which means
that they will never see the money again.

In recent years, and as the number of defectors has increased,
another defector organization, *T'ongilhoe* (Unification Organization),
has emerged, with about 40 members. *T'ongilhoe* is administered under
kimusa, another name for *poansa*, meaning "public security department." This has become the organization of choice for defectors who are
former or current soldiers, such as the former soldiers Yi Ŭng-p'yŏng
and Kim Nam-joon. In addition, several other organizations appear to
be emerging, much less formal than the others and apparently separate
from the government: *Wŏlnamkwisunyongsa Sŏnkyohoe* (Defector's Mission), an explicitly religious organization for Christians; *Tongyuhoe* (a
shortened name for *Tongŭrŏp Yuhakseanghoe*, meaning Eastern European Students Organization), a group of former north Koreans who had
lived and studied in eastern Germany, the Soviet Union, and other
Soviet-bloc nations; *Narasaranghoe* (literally, "Organization for the Love
of the Country"), for young defectors in their twenties and early thirties;
Paekhyanghoe (Toward Mount Paekdu), a very small group of defectors
in their mid-thirties; and *Hanpaekhoe* (From Halla to Paekdu), another
small but general group of defectors. According to Oh Hye-chŏng, more
than half of the defectors in her sample do not attend any meetings,
either because they are "out of the loop" or because they do not have the
time. My own opinion is that many defectors are afraid that meeting

with other defectors in a large group will be disadvantageous to their prospects for advancement in south Korea.

Many defectors are more active members in the north Korean provisional organizations, in part because these organizations consist primarily of south Koreans *(wŏlnammin)* who came from the north prior to, or during, the initial days of division and the subsequent war, and who therefore are not ordinarily classified as defectors. These groups are organized according to locality, from the highest level of province down to the level of township and neighborhood. The defectors from the home localities of an organization will attend meetings as guests and lecturers. The *wŏlnammin* who attend are always thrilled to meet someone from their hometown either to receive information about people and places with which they are familiar, or simply to reminisce.

According to my informants, the two formal defector organizations, and perhaps even some of the provisional organizations, make it much easier for the government to keep track of people who come from the north. This has been of some concern given three cases of attempted repatriation. Yi Su-kŭn, a newspaper editor in north Korea who had worked as a spy in P'anmunjŏm, defected back to the north after he came under suspicion in the south for continued spying; Kim Sin-jo, who led the infiltrators in the 1970's to assassinate Park Chung Hee at the Blue House, and who was the only survivor, was released from prison and later attempted to re-defect to the north. He has now become a pastor. Most recently, in 1995, Kim Hyŏng-dŏk, a 22-year-old defector well known to many of my informants, became so dissatisfied with his life in the south that he attempted, unsuccessfully, to re-defect; he was sentenced to prison in the south for a period of 2 years and 8 months and had his savings confiscated (by most news accounts, about $14,000, although Kim himself reported a higher figure of 14 million *wŏn*, or about $18,000, half as a resettlement payment and half for housing fees [Kim, H. D. 1997a: 394; 1997b]). At any rate, defectors are never entirely free of the government's suspicion, for they were born and raised in a completely different ideological system, and, from the government perspective, if they violated one law in crossing the border to the south, they may violate another law once they have defected. In other words, the defectors are forever tainted and, by the very act of defection, they will perhaps be forever observed.

CHALLENGES OF EVERYDAY LIFE

Money, as I have already noted, is a primary marker for differentiating between defectors—indeed, when policemen accompanied the higher-status defectors I interviewed, they often began their own remarks by reporting the settlement payment the defector had received, thereby heightening the status of both themselves and the defectors with whom they worked. In Oh Hye-chŏng's interviews, as in mine, money emerged as more than a marker of status—it had become a problem for people who claimed they previously had little need for money. I cite below some of the excerpts from her interviews:

> I was better off in the north because I came from a good family. Here I am not that well off, but I really have no need for money.

> The units of money here are too large. I cannot comprehend how much money there is, and I don't need money. When I have had a lot of money, I've just spent it because I don't understand how to use it.

> When I arrived in the south, I was amazed that this money could actually buy things. In the north you just don't carry money in your pocket. Shops don't even have any goods to buy if you did.

> I still don't know the value of 10,000 *wŏn*. (Oh, H. C. 1995: 22)

Money also involves choice, something with which the defectors say they are unfamiliar. They complain a lot about fashion, that they feel insecure about their tastes, and that they are overwhelmed by the diversity of goods available to them. The choices with which they are confronted extend to a variety of realms of life.

> In the north we wear uniforms to school, and in everyday life you don't need to decorate yourself. But in the south people wear short trousers and low-cut tops. Many clothes have different names. They all look the same to me, but I guess there is a difference between the names. (Oh, H. C. 1995: 25)

> In the north, I couldn't eat that much. The only side dishes were bean paste and red pepper paste. People dreamed of eating white rice

and beef soup, but most of the time they cannot even eat gruel *[chuk]*.
But in the south I can eat so much! (Oh, H. C. 1995: 25)

We don't know how to use the different ingredients. A whole family
that I know defected and one day his second child returned from
school upset because the other children ridiculed his lunch box. (Oh,
H. C. 1995: 27)

The lives of southerners are too diverse and complicated. Everyone
has a different personality. I can't understand it. And I am confused
that every item seems to have a different price. (Oh, H. C. 1995: 26)

In the north, I did what I was supposed to do. If I was supposed to
get in line, I got in line. If I was supposed to applaud, I applauded.
But in the south I never know what to do. People do whatever they
want to do. (Oh, H. C. 1995: 26)

Some defectors are also confused by language in south Korea. Not
only are there variations in the vocabulary with which they are unfamiliar, a subject I take up later in this chapter with reference to cultural
differences, but they are unable to comprehend many forms of writing
that use English and Chinese characters:

Many of us [defectors] feel that it is difficult to read a newspaper.
We don't read Chinese characters, and we are not used to reading
from top to bottom [reading characters vertically]. (Oh, H. C.
1995: 27)

Yet at the same time, language has been used by the defectors themselves
to mark difference. Some defectors have published books with titles that
use north Korean words. For instance, Kim Yong's *Mŏrirŭl ppanŭn
namja* (The man who washes his hair) employs the verb *ppalda* (to
wash); *ppalda* is used in the north to refer to washing hair, but in the
south it is used only to refer to washing clothes or sneakers. South
Koreans instead use *kamda*, and it would be wholly inappropriate to use
the verb *ppalda*. Several defectors opened a theater company in 1996
called *Omani* (Mothers), a distinctively north Korean way of saying
what south Koreans call *ŏmŏni*.

In defector narratives, these issue are blended together to give a picture of dissatisfaction. Here is how Mr. Chŏng (as I will call him), a former logger in Russia, described his frustrations:

> When I first came here I didn't think that much about money, but now I do. *Toni saram salinda* [people exist because of money—as if money is like air or blood]. But if a person is acknowledged by others, money will follow. There are many things I need to know. No one could understand my speech; I always had to repeat my words over and over again because of my accent. Here, if you have a lot of money you have a good life. In the markets I see people struggling more than me, and I try to help them. The government has helped me, even though I am a sinner, and I am grateful and owe them a debt I can never repay. Still, the government is wrong to discriminate between defectors. Some get more money than others, more respect than others. High-class defectors get a lot of money, but the loggers get so little. This is the major cause of "stress" *[stŭressŭ]* among the defectors. I used to not think about money, but since I am in the south all I think about is what other people have and what I don't have. Here you have to step on people to get to the top. It is an invisible war *[poiji anŭn chŏnjaeng]*.
>
> In the north, people live according to the times and the surroundings. But here there is no limit on greed. In the north people who are smooth talkers are called conmen, but in the south the people [defectors] who are smooth talkers [in initial negotiations with the ANSP] get a lot of money from the government. We get most of our support from other defectors, especially when we are lonely. You will say, "If you're lonely come visit me."
>
> In the south, living isn't fun.

I interviewed Mr. Kang, another man who had been a logger in Russia before his defection, in 1996. He works at a national agricultural organization. He has attended some computer classes and will soon enroll in night courses at a university in Seoul. He feels that he is adapting better to south Korea, that he is over his preliminary shock. When he first arrived, Seoul was utter chaos to him, and he feared for his life. Friends in Russia, where he eventually sought asylum, told him that if lower-class people like loggers tried to defect, the south Koreans would kill them. Mr. Kang complains that south Koreans ridicule him about having no sense of *hyo* or *hyoja*, that is, devotion to and respect for his family. This appears to hurt him a great deal, since he views his time in south Korea before unification as preparation for seeing his parents:

> We all worry about money, but I am happy that I do have a salary and a family here. But I am concerned about sustaining them and moving up. Maybe later I will be more concerned about money. . . . Every time I see a *Ch'ŏk'o Pai* [a chocolate cream pie with a sponge center, one of south Korea's leading exports to China, Russia, and Vietnam] I want to send it to my family, especially during the holidays. I know unification should happen soon, but this is just my wish. I am worried about seeing my family again. I don't have the guts to look them in the eye *[nun pol myŏng mok ŏpda]*. What do I have to show for the suffering I've caused them? And I cannot financially support them.

He spoke about the difficulties of leaving his family.

> KANG: I heard a KBS radio broadcast in Russia but I did not really think I would come to the south. I listened to all the news about developments in south Korea and it seemed to be true. I told a friend what I had heard, and soon we were both taken away by the authorities. Luckily, I escaped, but I was really hurt *[p'inŭnmulŭl hŭllida]*. I thought about [my family's] suffering too, but if I was arrested as a political criminal it would have made their future even worse. Then the decision was not that difficult. Either I become a criminal or a defector. Defection seemed to be the better of the two.

> ROY RICHARD GRINKER: Were you afraid?

> KANG: I have no idea what I felt at that time. Actually, I should have settled permanently in Russia but somebody said that in Russia too north Korean people who were of lower rank would be killed. I am still a Korean, even though I escaped. I don't think I am a north Korean. A person without a [country] is pitiful. There is no value to being north Korean. In the first couple of months in Korea there were lots of things to see. But these were not satisfactory for me.

When I saw the Yuksam building I thought it was somewhat small. On TV I saw some scenes of congressmen fighting each other and blaming the president. There was nothing to interest me, and everything seemed chaotic—no order, laws, balance, control.

RRG: Now you have been here for one year and five months. What do you think about south Korean people? Is the south's perspective on the north getting better?

KANG: South Koreans have a stereotypical view of north Koreans. They prefer to think of north Koreans as people from an underdeveloped country. They have pity toward us. There is no love.

RRG: What do you think about unification?

KANG: Currently there are lots of news stories about north Korea. I think it should happen quickly but I also worry that if unification came I might not have adapted enough. I would probably have no face with which to see my parents. I do not want to show them that I have no money, that I am not in a situation to help them. I can't even buy a box of ramen for them.

RRG: Do you know Kim Hyŏng-dŏk, who attempted to defect back into the north?

KANG: Yes, I do. He tried hard to adapt well, but it was too hard for him. He thought of me as a real brother. He mentioned that he wanted to escape, but I said, "You came here with a tough decision, and now you think it is hard to live so you want to go away? But wherever you go it will be the same. There is no country that is easy to adapt to." The problem with him is that he is so smart, so quick to understand what other people are thinking, and he always compares himself with others. He thought he was discriminated against. Once when we were out with some other people I told them that Hyŏng-dŏk needed help for employment. He was not in the conversation with us at that time, but he knew that I was telling his story to someone else. He complained that he was not happy to see me talking to south Korean people about his misery. Hyŏng-dŏk called me just before he tried to escape. I think I made a big mistake. I was not able to give him advice. I think it was totally my fault. Hyŏng-dŏk was too smart to forget how he was discriminated against.

RRG: How do you think south Koreans think about the defectors?

KANG: They think we are far behind them. They think we are relatively dull-witted but they don't understand the fundamental educational system in the north. The educational system in the elementary school, junior and high school, and even day care schools, were well developed, and not as bad as the southerners think. But in terms of employment the education I had in the north might not fit the qualifications a southern company requires. I understand the government has a hard time taking care of the defectors. They cannot do everything from one to ten for us, but it is not enough. We need something else.

Mr. Kang's story is typical, though most south Koreans I interviewed on the defectors had little sympathy for them. I commonly heard people say, "Well, aren't all defectors unhappy and lonely?" "Did you think it is easy to live in a divided nation?" "The north Koreans have to pay for what they have done."

Surveys conducted in south Korea have suggested that south Koreans do not overwhelmingly conceive of the defectors as "brothers and sisters" to be helped and cared for. While an unpublished 1993 survey conducted by the unification board, to which I was given access, noted that south Koreans were more likely to root for north Korean athletic teams than for teams from other countries, responses to its questions on brotherhood indicated that most respondents continue to think of the north as the enemy. Another poll, carried out by the Hyundai Institute among 800 south Koreans and 200 south Korean "experts" on north Korea in the 6 major south Korean cities, suggested that south Koreans have their sights set on potential problems of unification and are less concerned with brotherhood. Just 51.6 percent of citizens and 62 percent of "experts" said they consider the north Koreans as "brothers and sisters"; 39 percent of citizens and 33 percent of experts said that they had "no particular feeling toward north Koreans"; and 9.4 percent of citizens and 5 percent of experts considered north Korean people to be enemies of the south (Foreign Broadcast Information Service for East Asia, 95-049, 3.15.95: 42).

Kim Hyŏng-dŏk's attempted re-defection received a tremendous amount of public attention, however, and my impression is that many people who previously had not given much thought to the defectors began to consider whether the defectors were loyal to the south, and whether the south needed to put more effort into "Koreanizing" (*hankukhwa* or *inamhwa*) them. There are some Koreans, mostly students, who sympathize with the defectors, for in them they see many south Korean lives in microcosm: the poor person unable to fulfill the capitalist dream, the divided family member unable to see his or her family, or, as in a recent fictional depiction (Kim Chi-su 1996), the abused spouse who must flee her abusive husband for her own safety and yet is criticized for leaving him.

Kim Hyŏng-dŏk's actions are often cited as an example of potential criminal behavior among defectors, but the specifics of his case are not well known. He defected to south Korea in September of 1994 through China, and most people who knew him have said that his "adaptation process" was slow and confusing for him. Not long before he attempted to re-defect at Inchon on February 3, 1996, he became involved in an altercation and faced criminal charges for assault. He was sentenced to eight years in prison and two years' probation but was released about six months after beginning his sentence. On November 30, 1996, *Hanguk ilbo* reported that along with three other defectors (Yŏ Kŭm-yong, who is Yŏ Man-ch'ŏl's first son, Yi Wŏn-do, and Ch'oi Myŏng-nam) Kim Hyŏng-dŏk matriculated at Yonsei's business school, and the money the government had confiscated from him upon his arrest was returned to him. In a recent interview, Kim insists that he is now loyal to south Korea, but he remains disaffected. He believes he is the lowest-paid of all defectors and he states that he no longer has many defector friends (Kim Hyŏng-dŏk 1997a: 396; see also 1997b).

His story quickly appeared in fictional form as a short story in a very high-profile (and liberal) literary magazine, *Ch'angjakwa pip'yŏng*. The story, "*Mugŏun Saeng*" (Heavy life) by Kim Chi-su, portrays a day in the life of a sad and awkward man named Lee who befriends his landlord's daughter, Chŏng-un, when she flees her husband, who has been beating her. Lee appears naive, introverted, and lonely, and because of these features he is wrongly arrested for the burglary of a jewelry store. When the real thieves are caught, Lee is released and comforted by Chŏng-un, and in a drunken stupor he reveals that he is a north Korean defector. He had been a doctor of Oriental medicine in the north until, after the death of a high-status patient, he was sent to Siberia as a logger.

When he defected to the south, his southern relatives denounced his lack of loyalty to his northern family, and the south Korean government compensated him only with a settlement payment equal to a logger's salary. He secretly saved millions of *wŏn* so that he could return to his family and, he hoped, bring them to the south. His pain, as he describes it, is so unbearable that he must return to the north. The author thus carefully merges the lives of the two characters: both have fled for their personal safety, both realize that they cannot bear to live away from their families, and both take the risk of returning. Only after speaking with Lee does Chŏng-un finally realize that she cannot leave her son and must return home to give her ostensibly repentant husband a second chance. The next day she reads in the newspaper that Lee Myŏng-un, a thirty-five-year-old defector, had been arrested trying to illegally enter the north in a Chinese cargo ship.

The story's parallel between a south Korean woman and a north Korean man would no doubt have some appeal to defectors, since it emphasizes commonalities in a world in which they feel different. Despite the constant reminders in schoolbooks and other arenas of south Korean discourse that the north Koreans are of the same blood and ancestry as south Koreans, north Korea continues to be seen as another country, and north Koreans as immigrants. Indeed, some north Korean defectors told me that they feel they are treated less well than foreign workers from south and southeast Asia. No one can determine whether the north Korean defectors' beliefs about how south Koreans view them are justified by empirical evidence, but the discrimination certainly seems real to them.

The difference between defectors and south Koreans is curious amidst the ideology of homogeneity. As the anthropologist Hugh Gusterson commented recently in reaction to a conference presentation I made about the defectors, "The defectors' role as *symbols* is undermined by their role as *persons*" (personal communication). A conservative perspective may shed some light on the conflict. A conservative critic and editor of a leading journal on north Korea, Kim Chŏng-sun (1996: 25), has argued that Korean politics has been moving away from a conception of the nation as *minjok* (a national community defined by common ancestry), toward a conception of the nation as *kukminjŏk* (a political community). This is the only reason he can find to explain the nearly total agreement among the leaders of all political parties at the

October 7, 1996, summit on the submarine infiltrators. All could agree, he suggested, that north Korea must no longer be treated merely as a separate state containing innocent Korean people to be protected by south Korea; rather, north Korea has to be seen as if it were another country. Only then will real progress be made in limiting north Korean aggression and their plan to communize the peninsula. If Kim is right that this way of looking at north Korea is taking hold, then the increasing complaints of defectors may be attributable in some part to increasing intolerance in south Korea for the north Korean people's innocence. Are they truly blind people who have no ability to resist their oppressors? Isn't the persistence of the north Korean regime at least in part the result of the people's complicity?

As one response to their feeling of marginality, a defectors' theater company, "*Omani*," staged a play in Seoul entitled *K'orirang* (short for *Korea Arirang*). The stage was enveloped by an electric wire fence, along which were placed Russian, Japanese, Chinese, and American dolls. In the opening scene, five defectors appeared behind the fence in wheel-chairs, apparently symbolizing that they had been disabled by the foreign powers. They told a story about a man named Kim Yŏng-hwa who escaped from the north through China but preferred to be housed in a refugee camp for non-Koreans rather than to be treated like a defector. At the end of the play, all the defectors said that if the south Korean government embraces 200,000 illegal foreign workers, then why not several hundred Korean defectors? The audience was invited to participate in the play and to engage in a dialogue with the defectors. The eldest performer, Ho Ch'ŏl-su, talked about how he believed that his father lives somewhere in the south; another, Oh Myŏng-sun, talked of how north Koreans sing many south Korean popular songs, but said that south Koreans knew none of the north Korean songs. According to the director, Kim Sang-ch'ŏl, the play was designed to break the *ijilgam* between south and north in a safe environment where there were no government controls, and where people could talk candidly about their predicaments (Kim, H. S. 1996).[2]

In response to what they see as exaggerated reports of north Korean famine, the defectors have also argued publicly that only the poorest north Koreans are dying of hunger (Yi, T. L. 1996). According to some, even the poorest farmers in places such as Hwanghae-do and Sinuiju continue to produce enough rice for their subsistence. One defector, Yi

Chŏng-kuk, who claims to have been quite poor in north Korea before his 1996 defection, says that he had no problems getting through the winter. And in contrast to reports of north Korea's impending collapse, Park Ch'ŏl-ho says in the quotation that appears as the epigraph to this chapter: "Most people have been brainwashed since the day of their birth so that even though they may be miserable they believe that Kim Jong Il will save them. I was one of these people. I guarantee you there is no defector in south Korea who did not weep when Kim Il Sung died."

MISTRUST

Defectors with whom I spoke are for the most part suspicious of the south, just as southerners are suspicious of defectors. Some recent defectors think that Korean products may be American goods that are simply packaged in Korea, that the poorest Koreans are hidden from public view, and even more generally that when people appear warm and friendly they are in fact harboring much anger and resentment. One man told me that when people say to him in jest, "I'm surprised you don't have horns like the devil," he is saddened. For him, the statement shows that he is still marked in negative terms as north Korean. When people ask him about north Korea, they often imply that they think the north is a terrible place to live, and yet even those defectors who detest the north Korean political and economic system think of their home-land in fond terms. As one of Oh's interviewees said, "The north is neither a pack of wolves nor a socialist paradise; it is a place where human beings carry on their lives as best they can" (Oh, H. C. 1995: 61). When a defector commits a crime in south Korea, the press generally makes much of the fact that the criminal is also a defector, and this sort of publicity lowers morale among all the defectors and reaffirms their suspicions that southerners expect them to behave aberrantly.

According to the defectors, the south Korean public also views them as simple-minded and lacking in creativity and spontaneity. For this reason, they cannot trust their employers to promote them, or to give them positions with responsibility. Defectors say that south Koreans also view them in very contradictory ways: for example, although the defectors are viewed as physically strong, they are also seen as lazy. Similarly, although they are perceived as innocent, they are also perceived as potentially traitorous. They are seen as very emotional, and yet they are also seen as cold and stoic.

In general, the defectors discern that southerners believe the north is a place with little value. They fear that the 50-year history of nearly 30 million people will be discarded after unification, and yet, while loyal to the south, they are privately proud of many of the north's achievements, especially in education. There are currently few legal guidelines for south Korean recognition or validation of north Korean diplomas or job skill certifications. As a result, one defector I met, a doctor of Oriental medicine, was told that he would have to graduate from a south Korean school of Oriental medicine if he wanted an official license. He now works as an electronics repairman. Fortunately for people such as this man, the 1997 law supports the acknowledgment of diplomas acquired in the north or in other countries.

One area of profound mistrust is the south's ostensible wish for unification, and this is a subject that appears to take priority over all others in church organizations concerned with the plight of defectors. Nearly every defector I interviewed said firmly that there is a greater passion for unification in the north than in the south, and that they believed the south's statements in support of unification are intended solely to resonate with political constituencies and do not reflect true desires. Indeed, the defectors note that most south Koreans appear to enjoy the continued division of Korea because it means that nothing will change. Their taxes will not be raised, they will not fear acts of revenge, they will not lose their jobs, the economy will continue to grow, and they will remain victorious in the eyes of other nations as the "good" Korea.

Conservative voices in south Korea affirm these opinions. In my view, the content and tone of Seo Dong-ik's treatment of defector issues (1996: 50-57) comes close to equating north Korean defectors with rehabilitated prisoners. Seo, a prominent expert on north Korea, suggests four policies to care for larger numbers of defectors. First, he argues that although south Koreans need to welcome the defectors, the defectors must be compensated in a way that does not offend the lower classes—by which Seo means that the defectors should not be given amounts of money that place them in an economic position superior to poor south Koreans. Second, he states that south Koreans must never forget that the defectors were living in north Korea while south Korean students and civilians were fighting against the south Korean military dictatorships and working hard to build the south Korean economy. Seo thus asks: "What did the defectors do while our youths and civilians were fighting and bleeding in their protests? What did they do to change the Kim Il Sung/Kim Jong Il system? What were they doing while the children of low-income families in south Korea were struggling to build our economy?" (1996:52). Third, he says the defectors must understand that south and north Koreans are the "same people," and so they must learn to become more and more like south Koreans. Here is a passage from Seo in which north Koreans and south Koreans are likened to orphaned lion cubs and zoologists, respectively:

> A television program recently showed a zoologist feeding and train-ing a lion cub whose mother had died, in order to permit him to survive alone in the wild. When the zoologist released the grown cub into the wild, he was killed by other lions. This kind of natural phenomenon suggests to us that our government must adopt as a primary strategy the homogenizing [tongjilhwa] of north Korean defectors. (Seo 1996: 52)

I assume that Kim Il Sung and the north Korean state are the metaphorical "mother" in this analogy. Fourth, the defectors must "realize who they are" and cease complaining. In fact, Seo argues that if the defectors complain about their situation in the south, they will stand as a barrier to national unification.

Given this sort of conservative (and fairly widespread) reaction to the defectors, and the fact that defectors tell us quite explicitly about their unhappiness in south Korea, there is reason to fear that large numbers of defectors in the future will exacerbate the problem of achieving social harmony. At this point, the number of defectors is rather small, given that there are more than 44 million south Koreans and 27 million north Koreans. Yet defectors in south Korea have a considerable amount of visibility in the media, if only because each defection is touted by the south Korean government as evidence of its own superiority and of the terrible conditions in north Korea. Still, most analysts say that there are few signs of an impending flood of refugees across the south Korean border. But what if there is not a flood of thousands but a smaller influx of hundreds? What will the south Koreans do? What will south Korea ask of the United States? Since most defectors I have interviewed seem to believe that any large movement of people away from the north will head toward China (in part because many north Koreans suspect that defectors are imprisoned in south Korea), what will China do at its borders? These are perplexing questions because they are rather speculative, but they are also perplexing because they have not been adequately addressed and debated in south Korea.

Clearly, the new defector law makes some preparations for larger numbers of defectors. There are provisions for building new protection facilities in Ansŏng, Kyŏnggi Province, to be opened in 1999, that will house up to 500 "escapees" (as the defectors are now called).[3] This seems a small step, of course, especially since some officials in the south Korean government say that they expect as many as 4 million refugees to leave north Korea in the next few years (Foreign Broadcast Information Service for East Asia, 4.17.96: 242). However, there are some encouraging signs of preparation. For example, in order to prepare for the administration of a unified society and economy, the south Korean government will send about 20 officials to as many as 16 socialist or former communist countries on an annual basis to learn about socialist administration; there are some estimates that at least 35,000 new administrative personnel will be needed to work with the north Koreans on unification. Moreover, the law transfers many of the responsibilities for taking care of the defectors away from the Agency for National Security and Planning and toward other ministries—foreign affairs, justice, education, and health and social affairs. The south Korean government intends the interministerial management to provide a basis for coping with larger numbers of defectors and the complexities of their integration into south Korea. The transfer of powers away from the ANSP may also reflect an effort to make defector management appear less secretive or less tainted by covert intelligence operations. The law remains ambiguous and vague about the calculation of resettlement payments, no doubt because the government fears being bound to make payments to thousands or hundreds of thousands of escapees.

Yet most south Koreans continue to assume the end of the north Korean regime of Kim Jong Il and the eventual unification of Korea to be an endpoint rather than a beginning. The defectors tell us something very important about this assumption: if south Koreans think relations with north Korea are expensive now, wait until after unification.

TEN

CONCLUSION

PREPARING FOR UNIFICATION: THE PROBLEM OF COMPLICITY AND DIFFERENCE

Mother
You are ninety this year
But I've never dreamed
Of your death

—Yi Ki-hyŏng[1]

AS I HAVE NOTED SEVERAL TIMES, scholars and other writers who have taken on the subject of "unification theory" have seldom subjected the concept itself to critical examination and have instead explored new ways of reaffirming unification as Korea's paramount goal (Kang and Yu 1995).[2] There is nothing wrong with these reaffirmations. What is wrong is that unification discussions have been limited to them. As a result, Koreans are less prepared for the many dimensions and complexities of unification as an historical process, as opposed to a long-cherished desire.

What would it mean to prepare for unification? Clearly, there are economic, administrative, and public policy questions that have to be addressed, but these lie outside the scope of this particular study (see, for

example, Eberstadt 1995; Henriksen and Lho 1994). I have taken up
some of these more practical issues elsewhere.[3] I have been more
concerned here with discussing the conceptual contours of preparation—especially the ways in which unification is elevated to the level of
the sacred[4]—not only because this is an area that has been relatively
unexamined, but also because I want to show that unification "expenses"
cannot be limited to economics.[5] In an earlier part of this book, I
suggested that preparation might mean the conversion of *han* as enmity
into *han* as reconciliation. This process of conversion is analogous to the
mourning process, in which the present reconciles with the past,
recognizes what has changed, and adapts to the new situation. I have
argued that south Koreans have not conceived of themselves as situated
in a new context to which they must adapt, and that the past has not
been worked through sufficiently to accommodate a changed and
heterogeneous Korea. This issue of unresolved mourning, and in
particular the absence of discourse as a central feature of complicated or
unsuccessful mourning, may be somewhat new to Korean studies of
national division, but it has been addressed at length in the extensive
literature on Germany and the Holocaust. Some of the most important
questions concern the act of scholarship itself: Does understanding an
injustice in some way pardon it? What are the moral, aesthetic, or
theoretical reasons for writing about it? Having raised these questions,
let me discuss some differences and similarities between Korea and
Germany, drawing on some of the Holocaust literature but more
specifically on an exchange between Jurgen Habermas and Paik Nak
Chung. To some extent, the Habermas—Paik exchange evokes debate
about how to prepare for unification.

A number of scholars have noted that for many years after World
War II, few Jews or Germans wrote about the Holocaust. Some, such as
the Mitscherlichs, attribute much of the absence of literature to the
length of time between the end of the Nazi era and the beginning of a
time of healing and mourning. According to this thesis, Germans and
Jews needed time to repair some of the moral damage caused by the
extermination of the Jews. As Germans began to work through their
past, Germans, French, and Jews all over the world, among many others,
formed new political and literary relationships to struggle against racism
and genocide, and to represent the past in a way that would be
meaningful not only for the generation that lived through the Holocaust

but also for the later generations that inherited its legacies. This is not reconciliation; rather, it resembles what has been called *tikkun,* a Hebrew word meaning "mending" but not implying forgiveness, the resolution of dispute, or moral embrace. In other words, among Jews writing about the Holocaust, knowledge was emancipatory rather than conciliatory. To withhold forgiveness was not necessarily to attribute a collective guilt or a collective innocence—one can argue that the Holocaust is unforgivable—but to avoid the impotence and disingenuousness of a forced reconciliation.

Rather than accept a political and forced reconciliation, or forgive something that cannot be forgiven, Holocaust survivors engaged in a struggle to find literary, cinematic, and artistic ways to begin speaking about the unspeakable. This is one reason why President Reagan's controversial trip to the cemetery at Bitburg caused such an uproar among so many Jews: he was forcing a kind of forgiveness in his own terms on those who believe they hold exclusive rights to forgiveness in their own terms. Only Jews could forgive the Germans. Moreover, Holocaust survivors had to work through, on their own, the problem of the division of people and state (a division repeatedly reaffirmed by Reagan in justifying the laying of a wreath near the graves of former SS officers)—whether Nazis were to blame or whether the broader German public was to blame, either for active or passive complicity. If nothing else, memory was at stake in debates about Holocaust representations. How could the future generations know about Nazism if those who actually lived through it did not represent it themselves? The same question can be reframed a bit more elaborately: How can future generations liberate themselves from the burden of the past without simply denying, forgetting, or avoiding the tasks of mourning?

For Holocaust survivors, "working through" has meant an ongoing struggle to resist closure, a struggle that has involved painful acknowledgment of the failure to master the past or to arrive at incontestable truths. LaCapra (1994: 210) writes of Holocaust studies that "working through implies the possibility of judgment that is not apodictic or ad hominem but argumentative, self-questioning, and related in mediated ways to action." By this he also means that the binary oppositions between good and evil, innocent and guilty, among others, that were sufficient to sustain a biased and stereotyped perspective, no longer hold up in a process of working through trauma.

Working through also involves a relinquishment of prior forms of selfhood, because successful mourning has required that loss be, to some extent, externalized. Losses can be successfully mourned if they are consciously recognized as external events that impoverish the world; losses cannot be mourned if they are experienced primarily as internal losses that impoverish the self, or if they are so completely externalized that they are denied any connection with the living. At the level of the nation, acknowledgments of loss—whether through verbal expression, monuments, or some other vehicle—simultaneously retain loss as a part of national identity while also separating national identity from the object that was possessed and is now lost. The living do not forget the past, but they do move on. In a comment on Reitz's television series *Heimat,* discussed in chapter 2, Santner writes, "Mourning is understood here as that process whereby an object that is part of our ongoing lives is ritually guided into the past tense of our lives" (1990: 67). The Mitscherlichs also establish a linkage between mourning and externalization by noting that empathy, a vital component of any mourning process, is by definition an experience of an other, an object outside the self:

> Mourning arises when the lost object was loved for its own sake. Or, to put it somewhat differently, mourning can occur only when one individual is capable of empathy with another. This other person enriched me through his otherness, as man and woman can enrich each other by experiencing their difference.

It seems sad to suggest that the man cited in the epigraph to this chapter should begin dreaming of his mother's death. Yet some things can never be recovered, a point made clear in a poem by Don Pagis entitled "Written in Pencil in the Sealed Freight Car," which is included in an influential essay on closure by Irving Howe. The poem suggests that mourning does not involve resolution or completion. Far from it: mourning is about recognition, complexity, and enduring incompleteness. Pagis thus writes about loss without conveying closure.

Here in this transport
I Eve
and Abel my son

if you should see my older son
Cain son of man
tell him that I

Of the poem, the writer Irving Howe has said, "Cry to heaven or cry to earth: that sentence will never be completed."

IS SUCCESSFUL MOURNING A MATTER OF TIME?

We might argue, along with some Germanists, that mourning is a matter of time, and that south Koreans simply have not had enough time. After all, Koreans still live in a divided nation. However, the time thesis would be inaccurate not only for the obvious reason that it reduces complex phenomena to arbitrary intervals, but also because there are far too many differences between Korean and German histories to make the same argument for both.

First, there are many who would argue that whereas Jews may have made great strides in addressing the complexities of the Holocaust, Germans have been less successful because of their unwillingness to confront the issue of popular complicity and because of the persistence of anti-Semitism, which was articulated clearly by a large segment of the German public during the so-called Bitburg controversy when many Germans publicly denounced as trouble-makers the Jews who opposed Reagan's visit to the Bitburg cemetery, and when Germans asked if they would have to be reminded of the Holocaust forever. From this perspective, time has not helped the Germans' ability to mourn.

Second, despite the fact that Germany unified, German intellectuals were remarkably passive or silent about unification. Numerous scholars have commented on the absence of an intellectual debate on German unification until well after the Wall came down; political and academic discussion of the social and cultural dimensions of unification began in earnest only *after* the Berlin Wall was demolished. The current difficulties in developing an all-German national identity, blamed in part on what Andreas Huyssen (1991) has called "the failure of German intellectuals," led the eastern German writer Reiner Kunze to say that "after October 3, 1990, [Germany] will prepare itself for this day" (quoted in Mertes 1994: 25). In his response to Habermas's essay on

Germany and Korea, Paik cites an essay on unification by Hart-Landsberg and suggests that progressives in Germany simply did not have a national discourse to be employed and that the government took advantage of this weakness:

> Indeed, did not that neglect [of German intellectuals] give Kohl and the West German vested interests represented by him a more or less free hand in pursuing the "fast track?" To my mind, the fast track was more than a simply shortsighted or precipitous response to the collapse of "the alternative model of society" represented by the Soviet empire, but a deliberate and, in its own way, perspicacious move to ensure, if not actually strengthen, the economic and political hegemony of existing West German institutions in a new united Germany. (Paik 1996a: 19)

Koreans, as I have already noted, have been more vocal, but only in certain circles that have been marginalized, if not terrorized, by the government. Nearly every Korean argument for a federation, and nearly every warning that Korean unification might really be the imperialism of the south over the north, has been labeled in south Korea as radical and left-wing. Indeed, despite all the talk in both Germany and Korea about various small steps that needed to be taken to achieve cooperation or détente, it was simply not possible to discuss unification openly in Korea (or, for very different reasons, in Germany) prior to the late 1980s. What this coincidence of silence in south Korea and in Germany tells us is not only that Germany's "time" was not sufficient, but that what was at stake in conducting scholarly work on unification was a confrontation with reality, and perhaps also a confrontation with the uncomfortable possibilities of victory or defeat.

Third, as Habermas has pointed out, Germany and Korea's roles as pawns in the Cold War often led Germans and Koreans to focus more on ideological and military confrontations than on "internal political contradictions stemming from the past—colonial rule or the Nazi period" (1996: 4). How else to explain the continued employment of Japanese collaborators in Syngman Rhee's government? The conflict between the Western and the Eastern blocs, played out in both Germany and Korea, may be seen as having produced a defensive nationalism in which sovereignty and dependence vis-a-vis the superpowers tended to sideline internal problems. It was the end of the Cold War, not simply a matter of time, that gave Germans the opportunity to unify and Koreans an opportunity to embrace Roh's "northern diplomacy."

HABERMAS, PAIK, AND THE PROBLEM OF HOMOGENEITY

In their essays on the similarities and differences between Germany and Korea to which I have already referred, one of Germany's leading public intellectuals, Jurgen Habermas, and one of south Korea's most prominent literary and cultural critics, Paik Nak Chung, take on the troubling relation between homogeneity and the nation. Habermas (1996: 9), in particular, cautions Koreans against assuming too much common ethnic consciousness, even among a people with such a long history of political and cultural unity. No matter how much cultural homogeneity one may believe exists in any particular society, it is the form of political integration that is most crucial in determining freedom and equality. Habermas warns that democracies are conventionally assumed to require the "bonding energy" of a homogeneous nation, and that this is a dangerous assumption: "A government which bases its action on the premise that its citizens' loyalty must be rooted in the consciousness of a common nature and destiny, shared by a more or less homogeneous nation, would find itself having to enforce a certain uniformity against the actual complexity and the growing diversity of modern life" (1996: 10).

Habermas seems to believe that Germany moved too quickly to unify, marginalizing its citizens, especially those in the GDR, from meaningful participation in political decisions, and that, as one result, there is widespread discontent. The most recent literature and media reports out of Germany suggest that citizens of the former East Germany are increasingly unhappy about the ways in which their country has been "absorbed" or "assimilated," as if there is nothing good about the east to be preserved. Many eastern Germans have only reluctantly given up their old passports; a significant number of eastern Germans resent unification and want to return to division, and the term "wall of the mind" has come to stand for the many differences between the two sides. There are ecological debates about pollution in the former GDR, and intense criticisms of eastern Germans' consumerism; transitional justice is also a complicated problem, especially the question of how to handle disclosures about eastern German people's complicity with the *Stasi*, the state security police.

A December 1989 poll conducted in western Germany by the magazine *Der Spiegel* showed some striking answers to the question "Should the GDR form a state together with the FRG, or should the GDR continue to be a sovereign state?" Seventy-one percent said that they wanted GDR sovereignty while only 27 percent said they wanted unification (cited in Brockman 1991: 15 n.18). Perhaps one of the most profound problems is that unification in Germany was framed so much in terms of economics—the assumption that once east Germans saw the west they would be "converted" to capitalism (Habermas called this "Deutschmark Nationalismus")—that western Germans were unprepared for the social unrest that developed. For their part, eastern Germans began to mourn the loss of their country, including its isolation. We might look again at Ahrends's intriguing Sleeping Beauty metaphor:

> It has only been twenty-eight years [of sleep], and already it is coming to an end. Instead of the prince, some unauthorized person has turned on the light and started making nasty remarks about the slum in which one has been living. One wakes up blinking one's eyes and becomes aware of all the spider webs, the inch-thick dust, the worn-out carpets, the flaking paint. . . .
>
> One drives a shabby jalopy, walks around in simple clothes, eats gray bread and artificial honey. That did not use to be so important, but now it is shameful, now that there is no pride left in sacrifice, no dignity in poverty. . . . But it is not just the East, it is also the West that has been deprived of its dream: that there, in a dilapidated and not entirely couth castle the most beautiful of princesses is sleeping and waiting for the day of her liberation. Any real transfiguration of the East is possible only from the West; and it becomes even more powerful when it is assigned the role of an obituary. All right then, invest your capital and send in your construction crews, but think about what you are losing in the freedom of the East. (Ahrends 1991: 42)

In his own essay, Habermas goes on to suggest that some of this palpable resentment might have been avoided if there had been more active preparation before unification.

So I have no wish to argue that, in the other event, the balance-sheet would, all in all, have been more positive. What I have in mind is something rather different. A way of proceeding which permitted broader discussion and opinion formation, as well as more exten- sive—and, above all, better prepared—participation of the public, would have included citizens in both East *and* West in the eventual *responsibility* for the process. The allocation of responsibilities for unwanted side-effects would have been steered from the beginning in a different direction. It would have been the people's own mistakes that they would have had to cope with. (1996:12, emphasis in original).

Paik has responded to Habermas by noting that the euphoria in Korea after the end of the Cold War was quickly muted. If west Germany was being economically crippled by uniting with a country much stronger than north Korea, how could south Korea handle unification? Paik, sees this difference as an advantage, since, as he notes here and elsewhere, it would be a mistake to follow the German model: "It may therefore be a blessing in disguise that South Korea all too obviously lacks the resources even to begin to emulate the German model" (1996b: 199). Noting that neither the United States nor the south Korean government has any stated policy for Korean unification other than the very general concepts of "soft landing" or absorption, he asks how Korea can better prepare for unification when Germany could not do it. The answer to these questions is that preparation is difficult for a number of reasons that again engage us in comparisons between Germany and Korea.

First, Paik argues that whereas German unification has engendered disappointments and resentments, Korean unification, hindered as it is by military confrontation, could be truly disastrous. Second, Paik notes that Germans did not harbor the bitterness or military history of north Korea—Koreans had the Korean War and a long-standing political socialization that encouraged hatred of the other side. However, despite Paik's pessimism about the ability of Korea to follow the German model, the differences between Korea and Germany may also be advantages for Korea. Paik is optimistic that national solidarity can overcome division, that the common experiences of colonialism and imperialism in north and south will facilitate unification. For Paik, Koreans' history of vertical strength (that is, the ability to maintain a loyal citizenry) and lateral weakness (vulnerability to foreign interventions) provides opportunities for a peninsula-wide national consciousness. He does not believe, however, that north Korea will be easily absorbed into a south Korean system. Rather, a new system, an innovative state structure, must be implemented, one similar to a federation but that at the very least opens up the borders and provides a framework for a fuller unification, albeit through the detour of a federation and what might appear to some as a temporary perpetuation of the division system.

Paik and Habermas's analyses are also warnings. Habermas warns that Germans' euphoria after the wall came down masked the social and political differences between eastern and western Germans that soon engendered easterners' sense of having been conquered. It is true that Koreans in both north and south exhibit many commonalities, and one might even argue that the strength of the south and north Korean states has been correlated with the strength of those commonalities; that is, a strong state was required to prevent the people from establishing their own civil unification. Habermas warns, however, that Korea's sacred and naturalized sense of homogeneity (their *ethnos*) might easily usurp their voluntary sense of political organization *(demos)* and lead either to authoritarianism or, more likely, to the denial of difference and to forced assimilation into a uniform, homogeneous nation. Avoiding such a dangerous and coercive process might lead Korea to a future marked less by social conflict and suppressed emotion, and more by the conversion of resentment into virtue and compassion, and by the creativity of mourning. Despite their differences, Habermas and Paik similarly avoid talking about past identities to be resuscitated and instead focus on how new identities can be constructed out of the past.

TOWARD DIFFERENCE AND THE FUTURE

> *Yubi muhwan* [a proverb: "preparation avoids
> catastrophes"]: one seldom hears it these days.
> —Kim Tong-kil, 1996

In south Korea, adequate preparation, and successful mourning, would mean that Koreans would begin to talk more openly about unification, heterogeneity, and difference and would more freely debate the different perspectives that are found now only as unconscious ambivalence or as demonizing projections upon the north. Preparation might also mean inducing melancholia—that is, an intense sadness about the failure of the myth of homogeneity—as a precursor to mourning. Instabilities and differences may also have to be taken not as aberrations but as the reality of a new identity, a subject on which I will have more to say below.

Another facet of preparation is the need to debate the people-state division that I have argued is so fundamental to unification discourses. Recall that this was the division that made possible Roh Tae Woo's pardon of the terrorist Kim Hyun Hee. Yet already many questions appear to be emerging in the media about north Korean people's complicity with the state, some of which are specifically legal questions. Will some north Koreans face criminal charges? How will south Koreans determine which north Korean persons are part of the innocent "people" and which are part of the guilty north Korean "state"? The arrival in the south of Hwang Chang-yŏp, the highest-ranking north Korean to defect and an architect of the north Korean political ideology of chuch'e, will test the people-state divide. Despite his desire to defect, Hwang can also be blamed for continuing and strengthening the division of Korea. In Germany, it did not take long for the people-state division to collapse after unification. The enormous number of eastern Germans who had participated with the Stasi, or who had relatives and friends who collaborated with them, made it impossible to sustain a view of the people's innocence. The writer Christa Wolf, who revealed her own linkages with the Stasi, became the symbol of conformity with the state and was attacked quite viciously from all sides in the press. In western German unification discourses, Wolf came to stand for the eastern German people.

Many Koreans may want unification to be an endpoint, but we know that no matter where we arrive, it is always different than we imagined, and there is always someplace to which we can return. The German case shows this remarkably well, as many Germans from east and west now long for a return to the days of division. As noted above, the release of Stasi files has shown the people's complicity with the east German state; vigilante violence has increased; the costs of unity have been staggering; Germans find themselves bewildered by their potential strength amidst the ghosts of Auschwitz; the lowest common denominator appears to be capitalism, and this has led to a moral crisis in which the eastern Germans are damned as greedy if they embrace it and damned as backward if they do not; and the west has materialized as the masculine conqueror (embodied by Helmut Kohl) and the east as the feminine accomplice (embodied by the demonized Christa Wolf) to the former eastern state. One only has to look at the emerging literature on methods of making money in north Korea to realize the extent to which south Korean capitalism stands ready to conquer the north (see, for example, a 1996 best-seller by Yun Woong, the title of which translates as *108 Ideas for Making Money in P'yŏngyang*). Some defectors I have interviewed say they are afraid that south Koreans will continue to tacitly define unification as the finishing of the war by conquering the north and destroying everything that is distinctive about it. Some think that south Koreans believe there is nothing to be preserved in the north, and that the 50-year history of nearly 30 million people in the north will have been for nothing.

Arrivals, like borders, are not only endpoints but beginnings. They shatter preconceived images and point to new directions, sometimes forward and sometimes backward. Unfortunately, the forward-looking element of identity formation has received little scholarly attention. One of the purposes of this book is to show how certain visions of the future become integral aspects of identity. One might even suggest that the various arenas within which unification emerges as a central trope of national recovery lead us to see how some discourses promote unification while others seem to inhibit it. I hope that my analyses have shown that those discourses that promote a working through of loss are also those that promote unification; conversely, discourses on similarity tend to reinforce barriers to unification by highlighting fears and ambivalences and by constraining the process of mourning.

I would also like to point out two needs that are related to the subject of studies of the future. First, there is a need for social scientists outside the domain of policy studies, in which the orientation is always forward, to focus more directly on the study of the future, to establish, as Hebdige writes, "how particular discursive strategies open up or close down particular lines of possibility; how they invite or inhibit particular identifications for particular social fractions at particular moments" (1993: 275). Second, more research needs to be conducted on nations as cultural processes; just as cultures vary, so do nations, and just as cultures are always in flux, so are nations. Despite many scholars' best efforts (Tønneson and Antlöv 1996), a gap remains in studies of nations and nationalisms because non-Western nations continue to be seen either as static or as distorted reflections of essentialized Western precedents.

The goal of this study has not been to determine whether north Koreans and south Koreans are "different," although I know that my work is sometimes understood this way. On several occasions when I have presented my work at public lectures or conferences, someone in the audience has made the comment that north Koreans are not different, and that even if they are they could be transformed into south Koreans in a matter of only a couple of years. Conversely, when I have attended policy meetings in Washington, D.C., analysts have often treated north Korea as if it were a country completely foreign to south Korea, not as a part of a total Korea or as a place that contains the relatives and roots of millions of south Koreans. I try not to say that north and south Korea are similar or different. My intention rather, is to show that *concepts* of similarity and difference are central to south Korean thinking about the future and may have a powerful effect on the potential for reconciliation.

Many questions about Korean futures turn about the positive concept of homogeneity and the negative concept of difference, and so these concepts provide an important starting point for discussions of emerging identities in Korea (Grinker 1996a, 1997c; Cho H.J. 1997; Chung, J. K. 1997). The anthropologist Cho Hae Joang (1997) believes that such discussions are beginning in earnest, that unification is increasingly seen by young scholars less as a military or political process than as a cultural one. When contemplating unification myself, I find it troubling that Koreans do not employ a concept of difference that evokes the positive sense of a melting pot or multiculturalism often found in European and North American societies. Difference is assumed to be negative. I am not suggesting that societies with more value-neutral terms experience less conflict over diversity, but they may offer a greater potential for tolerance. To engage in more positive discussions of difference—that is, to develop a perspective on unification that focuses precisely on the myth of homogeneity—requires that difference be seen not simply as "otherness" (Hall 1990). Instead, difference might be seen as constitutive of new identities and communities whose worth lies not in how they diverge from an ideal purity but in how they bring together new cultural elements in a way that provides meaning for their members. It follows that cultural identity has to be seen as process rather than essence, movement rather than stasis.

However, it is not an easy task to generate discourses on identity that are loosened from the comfortable anchors of home, homogeneity, and stasis. Stuart Hall and James Clifford are among the numerous writers who note that all discourses are "placed" (Clifford and Dharewshar 1989), that, intentionally or not, people tend to frame their perspectives, beliefs, and identities in spatial and temporal terms. Yet it is also true that discourses are dis-placed, moved, and ruptured, especially in the contexts of modernity. Hall suggests that cultural identities can be framed by two axes: similarity and continuity, and difference and rupture: "The one gives us some grounding in, some continuity with, the past. The second reminds us that what we share is precisely the experience of a profound discontinuity" (1990: 224). This is undoubtedly true of diasporas. We can think of "Caribbean," "Korean-American," and "Indian-American" as distinct and unique identities precisely because they are cultural hybrids, because they are defined by traditions of displacement, discontinuity, and difference. But what of Korean national division? It too invokes narratives of displacement and discontinuity. But the desire to unify, to return home, and to realize the dream of homogeneity nonetheless stand by all the while as a shared Korean vision, a uniform backdrop against which north and south Koreans can compare their separate experiences and divergent meanings in history and the future. In contemplating this sacred desire, the defector Chang Yŏng-ch'ŏl (1997) has written critically about optimistic attitudes toward unification. In reaction to the customary platitudes about the inevitability of unification and the recovery of homogeneity, Chang suggests that, paradoxically, only through pessimism, and through the recognition that heterogeneity between north and south is enduring and fundamental, will Koreans achieve unification. He writes:

How can we talk about sameness unless we also talk about difference? How can we talk about possibilities without talking about impossibilities? I hope that differences, impossibilities, and heterogeneity will be stepping stones to finding unification. I'd like to be a spoke in the wheel of unification. But I will be willing to stand on the negative side of the wall if everyone else wants to be on the positive side. (1997: 263)

Paik Nak Chung may be right when he calls Korea a "division system," because, despite the many arguments to the contrary—that a divided Korea is a false or distorted Korea—national division and the unreachable ideal of unification have become constitutive of what it means to be Korean, and, more generally, what it means to live in the modernist age of provisional truths and homelands.

NOTES

PREFACE

1. I use the term "unification" rather than "reunification" out of convention. English translations of words for unification in Germany and China have frequently become central parts of political debate. For instance, Taipei wishes to translate the term *t'ongyi* as "reunification," while Beijing wants to translate it as "unification"; in Germany there have been heated debates on whether to use *Wiederverinigung* (reunification) or remove the prefix *wieder* (re-). On the German debate, see Brockman 1991. There has been much less debate in Korea, to my knowledge, and so I simply use the most conventional term, "unification."

2. In the context of the limits on academic freedom, the historian Charles K. Armstrong writes, provocatively: "Much of the scholarship on North Korea could be preceded with the following caveat: 'I am a South Korean. I have been educated all my life to hate communism in general and the North Korean regime in particular. Furthermore, if I stray from the official line and question assumptions about North Korea I will jeopardize my chances of employment and acceptability in South Korean society' " (1991: 185). As recently as October 1997, human rights groups in south Korea reported numerous arrests of professors, editors, bookstore owners and publishers for distributing works previously published in south Korea about Kim Il Sung and north Korea that are not sufficiently anti-communist or anti-north (see, for example, Mingahyŏp Human Rights Group, no. 1997-10, November 12, 1997).

3. The sound *tong* (in this specific case referring to sameness) is linguistically unrelated to *t'ongil*, which refers to unity.

4. At the time of this writing, a small number of films and literature, as well as some issues of the official north Korean newspaper, *Rodong sinmun,* are available at some university libraries; those willing to sign the check-out forms, to provide detailed personal information about their purpose in looking at the materials, and to give an identification card, address and phone number, can view them in the library. Moreover, from time to time, the Ministry of Unification shows north Korean films at a movie theatre in downtown Seoul. The showings are not advertised and that they are not well attended.

CHAPTER 1

1. In this book, I focus on a number of forms of difference, such as age, gender, and class, but I focus on these topics only to the extent that they are clearly linked with unification and division discourses.

2. See, for example, Kang and Wagner 1990; Kim D. et al. 1990, 1991; Cumings 1991, and Chai 1995. More specifically on the subject of unification, see Aspaturian 1994, Bae 1993, Hanguk Kaebal Yŏnguwŏn 1993, and Yang 1992. For an interesting study of some of the connections between Korean unification and unification in Germany and Vietnam, see Chun and So 1995.

CHAPTER 2

1. It should be pointed out that the contemporary political usage of many terms, such as the term for "unification," are of recent origin. *T'ongil* in Korean and *t'ongyi* in Chinese can be shown to derive from linguistic formulations constructed by the Japanese during the Meiji period (1868-1912).

2. Obviously, the reasons why south Koreans would not consider a confederation have to do with many conditions placed by north Korea. When the idea was first proposed by Kim Il Sung in August of 1960 an interim measure, it contained a provision for the removal of U.S. troops from Korea and the replacement of the south Korean government with a people's regime. In 1973 Kim Il Sung issued a five-point unification program that included a confederation system as the endpoint, not as an interim measure, and called for a system in which the "two sides mutually recognize and tolerate the difference in their ideologies and systems." But this provision was interpreted to mean that south Koreans had to accept communism as legitimate. South Korea's plans have included a commonwealth as an interim phase. The commonwealth would be headed by a council of the presidents of north and south and a council of ministers with equal participation from both sides. South Korean plans have not called explicitly for the dissolution of the north Korean government, at least in the interim phase of the commonwealth. The most recent south Korean plane, the "Korean National Community" suggests three steps: 1) reconciliation and cooperation, 2) a Korean commonwealth and 3) completion of the unified country. It appears that the primary disagreement with north Korea's confederation idea is that it seems to perpetuate division by advocating the coexistence of two states as an endpoint.

3. As an example of the sentiments about which Song writes, Korean-American supporters of north Korea and Korean-American supporters of south Korea clashed in Los Angeles, California, on February 3, 1997, at the former group's exhibition on north Korea's history and socialist achievements in honor of Kim Jong Il's fiftieth birthday. Clearly there are no national security laws operating in the United States with reference to representations of north Korea, yet the two groups engaged in a fistfight. About thirty anti-north demonstrators demanded that the exhibit be withdrawn (*Hanguk Ilbo*, Feb. 10, 1997: "Ttaeanin 'Kim Jong Il Sodong'" [Unexpected Kim Jong Il Disturbance]).

4. The people-state division transcends any particular political perspective, as it is taken for granted by conservatives and liberals alike.

5. This is not to say that sites of remembrance are absent. The most prominent site in Korea for national memory is the national cemetery, where Korean war dead are buried, including soldiers killed during the Korean War. Victims of the Korean War are remembered on Memorial Day (*Hyŏnch'ung-il*, June 6) when many Koreans pay their respects at the national cemetery. In addition, students have begun in recent years to eat a ritual meal, *6.25 ŭmshik mŏkki*, on the anniversary of the start of the war, consisting of grains, *kkongboripap* and *kaeddŏk*, that are usually eaten only in periods of severe food shortage.

6. On the demilitarized zone as a museum or monument of the Cold War, see Grinker 1995a.

7. As James Young notes, monuments help to master the past by becoming naturalized, and so also permanent and axiomatic: "In suggesting themselves as the indigenous, even geological outcrops in a national landscape, monuments tend to naturalize the values, ideals, and laws of the land itself. To do otherwise would be to undermine the very foundations of national legitimacy, of the state's seemingly natural right to exist" (Young 1990: 53).

8. Unless otherwise noted, all translations from the Korean are mine. I would like to thank Choi Song-hee and Shim Soo-in for their assistance in translating Korean-language texts.

9. A mineral, for instance, is *sunsuhan* because it is a naturally occurring homogeneous substance. Someone who is born and bred in Seoul may be termed a *sunsuhan seoulsaram* (a pure Seoul person); the actions of the north Korean state are sometimes said to be motivated by complex and dark drives, as opposed to an idealized pure motivation *(sunsuhan tonggi)* that is clear, clean, and follows a natural course of action.

10. *Ijil* can refer to the alien, the heterogenous, the different, or the exotic; for example, one might ask how south and north Koreans might build a bridge between their two different *(ijiljŏk)* ways of thinking. However, *ijil* can also refer to more mundane differences, such as the difference between the feel of silk and wool, *ijilgam* textures.

11. Similarly, Santner writes that one of the dangers of reaching one's destination is that it may require confronting the skeletons in the closet, like a homeopathic cure that introduces the same poison that has caused the problem. He writes of the show *Heimat* that it shows "how tempting the *path home* is . . . in the face of *homeopathic* cures that seem to promise only more suffering" (1990: 102, original emphasis).

12. On Freud's visit to the Acropolis, see Schur 1969; Slochower 1970; Homans 1989; Porter 1991.

13. There is, indeed, an enormous literature emerging on how the spatial and the social are mutually constituted (Massey 1993, 1994; Keith and Pile 1993; Bird et al. 1993; Duncan and Ley 1993) and on how travelers and traveling have become central metaphors for characterizing modernity (Robertson et al. 1994).

CHAPTER 3

1. Portions of this chapter appeared previously in English (Grinker 1995b) and in Korean (Grinker 1996b).

2. One way in which the exhibitors attempted to illuminate the purity of the north Korean people, and thereby unwittingly distort the reality of the north, was by excluding Kim Jong Il. Clearly, this was an exhibition about things "Korean," and this meant the north Korean "people," not the "state." Kim was excluded because he stands between north and south, between division and unification. Many south Koreans had pinned their hopes for unification on the death of Kim Il Sung because Kim Jong Il was "obviously" unfit to rule; among other things, Kim Jong Il was rumoured to be afflicted by various problems, including severe medical and psychiatric illnesses and mental retardation, that would ensure his failure. Precisely because so little is known about Kim Jong Il, he becomes the object of fantasy, symbolic elaboration and exaggeration, and the embodiment of an "anti-Korean" who threatens the integrity of the Korean nation. For example, the cover of a 1983 book, entitled *Chiguch'onŭi mangnani* (Villains of the Western World), published soon after the "Burma Incident" (in which 18 south Korean government ministers and advisors died in a terrorist bombing intended for President Chun), depicts Kim Jong Il as a little boy, holding his father's right hand and wielding a bloody axe. A 1985 cartoon shows Kim Jong Il lying in bed with a fever, sick from venereal diseases contracted through sexual promiscuity (Kim Y. H. 1990: 98). Some south Korean representations of Kim Jong Il's birth and early childhood deny him full Koreanness. In sharp contrast to the north Korean official versions, the official south Korean view of Kim's birth places him not only outside of Korea but outside of humanity, squarely in the animal world. According to *Kim Jong Il*, written by

the south Korean government research organ, the *Nam-Puk Munje Yŏnguso* (Institute for South-North Korea Studies), Kim Jong Il was born not in Korea but in the Siberian wilderness, "among the howls of wolves," and was delivered by an unlicensed veterinarian (1993: 8-9). As a child, while other children engaged in conflict by debating, arguing, boxing, or wrestling, Kim Jong Il knew only how to bite.

3. *Orenji jok* is a pejorative term that implies sexual freedom. Young men and women I interviewed at coffee shops in Apkujŏngdong say it comes from a method of dating in which a man or woman sends a glass of orange juice to someone he or she fancies; acceptance of the orange juice also means acceptance of a date.

4. For example, "Stars have disappeared along with cows and fields; children spend nights in libraries attempting to get into good schools in order to get good jobs. Amidst the superficial glitz and material plenty, a significant minority toils and lives in shacks, while new beggars roam around, trying in vain to catch the attention of the rapidly moving passers-by" (Lie 1992: 297).

5. The vast majority of south Koreans living today either did not live through the Korean War or were too young to be aware of it. At various conferences, I have heard that only 20 percent of south Koreans still living today can remember the war. The phrase "he/she doesn't know the war" is a common method used in everyday conversation for marking age.

6. This form of criticism is common in unified Germany. Former west Germans have repeatedly characterized east Germans in terms of their fascination with money. Jurgen Habermas thus echoed much popular sentiment among former west Germans when he coined the phrase *D-M-Nationalismus* (Deutsche-mark nationalism) to criticize east Germans' desire for the deutsche mark (Mertes 1994).

7. For discussion and criticism of the analogical equivalence drawn between north and south Korea and east and west Germany, see Cumings 1991: 120. See also Kim D. et al. 1990; 1991.

8. On the continuities between colonialism, orientalism, and Cold War discourse, see Pietz's article (1988) and Stephanson's response (1988) in the same issue of *Social Text*.

9. Such a process has already occurred in Germany, where an entrepreneur, Frank Georgi, is nearing completion of an expansive theme park in Germany that recreates everyday life in the former east Germany. Visitors would have to remain in the park for a full day and would be prevented from leaving by a high wall. Restaurants would have poor food, the waiters would be surly, and the only rental cars available would be Trabants and Volgas. People who worked for the park would circulate to find unhappy visitors who wanted to leave early and would help them escape. If caught, visitors would be imprisoned for up to two hours (Newman 1994: 33; and National Public Radio, *Morning Edition*, Nov. 16, 1994).

CHAPTER 4

1. Although I recognize the long list of psychoanalysts and psychoanalytically oriented social thinkers working between Freud and Kohut, namely, Winnicott and Klein, a more detailed consideration of psychoanalytic theory is beyond the scope of this study. Neither do I deal with how literary critics and philosophers have attempted to integrate modern psychoanalytic theory into literary analysis (see, for example, Kristeva 1987).

2. Deborah Lipstadt tells the story of when she visited a German bookstore to promote her book on the Holocaust, and an advertising display in the store window read "Books Commemorating the Fiftieth Anniversary of the Liberation of

Germany." Lipstadt writes: "The sign reflected the delusion that the Nazis were some foreign power who had invaded and occupied the country for 12 long years" (1997: 3).

3. "Auschwitz speaks against every trend born of manipulation of public opinion, against the purchasing power of the West German economy—for the hard currency of Deutschmarks even unification can be acquired—and yes, even against the right to self-determination granted without hesitation to other peoples. Auschwitz speaks against all this, because one of the preconditions for the terrible thing that happened was a strong, unified Germany" (Grass 1990: 122).

4. On the historians' controversy, see Santner 1990: 46-54; Brockmann 1991.

5. Santner writes, "The double bind of having to identify with figures of power one also at another level needs to disavow . . . leads to what the Mitscherlichs, in 1967, referred to as an 'Identifikationsscheu,' a resistance to identification with parents and elders, in the second generation" (1990: 45).

6. There is no relation between *han* as it has been defined in this chapter and the name of Seoul's Han River.

7. It should be pointed out, however, that prior to the unification of the two Germanies, there was virtually no discussion in Korea about the costs of unification. There may be many reasons for this absence, but it seemed to me, at the time, that Korean prosperity led to greater optimism about unification. "We are so rich," some of my interviewees said," we are now capable of unifying, and if we rose up from postwar poverty to become one of the most economically powerful societies in the world, there is nothing we cannot achieve." But economic prosperity incurred its own *han* in the form of shoddy construction and negligent inspection and maintenance of public facilities; more than thirty people died when the Songsu bridge collapsed, more than six hundred died when the Sampoong shopping center collapsed, more than three hundred died when the Sohae ferry capsized, and nearly two dozen people died as the result of an underground gas explosion in Taegu. All of these tragedies occurred within a matter of a few years during the Kim Young Sam administration when people were just feeling that they had truly achieved nearly everything they had hoped for, short of unification. These were man-made catastrophes. As for north-south relations, the greater economic prosperity of the south has not led, as expected, to reconciliation and dialogue. Despite the old line that south Korea needed to be prosperous before it could negotiate with the north, many Koreans now see unification as a threat to their economic well-being. If one can link economics and unification—and clearly the government has done so since the 1950s—then south Koreans' economic successes only exacerbate their preexisting *han*, making unification all the more elusive, all the more disruptive; conversely, north Korea's economic devastation has led not to greater dialogue with the south, as was expected, but to the marginalization of south Korea from north Korea's foreign relations.

CHAPTER 5

1. The demonization of the state can be considered a recent phenomenon. Although students and scholars during the Chosŏn Dynasty carried out protests, they were usually in support of the state. For example, in 1873, when a government official leveled harsh attacks against the government's morality, the students called a strike in support of the king and state, saying that an attack on the government was an attack against one's father: "Now, that whereby men are men and a state is a state is only that the laws of Heaven and human morality are carried out by the King. Therefore, if human relationships have crumbled and morality is in decay, then

this means there are no such things as ruler and subject, father and son [and the moral obligations that these relationships imply]. Being without ruler or father is the same as being barbarians and animals. How could men act like men and how could a state be a state?" (quoted in Palais 1975: 187).

2. The enormous sense of obligation to one's parents is illustrated in a folktale I was told in an interview during my research. A young woman conveyed a story her grandmother had told her of a starving family in which a son kills his child to prepare a soup for his parents. "I can always have another child," the main character says, "but my parents cannot be reborn."

3. Korean kinship and family norms during the Chosŏn Dynasty differed between the ideals of the *yangban*, or nobility, and the realities of commoners, the former being more closely modeled on Confucian patterns of marriage and filial piety. Yet far from being embraced without criticism, theologians and nationalists during the early twentieth-century argued that filial piety concentrated obligation only on one's kin at the expense of one's moral obligation to a wider public sphere such as the nation (Wells 1990: 54). In 1971 and 1972, Park Chung Hee's rural development movement, *saemaŭl undong* (new village movement), altered many aspects of Confucian practice: among other things, some ancestor worship rituals were abolished, and Confucian mourning periods were shortened. Despite his own authoritarianism, Park blamed the Chosŏn Dynasty for passing a rigid elitist, Confucianist, hierarchical social system to future generations that stood as a barrier to the growth of a more dynamic, progressive society, one that would be more attentive to the "people" than to family.

4. Eckert continues: "Since at least the seventh century the ruling classes in Korea had thought of themselves in cultural terms less as Koreans than as members of a larger cosmopolitan civilization centered on China. . . .To live outside the realm of Chinese culture was, for the Korean elite, to live as a barbarian" (1991: 227).

5. The colors of red and blue have special significance for Koreans. In past years, teachers instructed schoolchildren to draw maps of Korea with the north colored red and the south colored blue, and many interviewees say that school children commonly believed that north Koreans had red faces (with horns). Even today, north Koreans continue to be called *ppalgaengi* (reds).

6. Many works of art clearly show the body as severed, as in two works designed to make environmental statements about the DMZ: Kang Hee-chŏn's photograph of a naked man whose body is separated by a mound of sand, and Woo Chŏng-mee's photograph of a woman's nude figure separated by a mound of grass (Lee B. 1995: 143, 246).

7. A historical analysis of changes in schoolbooks' treatment of north Korea and unification over the past 30 years follows in chapter 6.

8. Similarly, one critic of unification discourses, the Korean-German philosopher Song Du-yul, has complained that concepts such as unification and division have become routinized and have merged with concepts that should be distinct (1995a: 137). It is useful to point out here his contention that unification has become conceptually indistinguishable from family reunions. *T'ongil* (unification) and terms such as *kohyangpangmun* (hometown visit) and *chinch'okpangmun* (relative visit) are often used in everyday language as if they have the same meaning, whereas Song believes that unification is a dynamic and multidimensional process that must be distinguished from the specific goals and linear movements implied by the latter terms. Indeed, other writers have suggested that it is time to discard the term *t'ongil* altogether. Song elaborates what he calls a "rule of identity," that is, the principle under which people assume that two will inevitably become one in a merging of equal parts (1995a: 138); it is because of this assumption, he suggests, that south

Koreans have so often spoken about unification by absorption *(hŭpsu t'ongil)* as the most likely and most desirable scenario; it is also why, I would suggest, the north Koreans are concerned that unification will destroy any of the distinctiveness they have developed over the past half century. If unification must be imagined in simple and abstract terms only as a merging of two into one, there is little hope that people will be able to cope with the complex realities of political and social change.

9. Armstrong says that south Korean representations of North Korea depict it as a "family state," that is, as an outgrowth of filial piety: "If Meiji Japan effectively transferred feudal loyalties to the nation as a whole, north Korea has done the same with familial loyalties; the modern state is able to tap into the strongest loyalties and emotional attachments of the traditional culture" (1991: 198).

10. On the north Korean family, see also Park K. S. 1972; Yi H. K. 1980; Soh 1987. For a bibliography on women's lives in north Korea, see Son 1991.

11. In 1949 north Korea abandoned all use of Chinese characters (Ko 1990: 493, 505). However, it should also be noted that south Koreans have long debated the use of Chinese characters. In 1948, when the Republic of Korea was founded, the new government fostered a failed policy of "exclusive *hangŭl* usage." In more recent years, student movements have struggled, with some success, to purify the Korean language of foreign words, including Chinese characters. Among the major national newspapers in south Korea, only the liberal *Hangyŏre sinmun* is published exclusively in *han'ul*.

12. In the Silla dynasty, loyalty between parents and children was established as a fundamental principle of human behavior. Koreans often followed a cosmopolitan moral order called *hwarangdo; hwarang* is a term that refers to a specific elite group of people who excelled in beauty, bravery, and military arts and adhered to a set of rules called *samgangoryun* (five principles of human relationship): *pujayujin* (intimacy between father and son), *kunshinyuŭi* (loyalty between the king and his followers), *punguyusin* (trust between friends), *changyuyusŏ* (hierarchical relationship by age and sex between brother and sister), and *pubuyubyŏl* (hierarchical relationship between husband and wife).

13. I am grateful to the KBS producer Ch'oi Sŏk-sul for giving me access to approximately sixteen hours of videotaped interviews with north Korean defectors, recorded during production of the fifteen-minute *Ch'ujŏk 60 Minutes* segment that aired on March 25, 1996.

14. Jager (n.d.) stresses a different aspect of the sibling metaphor by arguing that the focus on brotherhood is a narrative device for a culturally specific national project in which two brothers struggle for legitimacy: regenerating the nation, revitalizing manhood, connecting patriotism with filial piety, and celebrating unification as the continuity of Korea's ancestry and bloodline.

15. Of the brothers statue, Jager writes: "The rhetoric of fraternity was therefore not incompatible with an extremely strict sense of family hierarchy. This is because the unity of the nation could be secured only by acknowledging the true 'blood-line' descendants of the original ancestors: South Korea as the eldest brother and, hence, the *only* legitimate heir" (n.d.: 33).

16. Literally, "human heart."

17. *Minjung* literally means "the mass of the people" (*min* = "people"; *jung* = "mass") and is used to refer primarily to the oppressed, ruled, and exploited masses of people marginalized from the centers of intellectual and economic power (Moon 1985: 1).

18. Jager notes, interestingly, that the priest who accompanied Im Su-kyŏng on her travel to north Korea was well known for considering the love between spouses to be paramount, and for being devoted to remarrying elderly couples (1994: 156, n. 5).

19. The term *sadae,* or *sadaejuŭi* (the doctrine of *sadae*), was popularized as a very pejorative term with the establishment of the Independence Club in 1896 and the rise of early twentieth-century Korean nationalism (Robinson, 1988: 27; 33-34).

CHAPTER 6

1. This statue is described very briefly in chapters 3 and 5. For a more detailed analysis of the statue, see Jager n.d.

2. For each textbook reform, the editors and writers are selected by a school textbook development committee *(Kaebal uiwŏnhoe)* organized by Seoul National University at the request of the Ministry of Education. For more detailed information about government control of textbooks in both south and north Korea, see Linton 1989.

3. Ethics textbooks in high school are called *Yulli* (Ethics) or *Kukmin yulli* (National ethics).

4. In comparison to the literature on north Korean elementary, middle, and high school education, the literature on south Korean pre-school education is minuscule. On education and political indoctrination in north Korea, see the large number of articles on north Korean education that have appeared over the last 20 years in the journal *Pukhan;* see also Yang 1983. On the subject of how similar educational materials are taught to Koreans in Japan who are politically aligned with north Korea, see Ryang 1997.

5. The central feature of Japanese colonialist historiography in Korea—that Korea was stagnant until it was colonized by Japan—shares much with European historiography of Africa and other colonized regions of the world. According to this view, the backward traditions of colonized peoples prevented them from making substantial political, economic, and cultural achievements. James Palais writes: "The blame for the inability or incapacity of the Korean people to break the bonds that tied them to the premodern tradition with all its debilities could have been explained as the effect of contingent historical experience, but instead it was condemned as a permanent ethnic weakness. And it was reinforced by extending the period of Korean inferiority back in time. . . . The whole modern project for many Korean historians has been to reclaim their past, rebuild a basis for national pride, and reestablish a history that has meaning not only for themselves but for the world. The goal has been to rescue Korea from subjugation, degradation, and mediocrity by demanding new recognition of the value of Korean life and culture" (1995: 410). Nationalism in Korea provided a means of resisting not only Japanese oppression, but also those Japanese historical works that attributed value in Korean history only to the influence of outside cultures such as Japan and China. Indeed, as Palais tells us, Koreans used their first opportunity of revision to rid their standard textbooks of the mention of Han dynasty (108 B.C. to 313 A.D.) artifacts found in P'yŏngyang (1995: 410-411).

6. Ch'oe cites a north Korean study on the independent development of bronze culture entitled *Kochosŏn munje yŏngu* (A study of problems concerning Kochosŏn), in which the authors, Yi Sun-jin and Chang Chu-yŏp, write: "This [bronze culture] was the same that had been developed continuously since the Neolithic age by the people living in this region and had been further advanced. This culture carried unique and distinctive characteristics that were not only totally different from the culture of the Yellow River region but also clearly discernible from that of the area north of the Great Wall" (quoted in Ch'oe 1981: 506).

7. Indeed, the leaders of the Independence Club used the term *minjung* to refer to the masses; however, as Kang Man-kil notes, the term indicated "the general

populace" and was not identical to the contemporary usage of the term in which *minjung* referred to "an entity responsible for a historical task like the national movement" (1995: 32).

8. Among many other projects, they published the first newspapers to eliminate Chinese characters from print and to use only the Korean script. Although the membership was diverse and comprised of many conflicting voices, including Confucianists, farmers, fishermen, and students (even some pro-Japanese politicians), the members were, for the most part, intellectuals (leaders such as Yun Ch'i Ho and Yi Sang Jae) who were guided by Western liberalism, had received education in the United States, and had participated in the explicitly pro-Japanese reform movement known as *Kabo Kyŏngjang* (1894-1896).

9. Paek classified the pre - Three Kingdom period of Korean history as primitive communism, the Three Kingdom period as slavery, and the period from the Silla through the Chosŏn Dynasty as feudal—more specifically, "centralized feudalism" (Ch'oe 1980: 21).

10. Readers interested in a more thorough English-language account of Korean historiography should consult Em 1993. For my purposes here—setting the historiographic framework within which to understand historical representation of north Korea in southern school textbooks—it is important to recapitulate his general classification of some of the ways in which professional historians have represented division, the Korean War, and the events and processes that led to them. Two additional points should be noted, however. First, this is only one portion of his rather complex treatment of Korean historiography, and second, Em deals only with professional, academic historians. Religious historiographies, of which there are many, are an important concern for scholars of Korea, but it is nearly impossible to discern the degree to which religious writings on Korean history enter into the construction of state-sponsored schoolbooks. On the subject of religious historiography, see Walraven 1995.

11. The suffix -*ron*, used often in the pages that follow, means "doctrine" or "treatise" but can be more colloquially translated as "theory." *Pokhap* literally means "complex."

12. Perhaps the most notable characteristic of Korean historiography, however, is not any one specific perspective, but the relative absence of contemporary histories, in comparison to histories of pre-twentieth-century Korea. Indeed, at least until the 1980s courses offered in Korean universities on contemporary history were few and far between. Em reminds us that one of Korea's most progressive and creative historians, Kang Man-kil, argued that the few histories that were written remained embedded in the structure of division (in other words, the division system), and that they rationalized or legitimized division as the inevitable result of the concatenation of political events and forces at the end of World War II. As part of the developments in *chuch'eron*, historians such as Kang Man-kil, Song Kŏn-ho, and Pak Hyŏn-ch'ae attempted to bring postliberation Korea into sharper and more objective focus, eschewing the conventional periodizations of events leading to the war and illuminating instead the latent struggles in the revolutionary constellations that emerged before and after liberation (Em, 1993). In an influential essay (1989), the historians Choi Jang-jip and Chŏng Hae-gu emphasized what Em refers to as the "structure of conflict," thus avoiding both the conventional notion of *namch'imron* (that the north attacked the south), and the radical, prohibited notion of *pukch'imron* (that the south started the war by attacking the north), as well as the cause-and-effect relations common to most histories of the war. As Em puts it, Choi and Chŏng's essay "recaptured the dynamic nature of post-Liberation

politics" and was "self-reflective in the way it resisted creating a linear plot" (1993: 476).

13. Of the 20 schoolbooks I consulted for this chapter, all are published by Kukjŏng kyogwasŏ (Ministry of Education), and the vast majority are elementary-school texts. I would like to thank D. Yim Hyung-Bin of the Ch'u-gye School Foundation and Choong-ang Girls High School in Seoul for answering many of my questions about the structure and organization of school curricula in south Korea.

14. The difficult question of how much continuity or discontinuity there was between the Japanese textbooks and the texts that were then "nationalized" as "Korean" is beyond the scope of this study.

15. Some schools—those offering education to children with special needs, and those offering particular traditionalist curricula (for example, Minjok Sakwan Hakyo and Ch'onghakdong Sŏdang)—have the freedom to select their own texts.

16. Arrests of professors in 1997 will make the use of north Korean materials in the near future even more rare; in October 1997, the south Korean government banned a children's book entitled *Nanŭnya t'ongil sedae* (I am the unification generation) for providing too much neutral information about the north, even though the book had been published (by Ch'ŏnjae Kyoyuk publishing company) for some time, had been written in collaboration with members of the board of unification and had been selected by the board of unification for its own unification campaign. The editors, Lee Ch'ang-hee of Hanguk University of foreign studies and Kim Chi-hwa, were detained on November 27, 1997, on charges that they compiled the manuscript "in a manner not conforming to free democratic principles" (Hanguk Ilbo, 11, Nov. 1997). According to the *Hanguk Ilbo,* Lee introduced questions into the book such as "After unification, what would be the name of the country, what would be the new national flower, and what would be the new capital city?" Lee was further alleged to have reprinted in the book the north Korean national anthem and a song praising Kim Il Sung.

CHAPTER 7

1. On the methods of protest among student movements during the 1980s, see Jang, J. O. 1995.

2. The Japanese responded to the force of the movement by attempting to further assimilate Koreans into Japanese culture, requiring Koreans to wear Japanese clothing, convert to Shintoism, and abandon their names, and prohibiting Korean language instruction.

3. Carnegie Endowment Folio. George Washington University Special Collections.

4. Palais writes: "The yangban bureaucrats even turned the normative standards of Confucian thought against the throne. By insisting that the king conform to moral and ethical standards that transcended his right to the arbitrary exercise of power, by setting themselves up as arbiters of those standards by virtue of their knowledge of Confucian texts, and by insisting on their right to the king's obligation to tolerate remonstrance, yangban bureaucrats and literati sought to reduce kings to puppets of their own desires and interests" (1975:11).

5. This is not to suggest, however, that Marxism has not been influential in Korean scholarship. During the 1920s and 1930s, especially, historians had much use for Marxism, not only in order to juxtapose Korea's elites and peasants, but also to show that Korea was part of a dynamic world process, that it was not the stagnant civilization represented in Japanese histories of Korea (Palais 1995: 411-412).

6. South Korea's *minjung* national literature, too, has run a course distinct from any official or institutionalized political agenda such as socialist realism, Marxist literature, or communist literature (Choi, H. 1995: 171).

7. Oh B. (1975: 118) shows that the number of teachers in Korea could not accommodate the large number of students. Whereas in 1945 there were approximately 5 students per teacher in colleges and universities, by 1964 there were approximately 27 students per teacher.

8. At the very least, the term *yusin*, if not Park's regime, was doomed to failure. The word was used during Emperor Mutsuhito's Meiji era, and it also was used to mark the onset of Japan's military expansion (Ogle 1990: 67).

9. In a now-famous phrase, a police captain, Yi Kŭn-an, said about Pak, "*Tŏk'hani ŏk'hadŏra*" (I just tapped him—"*tok*"—and he fell—"*ok*"). Yi disappeared after the investigation, and to this day his whereabouts are unknown.

10. In contrast, a *Chŏndaehyŏp* history of the student movement suggests that unification became a central subject of protest much earlier in 1960. According to this history, a national unification students' union was organized on May 5, 1960, with the participation of 17 universities Korea-wide, and on May 13, students organized a rally to urge unification and encourage a north-south students' meeting (1991: 19). They also developed a number of unification slogans: *Kaja pukŭro!* (Let's go to the north!), *Ora namŭro!* (Come to the south!), *Mannaja P'anmunjŏmaesŏ!* (Let's meet at Panmunjŏm!), and *Itangi nŭi tangindae odokado mothanŭnga?* (Whose land is this land? Why can't we come and go [as we please]?).

11. In an extended treatment of the relationship between student activism and anti-American sentiment in south Korea, Shin writes that *Chamint'u* specified five struggles for a successful national liberation: "(1) struggle against American imperialism, (2) efforts to remove nuclear weapons from Korea, (3) moves toward peaceful reunification of the motherland, (4) struggle for the people's rights in the workplace, and (5) resistance to American economic imperialism" (1995: 523-24). *Chamint'u* idealized north Korea and advocated a policy with terms similar to those used by Kim Il Sung: "National liberation people's democratic revolution" (NLPDR).

12. On some public responses to the crackdown, see Kim J.K. "Responses from every walk of life," *Hanguk ilbo*, August 21, 1996: 16. See also Chŏng M. K. 1996 for the *Hanchongryŏn* chairman's response.

13. This is especially true of the students in the 1980s, who were far more enveloped by campus activism than students in the 1990s. In her study of the Kochong Farmer's social movement in Chŏlla-do, Nancy Abelmann cites Cho Hae Joang's study of 1990s university students: "Although many people have charged that this [new] generation is more individualistic and even selfish, Cho (1994: 152-53) argues that like their activist predecessors, they too are resisting. They ask, 'Why,' not about military authoritarianism, but about 'me' and they assert, 'I don't want to do [this or] that.'"

Abelmann comments on Cho: "I think Cho meant to say that their individualistic orientation itself is a resistance against the cultural and political matrix that fashioned their predecessors: military authoritarian schooling and childhood. Raised under 'another order,' they know little of the freedom or autonomy they would like to achieve. Their enemy, Cho (1994: 200) declares, 'is within themselves: There is a huge distance between what they want to become and what they are able to become.'"

Precisely because of students' importance to their families and to society at large, the government finds it valuable and appropriate to describe the students as good or bad, pure or impure. I get the impression that many students wonder what all the fuss is about.

14. For some additional English-language comments on the film, see Standish 1994. For a considerable amount of information on Korean cinema and its relationship to nationalism, democracy, and unification, see the Korean cinema web-site at http://www-scf.usc.edu/~khkim/kyung2.html.

15. I do not know how many students have participated in *nonghwal* programs, although the proportion of students who participate appears to have decreased considerably each year since the height of the movement in 1987.

16. In the quantitative component of his 1995 study of more than eleven hundred students at ten south Korean universities, Park Byeong-chul shows that social relationships between peers are far more influential than any other factor (family decision-making styles, parental party identification, or social class, among others) in motivating student activism (1995: 237-43).

17. Kang Man-kil writes: "The *minjung* is centered around workers and farmers but includes minor landowners, national capitalists, and the urban middle class. Changes must be made in the national view of history so that the *minjung* can become the standard by which to see history, and furthermore embraces all classes of the nation. The *minjung* is transcendent, encompassing categories like class, nation, and citizen" (1995: 36).

18. One of the primary vehicles for conveying *minjung* nationalism is through poetry and fiction. Thus Kim Chi Ha wrote: "One must submerge oneself in the *minjung*, affirm the self living and breathing with them, and accept oneself as *minjung*. A poet must educate the people through *minjung* satire, awaken them, and show them the direction of their vital spirit by focusing on satire and violence, which expresses the explosion of the people's dissatisfaction" (quoted in Choi, H. 1995: 173). It is necessary to point out here a reluctance among some writers to employ the term *minjung munhak* (people's literature); they favor instead the term *minjok munhak* (national literature), since the former term, according to Paik Nak Chung, risks mystifying the people as "an undifferentiated mass rather than recognizing them as groups of actual men and women with particular (and often conflicting) national, regional, class, and gender interests" (1988:2). At the same time, however, the coexistence of the two terms can express the dialectical nature of the literature movement. Paik again: "'National literature' stresses how, in claiming to be a literature of the people, it yet negates an oversimplified class concept, while the name 'people's literature' brings out how this particular national literature refuses an idealistic conception of the nation or national culture" (1988: 5).

19. It should be pointed out that the author, Kim Ha-ki (born Kim Yŏng in 1958), is himself a "dissident," imprisoned between 1980 and 1988 for writings the government considered "anti-state," and in 1996 for violating the national security law prohibiting travel to north Korea. In August 1996 he entered north Korea through China and was held in a north Korean prison for two weeks for violating the border until he was returned to the authorities in Seoul. Although Kim contends that he accidentally entered the north in a drunken stupor, prosecutors argue that his visit to the birthplace of Kim Jong Il's mother proves that he went to the north of his own free will. On February 7, 1997, Kim Ha-ki was sentenced to seven years in prison.

CHAPTER 8

1. Such reactions can be found throughout the world. Interestingly, in 1994, former president Jimmy Carter, then a private citizen, was criticized by much of the

American and south Korean media for what American and Korean conservatives variously called a careless, naive, and destabilizing trip to north Korea to see Kim Il Sung. The conservative Korean media accused Carter of not understanding the *silje* of the north, of being overly respectful to Kim, of giving away too much, and of undermining the increasingly strong and intransigent positions of the U.S. State Department and the south Korean government. Ironically, during his own presidency Carter had himself reacted angrily when the mother of a hostage held in Iran ignored the U.S. government and traveled alone to Iran to meet with Iranian officials, thus polluting the categorical positions of state and citizen.

2. The writings of all three, it should be stressed, are laden with the religious imagery of returns and resurrections found in the works of *minjung* theologians. Suh Namdong writes: "It is our conviction that the Risen Jesus lives among the *minjung*, who have been continually oppressed and alienated in the course of socio-economic history" (1983: 161). Thus, Mun refers repeatedly to Im as a "little lamb" (a reference to Christ) and tells us that Chun Tae-il (a tailor who burned himself to death in November 1970 protesting government policies) is the resurrection of Jesus, and that student demonstrators today are the resurrection of Chun Tae-il.

3. In 1980, at the third meeting of the Chosŏn Writers Solidarity (Chosŏn Chakka Dongmaeng daehoe), Kim Jong Il outlined his own version of reality: "reality [*hyŏnsil*] is the foundation of all written work" (quoted in Kim C. Y. 1992: 81). According to Kim Jong Il, writers should find the "boiling hot reality" *(hyŏnsil)*, determine the true *(ch'amdoen)* form of communism—that is, those hidden heroes among the masses who are endlessly loyal to the Party and their people *(taejung)*— and, finally, to take this true form of communism and use it to shape a beautiful "mental world" *(ch'ŏngsin segye)* (Kim C. Y. 1992: 81).

4. *Hyŏnsil* implies fact, actuality. For example, one might urge that people think not ideally but realistically *(hyŏnsil)*, or one might stress to someone younger that he or she doesn't understand the "real [*hyŏnsil*] world," or bemoan that, "practically speaking [*hyŏnsilchŏgŭro*], it is impossible to take a long vacation this year." But the term is also used in a more abstract sense as well. In her account of her travels to north Korea, Im Su-kyŏng says: " I had to fly 36 hours to go to P'yŏngyang, go around the earth to come back to my own nation. This is our reality [*hyŏnsil*]" (1989: 548). In this instance, *hyŏnsil* refers to the structural and symbolic distance between north and south Korea. *Silje* is equally polysemous. The word usually denotes the actual condition of things. For example, one might say, "The journalists tried to record as much of the reality [*silje*] of north Korea as possible"; "Far from Kim Il Sung's propagandized image, I found his *silje* to be different"; or "Don't give me vague and general information, I need concrete details [*silje*]." But a more abstract sense also appears, particularly in the writings of the so-called sentimental *(kamsangjŏk)* unificationists, who write about discovering the "*silje*" of the Korean people in north Korea.

5. An additional word to mentioned here is *silsang*, a variant of *silje*, frequently used in literature on unification to refer to states of being, circumstances, and conditions: for example, "The state *(silsang)* of the economy is not as bad as we think."

6. The words themselves, it seems, suggest ambivalence about unification not only because they refer both to the lost truth and current reality, but also because they simultaneously denote the real as both abstract and concrete, dream and actual: for example: "This exhibit of north Korea is not the real *(silje)* north Korea"; "North Korea distorts the reality *(hyŏnsil)* of our situation"; "We are in conflict over our distorted reality *(hyŏnsil)*"; "Our reality *(hyŏnsil)* can be found through scientific, not sentimental, means"; "Student protesters are not realistic *(hyŏnsil)*." Words

such as *hyŏnsil* and *silje* can also refer to the real as something elusive or unattainable; for example: "How can we achieve homogeneity when the reality of our situation is war?"; "Given all the differences that have developed [between north and south], even when we unify, we'll only achieve a part of reality *(hyŏnsil)*."

7. Images of the return home can be found in popular music: as one explicit example, in a recent song, " *Kajang arŭmdaum p'unggyŏng* " (The most beautiful scene in the world), the songwriter Ha Dŏk-kyu sings: "The most beautiful scene in the world is everything going back to its own place."

CHAPTER 9

1. South Korean media are famous for incorrect reporting about north Korea. In addition to the false report about Sŏng Hye-rim and the dozens of false reports that appeared in south Korea during the 1970's and 1980's stating that Kim Jong Il had been killed or brain-damaged in automobile accidents, a more recent fabrication concerns insurance claims for damaged crops. Beginning on June 8, 1996, just before south Korea, the United States, and Japan agreed to provide food aid to north Korea through a United Nations organization, news articles in south Korea reported that north Korea had collected nearly $130 million U.S. dollars from eight European insurance company for crops damaged by floods, and that the money was not being used for famine relief (see Chang In-ch'ul, 1996: 2).

2. It is my impression that south Korean complaints about the treatment of defectors is increasing. See, for example, Seo Dong-ik (1995) and Yi Ch'ŏl (1996); Yi fears that the defectors will one day be saying, "Once when I lived in south Korea. . . .'"

3. Some media reports in 1997 have suggested that the Chinese have begun construction on their border to house as many as 100,000 north Korean refugees in the event of a massive exodus from north Korea.

CHAPTER 10

4. From *Samohan* (The *han* of longing for my mother), in an unpublished collection of writings by alumni of a high school in Hwanghae-do, north Korea, who are citizens of south Korea.

5. Some notable exceptions include Tto Hanaŭi Munhwa (Another Culture)—a group of scholars that seeks to frame political issues in new and innovative ways (see, for example, Tto Hanaŭi Munhwa 1996; Cho H. J. 1992, 1994)—and the artist Lee Bann's "Front DMZ" group (1995), which is concerned largely with ecological aspects of north-south relations. It should also be noted that Yu Dong Hee of the Munhwa Broadcasting Company (MBC) has produced numerous books on the relationship between unification and broadcasting, politics, and public culture, books which are far more anthropological in orientation—to the extent that they focus on culture and people—than anything one sees in the conventional work of political scientists at Korean think-tanks and policy institutes (Yu 1996).

6. In English, see Grinker 1997a; in Korean, see Grinker 1997b.

7. For a comprehensive collection of contemporary Korean affirmations of the need for unification, see Kang and Yu 1995; Yi H. Y. 1995.

8. On the subject of unification cost as a denial of other, more abstract, sacrifices, see Song D. Y. 1995b: 96).

REFERENCES CITED

Abelmann, Nancy. 1993. "*Minjung*Theory and Practice." In Harumi Befu, ed. *Cultural Nationalism in East Asia: Representation and Identity,* pp. 139-166. Berkeley: Institute of East Asian Studies, Research Papers and Policy Studies, no. 39.

———. 1995. "The English Language Ethnographic Legacy on Village Korea." Unpublished ms.

———. 1996. *Echoes of the Past, Epics of Dissent: A South Korean Social Movement.* Berkeley and Los Angeles: University of California Press.

Abelmann, Nancy, and John Lie. 1995. *Blue Dreams: Korean-Americans and the Los Angeles Riots.* Cambridge: Harvard University Press.

Ahrends, Martin. 1991. "The Great Waiting, or the Freedom of the East: An Obituary for Life in Sleeping Beauty's Castle." *New German Critique* 52 (Winter): 41-49.

Alloula, Malek. 1986. *The Colonial Harem.* Minneapolis: University of Minnesota Press.

An Myŏng-ch'ŏl. 1995. *Kŭdŭli ulgo idda* [They are crying]. Seoul: Ch'ŏnji Media.

Anderson, Benedict, ed. 1990. *Language and Power: Exploring Cultures in Indonesia.* Ithaca: Cornell University Press.

———. 1991 [1983]. *Imagined Communities: Reflections on the Origin and Spread of Nationalism.* London: Verso.

Armstrong, Charles K. 1991. "The Myth of North Korea." In Bruce Cumings, ed. *Chicago Occasional Papers on Korea,* no. 6, pp. 177-203. Chicago: Center of East Asian Studies, University of Chicago.

Aspaturian, Vernon V. 1994. "The Collapse of Communism in the USSR and Eastern Europe and Its Impact on Developments in China and North Korea." *Journal of East Asian Affairs* 8 (2): 256-295.

Bae Jin-young, ed. 1993. *Two Years Since German Unification: Economic Evaluations and Implications for Korea.* Seoul: Korea Institute for International Economic Policy.

Bakhtin, Mikhail. 1984 [1965]. *Rabelais and His World.* Trans. Helene Iswolsky. Bloomington: Indiana University Press.

Barthes, Roland. 1981. *Camera Lucida.* Trans. Richard Howard. New York: Hill and Wang, Noonday Press.

Berger, Peter, Brigitte Berger, and Hansfried Kellner. 1974. *The Homeless Mind: Modernisation and Consciousness.* Harmondsworth: Penguin.

Berman, Marshall. 1983. *All that Is Solid Melts into Air: The Experience of Modernity.* London: Verso.

Bhabha, Homi. 1994. *The Location of Culture.* London: Routledge.

Bird, Jon, Barry Curtis, Tim Putnam, George Robertson, and Lisa Tickner, eds. 1993. *Mapping the Futures: Local Cultures, Global Change.* London and New York: Routledge.

Borneman, John. 1989. "Narratives of Belonging in the Two Berlins: Kinship Formation and Nation Building in the Context of the Cold War, 1945-1989." Ph.D. dissertation, Department of Anthropology, Harvard University.

Bourdieu, Pierre. 1977. *Outline of a Theory of Practice.* Cambridge: Cambridge University Press.

Bourdieu, Pierre, and Jean-Claude Passeron. 1977. *Reproduction in Education, Society and Culture.* Trans. Richard Nice. London and Beverly Hills: Sage Publications.

Boyarin, Jonathan. 1994. "Ruins, Mounting Toward Jerusalem." *Found Object* 3: 33-48.

Brandt, Vincent. 1971. *A Korean Village between Farm and Sea.* Cambridge: Harvard University Press.

————. 1991. "The South Korean Student Movement in a Transitional Society." Unpublished ms.

Brockmann, Stephen. 1991. "The Reunification Debate," *New German Critique* 52 (Winter): 3-30.

Carnegie Endowment Folio. 1919. *Declaration of the People of Korea to the Paris Peace Conference.* George Washington University Special Collections. The Gelman Library, Washington, D.C.

Caruth, Cathy, ed. 1994. *Trauma: Explorations in Memory.* Baltimore and London: Johns Hopkins Univiersity Press.

Chai Goo-mook. 1995. "National Unification: A Comparison of German Experience and Korean Possibilities." Ph.D. dissertation, University of Utah.

Chang In-ch'ul. 1996. "Pukhan hyungjak pohŏmkŭm hep'ŭning" [The north Korean poor crop insurance money happening]. *The Korea Times,* Washington edition, July 18, part 2: 2.

Chang Myŏng-su. 1995. "Anaeŭi sajin tuchang" [Two pictures of his wife]. *Hanguk ilbo,* Washington edition, December 27, 1995: 2.

Chang Yŏng-ch'ŏl. 1997. *Tangsindŭli kŭrŏge chalnassŏyo?* [Has Your Life Really Improved?]. Seoul: Sahoe P'yŏngrul.

Chin Hyŏng-yŏng. 1993. "Kichaŭi nun" [Correspondent's eye]. *Pukhan,* 8: 136-139.

Chira, Susan. 1988. "Tortured Dissenter Lives to See Far Better Days." *New York Times,* September 2: 4.

Cho Hae Joang. 1992. *T'alshikminji side jisikinŭi kŭl ilgiwa sam ilgi 1: paro yŏgi kyosilaesŏ* [Reading texts and reading everyday lives in the post-colonial era 1: From the classroom]. Seoul: Tto Hanaŭi Munhwa.

———. 1994. *Kŭl ilgiwa sam ilgi* [Reading sentences and reading life]. Seoul: Tto Hanaŭi Munhwa.

———. 1997. "A Discourse on the Cultural Aspect of North-South Korean Unification: the Cultural Homogeneity and Heterogeneity of 'Puk (North) Chosŏn' and 'Nam (South) Han,' Nationalism and Progressivism." Seoul: Ministry of National Unification.

Cho Myŏng-hun. 1988. "Interview." *Wŏlgan Kyŏnghyang,* August: 514 - 553.

Ch'oe, Yŏng-ho. 1980. "An Outline History of Korean Historiography." *Korean Studies* 4: 1-27.

———. 1981. "Reinterpreting Traditional History in North Korea." *Journal of Asian Studies* 40 (3): 503-523.

Choi, Chungmoo. 1993. "The Discourse of Decolonization and Popular Memory: South Korea." *Positions* 1 (1): 77-102.

———. 1995. "The Minjung Culture Movement and the Construction of Popular Culture in Korea." In Kenneth M. Wells, ed. *South Korea's Minjung Movement: The Culture and Politics of Dissidence,* pp. 105-118. Honolulu: University of Hawaii Press.

———, ed. 1997. "The Comfort Women: Colonialism, War, and Sex." Special Issue of *positions: east asia cultures critique:* Volume 5, no. 1.

Ch'oi, Eun-hee. 1988. *Chogukŭn chŏ hanŭl chŏ mŏlri* [My country far beyond those skies], vol. 1. Pacific Palisades, Calif.: Pacific Artists Cooperation.

Choi Hyun-moo. 1995. "Contemporary Korean Literature: From Victimization to Minjung Nationalism" trans. Carolyn U. So. In Kenneth M. Wells, ed. *South Korea's Minjung Movement: The Culture and Politics of Dissidence,* pp. 167-178. Honolulu: University of Hawaii Press.

Ch'oi Il-nam. 1989. "Kkŭmgil kwa malgil" [Dream-way and language-way]. *Ch'angjakkwa pip'yŏng* 78: 202-23.

Choi Jang-jip and Chung Hae-koo. 1989. "Haebang 8-nyŏnsaŭi ch'ongch'ejŏk insik" [A structural understanding of the 8 years following liberation]. In Choi Jang Jip et al., eds. *Haebang chŏnhusaŭi insik* [Understanding before and after liberation], volume 4. Seoul: Hangilsa.

Choi, Jang-jip. 1993. "Political Cleavages in South Korea." In Hagen Koo., ed. *State and Society in Contemporary Korea*, pp. 13-50. Ithaca, N.Y.: Cornell University Press.

Ch'oi Je-bong. 1993. Review of Yi Ch'ŏng Joon's "Hŭin ot" (White clothes). *Hangyŏre sinmun*, November 7: 12.

Ch'oi Min-hong. 1984. *Han Ch'ŏlhak* [Philosophy of han]. Seoul: Sŏngmunsa.

Ch'oi Yŏl. 1994. *Minjung Misul 15 nyŏn: 1980-1994* [15 years of minjung art: 1980-1994]. Seoul: Samkwa Kkum.

Ch'oi Yong-muk. 1993. "Nampukŭi ch'ang" / "Tong-il chŏnmangdae," [North-south window/Observatory of unification]. *Hangyŏre sinmun*, April 21: 9.

Chŏn Ch'ŏl-woo. 1994. *P'yŏngyang nolse / Seoul orenji* [P'yŏngyang birds / Seoul oranges]. Seoul: Chayusidaesa.

Chŏndaehyŏp. 1991. *Chŏndaehyŏp*. Seoul: Tolpaege.

Chŏn Duk-joo. 1994. "Hangukŭi t'ongilchŏngch'aek" [Korean unification policy]. In Chŏn Duk Joo et al., *Siminkwa kukka* [Citizen and state], pp. 345-374. Seoul: Hakmunsa.

Ch'ŏn Su-il. 1996. Shiron. *Hanguk ilbo* (Washington edition), February 10: 12.

Ch'ŏn Yi-du. 1993. *Hanŭi kujo yŏngu* [Research on the structure of han]. Seoul: Munhakwa Chisŏngsa.

Chŏng Myŏng-ki. 1996. "Kim Dae Jung Ch'ongjaeŭi sagwarŭl yoguhanda." [Demanding an apology from Kim Dae Jung]. *Sisa Journal* 360 (Sept.): 12-13.

Chow, Rey. 1991. "Violence in the Other Country: China as Crisis, Spectacle, and Woman." In Chandra Mohanty, Ann Russo, and Lourdes Torres, eds. *Third World Women and the Politics of Feminism.* Bloomington: Indiana University Press.

Chu Wan-su. 1989. *Pot'ong gorilla* [Ordinary gorilla]. Seoul: Segye.

Chun Kyung-soo and Sŏ Pyŏng-ch'ŏl. 1995. *T'ongilsahoeŭi chep'yŏn kwajŏng: Togilkwa paetŭnam* [Processes of reorganization in a unified society: Germany and Vietnam]. Seoul: Seoul National University Press.

Chung Jean-kyung. 1997. "The Culture Assimilator: Unification and Social Harmony." Seoul: Ministry of National Unification.

Chung Tal-yŏng. 1989. "Munmoksaga Kattŭnkil." (The road on which Pastor Mun walks"). *Hanguk ilbo,* April 1: 5.

Clifford, James and Vivek Dhareshwar. 1989. "Traveling Theories, Traveling Theorists." Special Issue of *Inscriptions.* Volume 5. Santa Cruz: Group for the Critical Study of Colonial Discourse and the Center for Cultural Studies, University of California, Santa Cruz.

Cohn, Bernard S. 1987. *An Anthropologist among Historians and other Essays.* Oxford: Oxford University Press.

Comaroff, Jean, and John Comaroff. 1991. *Of Revelation and Revolution,* vol. 1: *Christianity, Colonialism, and Consciousness in South Africa.* Chicago: University of Chicago Press.

Crimp, Douglas. 1989. "Mourning and Militancy." *October* 52: 3-18.

Cumings, Bruce. 1981. *The Origins of the Korean War,* vol. 1: *Liberation and the Emergence of Separate Regimes.* Princeton, N.J.: Princeton University Press.

———. 1990. *The Origins of the Korean War,* vol. 2: *The Roaring of the Cataract, 1947-1950.* Princeton, N.J.: Princeton University Press.

——— .1991. "Illusion, Critique, and Responsibility: The 'Revolutions of '89' in West and East." In Daniel Chirot, ed. *The Crisis of Leninism and the Decline of the Left: The Revolutions of 1989,* pp. 100-128. Seattle: University of Washington Press.

——— 1992. *War and Television.* London: Verso.

Daniel, E. Valentine, and John Chr. Knudsen, eds. 1995. *Mistrusting Refugees.* Berkeley and Los Angeles: University of California Press.

Derrida, Jacques. Trans. Gayatri Chakravorty Spivak. 1976. *Of Grammatology.* Baltimore: Johns Hopkins University Press, p. 306.

Duncan, James. 1993. "Sites of Representation: Place, Time, and the Discourse of the Other." In James Duncan and David Ley, eds. *Place/Culture/Representation,* pp. 39-57. London and New York: Routledge.

Duncan, James, and David Ley, eds. 1993. *Place/Culture/Representation.* London: Routledge.

Eberstadt, Nicholas. 1996. *Korea Approaches Reunification*. Armonk, NY. and London: M.E. Sharpe.

Eckert, Carter. 1991. *Offspring of Empire: The Koch'ang Kims and the Colonial Origins of Korean Capitalism, 1876-1945*. Seattle: University of Washington Press.

Eckert, Carter, Ki-baik Lee, Young Ik Lew, Michael Robinson, and Edward W. Wagner. 1990. *Korea Old and New: A History*. Seoul: Ilchogak.

Em, Henry H. 1993. "'Overcoming' Korea's Division: Narrative Strategies in Recent South Korean Historiography." *Positions* 1 (2): 450-485.

————. 1995. "The Nationalist Discourse in Modern Korea: *Minjok* as a Democratic Imaginary." Ph.D. dissertation, Department of History, University of Chicago.

Fine, Ellen S. 1988. "The Absent Memory: The Act of Writing in Post-Holocaust French Literature." In Berel Lang, ed. *Writing and the Holocaust*, pp. 41-57. New York and London: Holmes and Meier.

Foster-Carter, Aidan. 1994. "Korea: Sociopolitical Realities of Reuniting a Divided Nation." In Thomas H. Henriksen and Kyongsoo Lho, eds. *One Korea: Challenges and Prospects for Reunification*, pp. 31-48. Stanford, Calif.: Hoover Institution Press.

Freud, Sigmund. 1917. "Mourning and Melancholia." In J. Strachey, ed. *Standard Edition of the Complete Psychological Works of Sigmund Freud*, vol. 14: 154-167. London: Hogarth Press.

————. 1936. "Disturbance of Memory on the Acropolis." In J. Strachey, ed. *Standard Edition of the Complete Psychological Works of Sigmund Freud*, vol. 22: 239-249. London: Hogarth Press.

Friedlander, Saul. 1993. *Memory, History and the Extermination of the Jews in Europe*. Bloomington and Indianapolis: Indiana University Press.

Gellner, Ernst. 1983. *Nations and Nationalism*. Oxford: Blackwell.

Ghosh, Gautam. 1993. "Catastrophes and Categories." *Economic and Political Weekly* (Bombay), October 30: 2374.

Giddens, Anthony. 1990. *The Consequences of Modernity*. Cambridge: Polity.

Glaser, Hermann. 1993. "The Future Requires an Origin: East-West German Identity, the Opportunities and Difficulties of Cultural Politics." In Friederike Eigler and Peter C. Pfeiffer, eds. *Cultural Transformations in the New Germany*, pp. 64-80. Columbia, S.C.: Camden House.

Goldhagen, J. 1996. *Hitler's Willing Executioners: Ordinary Germans and the Holocaust.* London: Little, Brown.

Grass, Gunter. 1990. *Two States—One Nation?* Trans. Krishna Winston with A. S. Wensinger. New York: Harcourt Brace Jovanovich.

Greenblatt, Stephen. 1991. "Resonance and Wonder." In Ivan Karp and Steven D. Lavine, eds. *Exhibiting Cultures: The Poetics and Politics of Museum Display,* pp. 42-56. Washington, D.C.: Smithsonian Institution Press.

Grinker, Roy Richard. 1994. *Houses in the Rainforest: Ethnicity and Inequality among Farmers and Foragers in Central Africa.* Berkeley and Los Angeles: University of California Press.

———. 1995a. "The 'Real' Enemy of the Nation: Exhibiting North Korea at the Demilitarized Zone." *Museum Anthropology* 19 (2): 30-42.

———. 1995b "Mourning the Nation: Ruins of the North in Seoul." *Positions* 3 (1): 192-223.

———. 1996a. Op-ed ("*Shiron*"): "Understanding 'Difference' in North-South Korean Relations." *Joong-Ang ilbo,* June 19, 1996: 6. In Korean.

———. 1996b. "Imagining the North: Unification and Colonial Discourses in a South Korean Exhibition." In Cho Hyŏng, ed. *T'ongildoen ddangaesŏ tŏburŏ sanŭn yŏnsŭp* [Learning to live together in a unified land], pp. 189-207. Trans. Yu Seung-hee. Seoul: Tto Hanaŭi Munhwa. In Korean.

———. 1997a. "*T'ongilhanguksahoe: miriponŭn kŏulinga*" [Korean unification society]. *Shindonga* (April): 136-145. In Korean.

———. 1997b. "Engaging the Hermit Kingdom: U.S. Policy toward North Korea." *Prepared and Oral Testimony Before the United States House of Representatives,* February 26, 1997. House International Relations Committee, Subcommittee on Asia and the Pacific. Washington, D.C.: Government Printing Office.

———. 1997c. Interview. In Yu Dong-hee, ed. *Nampukhanŭi t'onghapkwa pangsong* [North-south unification and broadcasting], pp. 89-96. Seoul: Munhwa Broadcasting Company. In Korean.

Grinker, Roy Richard, and Christopher B. Steiner, eds. 1997. *Perspectives on Africa: A Reader in Culture, History and Representation.* Oxford and Cambridge, Mass.: Blackwell Publishers, Inc.

Habermas, Jurgen. 1996. "National Unification and Popular Sovereignty." *New Left Review* 129: 3-13.

Hall, Stuart. 1990. "Cultural Identity and Diaspora." In J. Rutherford, ed. *Identity: Community, Culture, Difference.* London: Lawrence & Wishart.

Han, Kyŏng Koo. 1994. "Some Foods Are Good to Think: Kimchi and the Epitomization of National Character." Paper presented at the annual meeting of the Asian Studies Association, Boston.

Hanguk Kaebal Yŏnguwŏn [Korean Development Research Institute]. 1993. *Togil t'ongil 3 nyŏnŭi kyŏngjejŏk p'yŏnggawa nampukhan kyŏngje kwangye'e taehan sisajŏm* [The implications of German unification for North-South Korean economic relations]. Seoul: Korean Development Research Institute.

Harrell-Bond, B. E., and E. Voutira. 1991. "Anthropology and the Situation of Refugees." *Anthropology Today* 8 (4): 6-10.

Hebdige, Dick. 1993. "Training Some Thoughts on the Future." In Jon Bird, Barry Curtis, Tim Putnam, George Robertson, and Lisa Tickner, eds. *Mapping the Futures: Local Cultures, Global Change,* pp. 270-279. London and New York: Routledge.

Henriksen, Thomas H. and Kyongsoo Lho, eds. 1994. *One Korea: Challenges and Prospects for Reunification.* Stanford, Calif.: Hoover Institution Press.

Hirsch, E. D., Jr. 1987. *Cultural Literacy: What Every American Needs to Know.* Boston: Houghton Mifflin.

Hŏ In-hoe. "Haksaeng undong, Todŏksŏng sunsusŏng sŏnhaenddoeya handa" [Students should put morality and purity first]. *Shindonga* (October 1996): 278-283.

Homans, Peter. 1989. *The Ability to Mourn: Disillusionment and the Social Origins of Psychoanalysis.* Chicago: University of Chicago Press.

Howe, Irving, 1988. "Writing and the Holocaust." In Berel Lang, ed. *Writing and the Holocaust.* pp. 175-199. New York and London: Holmes and Meier.

Hwang In-sŏng. 1989. "*Pangongkyoyukŭi naeyonggwa hyogwa'ae kwanhan yŏngu*" [A study of the contents and effects of anti-communist education]. M.A. thesis, Department of Education, Hanyang University.

Hwang Sŏk-yŏng. 1989a. "Sarami Salgoitsŏtne!" [There are people there!]. Two parts. *Shindonga* (June) 242-261; (July): 260-289.

———.1989b. "*Nampuk tokjaroput'ŏ hamgge sarang patko sipda*" [I want to be loved by readers from both north and south]. *Shindonga* (June): 262-285.

Hyŏnsilkwa parŏn. 1990. *Minjungmisulŭl hyanghayŏ* [Toward minjung art]. Seoul: Kwahakkwa sasang.

Im Su-kyŏng. 1990a. "Paekdusanaesŏ Hallakkachi hanaga Toeŏ" [Becoming one from Paekdu mountain to Halla]. *Shindonga* (June): 543-579.

————. 1990b. Ŏmŏni, hanadoen chogukae salgo sip'ŏyo [Mother, I want to live in a Unified Country] Seoul: Tolpegae.

Inkeles, Alex, and Donald B. Holsinger, eds. 1974. *Education and Individual Modernity in Developing Countries.* Leiden: E. J. Brill.

Ivy, Marilyn. 1995. *Discourses of the Vanishing: Modernity, Phantasm, Japan.* Chicago: University of Chicago Press.

Jager, Sheila Miyoshi. 1994. "Narrating the Nation: Students, Romance, and the Politics of Resistance in South Korea." Ph.D. dissertation, Department of Anthropology, University of Chicago.

————. 1996. "Women, Resistance and the Divided Nation: The Romantic Rhetoric of Korean Reunification." *Journal of Asian Studies* 55 (1): 3-21.

————. n.d. "The Genealogy of Patriotism: Making Family Histories in Modern Korea." Unpublished ms.

————. In press. "Monumental Histories." Museum Anthropology.

Jang Joon Oh. 1994. "Discourses on the Korean Student Movement in the 1980's: Democracy as a Master Frame." Ph.D. dissertation, University of Kansas.

Janelli, Roger, and Dwanhee Yim Janelli. 1982. *Ancestor Worship and Korean Society.* Stanford: Stanford University Press.

Jee, Man Won. 1994. "Forging a Common Security View: Prospects for Arms Control in Korea." In Thomas H. Henriksen and Kyongsoo Lho, eds. *One Korea: Challenges and Prospects for Reunification,* pp. 81-98. Stanford, Calif.: Hoover Institution Press.

Kang, Hugh H. W. 1974. "Images of Korean History." In Andrew C. Nahm, ed. *Traditional Korea: Theory and Practice.* Kalamazoo: Western Michigan State University.

Kang Man-kil. 1995. "Contemporary Nationalist Movements and the Minjung." In Kenneth M. Wells, ed. *South Korea's Minjung Movement: The Culture and Politics of Dissidence,* pp. 31-38. Honolulu: University of Hawaii Press.

Kang Man-kil and Yu Chae-hyun, eds. 1995. *T'ongil: Kŭ paraemesŏ hyŏnsilro* [Unification: From wish to reality]. Seoul: Pibong Ch'ulpansa.

Kang Myoung Kyu and Helmut Wagner, eds. 1990. *Korea and Germany: Lessons in Division.* Seoul: Seoul National University Press.

Kangwŏn University. 1982. *Survey of Nonghwal Participation.* Ch'unch'ŏn: Kangwŏn University.

Karp, Ivan, and Steven D. Lavine, eds. 1991. *Exhibiting Cultures: The Poetics and Politics of Museum Display.* Washington, D.C.: Smithsonian Institution Press.

Keith, Michael, and Steve Pile, eds. 1993. *Place and the Politics of Identity.* London and New York: Routledge.

Kendall, Laurel. 1988. *The Life and Hard Times of a Korean Shaman: Of Tales and the Telling of Tales.* Honolulu: University of Hawaii Press.

——— 1996. *Getting Married in Korea: Of Gender, Morality and Modernity.* Berkeley and Los Angeles: University of California Press.

Kihl, Young Hwan. 1984. *Politics and Policies in Divided Korea.* Boulder, Colo.: Westview.

Kim, Byoung-Lo Philo. 1992. *Two Koreas in Development.* New Brunswick, N.J.: Transaction.

Kim Chae-yŏng. 1992. "80 Nyŏndae Pukhan Sosŏlmunhakŭi T'ŭkchingkwa Munchaejŏm" [Characteristics and problems of north Korean novels in the 1980s]. *Ch'angjakwa pip'yŏng* 20 (4): 76-95.

Kim Chi-soo. 1996. "Mugŏŭn saeng" [Heavy life]. *Ch'angjakkwa pip'yŏng* 93: 115-148.

Kim Chin-myŏng 1995. *Kajŭoŭi nara* [Kajuo's country]. Seoul: Premium Books.

Kim Chŏng-hae. 1994. "Pukjosŏnŭi pitjang" [North Korea's crossbar]. *Munhak Sasang* (January): 206-211.

Kim, Choong Soon. 1988. *Faithful Endurance: An Ethnography of Korean Family Dispersal.* Tucson: University of Arizona Press.

Kim Dae-mun. 1989. Tokjaŭi P'yŏnji. [Readers Section]. *Tonga ilbo,* July 8: 11.

Kim Dalchoong et al., eds. 1990. *Divided Nations and East-West Relations on the Threshold of the 1990's.* Seoul: Institute of East and West Studies, Yonsei University.

———. 1991. *Europe in Transition and the Korean Peninsula.* Seoul: Institute of East and West Studies, Yonsei University.

Kim, Doh Jŏng. 1991. "The Politics of the Korean Student Movement: Its Tradition, Evolution, and Uniqueness." Ph.D. dissertation, Arizona State University.

Kim, Eugene C. 1973. "Education in Korea." In Andrew C. Nahm, ed. *Korea under Japanese Rule: Studies of the Policy and Techniques of Japanese Colonialism,* pp. 137-156. Kalamazoo: Center for Korean Studies/Institute of International and Area Studies, Western Michigan University.

Kim Ha-ki. 1993. *Hangro ŏpnŭn piheng* [Flying without direction]. 2 vols. Seoul: Ch'angjakkwa pip'yŏngsa.

Kim Ho-sŏp. 1996. "Ah, Puknyŏgŭi omani!" [Ah, north Korean mother!]. *Chugan Hanguk* (September) 5: 36.

Kim Hyŏng-dŏk. 1997a. Interview by Lee Chong Hwan. *Shindonga* (May): 394-398.

———. 1997b. *Abŏjiwa hamkke salgo sipŏyo* [I want to live with father]. Seoul: Ch'anghe.

Kim Hyun Hee. 1991. *Ijen yŏjaga toego sip'ŏyo* (Now I want to be a woman). Seoul: Chajaknamu.

———. 1993. *The Tears of My Soul.* New York: William Morrow and Co.

Kim, Ilsoo. 1981. *New Urban Immigrant: The Korean Community in New York.* Princeton, N.J.: Princeton University Press.

Kim Tong Kil. 1996. "Hanatoegi ŏryŏun minjok" [The people have difficulty becoming one]. *Shindonga* (April): 100-106.

Kim, Yong. 1992. *Mŏrirŭl ppanŭn namja* [The man who washes his hair]. Seoul: Chajaknamu.

Kim Yŏng-ch'un. 1996. "Chuch'e sasang, hŏddoen kkumaesŏ kkeŏnara" [Wake up from the vain dream of *chuch'e sasang*]. *Shindonga* (October): 272-277.

Kim Yong Hwan. 1990. *Y. H. Kim's Editorial Cartoons, 1983-1989.* Seoul: Minmungo.

Kim Yŏng-sŏng. 1995. *O, Suryŏngnim hedo nŏmuhamnida* [Oh, Great Leader, this is too much!]. Seoul: Chosŏn ilbosa.

Kim Young Sam, 1993. "Address Marking the First 100 Days in Office, June 3, 1993." Reprinted in *Korea Observer* 24 (2): 1-5.

Kim-Renaud, Young-Key. 1993. "Sŏp'yŏnje: A Journey into the Korean Soul and Human Existence." *Korea Journal* 33 (4): 112-117.

Kristeva, Julia. 1987. "On the Melancholic Imaginary." Trans. Louise Burchill. In Schlomth Rimmon-Kenan, ed. *Discourse in Psychoanalysis and Literature*, pp. 116-137. London: Methuen.

Ko Yong Kŭn. 1990. "Development of Language Policies in South and North Korea." In Kang Myoung Kyu and Helmut Wagner, eds. *Korea and Germany: Lessons in Division.* pp. 489-520. Seoul: Seoul National University Press.

Koh T'ae Woo. 1993. "T'ongil Chŏngch'egŭn Kwihyang Chŏngch'egida" [Unification policy is a homecoming policy]. *Pukhan* 6: 68-76.

Kohut, Heinz. 1971. *The Analysis of Self: A Systematic Approach to the Psychoanalytic Treatment of Narcissistic Personality Disorders.* New York: International Universities Press.

Koo Hagen. ed. 1993a. *State and Society in Contemporary Korea.* Ithaca, N.Y.: Cornell University Press.

———. 1993b. "The State, *Minjung*, and the Working Class in South Korea." In Hagen Koo, ed. *State and Society in Contemporary Korea*, pp. 131-162. Ithaca, N.Y.: Cornell University Press.

Krulfeld, Ruth M., and Linda A. Camino, eds. 1994. *Reconstructing Lives, Recapturing Meaning: Refugee Identity, Gender and Change.* New York: Gordon and Breach

Kwŏn Han-suk. 1995. *Inshalla.* Seoul: Hangyŏre Sinmunsa.

Kukjŏng kyogwasŏ [Ministry of Education]. 1965. *Sŭng'gong* [Defeating communism]. 2nd Year. Elementary. Seoul: Ministry of Education.

———. 1966. *Sŭng'gong* [Defeating communism]. 3rd Year. Elementary. Seoul: Ministry of Education.

———. 1965. *Todŏk* [Ethics]. 2nd year. Elementary. Seoul: Ministry of Education.

———. 1965. *Todŏk* [Ethics]. 4th year. Elementary. Seoul: Ministry of Education.

———. 1974. *Todŏk* [Ethics]. 2nd year. Elementary. Seoul: Ministry of Education.

———. 1974. *Todŏk* [Ethics]. 5th year. Elementary. Seoul: Ministry of Education.

———. 1993. *Saenghwalŭi kiljabi* [Guide to everyday life]. 4th year, Elementary. Seoul: Ministry of Education.

———. 1993. *Todŏk* [Ethics]. 2nd year. Middle school. Seoul: Ministry of Education.

———. 1993. *Todŏk* [Ethics]. 2nd year. Elementary. Seoul: Ministry of Education.

———. 1993. *Todŏk* [Ethics]. 4th year. Elementary. Seoul: Ministry of Education.

———. 1993. *Todŏk* [Ethics]. 5th year. Elementary. Seoul: Ministry of Education.

———. 1993. *Todŏk* [Ethics]. 1st year. Elementary. Seoul: Ministry of Education.

———. 1996. *Todŏk* [Ethics] 2nd year. Middle School. Seoul: Ministry of Education.

———. 1996. *Todŏk* [Ethics]. 2nd year. Elementary. Seoul: Ministry of Education.

———. 1996. *Todŏk* [Ethics]. 3rd year. Elementary. Seoul: Ministry of Education.

LaCapra, Dominick. 1994. *Representing the Holocaust: History, Memory, Trauma.* Ithaca, N.Y.: Cornell University Press.

Lacan, Jaques. 1987. "Television." Trans. Denis Hollier, Rosalind Krauss, and Annette Michelson. *October* 40: 5-50.

Laclau, Ernesto, and Lilian Zac. 1994. "Minding the Gap: The Subject of Politics." In Ernesto Laclau, ed. *The Making of Political Identities,* pp. 11-39. London: Verso.

Lambek, Michael, and Paul Antze. 1996. "Introduction: Forecasting Memory." In Paul Antze and Michael Lambek, eds. *Tense Past: Cultural Essays in Trauma and Memory.* pp. xi-xxxviii. London: Routledge.

Lang, Berel, ed. 1988. "Introduction." In Berel Lang, ed. *Writing and the Holocaust,* pp. 1-16. New York and London: Holmes and Meier.

Lee Bann, ed. 1995. *DMZŭi: Kwagŏ, hyŏnjae, mirae* [Front DMZ: past, present, future]. Seoul: International Forum for Conservation of the Korean Demilitarized Zone.

Lee, Chong Sik. 1963. *The Politics of Korean Nationalism.* Berkeley: University of California Press.

Lee, Jae Hoon. 1994. *The Exploration of the Inner Wounds: Han.* Atlanta: Scholar's Press.

Lee, Jonathan Scott. 1990. *Jaques Lacan.* Amherst, Mass.: University of Massachusetts Press.

Lee, Ki-baik. 1984. *A New History of Korea.* Trans. Edward Wagner with Edward Shultz. Cambridge: Harvard University Press.

Lee Kwang Kyu. 1975. *Hanguk kajogüi kujo punsŏk* [Analysis of the Korean family structure]. Seoul: Ilchisa.

Lee, Namhee. 1991. "The South Korean Student Movement, 1980-1987." In Bruce Cumings, ed. *Chicago Occasional Papers on Korea,* no 6. pp. 204-245. Chicago: Center of East Asian Studies, University of Chicago.

Lee, Peter, ed. 1987. *Anthology of Korean Literature: From Early Times to the Nineteenth Century.* Honolulu: University of Hawaii Press.

————, ed. 1990. *Modern Korean Literature: An Anthology.* Honolulu: University of Hawaii Press.

Lee Woo-young. 1997. "Northern Defectors in South Korea." *Korea Focus,* 5 (3): 31-40.

Lee Yong Hwan. 1993. "Minjok tongjilsŏng hoebokŭl wihan t'ongil kyoyukŭi paljŏn panghyang" [The direction of the development of unification education and the recovery of national homogeneity]. *Pukhan* 4: 184-199.

Lie, John. 1992. "The Political Economy of South Korean Development." *International Sociology* 7 (3): 285-300.

Light, Ivan, and Edna Bonacich. 1988. *Immigrant Entrepreneurs: Koreans in Los Angeles, 1965-1982.* Berkeley and Los Angeles: University of California Press.

Linton, Stephen Winn. 1989. "Patterns in Korean Civil Religions." Ph.D. Dissertation, Columbia University.

Lipstadt, Deborah. 1997. "Why the Holocaust Keeps Coming Back." *Washington Post,* March 23: C3.

Lukes, Steven. 1992. *Emile Durkheim, His Life and Work: A Historical and Critical Study.* Harmondsworth: Penguin.

Maier, Charles S. 1988. *The Unmasterable Past: History, Holocaust, and German National Identity.* Cambridge: Harvard University Press.

Malkki, Lisa. 1995. *Purity and Exile: Violence, Memory, and National Cosmology Among Hutu Refugees.* Chicago: University of Chicago Press.

Massey, Doreen. 1993. "Power Geometry and a Progressive Sense of Place." In Jon Bird, Barry Curtis, Tim Putnam, George Robertson, and Lisa Tickner, eds. *Mapping the Futures: Local Cultures, Global Change,* pp. 59-69. London and New York: Routledge.

————. 1994. "Double Articulation: A Place in the World." In Agelika Bammer, ed. *Displacements: Cultural Identities in Question.* Bloomington: Indiana University Press.

McClintock, Anne. 1994 [1992]. "The Angel of Progress: Pitfalls of the Term 'Post-colonialism.'" Reprinted in Patrick Williams and Laura Chrisman, eds. *Colonial Discourses and Post-colonial Theory: A Reader,* pp. 291-304. New York: Columbia University Press.

McVey, Ruth. 1982. "The *Beamtenstaat* in Indonesia." In B. Anderson and A. Kahin, eds. *Interpreting Indonesian Politics: Thirteen Contributions to the Debate.* Ithaca: Cornell University Press.

Mertes, Michael. 1994. "Germany's Social and Political Culture: Change Through Consensus?" *Daedalus* 123 (1): 1-32.

Min Pyŏng-ch'ŏn. 1980. *Wŏlnam Kwisunjaŭi chayusahoe chŏkŭng kwajŏng silt'ae chosa* [Research on the defector's adaptation into liberal society.] Seoul: Kukt'o T'ongilwŏn Chosayŏngusil.

Mitchell, W. J. T. 1986. *Iconology: Image, Text, Ideology.* Chicago: University of Chicago Press.

Mitscherlich, Alexander, and Margarete Mitscherlich. 1975. *The Inability to Mourn: Principles of Collective Behavior.* Trans. Beverly R. Placzek. New York: Grove Press.

Moon, C. H. S. 1985. *A Korean Minjung Theology: An Old Testament Perspective.* Maryknoll, N.Y.: Orbis.

Morley, David, and Kevin Robins. 1990. "No Place Like *Heimat:* Images of Home(land) in European Culture." *New Formations* 12: 1-25.

Mosse, George L. 1985. *Nationalism and Sexuality: Respectability and Abnormal Sexuality in Modern Europe.* New York: Howard Fertig.

Mudimbe, V.Y. 1988. *The Invention of Africa: Gnosis, Philosophy, and the Order of Knowledge.* Bloomington: Indiana University Press.

————. 1994. *The Idea of Africa.* Bloomington: Indiana University Press.

Mun Ik Hwan. 1990. *Kasŭmŭromannan P'yŏngyang* [P'yŏngyang that I met with all my heart]. Seoul: Samminsa.

Mushaben, Joyce Marie. 1993. "Citizenship as Process: German Identity in an Age of Reconstruction." In Friederike Eigler and Peter C. Pfeiffer, eds. *Cultural Transformations in the New Germany,* pp. 42-63. Columbia, S.C.: Camden House.

Myers, Brian. 1994. "Han Sorya and North Korean Literature." Paper presented to the Korea Society, Georgetown University, Washington, D.C., April 5.

Nam Sang-ch'ŏn. 1994. "Minjokhon toech'atŭl ddaeda" [Time to revive the Korean spirit]. *Chugan Washington,* June 28: 20-21.

Nampuk Munje Yŏnguso [Institute for South-North Korean Studies], ed. 1993. *Kim Jŏng Il kŭnŭn ŏddŏn inmulinga?* [Kim Jong Il, what sort of person is he?). Seoul: Nambuk Munje Yŏnguso.

Nandy, Ashis. 1988. *The Intimate Enemy.* Delhi: Oxford University Press.

Newman, Peter C. 1994. "Berlin: Europe's New Commercial Cabaret." *Maclean's,* February 14: 33.

Oberdofer, Don. 1997. *The Two Koreas: A Contemporary History.* Reading, MA.: Addison-Wesley.

Ogle, George E. 1990. *South Korea: Dissent Within the Economic Miracle.* London: Zed Books.

Oh, Byung-hun. 1975. "Students and Politics." In Edward R. Wright, ed. *Korean Politics in Transition.* Seattle: University of Washington Press.

Oh Hye-chŏng. 1995. "Kwisun pukhantongpoŭi namhansahoe chŏgŭng silt'ae" [Reality of defector's adaptation to southern society]. M.A. Thesis, Dept. of North Korean Studies, Sŏgang University.

Oh Sae Yŏng. 1976. "Hanŭi nolliwa kŭ yŏksŏljŏk ŭimi" [The logic of *han* and its paradoxical meaning]. *Munhak Sasang* 51: 218.

Osborne, Peter. 1995. *The Politics of Time: Modernity and Avant-Garde.* London and New York: Verso.

Paige, Glenn D. 1970. "Some Implications for Political Science of the Comparative Politics of Korea." In Fred Riggs, ed. *Frontiers of Development Administration,* pp. 139-168. Durham, N.C.: Duke University Press.

Paik, Nak Chung. 1988. "What the Other Korean Writers Think." Message to the foreign participants at the 1988 Seoul PEN Congress, Seoul, Korea, August 1988.

———. 1991. "Korea and the United States: The Mutual Challenge." Paper presented at the symposium "America, Asia and Asian Americans," Center for East Asian Studies, University of Chicago, November 18.

———. 1993a. "Japan and Korea as Each Other's Problem in the Age of Globalization." Paper presented to the Peace Research Institute, Meigaku, Yokohama, Japan, March.

———. 1993b. "South Korea and the Democratic Challenge." *New Left Review* 197: 67-84.

———. 1994. *Pundanch'eje pyŏnhyŏngŭi kongbugil* [How to study and transform the division system]. Seoul: Ch'angjakkwa pip'yŏngsa.

———. 1995. "The Reunification Movement and Literature." Trans. Kenneth M. Wells. In Kenneth M. Wells, ed. *South Korea's Minjung Movement: The Culture and Politics of Dissidence,* pp. 179-208. Honolulu: University of Hawaii Press.

———. 1996a. "Habermas on National Unification in Germany and Korea." *New Left Review* 129: 14-21.

———. 1996b. "Continuity and Transformation." In Cynthia C. Davidson, ed. *Anywise.* pp. 194-199. Cambridge and London: the MIT Press.

Pak Hyŏn-ch'ae. 1988. *Minjok kyŏngjewa minjung undong* [The national economy and the *minjung* movement]. Seoul: Ch'angjakkwa pip'yŏngsa.

Palais, James B. 1975. *Politics and Policy in Traditional Korea.* Cambridge: Harvard University Press.

———.1995. "A Search for Korean Uniqueness." *Harvard Journal of Asiatic Studies* 55: 409-426.

Park, Byeong Chul. 1995. *Motivational Dynamics of Student Movement Participation in Contemporary South Korea.* Ph.D. dissertation, Department of Sociology, Syracuse University.

Park Dong-un. 1996. "Hankwa hanp'uli" [*Han* and its resolution]. *Pukhan* 2: 74-83.

Park Il Sung. 1983. "Legitimacy in Political, Economic, and Social Systems." In Kuk Sung Suh et al. *The Identity of the Korean People: A History of Legitimacy on the Korean Peninsula,* 171-208. Trans. Chung Chung Ho. Seoul: National Unification Board, Republic of Korea.

Park Kwan-su. 1972. *Pukhanŭi kajŏngkwa punyŏja* [North Korean families and married women]. Seoul: Kongsangwŏn Munje Yŏnguso.

Phelan, Peggy. 1997. *Mourning Sex: Performing Public Memories.* London and New York: Routledge.

Pietz, William. 1988. "The 'Post-Colonialism' of Cold War Discourse." *Social Text* 7 (1-2): 55-75.

Porter, Dennis. 1991. *Haunted Journeys.* Princeton, N. J.: Princeton University Press.

Pratt, Mary Louise. 1992. *Imperial Eyes.* London: Routledge.

Price, Sally. 1989. *Primitive Art in Civilized Places.* Chicago: University of Chicago Press.

P'yŏnghwa Munje Yŏnguso, eds. 1997. *T'ongil / Pukhan Haendŭbuk* [Unification/North Korea handbook]. Seoul: P'yŏnghwa Munje Yŏnguso.

Reynolds, Donald Martin, ed. 1996. *"Remove Not the Ancient Landmark:" Public Monuments and Moral Values.* Langhorne, PA: Gordon and Breach.

Riew, Yong Kiew. 1985. *The Theology of Mission Structures and Its Relation to Korea's Indigeneous Student Movements.* Ph.D. dissertation, Fuller Theological Seminary.

Robertson, George, Melinda Mash, Lisa Tickner, Jon Bird, Barry Curtis, and Tim Putnam, eds. 1994. *Traveller's Tales: Narratives of Home and Displacement.* London and New York: Routledge.

Robinson, Michael E. 1988. *Cultural Nationalism in Colonial Korea, 1920-1925.* Seattle: University of Washington Press.

Roth, Michael S. 1995. *The Ironist's Cage: Memory, Trauma, and the Construction of History.* New York: Columbia University Press.

Rushdie, Salman. 1991. "Imaginary Homelands." In *Imaginary Homelands: Essays and Criticism, 1981-1991.* London: Granta.

Ryang, Sonia. 1997. *North Koreans in Japan: Language, Ideology and Identity.* Boulder: Westview.

Said, Edward W. 1995. "East Isn't East: The Impending End of the Age of Orientalism." *Times Literary Supplement,* February 3: 3-6.

Santner, Eric. 1990. *Stranded Objects: Mourning, Memory, and Film in Postwar Germany.* Ithaca and London: Cornell University Press.

Schneider, Peter. 1996. "For Germans, Guilt Isn't Enough." *New York Times,* December 5: A35.

Schur, M. 1969. "The Background of Freud's 'Disturbance' on the Acropolis." *American Imago* 26: 303-323.

Seo Dong-ik. 1996. "T'alpuk kwisun tongp'o ŏddŏge ch'ŏriheya hana" [How to take care of the defectors]. *Pukhan* 5: 50-57.

Shapiro, Michael. 1990. *The Shadow in the Sun.* New York: Atlantic Monthly Press.

Shin Gi-Wook. 1995. "Marxism, Anti-Americanism, and Democracy in South Korea: An Examination of Nationalist Intellectual Discourse." *Positions* 3 (2): 508-534.

Shin Sang Ok. 1988. *Choguk-ŭn chŏ hanŭl chŏ mŏlri* [My country far beyond those skies]. Pacific Palisades, Calif.: Pacific Artists Cooperation.

Shin Yŏng-kil. 1993. Letter to the Editor. *Hangyŏre Sinmun,* April 17: 4.

Slochower, H. 1970. "Freud's 'Deja Vu' on the Acropolis: A Symbolic Relic of 'Mater Nuda.'" *Psychoanalytic Quarterly* 39: 90-101.

Snyder, Scott. 1997a. "How North Korea Negotiates: Patterns in Recent U.S. - North Korean Negotiations." Paper presented at the Virginia Consortium of Asian Studies, College of William and Mary, February 8, 1997.

————.1997b. "North Korean Crises and American Choices: Managing U.S. Policy Toward the Korean Peninsula." Paper presented at the annual meeting of the International Studies Association, March 19, 1997.

Soh Sŏng-wu. 1987. "Tongt'oŭi ddang, pukhan kŭ pich'amhan saenghwalsang: Kim Man-ch'ŏlssi ilga chayuŭi p'umae angin kŏsŏl pogo" [Land of frozen soil, tragic lives in north Korea: watching Kim Man Ch'ŏl's family discover freedom]. *Hoguk,* March: 159: 9.

Son Bong-suk, ed. 1991. *Pukhanŭi yŏsŏng saenghwal* [Women's daily lives in north Korea]. Seoul: Nanam.

Song Du-yul. 1995a. *Yŏksanŭn kkŭtnatnŭnga?* [The end of history?]. Seoul: Tangdae.

————.1995b. "T'ongile yŏngmarue sŏsŏ chogugŭl saengkakhanda" [Standing at the peak of the mountain pass of unification and thinking about the fatherland]. *Mal* (August): 94-99.

Song Kwŏn-ho et al. 1989. *Haebang chŏnhuŭi yŏksajŏk insik* [Historical consciousness before and after liberation]. Seoul: Hangilsa.

Sŏnu Chŏng-wŏn. 1993. "Kamsangjŏgin T'ongil Chisangchuŭi Kyŏnggyae" [Guarding against a sentimentalist unification]. *Pukhan* 11: 18 -21.

Sorenson, Clark W. 1988. *Over the Mountains There Are Mountains: Korean Peasant Households and Their Adaptations to Rapid Industrialization.* Seattle: University of Washington Press.

Standish, Isolde. 1994. "Korean Cinema and the New Realism: Text and Context." In Wimal Dissanayake, ed. *Colonialism and Nationalism in Asian Cinema,* pp. 65-89. Bloomington: Indiana University Press.

Steiner, Christopher B. 1994. *African Art in Transit.* Cambridge: Cambridge University Press.

Stephanson, Anders. 1988. "Reply to Pietz." *Social Text* 7 (1-2): 77-84.

Stewart, Susan. 1993. *On Longing: Narratives of the Miniature, the Gigantic, the Souvenir, the Collection.* Durham and London: Duke University Press.

Suh Nam Dong. 1983. "Towards a Theology of Han." In Commission on Theological Concerns of the Christian Conference of Asia (CTC-CCA), eds. *Minjung Theology: People as the Subjects of History,* pp. 55-73. Maryknoll, N.Y.: Orbis.

Thom, Martin. 1990. "Tribes Within Nations: The Ancient Germans and the History of Modern France." In Homi Bhabha, ed. *Nation and Narration,* pp. 23-43. London: Routledge.

Tønneson, Stein and Hans Antlöv, eds. 1996. *Asian Forms of the Nation.* Nordic Institute of Asian Studies, Studies in Asian Topics, No. 23. Surrey: Curzon.

Tto Hanaŭi Munhwa, ed. 1996. *T'ongildoen Ttangaesŏ tŏburŏ sanŭn yŏnsŭp* [Learning to live together in a unified land]. Seoul: Tto Hanaŭi Munhwa.

Walraven, Boudewijn. 1996. "Putting on Bifocals: Group Historiography and the Nation." Paper presented at the conference "Identity through History." University of Leiden, the Netherlands, August 29-September 1, 1996.

Wells, Kenneth M. 1990. *New God, New Nation: Protestants, Self-Reconstruction and Nationalism in Korea, 1896-1937.* Honolulu: University of Hawaii Press.

———.1996. "Nationalist Historiography in South Korea: Is There an Alternative?" Paper presented at the conference "Identity through History." University of Leiden, the Netherlands, August 29–September 1, 1996.

———, ed. 1995. *South Korea's Minjung Movement: The Culture and Politics of Dissidence.* Honolulu: University of Hawaii Press.

Williams, Raymond. 1973. *The City and the Country.* New York: Oxford University Press.

Winter, Jay. 1995. *Sites of Memory, Sites of Mourning: The Great War in European Cultural History.* Cambridge: Cambridge University Press.

Yang, Sung Chul. 1983. "Socialist Education in North Korea." In Eugene C. I. Kim and B. C. Koh, eds. *Journey to North Korea: Personal Perceptions,* p. 63-83. Berkeley: Institute of East Asian Studies.

———.1992. "United Germany for Divided Korea: Learning from Euphoria and Dysphoria." *Korea and World Affairs* 16 (3): 436-462.

————.1994. *The North and South Korean Political Systems: A Comparative Analysis.* Boulder and Seoul: Westview Press and Seoul Press.

Yi Ch'ŏl. 1996. *"Muchangkongbi"* [Infiltrators]. *Hanguk ilbo,* October 1: 4.

Yi Chŏng-hun. 1996. "Kwisun pukhantongp'oŭi namhansahoe yŏngu." Unpublished ms.

Yi Ch'ŏng-jun. 1993. "Hamggae ap'ahagi" [Agonizing together]. *Munye Chungang* (winter): 285-287.

Yi Chong-woo. 1993. "Maŭmsokŭi changbyŏk" [War in the Heart]. *Pukhan* 11: 166-171.

Yi Ha-sŏk. 1994. "Pakkatae Toladaniki" [Wandering around outside]. *Munhak Sasang,* March: 66-69.

Yi Han-yŏng. 1996. *Taedonggang royŏl p'aemilli Seoulchamhaeng 14nyŏn* [Fourteen years of traveling in disguise in Seoul, by a member of the royal family of the Taedong River]. Seoul: Tonga Ilbosa.

Yi Hang-ku. 1980. "Pukhan Chuminŭi Yŏgasaenghwal" [Leisure life of north Korean residents.] *Pukhan,* 102: 35-43.

————. 1993. *Kim Il Sung.* 2 vols. Seoul: Sint'aeyangsa.

Yi Ho-ch'ŏl. 1988 [1961]. "P'anmunjŏm." In *Yi Hoch'ŏl chŏnjip* [Collected works of Yi Ho Ch'ŏl], vol. 1, pp. 57-87. Seoul: Ch'ŏnggye Yŏngusŏ.

Yi Hyŏn-yŏng. 1995. *Siminŭl wihan t'ongilron* [Unification theories for citizens]. Seoul: Saegilsinsŏ.

Yi Kŏn-ch'ang. 1994. "Sŏp'yŏng: Song, Sŏk-wŏn" *Munhak Sasang* (May): 249-251.

Yi Pyŏng-kwan, ed. 1995. *O, kŭrae? Pukhan p'yŏn* [Oh, really? About north Korea]. Seoul: Saeroun saramdŭl.

Yi Sun-kyo. 1994. "Hakkyo t'ongil kyoyuk silt'ae mit kyosaŭi taepukhan insikpunsŏk" [Reality of unification education and analysis of school teachers' perspectives]. M.A. thesis, Department of North Korean Studies, Sŏgang University.

Yi Sung-wu. 1988. Interview. *Wŏlgan Kyŏnghyang* (August): 514 - 537.

Yi Tong Lip. 1996. "Chugŏnanŭn kŏsŭn nodongja nongminbbun" [Only workers and farmers are dying] *Wŏlgan Chosŏn:* 142-150.

Yu Dong-ryŏl. 1996. *"Hanch'ongryŏn* and the North's Strategy against the South," *Pukhan* 12: 70-87.

Young, James E. 1990. "The Counter-Monument: Memory Against Itself in Germany Today." In W. J. T. Mitchell, ed. *Art and the Public Sphere,* pp. 49-78. Chicago: University of Chicago Press.

————.1993. *The Texture of Memory: Holocaust Memorials and Meaning.* New Haven and London: Yale University Press.

————ed. 1994. *The Art of Memory: Holocaust Memorials.* New York and Munich: Prestel.

Yu Dong-hee, et al. 1996. *T'ongil pangsong yŏngu.* 3 vol. Seoul: Munhwa Broadcasting System.

Yun Sun-hwan, 1996. "*Kim miyŏk mŏgŭmyŏ panch'anirŭmmutnya?*" [Eating seaweed, they ask, what are the names of these side dishes?]. *Hanguk ilbo,* December 11: 3.

Yun Wung. 1996. *P'yŏngyangkasŏ tonpŏnŭn 108 kaji aidiŏ* [108 ideas for making money in P'yŏngyang]. Seoul: Pressville.

Yun Yŏ-sang. 1994. "Kwisun Pukhan tongp'oŭi namhansahoe chŏgŭnge kwanhan yŏngu" [Research on defectors' adaptation to southern society]. M.A. Thesis, Department of Politics, Yŏngnam University.

Žižek, Slavoj. 1991. *Looking Awry.* Cambridge and London: MIT Press.

INDEX

Tonga ilbo (newspaper), 212, 213, 219
Tonghak rebellion (1893-1894), 177,
    178, 200
t'ongil, ix, xiii, 19-20, 273n3, 274n1,
    278n8
T'ongilwŏn, 56
3.15 election fraud, 178
travelers and travel writings, 14,
    175n13

Unification
    costs of, 255-56
    and economics, 36, 226, 277n7
    and modernity, 43-45
    preparation for, 257-58, 266-71
    See also t'ongil
United States, 32, 183, 220
    troops in Korea, 124, 182,
        274n2
universities, 129, 174
    as boundary, 188
    enrollment in, 179
    as means to higher social status,
        186
    See also student protests; educa-
        tion

Vietnam, 43
    and *t'ongil*, 19
Vietnam Veterans Memorial, 83
violence, 2, 125, 137, 185

Wells, Kenneth, 140, 197, 199
Winter, Jay, 33
Wolf, Christa, 267-68
Woo Chŏng-mee, 278n6
working through, 10, 259-60
World War II, 33

Yang Sŏng-wu, 84
Yang Sung-chul, 26

Yemen, 43
Yi Ch'ŏl-su, 233
Yi Chŏng-hoon, 237
Yi Ch'ŏng Joon, 42-43
Yi Chŏng-kuk, 251-52
Yi Han-yŏl, 183
Yi Han-yŏng, 24, 231
Yi Ho-ch'ŏl, 28
Yi In-mo, 185
Yi Kŭn-an, 283n9
Yi Min-bok, 231
Yi Sang Jae, 281n8
Yi Su-kŭn, 242
Yi Sŭng-bok, 51-53
Yi Ung-pyŏng, 233, 235, 241
Yi Wŏn-do, 249
Yim Hyung-Bin, 282n13
Yŏ Kŭm-chu, 232
Yŏ Kŭm-yŏng, 249
Yŏ Man-ch'ŏl, 232, 249
Yonsei University, 203
    1996 riots, 1-2, 187
    and *t'ongil*, 19
Young, James, 30, 274n7
Yu Dong Hee, 286n5
Yu Kwan-sun, 176, 184
Yu Sun-jin, 280n6
Yun Ch'i Ho, 281n8
Yun Wŏn-chŏl, 120-21, 220
Yun, Woong: *108 Ideas for Making
    Money in P'yŏngyang* (book),
    268
Yun Yŏ-sang, 237
yusin, 283n8
Yusin Constitution, 147, 148, 155,
    179, 180

Žižek, Slavoj, 45, 73